THE
COURT
AND THE
CONSTITUTION

BOOKS BY ARCHIBALD COX

Law and the National Labor Policy

Civil Rights, the Constitution, and the Courts
(with Mark DeWolfe Howe and J. R. Wiggins)

Crisis at Columbia
(The Cox Commission Report)

*The Warren Court: Constitutional Decision
as an Instrument of Reform*

*The Role of the Supreme Court
in American Government*

Freedom of Expression

Cases and Materials on Labor Law
(with Derek Curtis Bok and Robert A. Gorman)

The Court and the Constitution

THE

COURT

AND THE

CONSTITUTION

———

ARCHIBALD COX

Houghton Mifflin Company

BOSTON

1987

LIBRARY OF CONGRESS CATALOGING-IN-PUBLICATION DATA

Cox, Archibald, date.
The court and the constitution.

Includes index.
1. United States — Constitutional law — Interpretation and construction — History. 2. Judicial review — United States — History. 3. United States. Supreme Court — History. I. Title.
KF4550.C69 1987   347.73′26   87-3772
ISBN 0-395-37933-4   347.30735

PRINTED IN THE UNITED STATES OF AMERICA

P 10 9 8 7 6 5 4 3 2 1

Acknowledgments

IN WRITING this book I benefited immeasurably from discussions with Adrian Malone and Gregory W. Smith looking toward the production of a thirteen-part television series presenting the role of the U.S. Supreme Court in the development of American life. Although the plans did not come to fruition, both men contributed to my ideas and especially to their expression. Gregory W. Smith and Adrian Malone's staff also provided a wealth of factual research.

I am also indebted to Jonathan Berek, a Harvard Law School student, and Marlene Roeder, my secretary and research assistant, for their helpful research.

Contents

CONTENTS

PART FOUR

Constitutionalism and the Rule of Law

THE
COURT
AND THE
CONSTITUTION

Prologue

IN CELEBRATING the bicentennial of the Philadelphia Convention that drew up the Constitution in 1787, Americans will once again reassert their faith in constitutionalism and the rule of law. We take pride in the Framers not only for outlining an ingenious plan of government but also for providing guarantees of individual liberty and dignity against government oppression. That faith attaches to the Supreme Court of the United States and, in a lesser degree, to the lower courts as the mechanism for interpreting the commands of the Constitution and preserving the rule of law.

A court, in deciding the case before it, will disregard an Act of Congress that it finds inconsistent with the Constitution. A court may also issue a decree commanding an executive officer to refrain from unconstitutional or otherwise illegal conduct against an individual or to perform any nondiscretionary duty required by law. In these ways the courts, and ultimately the U.S. Supreme Court, preserve the basic frame of government and protect individual rights.

The Court's constitutional decisions often shape the course of our national life. Recall, for example, the School Desegregation Cases,[1] the School Prayer Cases,[2] or the earlier decisions, in 1937, validating an enormous expansion of the powers of the federal government that enables it to regulate virtually all business activity as a regulation of "commerce among the several States."[3]

What is the foundation of this power of judicial review—more broadly, of constitutionalism and the rule of law? One may answer that the Court asserted the power of judicial review in *Marbury* v. *Madison*,[4] and gradually the country came to accept it. But does the answer probe deep enough? Suppose that executive officials,

I

perhaps backed by legislative sentiment, persist in enforcing an unconstitutional law or engaging in their own illegal conduct. If the official stands alone, perhaps the marshal or other court officials will have the physical power to deal with him. If he is too strong for them—if, for example, he is a State Governor—the court may obtain the physical support of the President of the United States, who can call out the armed forces, as did Presidents Eisenhower and Kennedy to enforce desegregation decrees at the schools in Little Rock, Arkansas, and the University of Mississippi. But suppose that the President refuses to enforce the decree? Or that the President himself is found to be disobeying the Constitution? What then is the protection for constitutional liberties? What, in the final analysis, is the foundation of our constitutionalism—of the rule of law?

From time to time lawyers and political philosophers have speculated about these questions. They became vital in the autumn of 1973, during the Watergate investigation.

The stage for that showdown was set in July 1973, in Judge John Sirica's courtroom in Washington, D.C. A grand jury was investigating various charges of wrongdoing by officials high in the Nixon Administration or in President Nixon's Committee to Re-elect the President. In June 1972 James McCord, Howard Hunt, and some anti-Castro Cuban refugees had been caught attempting to break into the Watergate offices of the Democratic National Committee for the purpose of planting an electronic bug through which to eavesdrop upon conversations in the office or on the telephone. McCord and Hunt were quickly linked to the White House and the Republican Party. Gradually there developed grounds for reasonable suspicion that the ultimate responsibility for the Watergate break-in reached as high as President Nixon's chief aide, Robert Haldeman, his former Attorney General, John Mitchell, and perhaps the President himself. Other charges of wrongdoing by high officials were in the air, including the corrupt settlement of a major antitrust case in return for financial support of the 1972 Republican Convention, the receipt of unlawful corporate campaign contributions, the "bugging" of newspaper reporters, and sundry violations of the civil liberties of vocal critics of the President.

By the spring of 1973 it became apparent that the Department of Justice was not investigating the charges as vigorously as the evidence warranted. Attorney General Richard Kleindienst, Robert

Haldeman, and another high White House aide, John Ehrlichman, resigned under fire. The President's Legal Counsel, John Dean, was dismissed. President Nixon then nominated Elliot Richardson, a man of great experience and unimpeachable integrity, to be Attorney General. The Senate Judiciary Committee required Richardson, as a condition of confirmation, to appoint a Special Prosecutor to investigate these and related charges, to present evidence to the grand jury, and to prosecute any resulting indictments.

Richardson's choice for Special Prosecutor fell upon me. I accepted the post out of belief in the importance of trying to demonstrate that our system of law and government is capable of investigating, thoroughly and fairly, any plausible charges of wrongdoing, even at the very highest levels of government, and also capable of dealing, vigorously but impartially, with any demonstrated wrongs. Appearing with Richardson before the Senate Judiciary Committee, I promised that I would pursue the trail wherever it led, even to the Presidency. I also promised to challenge by appropriate judicial proceedings any claim by the President of a power to withhold evidence under the constitutional doctrine called "executive privilege." The terms of my appointment contained unequivocal assurance of independence and a guarantee that I would not be removed from office unless guilty of gross misconduct.

By July 6, 1973, there was considerable evidence to show not only that the ultimate responsibility for the Watergate break-in reached high in the circle of White House officials, but also that there had been a deliberate effort to cover up the links between the break-in and the White House and Republican campaign officials. John Dean, the discharged Legal Counsel to the President, had given detailed testimony before a Senate Investigating Committee which, if believed, showed that President Nixon, Haldeman, and others in the Administration had engaged in planning a "cover-up" to hide the responsibility for the break-in. If so, they were guilty of the felonious crime of conspiring to obstruct justice. Those whom Dean accused vigorously denied his allegations. We of the Watergate Special Prosecution Force could and would continue the investigation, but at that point it looked all too likely that the matter would come down to a question of credibility.

Suddenly Alexander Butterfield, another former White House aide, revealed in testimony before the Senate Investigating Committee that all the conversations in which President Nixon had taken part were recorded on tape. Here was a way of resolving the question of credibility—if we could obtain the tapes.

But could we obtain the tapes? The President quickly made a public statement that he would keep them confidential. He also said that he had taken the tapes into his personal custody. The latter statement had central legal significance. A court or a congressional committee obtains records, papers, and other physical evidence by issuing a subpoena *duces tecum* to the person who has possession of the evidence, commanding him or her to bring the evidence before the tribunal. The attempt meant that a subpoena for the tapes must be addressed to the President himself. "What right," his lawyers would ask, "has a congressional committee or a court to issue a subpoena to the President of the United States?"

At the Watergate Special Prosecution Force we resolved to press ahead. Subpoenas are printed legal forms issued in the name of the court. We filled in "Richard M. Nixon, 1600 Pennsylvania Avenue," and designated as the required evidence the tape recordings of the nine specific conversations that seemed most likely to deal with the Watergate break-in and any cover-up. The paperwork was simple, but even at this stage we began to have the awful sense that we were setting in train an historic confrontation that we could not easily control. No President of the United States had ever been forced to give evidence in response to a subpoena. No court had ever successfully directed any other kind of order to a President of the United States. Nevertheless, we must try.

When the subpoena was received by the President, he sent the court a letter refusing to comply. The courts, he respectfully argued, have no more power to direct the conduct of the President than the President has power to interfere with the courts. As President, the letter continued, he had a constitutional duty to maintain the integrity of his office; one of its responsibilities was to decide without outside interference what papers and like documents should be kept confidential in order to protect the public interest. These were *Presidential* papers; the public interest demanded confidentiality.

The grand jury investigating the Watergate affair was sitting under the direction of U. S. District Judge John Sirica. The next step would be to ask Judge Sirica for an order directing Richard M. Nixon to show cause why the court should not require him to comply with the subpoena. But while in practice a prosecutor may guide and even dominate a grand jury, in legal theory he is the grand jury's servant and the investigation is the grand jury's investigation. To guard my flank, I went before the grand jury, explained the importance of the tapes, recommended that the grand jurors authorize me to seek the order to show cause, and asked for their approval. There was general acquiescence. I was then ready to file the formal application to show cause, but in view of the extraordinary daily publicity, it seemed courteous first to tell Judge Sirica. When we met in his chambers, I was not a little surprised to have him say that, while he did not doubt my word, he thought he should have the grand jury polled in open court to ascertain whether the grand jurors really did wish to press ahead with a subpoena to the President of the United States.

A day was set. The courtroom was jammed with reporters. Lawyers crowded the seats within the bar. The grand jury lined up on one of the spectators' benches. According to legal tradition, the grand jurors represent the people of the vicinity. The eighteen or twenty men and women then serving on the Watergate grand jury were truly a cross-section of the people of Washington: black and white, men and women, workers, unemployed and retired, one or two, but no more, educated for a profession. I rose and addressed Judge Sirica, stressing the importance of the tapes to the Watergate investigation and the necessity for an order to show cause. Judge Sirica turned toward the grand jury and asked the foreman, Vladimir Pregelj, to stand forward.

"Mr. Pregelj, you heard the statement of Mr. Cox?" Judge Sirica asked.

"I have, Your Honor," Pregelj said.

"This has been explained to the grand jury I take it?"

"It has."

"Is it the desire and wish of each grand juror, including yourself, that the court sign this order to show cause?"

"Your Honor, we have not polled the grand jury, but the question was asked informally and no objections have been raised."

"Will you call the names of the grand jurors, Mr. Clerk. I will ask each grand juror as your names are called to please stand."

The moment dramatized the American philosophy of government. Here were eighteen or twenty typical citizens, none titled, rich, or powerful, deciding whether to require the President of the United States, the holder of the Nation's highest office and probably the most powerful man in the world, to come before them in order to help them in the administration of justice, and either to give an account of himself or to plead the privilege against self-incrimination if there were evidence that he had violated a criminal law. I can recall no more symbolic scene in American history. At the time, and for me, its intensity was fed by the fear that the grand jurors, when called upon to stand individually in open court before the eyes of the Nation, might not be quite as ready to challenge the President as they had been in the secrecy of the grand jury room. It is not easy to stand up to the President of the United States. I would learn that at first hand a few months later.

I should not have worried. The jurors were unanimous. Judge Sirica signed the order directing President Nixon to show cause why he should not be required to comply with the subpoena calling for production of the nine tapes. The order set the stage, first, for courtroom battles over whether the courts could and should order the President to produce the tapes, and, later, for a test of the ultimate foundations of our constitutionalism.

II

Years later the imagination is inadequate to revive the tension in Judge Sirica's courtroom on the day of oral argument. Never before had a federal court issued and enforced an order addressed personally to the President of the United States.

Once before, in a time of great national excitement, the question had arisen whether a court may require the President to produce evidence relevant in a criminal proceeding. In 1807 Aaron Burr was put on trial in the federal court in Richmond, Virginia, charged with committing treason against the United States by plotting to form a new nation out of the area in the lower valley of the Mississippi River. Burr had been Vice President during President Jefferson's first term in office, but the two had become enemies. Jefferson was pushing hard for a conviction. He had taken the extraordinary step of sending a special message to Congress, building an air of national crisis and telling the country that Burr's "guilt is placed beyond question." Burr's chief accuser was a General James Wilkinson, the U.S. commanding general in New Orleans, himself a traitor in the pay of the Spanish government. Wilkinson had reported Burr's activities to President Jefferson by letter. Burr's lawyers, believing that the letter might aid the defense, applied for a subpoena *duces tecum,* requiring the President to produce the letter. Chief Justice John Marshall presided at the trial, sitting on circuit in accordance with a custom now abandoned. After three days of argument, the court granted the subpoena. Under the rules of evidence, the Chief Justice reasoned, the "propriety of introducing any paper into the case, as testimony, must depend upon the character of the paper, not on the character of the person who holds it." The President had no immunity. "The court perceived no legal objection to issuing a subpoena *duces tecum* to any person whatever, provided the case be such as to justify the process." But then Marshall grew more cautious, perhaps fearing a conflict between the Executive and the Judiciary: "[W]hatever difference may exist with respect to the power to compel the same obedience to the process [that is, the subpoena], as if it had been directed to a private citizen, there exists no difference with respect to the right to obtain it."[5]

Before Judge Sirica, the Watergate Special Prosecution Force cited as a precedent the subpoena addressed to President Jefferson. President Nixon's lawyers replied by pointing to the Chief Justice's reservation of judgment upon whether the subpoena could be enforced. Jefferson's reply cut both ways. He would not comply with the subpoena either by traveling to Richmond or by furnishing all the papers: "All nations have found it necessary, that, for the advantageous conduct of their affairs, some of these proceedings at least, should remain known to their executive functionary only." But Jefferson was ready to furnish voluntarily whatever the courts might need, "reserving the necessary right of the president of the United States, to decide, independently of all other authority, what papers coming to him as president, the public interest permits to be communicated."[6] No one had moved precipitously to enforce the subpoena. Later the prosecutor furnished parts of the material to the defense. The issue was then allowed to slide into history without resolution.

In 1973 two lines of argument were presented by President Nixon's lawyers.

One was a claim of absolute Presidential immunity from legal process. After the event, in the quiet of Old Schools at Cambridge University, England, a Scandinavian legal scholar vehemently protested to me, "It is *unthinkable* that the courts of any country should issue an order to its Chief of State."

His outrage reflected an ancient postulate of many legal systems, including some that declared the monarch's duty to obey the laws but provided no means of enforcement. The sovereign can do no wrong. The Chief of State inherited the sovereign's immunity. The theme found its way into American law. In *Marbury* v. *Madison*,[7] counsel seeking the mandamus against the Secretary of State were careful to acknowledge that the situation of the President was different:

> I declare it to be my opinion . . . that the President is not amenable to any court of judicature for the exercise of his high functions, but is responsible only in the mode pointed out in the constitution [that is, by impeachment].[8]

A century before Watergate, in a case brought by the State of Mississippi against President Andrew Johnson, Attorney General Henry Stanberry invoked sovereign immunity in arguing in the U.S. Supreme Court that the President is beyond the reach of legal process:

> I deny that there is a particle less dignity belonging to the office of President than to the office of King of Great Britain or of any other potentate on the face of the earth. He represents the majesty of the law and of the people as fully and as essentially, and with the same dignity, as does any absolute monarch or the head of any independent government in the world.[9]

The Court dismissed the complaint, albeit upon somewhat different grounds, but most lawyers and scholars concluded that in performing what he deems his constitutional duties the President is indeed immune from legal process.

In 1973 President Nixon's lawyers put the claim of immunity in terms more pleasing to American ears. The Constitution is framed upon a theory of the separation of powers. The federal legislative power is vested in Congress, the executive power in a President elected separately from the Congress, and the judicial power in the courts. Each of the three branches is independent and coordinate with the others. A holding that the President is personally subject to the orders of a court, President Nixon's lawyers contended, would effectively subordinate the Executive Branch.

Our answering argument was that all executive officials are subject to law and therefore have no immunity from court orders. The principle, drawn from earlier English history, had first taken shape in *Marbury* v. *Madison* in the ruling that the Secretary of State was subject to judicial command when necessary to enforce the vested legal right of a citizen to his commission as Justice of the Peace, even though the Secretary was withholding the commission under orders from the President.[10] In that case the Court had turned away from confrontation, but in later years the judiciary had often issued decrees requiring high executive officials to desist from unconstitutional or otherwise illegal action, even when directed by the President.[11]

The most dramatic instance had developed under President Truman. In order to limit wage and price inflation and to provide a method of resolving major labor disputes without recourse to strikes, which would interrupt the flow of weapons to the armed forces, President Harry S. Truman had established the National Wage Stabilization Board. When the production of virtually the entire supply of steel was threatened by a strike of the United Steelworkers against the major steel companies, the board intervened, heard the dispute, and recommended a settlement. The steel companies refused to comply with the recommendations. The Steelworkers struck. President Truman, fearful of the effect on the flow of war matériel and acting as the Nation's Chief Executive and Commander-in-Chief of the Armed Forces, directed his Secretary of Commerce to seize and operate the steel mills. The Secretary accomplished the seizure without physical interference from the steel companies, and the Steelworkers returned to work. The steel companies then sued the Secretary of Commerce, alleging that the Presidential order of seizure was unconstitutional and asking for a decree requiring return of the mills. Even though the suit was nominally against the Secretary of Commerce, no one doubted that the real party in interest was the President of the United States. The U.S. Supreme Court affirmed the trial court's decree ordering the Secretary to terminate the seizure of the steel mills as an unconstitutional effort of the President, without statutory authority, to exercise the legislative powers that the Constitution entrusts to Congress alone.[12] President Truman regarded the decision as a personal affront. There was speculation that he might disregard the decision. The President put an end to it quickly, telling the country that it was his duty to obey the law as declared by the Court.

Justice Robert H. Jackson's concurring opinion best expressed not only the dominant constitutional theme but the long history behind it, running back to Magna Carta:

With all its defects, delays and inconveniences, men have discovered no technique for long preserving free government except that the Executive be under the law, and that the law be made by parliamentary deliberations.[13]

In a footnote the Justice recalled Chief Justice Coke's reply to King James I: "The King ought not to be under any man, but he is under God and the Law." I quoted the words again in closing my argument before Judge Sirica.

The opposing traditions—Presidential immunity, on the one hand, and subjection of the Executive Branch to judicial interpretations of the Constitution and laws, on the other hand—were scarcely compatible. It would make little sense to conclude that the President is subject to the rule of law when he acts, as he usually must, through other officials, but that the President is above the law if he personally violates the rights of other citizens or refuses to perform a personal legal duty. Yet the law is filled with compromises between policies that, when pressed to their extremes, are logically inconsistent. No President had been subjected to legal process since the subpoena in the Burr trial. No President had ever been successfully sued. And Judge Sirica would be bound to foresee down the road the awesome question "If I order compliance with the subpoena and President Nixon refuses, how can compliance be achieved?"

The second line of defense presented by President Nixon's lawyers was a claim of "executive privilege." The Constitution says nothing about the subject, but a number of prior Presidents, including Dwight D. Eisenhower, had asserted that the Chief Executive has the right to decide finally and for all purposes what information, documents, or other papers in the Executive Branch of the government shall be kept confidential. The argument is partly in terms of the equality and independence of the three branches: no one branch, it is said, may control the documents or papers of another. The argument is also practical: in order to perform his constitutional duties the President needs aides and advisers with whom he can debate policy freely and candidly; freedom and candor depend upon assurance of the confidentiality that protects a man from public or political reprisals because of what he has said or thought. The privilege had been claimed and disputed every now and then throughout U.S. history, usually by a President against the Senate or House of Representatives. No constitutional principle

had emerged, because the courts were supposed to have no power
to resolve such controversies between the two political branches.

The Special Prosecution Force conceded that those considerations are important enough to give rise to a right to confidentiality
except when weightier public interests require disclosure. In a
grand jury investigation those weightier interests are present and
so defeat the prima facie privilege, we argued, when there is already
other evidence that the deliberations may themselves have involved
the commission of crime by high executive officials. In such a case,
we said, any danger that the compelled disclosure would discourage
candor in future executive deliberations is far outweighed by the
need to preserve the integrity of the office of the President from
the taint of suspicion of criminal conduct. Whether we had made
a sufficient showing was for the court, not the President, to decide.
Everyone knew that President Nixon's good faith was in question,
but it seemed unnecessary and unwise to attack him explicitly.
Even if a President could judge impartially the relative public ad-
vantages of secrecy and disclosure without regard to the consequences for himself or his associates, we concluded, confidence in
the Presidency as well as in the integrity and impartiality of the
legal system as between the high and the lowly would be impaired
by violation of the ancient precept that no man shall be judge of
his own cause.

A week after the argument Judge Sirica unequivocally rejected
the claim of Presidential immunity. Invoking the line of precedents
beginning with *Marbury* v. *Madison* and culminating in the Steel
Seizure Case, he reasoned that to give a President a personal
immunity denied to executive officials acting on the President's
instructions "would exalt the form . . . over its substance."[14]

Judge Sirica also rejected the claim of an absolute executive
privilege. The tapes must be submitted to the court for its secret
inspection without the participation of the Watergate Special Prosecution Force. The court would then determine what portions, if
any, were privileged and what portions should be submitted to the
grand jury.

Both parties appealed. In the U.S. Court of Appeals the specter
of Presidential disobedience began to move out of the shadows.
The White House was hinting that the President might simply
ignore Judge Sirica's order. How could compliance be achieved?
And if compliance could not be forced, how did that affect the

court's jurisdiction? Judge David Bazelon put the question during the oral argument.

> JUDGE BAZELON: Assuming that the President is not subject to punishment for contempt, what significance would that have to the question now before the court?
>
> COX: I think no real relevance, Your Honor. . . . The question of the court's duty to decide is determined not by its power to enforce its decrees but by whether the issue is one that lends itself to adjudication.

After citing U.S. Supreme Court precedents enunciating the principle, I continued:

> Our country is blessed, of course, Chief Judge Bazelon, by the fact that Presidents, when the time came, have always bowed to a decision of the Supreme Court and complied with it. . . . I at least have every confidence that the same spirit which has characterized our history would prevail here, both with respect to this Court or the Supreme Court, if the case should go higher.

The answer suppressed a worry that would soon turn to anguish.

While the Court of Appeals deliberated, tension built in Washington. In late September, the Vice President, Spiro Agnew, was charged with receiving while he was Vice President continuing payments of graft exacted from contractors while he was Governor of Maryland. On October 10 he acknowledged his guilt in a federal court in Baltimore. His resignation left the country without a Vice President even while the cloud over the President led to talk about impeachment. Four days earlier the Middle East had erupted in war. There were daily reports both that White House aides would be indicted and that the Special Prosecutor would be fired.

Two days later, on October 12, the Court of Appeals rendered its decision.[15] Like Judge Sirica, it rejected the claims of Presidential immunity and absolute executive privilege. The opinion acknowledged that Presidential conversations are normally to be regarded as privileged, but held that the normal privilege must yield "in the face of the uniquely powerful showing made by the special prosecutor in this case" that the tapes were evidence "peculiarly necessary" to the grand jury's Watergate investigation. The opinion laid down the procedure to be followed, with active participation by the Special Prosecutor in separating the admissible from the privileged parts of the tapes. Later, Special Prosecutor Leon

Jaworski would subpoena a second set of tapes, and the U.S. Supreme Court would approve the core of the earlier decisions by Judge Sirica and the Court of Appeals.[16]

The rulings as a group settled the principle that even the President of the United States is subject to the Constitution and other legal obligations as interpreted by an independent judiciary.

III

"Settled the principle," I should say, "insofar as judicial decisions can." Judicial decisions could not determine what would happen if President Nixon refused to comply with the subpoena for the tapes, couching his refusal in respectful words for the courts but asserting his own sworn Presidential duty to uphold the Constitution and laws as he understood them. What could I do? What could Judge Sirica or the Court of Appeals do? Was the law helpless if the President chose to ignore its commands?

I had begun to worry about those questions when we first considered subpoenaing the tapes. As hints of noncompliance began filtering out of the White House in response to Judge Sirica's decision, we discussed in staff meetings the steps we could take. We could seek a citation for contempt of court; that would highlight the President's disobedience but accomplish no more. Should we ask Judge Sirica to impose a coercive fine for each day of noncompliance? If President Nixon would not produce the tapes, he was unlikely to pay a fine. If he refused, legal theory might permit attachment of his property, but it seemed to me that reducing the issue to dollars and cents would cheapen it. "Send a group of U.S. Marshals to the White House to seize the tapes," one lawyer suggested. "They'd be met by the White House guards or the Marines in their fancy uniforms," another replied. Scenes from Gilbert and Sullivan operettas floated through my mind.

In both academic and governmental posts, I had previously been required to think about the ultimate sanctions for law in a free society, especially about the enforcement of judicial rulings against a State or another branch of the federal government. The Supreme Court may interpret the Constitution; it may even refuse to give effect to an unconstitutional law or executive order; but lacking the power of the purse or the sword, a court is helpless to enforce its own commands. Their effectiveness, like the effectiveness of all law in a free society, depends for the most part on voluntary compliance. In cases affecting a few recalcitrant individuals, whether civil or criminal, the sheriff stands behind the court's decree; but even against individuals, force can be invoked only in exceptional cases. Force supports, but cannot take the place of, voluntary compliance, because freedom and force on a large scale are antithetical.

When the Executive Branch is willing to support the court decree, coercion may sometimes be available even against a recalcitrant State. President Eisenhower sent troops to Little Rock, Arkansas, in 1957 to quell mob violence that was frustrating a decree ordering desegregation of the Little Rock schools. President Kennedy used the Army to force the admission of James Meredith, a black student, to the University of Mississippi in the face of obstructive violence encouraged by Governor Ross Barnett.

But if the President will not support the courts against a recalcitrant State, the courts have no coercive power. In 1831 the State of Georgia convicted two missionaries living in Cherokee country of violating a State law requiring persons living in Cherokee country to take out a license and swear allegiance to the State of Georgia. The missionaries were sentenced to four years' imprisonment. The U.S. Supreme Court held that the Georgia statute infringed on the exclusive power of the federal government to pass laws dealing with Indian affairs, and ordered release of the missionaries.[17] Georgia refused. The country was in the throes of excitement over the power of the U.S. Supreme Court to review or reverse decisions by a State's highest court. South Carolina was preaching and beginning to practice nullification. In the South and West, public opinion ran strongly against the Indians. An old Indian fighter from the Southwest, Andrew Jackson, was President. Amidst the speculation over whether he would enforce the Court's decree, he was reported to have said, "John Marshall has made his decision. Now let *him* enforce it." Before the dispute with Georgia was resolved, South Carolina attempted to block collection of the federal tariff. South Carolina's attempt at nullification led President Jackson to take a more nationalistic stance and made it improbable that he could allow Georgia to continue its defiance of the Court. A showdown was averted by face-saving compromise. Georgia, while standing fast on principle, granted pardons to the missionaries, making the question of compliance moot.

Some judicial decrees cannot be carried out by force, even if the

Executive is willing. In 1963, just as school desegregation was coming to a crisis in Alabama and U.S. Attorney General Robert Kennedy was arranging for federal troops to bar Governor George Wallace from blocking the entrance of the black children through the schoolhouse door, the Supreme Court of the United States, in cases from Pennsylvania and Maryland, ruled that to open the day in the public schools by reading from the Bible or saying a prayer violated the constitutional ban against "an establishment of religion."[18] Governor Wallace announced that Alabama teachers would continue to open the schoolday with prayer. He then fired off a telegram to Attorney General Kennedy, demanding to know whether the Attorney General would send the army to Alabama to stop the teachers and children from praying. The Attorney General asked me what reply he should make and whether he was required to send troops to Alabama to enforce the Supreme Court decision. I answered, "Of course not," but when he went on to ask "What should I do," I could only murmur that there was no decree against any Alabama official for him to enforce, that the problem was a long way off, and that perhaps it would never arise.

My answer was technically correct but it was also lame, both politically and philosophically. Much later, I realized that I should have gone on to say "Mr. Attorney General, often there is no satisfactory answer to the question how should the law be enforced, either because there is no physical power or because the use of the only available power is morally unacceptable. Constitutionalism works, our liberties are protected, and our society is free because officials, individuals, and the people as a whole realize that liberty for the weak depends upon the rule of law and the rule of law depends upon voluntary compliance. When the test comes, that realization must be strong enough for the people to rise up, morally and politically, and overwhelm the offender. The roots of constitutionalism lie in the hearts of the people."

The incident came back to mind as the crisis approached in the case of the Watergate Tapes. A Presidential refusal to comply with the order of the court would lift the controversy beyond the courts into a trial before the people. But would the people, consciously, half consciously, or intuitively, realize that constitutionalism and therefore, for the long run, the bulwarks of their liberties were at risk? Would they see the issue as I saw it? Did I see it right?

History was far from encouraging. There was good reason to

believe that if the Court had issued a mandamus in *Marbury* v. *Madison,* President Jefferson and Secretary of State Madison would have defied the Court. Probably they would have succeeded, and the Court would never have achieved supremacy in applying the Constitution. President Lincoln directed the military to disregard writs of habeas corpus issued by the federal court sitting in Maryland at the start of the Civil War. In 1935, fearing a Supreme Court ruling invalidating his abandonment of the gold standard, President Franklin D. Roosevelt had prepared a "fireside chat" to be broadcast on national radio following the decision and explaining to the country his decision to disregard the ruling of the Court. He did not have to deliver the address, because the decision was unexpectedly favorable. Suppose, I asked myself, that President Nixon, invoking the examples of Jefferson, Lincoln, and Roosevelt, stood on his duty to carry out the Constitution as he understood it. He had received an overwhelming popular endorsement in the 1972 election, less than a year earlier. A Harvard professor seemed an unlikely figure to challenge successfully the President of the United States.

My fears went further. Suppose that President Nixon did disobey the order to produce the Watergate Tapes, suffered no penalties, and thus revealed the impotence of law. Later, given that precedent of successful disregard of the judicial command, might not President Nixon himself or his early successors all too easily disregard other judicial orders enforcing constitutional safeguards and so erode the judicial supremacy underpinning our constitutionalism? President Nixon had already given signs of holding the philosophy he later bluntly acknowledged: "If the President does it, it can't be against the law. The President does it."

Given the costs of losing, perhaps it would be wrong to force the issue and thus precipitate a constitutional crisis. Winston Churchill once observed that a democracy must never expose its weakness. Surely it would be irresponsible to play the part of the little boy who destroyed the myth of the emperor's marvelous raiment by blurting out that the emperor wore no clothes. On the other hand, what good was the principle that even our highest official is subject to the Constitution and laws if one dared not invoke the principle over executive opposition?

The dilemma seemed unresolvable. The only means of escape would be to evolve a compromise that would provide the Watergate

Special Prosecution Force with all parts of the tapes relevant to its inquiries in a form acceptable as evidence yet withhold all other portions whose release would threaten national security interests or otherwise embarrass the proper conduct of Presidential business. And plainly the White House would not agree to any solution that called for Judge Sirica to make the separation.

Time was short. The Court of Appeals had stayed its order for only five days in order to allow the President to seek review by the U.S. Supreme Court. The tension, fueled by war in the Middle East and the forced resignation of Vice President Agnew, was near the breaking point. There was talk of the impeachment of President Nixon and, contrariwise, of my dismissal. The grand jury had just indicted Egil Krog, a White House aide, for perjury in the course of an investigation into whether there had been a White House conspiracy to break into the office of a Dr. Fielding, Daniel Ellsberg's psychiatrist, in the hope of stealing his files and using them to discredit Ellsberg as a hero of the movement seeking to end the war in Vietnam. The press carried rumors that the Watergate Special Prosecution Force would shortly charge such senior White House aides as Charles Colson and John Erhlichman with the conspiracy. The press also carried repeated rumors that I would soon be fired.

Against this background I met with Attorney General Elliot Richardson late in the afternoon of Monday, October 15. We enjoyed an easy informal relationship, each confident of the basic integrity of the other, even when his place in the President's Cabinet and mine as Special Prosecutor came into opposition. Elliot had been a brilliant student at the Harvard Law School when I was a young professor. A common interest in government brought us together. We both lived in Boston. We had served as law clerks to Judge Learned Hand. We had been associated with the same Boston law firm. As we talked that evening, Elliot changed into formal evening clothes for a White House dinner, the first to which he had ever been invited, despite his years in the President's Cabinet.

But the informality did little to lift the weight of the business. A few days earlier, Elliot had musingly observed to me that it "is better to lose your job than to have your head cut off." I could not tell whether he was reflecting on his own stand in the Agnew affair or was preparing me for my dismissal. I was blunter. "You realize that the President has no power to fire me," I said; "only you can do it." I then recalled how President Andrew Jackson had found it necessary to force a Secretary of the Treasury out of office and appoint a successor in order to carry out his wish to remove all government deposits from the Bank of the United States. "Yes," Elliot replied a little wryly, "that's what the lawyers here in the Department tell me."

That Monday evening we talked of the need for a compromise that would avoid a constitutional crisis. Years later I learned that he had spent much of that day and the preceding Sunday conferring with General Alexander M. Haig, the White House Chief of Staff, about the President's determination to get rid of me. Out of their discussion and disagreements had emerged Elliot's undertaking to persuade me to accept a plan of third-party review that came to be called the Stennis compromise.

The details of the plan emerged gradually as Elliot and I talked late Monday afternoon and again on Tuesday and as he wrote them down on Wednesday, October 17. J. Fred Buzhardt, Counsel to the President, would prepare a transcript of those portions of the nine specific tapes covered by the subpoena which he concluded were relevant to the Watergate investigation. Senator John Stennis would then authenticate the transcript by listening to the tapes, transcript in hand, excluding portions that should be withheld in the interests of national security or international relations. The transcript would be phrased in the third person, and the President's language would be sanitized to avoid embarrassing him. How far the authenticated transcript would be a paraphrase and how far it would be a verbatim copy of the tape was unclear.

I was not averse to third-party review of the tapes. Indeed, I had first proposed it to President Nixon's lawyers before the decision of the Court of Appeals, but they had responded by insisting that I agree to accept whatever transcript the President submitted as containing all Watergate material not required to be held in secret to protect the defense or international interest of the United States. It was plain, however, that the Attorney General's proposal, as authorized by the White House, fell short of an acceptable compromise.

First, Senator Stennis was not an acceptable third party. I had complete confidence in his personal honesty and integrity. He would not deceive either the Special Prosecution Force or the country. But Senator Stennis had been an admirer of President

Nixon, and they shared strong views about the requirements of secrecy in matters affecting the national interest. Buzhardt, the President's Counsel, was to prepare the typed transcript. His version was certain to be favorable to the President. Under the best of circumstances the Senator would tend to rely upon Buzhardt, who had previously worked for him. In fact, Senator Stennis was hardly in a position to be alert to omissions or distortions. He was still recovering from gunshot wounds received in an attempted holdup. He would hear the tapes only once, with no opportunity to enhance a poor recording. While members of the Senate would be well pleased to have Senator Stennis as authenticator, he lacked the confidence of the general public. I could not reject Senator Stennis without offending the Senate, but I proposed additional names.

Second, it was essential that any procedure for editing the tapes and supplying the relevant portions yield evidence admissible in a criminal trial. The Attorney General's proposal was almost surely inadequate in this respect. Furthermore, any defendant charged with the cover-up would undoubtedly demand access to the tapes on the ground that they might contain exculpatory evidence; and under established Supreme Court doctrine we would be required either to furnish the tapes or to dismiss the indictments. I proposed a procedure that would make the authenticators officers of the court.

Third, the proposed compromise made no provision for access to relevant portions of other tapes or other documentary evidence in the White House files. The subpoena covered only nine tapes. If some of those nine sustained John Dean's testimony, then other recorded conversations would surely be important evidence. It would be foolish to compromise the case then in court, in which we had obtained a favorable order, without some provision for future access to other tapes.

On Thursday afternoon I responded to the Attorney General's proposals in writing, explaining the need for changes to meet my objections and expressing my earnest hope that we could work out a solution. Then, because nothing seemed likely to happen before morning, I sought relief in cocktails and dinner with my brother, Louis, his wife, and children. As we sat down to the table, the phone rang. Louis answered and came back to say that it was my deputy, Henry Ruth, with a message to call the White House

operator and ask for Marshall Wright. I was mystified. I knew no
Marshall Wright but made the call and after some confusion heard
the familiar voice of Charles Wright, a fellow law professor who
had been advising President Nixon on questions of constitutional
law and who had made the arguments on his behalf before Judge
Sirica and the Court of Appeals. No chair near the telephone. I sat
on the floor. Three little nieces, excited by the mention of the
White House, crowded about me. Kathy, the youngest, climbed
into my lap. "Is it the President?" "What did he say?" "Let me
hear, Uncle Archie." "What did he say?"

At the White House Wright had argued that my refusal to accept
the so-called Stennis compromise left no alternative to firing me.
He had telephoned in a final effort to persuade me that the proposal
was fair. To my ears his words sounded more like an ultimatum as
he listed four points that I must categorically accept:

1. Only Senator Stennis would be permitted to hear the tapes.
2. He could not be made an officer of the court.
3. No portion of the actual tapes would be provided to the courts
   or to anyone under any circumstances.
4. I must agree not to subpoena any additional Presidential tape,
   paper, or document.

The conditions were obviously unacceptable. The fourth condition alone would have made them intolerable. I had learned the
importance of additional tapes from testimony. Before the Senate
Judiciary Committee I had promised to challenge claims to executive privilege. I had won two courtroom battles. I could not cry
a halt now without violating my promise and virtually abandoning
the Watergate investigation. Yet I was reluctant to be the one to
break off the effort to find some mutually acceptable solution. It
seemed irresponsible to take the final step toward precipitating a
constitutional crisis while sitting on the floor at a family party. I
told Wright that his conditions seemed unacceptable but that the
matter was too important to settle then and there. "Put them in
writing," I said. "Send them over to me tomorrow morning and I'll
give you a more thoughtful answer."

Wright's letter was an apologia for the Stennis compromise. It
omitted the four points upon which he had insisted in the telephone
conversation, but it assumed that I was rejecting "the very reason-

able proposal." I quickly wrote back, stating the four points on which he had insisted and explaining why I could not honorably accept them. Wright's reply gave a slightly different version of the four points, but the thrust of his position remained firm. Further negotiations, he said, would obviously be futile.

Between letters, those of us at the Watergate Special Prosecution Force hurried to Judge Sirica's courtroom. John Dean had secured a promise of immunity from any criminal prosecution resulting from the testimony he gave before the Senate Investigating Committee. But James Neal and other lawyers on the Special Prosecution Force had had the foresight to gather and seal the evidence available against Dean before the promise of use immunity was given. They had also separated out the evidence that Dean had supplied while he was negotiating earlier with the office of the United States Attorney. Enough remained to convince both Dean and his lawyers that he could and would be convicted of the felony of conspiring to obstruct justice by participating in the Watergate cover-up. That Friday morning at 10:00 A.M. he was to plead guilty. The hearing was brief but dramatic. Dean was sentenced to five years' imprisonment. The White House had visible proof that the Watergate Special Prosecution Force would pull no punches.

Back we went to wait in the office. The stay that the Court of Appeals had granted the President was to expire in a few hours. Surely some White House announcement was imminent; perhaps word of the President's appeal to the Supreme Court of the United States. Rumors and telephone calls from the press added to the tension, but nothing happened. The Supreme Court closed. Still nothing happened. In such times anxiety easily leads to mistakes. I had sought to break the tension by browsing in Brentano's during the lunch hour. Now I told my staff that I was going home and urged them to follow my example.

About 7:45 P.M. the telephone rang. It was Attorney General Richardson, calling to bring me up to date. A letter was on its way to him from President Nixon, announcing that Senators Sam Ervin and Howard Baker, Chairman and Vice Chairman of the Senate Investigating Committee, had endorsed the Stennis compromise. He then read part of the President's letter "for your information":

As part of these actions I am instructing you to direct Special Prosecutor Archibald Cox of the Watergate Special Prosecution Force that he is to make no further efforts by judicial process to obtain tapes, notes, or memoranda of Presidential conversations.

Elliot said that he would get back to the White House and seek to persuade the President to withdraw those instructions.

I hurried back to the office to meet James Doyle, officially my Special Assistant for Public Affairs but now a friend whose suggestions and support were of inestimable value. Nothing happened. The deadlines for the morning newspapers were approaching. Still nothing happened. Jim called the Washington Bureau of the *Los Angeles Times* and thus learned that the White House had indeed announced that Senator Stennis would prepare summaries of the relevant portions of the tapes and that Senators Ervin and Baker had approved this solution on behalf of the Senate Investigating Committee. The White House statement noted "with regret" that I had rejected the proposal and said that the President was now ordering me to make no further attempts to get any more Presidential documents by judicial process.

In the moments remaining I dictated a short reply for Jim Doyle to type.

In my judgment the President is refusing to comply with the Court's decree.

A summary of the content of the tapes lacks the evidentiary value of the tapes themselves. No steps are being taken to turn over the important notes, memoranda and other documents that the Court orders require. I shall bring these points to the attention of the Court and abide by its decision.

Referring to the instruction not to seek further judicial process, I said:

For me to comply with those instructions would violate my solemn pledge to the Senate and the country to invoke judicial process to challenge exaggerated claims of executive privilege. I shall not violate my promise.

I also undertook to hold a press conference the next afternoon.

Shortly afterward, the telephone rang. It was Elliot Richardson, asking, "Can you tell me what happened to my letter from the President?"

The morning headlines carried the message COX DEFIANT. If the writers could have seen me, they would not have said I was defiant. I was in tears, complaining to my wife, Phyllis: "I can't fight with the President of the United States. I was brought up to honor and respect the President of the United States." Phyllis helped me pull myself together. I went to the office. The staff was there—anxious, excited, and supportive. We went into my room and sat around the conference table as I asked for advice. Each had something different to propose. "Be tough; kick him in the teeth." "Don't be arrogant; be restrained." The advice was worse than useless. All of it pertained to my demeanor or style. There was no use advising me about that. I knew that the only thing that would show through was my true nature, whatever that might be. After a while I stopped the discussion. "You can help me most by putting it in writing," I said.

As they left the room, I settled down to prepare myself for the press conference that afternoon much as I would prepare for an oral argument before the Supreme Court. Putting my thoughts into a familiar mold eased the tension. Later the staff assembled in our library. It was an emotional moment. We knew that a crisis was upon us. It might even be the end. Again, emotion almost overwhelmed me. I did not know what would happen, I said. Perhaps I would be dismissed. The one thing that was clear was that whatever happened to me, the staff must be sure to stay on the job together. If the staff did that, I said, the investigation would go forward, whatever the President might seek to do.

We went to the National Press Club. The tension was bearable because Phyllis went with me and I could draw on her for strength. The room was crowded. NBC and CBS had pre-empted the time and were carrying the interview live. I told of my efforts to get evidence from the White House and the repeated frustration. I explained the negotiations with Elliot Richardson and the telephone conversations with Charles Wright. I also explained my reasons for rejecting the so-called Stennis compromise and then took up the instructions not to go back to court in pursuit of evidence:

> It is that there is a basic change in the institutional arrangement that was established. . . . It wouldn't be right to continue with the pretense that we have the old arrangements. . . . I'm afraid that if I acquiesced once in the hope of avoiding confrontation—and as I say, I don't like confrontations—then I would find myself saying, Well, it isn't worth doing this time, either.

In answer to questions, I acknowledged that the President could have me dismissed, but said that in the meanwhile I would go about my duties "on the terms on which I assumed them."

> I do not mean to seem to cling to power or office. If my personal ease were the test, I would be on the coast of Maine and not here. But I do think it important to do everything I can to emphasize the extent of the departure from the kind of detached, independent public inquiry which the Senate caused to be set up. Once I have done everything I can to make that clear, then I will be happy to relax.

The press conference over, it was again time to wait. That evening after dinner the telephone rang. Again, it was Elliot Richardson to tell me what was going to happen. President Nixon has asked me to fire you, he said, and I have resigned. Deputy Attorney General William Ruckleshaus, the next in line, was also asked to fire you and he has resigned. The Solicitor General, Robert Bork, has agreed to dismiss you.

A little later the phone rang again. It was the White House, calling to ask our address. "I should have told them that you had gone away," my daughter Sally laughingly said. "I wonder what they would have done then." An hour later there was a knock on the door. It was a letter from Robert Bork dismissing me.

In answer to inquiries from the press, I made one last statement: "It is now for the Congress and the people to decide."

Sunday and Monday a firestorm of public outrage overwhelmed the White House. The President's defiance of the courts and the Saturday night massacre dominated the media. There were special bulletins. Senators, Representatives, newspaper editors, and columnists called for impeachment. Cars streamed by the White House, honking for impeachment. Telegrams streamed into Washington at the rate of thirty thousand a day. Tuesday morning, while Charles Wright was appearing on the *Today* show to describe how surprised and pleased he had been by the President's generous offer of compromise—the compromise Cox had so unreasonably rejected—John Anderson, the leader of the House Republican Conference, was coldly telling the President's legislative assistant, "If you want Republican members to support you, tell the President he has to turn over the tapes."

Tuesday afternoon Wright rose in Judge Sirica's courtroom. "I am . . . authorized to say that the President of the United States will comply in all respects with the order of August 29 as modified by the order of the Court of Appeals. . . . [T]his President does not defy the law."

Because the people did rise up morally and politically, the rule of law prevailed. The response doubtless flowed from many sources: disgust at the evidence already published, distrust engendered by the withholding of evidence, outrage that President Nixon should insist upon the dismissal of a man whose sole offense was to pursue the assignment given him, and should thus force Richardson and Ruckleshaus from office, determination that despite the President's interference the Watergate investigation should go forward under an independent Special Prosecution Force. I like to think that there was also present something deeper and more enduring—a realization that all our liberties depend upon compliance with law. By the Watergate investigations and the public response, the principle that even the highest executive officials are subject to the Constitution and laws as interpreted by an independent judiciary was confirmed and strengthened, not only in legal theory but in fact. Ultimately, their support is the only sanction for constitutionalism and the rule of law.

Why do the people support constitutionalism and the rule of law, and, as their instrument, the courts? Will the support continue?

Surely, some part of the answer to the first question is that law, as it binds officials, is seen as a check on both executive oppression and bureaucratic caprice. "Law" takes its meaning partly from traditional and evocative precepts that in fact symbolize historic struggles for freedom from oppression: "Liberty under Law," for example, and "A government of laws, not of men." Surely, too, some part of the answer lies in the ancient and deep-seated belief that there are individual human rights that ought to be beyond the reach of any government, even the majority of a representative legislature. A third ingredient, I think, is the faith that law is reaching for equal justice. And perhaps it is not too romantic to suggest that the idea of "law" is also a response to an enduring human belief that in applying general rules to particular individuals, and also in protecting fundamental human rights against oppression by government, questions should be resolved not by force, not by the pressures of interest groups nor even by votes, but by what reason and a sense of justice tell is right. An unattainable ideal.

But reaching for ideals is part of reality, even though our reach exceeds our grasp.

Behind such beliefs lies the fragile faith that "law" has a separate existence not merely because it applies to all men equally but because it binds the judges as well as the judged, not just today but yesterday and tomorrow. Learned Hand, one of the great federal judges who never reached the Supreme Court, once put the point to me, a young law clerk, from a judge's perspective. "Sonny," he asked, "to whom am I responsible? No one can fire me. No one can dock my pay. Even those nine bozos in Washington, who sometimes reverse me, can't make me decide as they wish. Everyone should be responsible to someone. To whom am I responsible?" Then the Judge turned and pointed to the shelves of his law library. "To those books about us. That's to whom I'm responsible."

Judge Hand was no slave to precedent. He served a continuing body of law, but he also knew that the law must grow and change to meet the needs of men. New conditions may rob old legal concepts, old rules, and even old principles of their former meaning, so that the old ideals and even traditional principles call for new applications. Better perception of the true meaning of basic ideals also may call for new developments. On another occasion the Judge spoke of the dilemma at the bottom of a judge's work: "He must preserve his authority by cloaking himself in the majesty of an overshadowing past, but he must discover some composition with the dominant needs of his times."[19]

Devotion to the Constitution and the rule of law go hand in hand among the American people. The original Constitution still serves us well, despite the tremendous changes in every aspect of American life, because the Framers had the genius to say enough but not too much. They outlined a unique federal form of government; and shortly later, by amendments to the Constitution, they identified the basic individual rights they wished to guarantee against government oppression. In both areas important questions were left open, questions that the Framers could not foresee and questions on which they could not agree. Yet they said enough to provide points of reference. Then, perhaps by chance, perhaps by the wisdom and force of John Marshall, perhaps because it was intended though not written in the beginning, the great unanswered questions of federalism and individual right fell to the judiciary, and in the final analysis to the Supreme Court of the United States, to be decided "according to law." As the plan outlined in the Constitutional Convention succeeded, as the country grew and prospered both materially and in the realization of ideals, the Constitution gained majesty and authority far greater than those of any individual or body of men. Because enough was written and because decision "according to law" calls for building upon a continuity of principle found in the instrument, its structure and purposes, and in judicial precedents, traditional understanding, and historic practices, the Court, by always referring back to the sacred document, could bring to its resolution of the new and often divisive constitutional issues of each generation the momentum and authority of the overshadowing past yet could also accommodate the dominant needs of the times.

The genius of American constitutionalism, which supports the rule of law, lies, first, in the Constitution, which provides the opportunity for both change and continuity; second, in the method of judicial interpretation; and third, in the skill with which the generations of Justices, despite a few bad mistakes, have steered between the horns of their dilemma.

Perhaps the story of their work will clarify my meaning.

PART ONE

Building a Nation

· I ·

Miracle at Philadelphia

ON SEPTEMBER 17, 1787, stout old Ben Franklin's sedan chair was carried up the steps of Independence Hall for the last day of the Constitutional Convention. He wept as he signed. Sitting back while others signed, his eye fell on a painting, and he noted the difficulty artists have in distinguishing between a rising and setting sun. Franklin had labored unsuccessfully for a lifetime to bring the North American colonies together. Each movement toward union had been followed by retreat. For four hot and humid months the Convention had often teetered on the brink. "But now at length," he said, "I have the happiness to know that it is a rising not a setting sun."

In a nation unified by instant communication, nationwide markets, and a common heritage, it is hard to imagine the disunity prevailing when the delegates from thirteen independent States assembled in Philadelphia. The former colonies, freed from British rule in 1783 by the Treaty of Paris, were strung out along the eastern seaboard of North America from near the St. Lawrence River to the Florida peninsula, which then belonged to Spain. The population was a bit more than three million, thinly scattered over an area now holding seventy million people. Settlement had gone above tidewater, and in some regions it was rapidly pushing through the Appalachian Mountains to the valleys of rivers flowing westward into the Mississippi, such as the Ohio and the Cumberland. Distances were great. Roads were bad or nonexistent. Travel was both slow and painful. The journey from Boston to New York, which one now flies in forty-five minutes, might take a week. It would have taken months to travel by stagecoach from Boston to Savannah, if any man were strong enough to withstand the rigors of the journey without interruption.

The people of the rival States were also divided by differences of religion, environment, and custom that bred fierce jealousy and local pride. A man thought of himself as a Georgian, a Virginian, or a New Yorker but hardly ever as an American. Economic interests clashed. The one-family, self-sufficient farms of the States above the Potomac (where Washington, D.C., lies today) had different needs and produced an altogether different style of life from the great one-crop plantations of Virginia and South Carolina. In and around the port cities like Boston and New York, commercial interests were developing. Their needs were different from those of the farmers, and there was also bitter rivalry among them. In the North there were already very small, faint stirrings of local manufacturing industries, with their own special interests. The frontier clashed with the settled, coastal tidewater. The deepest cleavage—a division destined to split the States in a bloody civil war—was between the eight northern States and the five slave-holding States to the south.

The citizens having thrown off British rule at least for the moment, few men were willing to trade their local independence for a central government. Union among all thirteen States was unlikely on any terms. Unity was manifestly impossible.

Previous attempts to achieve a measure of united action had been halting. In 1775 a call had been issued for the several colonies to send delegates to a Continental Congress. It was the Continental Congress that adopted the Declaration of Independence, appointed George Washington to be Commander-in-Chief of the Continental Army, attempted to manage the war and to raise troops and money, issued a currency, floated loans at home and abroad, and negotiated the French treaty of alliance, which in turn provided the sinews of victory in the War for Independence. But the Continental Congress had little real power. It could lay requisitions on the State governments for men and money, but it was impotent when States chose to disregard the requisitions, as they often did.

The year 1781 brought the final adoption of the Articles of Confederation, by which the former colonies formed a loose alliance named the United States of America. The Articles gave the alliance no coercive power vis-à-vis any State. When a State ignored a fiscal levy, nothing could be done. The *New York Packet* for October 1, 1787, carried a representative notice:

> The subscriber has received nothing on account of the quota of this State for the present year.
>
> (*Signed*) Alexander Hamilton
> *Receiver of Continental Taxes*

New Hampshire had not paid a penny since the end of the war. When a State ignored treaty obligations, again there was nothing to be done. In the Treaty of Paris, for example, the United States promised respect for British claims against debtors and for British titles to property located in the United States. State governments, including State courts, all too often ignored the obligation. Likewise, under the Articles of Confederation the United States was powerless to protect commercial and mercantile interests, because it had neither the power to regulate interstate and foreign commerce nor the ability to require the individual States to respect commercial treaties with foreign nations.

As the 1780s wore on, James Madison, Alexander Hamilton, John Marshall, and other men of vision perceived the need for stronger federation if the American States were to survive in a rapacious world. Britain to the north in Canada and Spain in Florida and at the mouth of the Mississippi were waiting to gobble up all or parts of the States. The western lands—the region between the Appalachians and the Mississippi—furnished another persuasive reason for a better union. The old colonial charters had sometimes been carelessly drafted or based on misleading maps. A number of States had vast but vague and often overlapping claims to areas in the West. Strong sentiment developed for turning all the western areas over to the United States, but for that plan to succeed a more effective federal establishment was needed.

Mercantile and propertied interests were distraught by the weakness of some State governments and the irresponsibility of others. Even Massachusetts was barely able to maintain order against Shay's Rebellion. Domination by frontier and debtor classes often imperiled mercantile activity. Men concerned for property, trade, and commerce—even for physical security—began to look to the creation of a stronger central government. One group had a more direct concern. The Continental Congress had sought to establish a currency; it had also borrowed vast sums of money both at home and abroad. The creditors felt a money interest in a stronger central government because only a stronger central government could possibly assume and pay off the debts. Other merchants must have realized that assumption of these debts would create an atmosphere vastly more encouraging to trade and commerce.

Commercial warfare furnished the immediate occasion for the Philadelphia Convention. The taxes levied upon goods moving through the Ports of New York and Philadelphia were bleeding portless New Jersey white. Virginia and South Carolina were bleeding North Carolina. Baltimore was fattening on the people of the interior valleys. When Virginia passed a law declaring that vessels failing to pay duty in her ports were subject to seizure, she was aiming at cargoes from Massachusetts, New York, and Pennsylvania. In 1786 delegates from the States bordering on Chesapeake Bay met at Annapolis in an effort to stop the commercial warfare on the bay. The Annapolis Convention led to the broader summons to Philadelphia.

II

The assemblage over which George Washington presided in Independence Hall in the summer of 1787 was a bright constellation. Along with Benjamin Franklin were other veterans of the colonial and revolutionary periods, but most of the delegates were young men of the rising generation. Many were well educated and widely read, with their learning seasoned by local political experience. They were familiar with the idea that every government has a "constitution," meaning a set of laws or other rules fixing the powers and relationships of its several parts. In the Old World there were no written constitutions. In the New World there were the examples of the old colonial charters issued by the sovereign, outlining the frame of the colonial governments. The charters were followed by written State constitutions, drawn up after Independence, that carried forward the colonial regime. But the idea of creating a whole new sovereignty, an entire new government, by writing upon a blank sheet and securing its ratification by conventions of representatives of the people was utterly untried.

Two shrewd decisions were taken at the start of the Philadelphia Convention: to draw up a new constitution instead of amendments to the Articles of Confederation, and to maintain secrecy until the work was done. Possibly the first decision required the second, for the delegates had no authority to do more than propose amendments. After three months the work was done. The proposed Constitution was submitted to conventions in the separate States and, after tense battles, was ratified.

The Philadelphia Convention faced and resolved many divisive issues: between the large and small States, for example, and between the slave States and the free. No problem was more difficult, however, than the conflict between the demands of unity and diversity, between the one and the many. Unity was required lest the States and localities exhaust themselves in economic warfare and allow Great Britain and Spain to gobble up their territory. The very size of the area, the diversities among the people of different States, and the distrust of any distant central government called for local control.

Miraculously, the Framers solved the problem by inventing a unique form of federalism that met the needs of 1787 yet could be gradually transformed by interpretation under the pressure of events to meet the very different needs we know today.

The story of the transformation by interpretation is a major theme in the story of both the Supreme Court and the American people. The invention itself comprised four elements:

1. Let there be two governments within each State, conceived as a geographical area: the existing State government and a new federal government, each with its own laws and courts and its own Legislative and Executive Branches. Make every individual a citizen not only of the State in which he lives but also of the United States, with direct rights against, and under direct obligations to, each. All of this we now absorb with our first breath. The key idea was extraordinarily imaginative two hundred years ago. Even today those who grow up in other countries find the concept difficult to comprehend.

2. Divide the full range of governmental functions between the federal and State governments, giving the national government total responsibility for foreign relations but only certain assigned domestic powers. Leave all other law and business of government to the States. As the direct relation between the citizen and the new federal government was and is the foundation of unity, so the division of the functions of government was and is essential to

diversity—to the freedom of the people of each State to write their own laws suited to their own peculiar environment, activities, customs, and needs; to the freedom of the people of California and Colorado, for example, to reject the old law of riparian rights to flowing waters that prevailed in the East in favor of water laws suitable to conditions in the West.

3. Provide that if a State law conflicts with the Constitution or with a law of the United States adopted within the sphere of limited functions allocated to the United States, then the latter shall prevail. The idea of federal supremacy is simple enough. Without it, a workable degree of unity could never have been achieved. The rule is plainly set forth in the Supremacy Clause of Article VI of the Constitution, but more than eight decades would have to pass and a bloody civil war be fought before it was fully accepted in all the States.

4. Establish a vast nationwide common market, free from tariffs and local obstacles to trade, on which to build economic unity as a foundation for political unity. Not all the Framers shared this vision. Probably very few thought about the problem of practical realization. But the seed was sown in the stipulation that "[t]he Citizens of each State shall be entitled to all the Privileges & Immunities of Citizens in the several States," and also in the simple words of the Commerce Clause:

Congress shall have power to regulate commerce . . . among the several States.

Much future creativity would be required in the Supreme Court to work out mechanisms for realizing and protecting the dream by striking a proper balance between State rights and freedom of interstate trade.

For the basic frame of the new federal government, the Convention looked to the example of the colonial governments and to the writings of Locke and Montesquieu. The central theme, designed to keep the new government from becoming too strong, called for the separation of powers among the Legislative, Executive, and Judicial Branches, each coordinate with and in some degree a check on the others.

Article I put the limited legislative powers of the federal government in the hands of a Congress of the United States. Its composition reflects the compromise of disputes that nearly terminated the Convention. The small States—Delaware and New Jersey, for example—had insisted upon the equality of sovereign States and demanded equal representation. The large States argued for *per capita* representation, stressing the sovereignty of the people. The first principle is reflected in the Senate; the second, in the House of Representatives. The true believers in popular government compromised with those whose trust was in the property holders and educated men of the community. The term of the Senator is longer, the qualifications are higher, the number of Senators is fewer, and the original method of election by the State legislatures that prevailed until 1913 was thought likely to reduce the effects of popular clamor.

Article II deals with the Executive Branch. The method provided for choosing the President again reflects compromises between the large and small States and the democratic and aristocratic concepts. The election is by an Electoral College. Each State is allocated electors equal in number to its Representatives in Congress plus its Senators. If no candidate receives a majority in the Electoral College, the election is thrown into the House of Representatives, where the vote is taken by States. It was expected that the Electoral College could canvass the candidates and truly make a selection. In fact, the electors have come to be pledged or bound by law to designated candidates, and their ballots are sheer formality.

The important, stated powers of the President are four:

1. He is Commander-in-Chief of the Armed Forces.
2. He conducts the entire foreign policy of the United States, but treaties require ratification by two thirds of the Senate.
3. He appoints federal judges and other executive officials, but all major appointments require confirmation by majority vote of the Senate.
4. He is charged with the faithful execution of the laws.

The formal prescription of the President's functions is plainly inadequate to describe the enormous power and prestige the Presidency has achieved.

The "judicial power of the United States" is vested by Article III "in one Supreme Court and such inferior courts as the Congress may from time to time ordain and establish." The judicial power is defined to include "cases, in law and equity, arising under the Constitution, the laws of the United States, and treaties made, or which shall be made under their authority." There is scarcely a hint in the text of the enormous power now exercised by the Supreme Court of the United States. Not a word indicates that the Court may review the constitutionality of Acts of Congress or of the President. Nothing expressly empowers the Court to sit in review of constitutional rulings made by the courts of the States.

The Bill of Rights that now protects the freedom of speech, the security of our homes, and other fundamental liberties was not part of the original Constitution but was added by Amendments I through X, adopted in 1791. The two documents may fairly be treated as one. The Framers were deep believers in "natural rights." The Revolution had been fought to secure traditional individual liberties against Parliamentary oppression. The Philadelphia Convention omitted a Bill of Rights only because its members thought that very limited powers were granted to the new federal government. They supposed that confining Congress to the exercise of the delegated powers would itself eliminate any threat to fundamental rights, and that the inclusion of a Bill of Rights would therefore suggest a loose construction of the delegated powers, which would be an even greater threat to liberty.

The people were not satisfied by this rather technical, lawyers' argument. Ratification was secured only by promises of a Bill of Rights. The Bill of Rights added pursuant to those promises protects the individual against oppression by the federal government. It would be three quarters of a century before the Constitution of the United States was amended to safeguard individual rights against violation by a State. In the beginning nearly everyone believed that protection against State legislation interfering with freedom of speech or other fundamental rights of individuals must come from State constitutions interpreted by State courts without federal intervention.

It is enough for the present, therefore, merely to note the most important guarantees against federal intrusion on individual liberty. The First Amendment forthrightly provides that

> Congress shall make no law respecting an establishment of religion or prohibiting the free exercise thereof, or abridging the freedom of speech, or of the press.

Procedural safeguards for persons suspected or charged with crime are set out in the Fourth, Fifth, Sixth, and Eighth Amendments. The Fourth Amendment, for example, prohibits "unreasonable searches and seizures." A search without a judicially authorized warrant is usually held "unreasonable." The Fourth Amendment prohibits the issuance of warrants except upon a showing of probable cause and a particular description of the persons or things to be seized. The Fifth Amendment requires criminal prosecutions to be commenced by indictment by a grand jury, prohibits putting a person in double jeopardy for the same offense, and secures the privilege against self-incrimination. It also contains the broad guarantee:

> [N]or shall any person . . . be deprived of life, liberty or property without due process of law. . . .

The words are majestic and evocative, yet also open-ended. What is the meaning of "liberty" beyond freedom from imprisonment? What restrictions on the use of property are deprivations? And what is or is not "due process of law"? The Due Process Clause is more open to interpretation than most constitutional provisions, but it is illustrative of a pervasive characteristic. What is "the freedom of speech, or of the press"? How is one to recognize a "law respecting an establishment of religion?" History provided a few answers to such questions even in the last quarter of the eighteenth century, but for the most part the questions were left to the future. The Framers did not even designate a certain means for getting answers.

In laying the proposed Bill of Rights before the First Congress, James Madison declared that if the amendments were adopted, "independent tribunals of justice will consider themselves in a peculiar manner the guardians of those rights, they will be an unpenetrable bulwark against every assumption of [excessive] power in the Legislative or Executive."[1] Madison's prediction was confirmed by events, but nothing in the original document or the Bill of Rights ordained that the Supreme Court should have the ultimate authority to interpret the Constitution and thus to strike the balance between organized society and individual right.

The original Constitution likewise left to the future major questions concerning the plan of government. Shortly after ratification and despite the agreements reached in the Convention, sharp controversies developed concerning the relationship between the new federal government and the States. The bold outlines of the federal plan were plain enough, but they left room for political warfare to break out over four critical issues:

1. *Should the domestic role of the new federal government be great or small?* Article I, Section 8, listed the powers delegated to Congress; for example:

· To lay and collect taxes . . . to pay the debts and provide for the common defense and general welfare of the United States.
· To borrow money on the credit of the United States.
· To establish post offices and post roads.
· To regulate commerce among the several States.

Even though there was, and is, general agreement that Congress may constitutionally exercise only the delegated powers, their scope and character have always been subject to dispute. Should the interpretation be strict or liberal? Might Congress levy a protective tariff on imports even though the revenue is not required? Establish a national bank? Appropriate funds to build roads and improve rivers and harbors within a single State? Prohibit racial segregation in local restaurants?

The scope and character of the activities of the federal government are not simply a constitutional question. Congress may and often does make the political decision to leave to the States matters that it has power to regulate. When legislation is offered that pushes close to constitutional limits, especially when there is uncertainty about the limits, the question may be debated and resolved in constitutional terms. The scope of federal domestic activity is determined by the courts in terms of constitutional law only after Congress actually legislates in an area claimed to lie beyond its delegated power.

2. *What is the significance of the grant of power to Congress "to regulate commerce . . . among the several States"?* One aspect of the debate on this question concerned the extent of the regulatory power granted to Congress—a question that would recur and receive different answers throughout our history. In a second aspect the Commerce Clause raised and still raises questions concerning the limits that the Constitution imposes upon the powers of the States. For example, when Congress has not acted, may a State tax and regulate interstate commerce? Did the Commerce Clause

bar New York from determining who might have the privilege of operating steamboats on the inland waters of New York? Did the Commerce Clause bar slave-holding South Carolina from restricting the freedom of foreign Negro seamen to roam about on her streets? Does it bar New Jersey from excluding garbage and other wastes from Philadelphia and New York?

3. *Under the Constitution, where did the ultimate sovereignty lie? Was the United States simply a league of once-independent States that retained their ultimate sovereignty? Or did the Constitution establish an indissoluble union with the ultimate sovereignty resting in the people of the United States?* The matter of ultimate sovereignty lay behind many constitutional questions of the first half of the nineteenth century. The issues were often bitterly debated in Congress, in State legislatures, on the hustings, and in the press. The courts grappled with many of those issues when shaped by litigation. The U.S. Supreme Court's rulings tended to become final, short of recourse to nullification, secession, and war. The trend was toward broad assertions of congressional power, national supremacy, and the development of an open, continentwide economy, binding the States in the Northeast and old Northwest together in a burgeoning economy and isolating the aristocratic, one-crop, slave-holding South.

But the question of ultimate sovereignty would not yield to a peaceful solution, either political or judicial. In time, dispute led to nullification; nullification led to secession; and secession led to the civil war that ultimately solidified the Union for which the delegates in Independence Hall had laid the groundwork but which, in 1787, they could only dimly foresee.

4. *Where rests the final authority to interpret the Constitution?* The forms of government under the Constitution are extraordinarily complex. The total sum of governmental power is divided, as we have seen, between the federal government and the States. In accordance with the political theory of the separation of powers, the powers assigned to the federal government are divided among the Legislative, Executive, and Judicial Branches. In both instances the prescribed lines of division left much room for conflict, inconsistency, and disputes among the several parts. Often two or more arms of government could act in the same area, creating uncertainty about the significance of the interplay. Without some body to act as umpire, the several parts must inevitably fall to

squabbling, and the enterprise launched in Philadelphia break up on the reefs. Yet the Constitution nowhere specifically and explicitly stated who, if anyone, was to have the final word.

Similarly, again as we have seen, after ratification of the Bill of Rights, the Constitution pronounced broad guarantees of individual liberty and fair procedure protecting citizens against federal oppression. But the Bill of Rights neither particularized the broad generalities nor provided machinery for their interpretation.

It seemed a miracle in 1787–1789 that the delegates to the Philadelphia Convention were able to agree on a Constitution that would be ratified by thirteen diverse, jealous, and squabbling States.[2] It seems even more miraculous today that a plan of government drawn up two hundred years ago for eighteenth-century North America should, with the addition of the Bill of Rights and the post–Civil War Amendments, prove suitable for a greatly expanded country in the very different conditions of the nineteenth century and also for the new and unprecedented conditions of today.

In retrospect we can see that much of the genius of the Founding Fathers, perhaps forced upon them by their very differences, lay in their remarkable capacity for saying enough but not too much— just enough to give those who would come after them a point of reference and a strong foundation on which to build, but not so much as to inhibit their successors, who would live in changed and changing worlds. Many forces, many institutions, many men and women, would do the building of a great nation of free people. Many of the natural resources with which North America is blessed would be required.

Coherence—vision and direction—were also required. The Supreme Court of the United States came to be like Galen's great ganglion of the nerves of American society, receiving messages from all parts of the body politic, appreciating their meaning and its needs—comprehending the body within itself, as it were—and sending back the critical impulses to shape the body's growth and action. Who controls the center makes all the difference. So too does the process by which critical decisions are made.

The Constitution contains no hint of the role that the Court would come to play. It might have been left as a document to which individuals and governmental authorities would refer for moral authority in fighting out their differences, but without other sanction. The great questions left to the future, both the questions of federalism and those of individual liberty, would then have been answered in political forums, by economic pressures, or by force of arms. For the genius of American constitutionalism to develop, the Court had first to assert, and then win, the people's support for the Court's power of interpretation "according to law."

· 2 ·

Judicial Supremacy

FEW DELEGATES to the Philadelphia Convention can have even dimly perceived the future role of the Supreme Court of the United States. *The Federalist* papers, in urging ratification of the Constitution, described the proposed federal judiciary as "the least dangerous" branch.[1] John Jay, the first Chief Justice of the United States, resigned the office in order to serve as the Governor of New York. Robert H. Harrison, one of President Washington's initial choices for Associate Justice, resigned five days later to become Chancellor of Maryland. Two centuries later the Court would exercise a degree of power unique in judicial history.

In 1954 the Supreme Court overturned the educational systems of many States by ruling that racial segregation in the public schools is inconsistent with the Fourteenth Amendment's command that no State shall deny any person "equal protection of the law."[2] Few Acts of Congress—perhaps only declarations of war—have so vitally affected so many individuals.

For generations, millions of Americans attended public schools, where it was customary to begin the day with exercises including prayer or Bible reading. In 1962 the Supreme Court stopped the exercises.[3]

In 1973 a decision barring enforcement of State anti-abortion laws during the first three months of pregnancy enhanced a woman's freedom of choice, but the decision, based on the divided votes of nine Justices, also swept away established laws enacted by State legislatures and supported by moral themes dominant in American life for more than a century.[4]

No other country has given its courts such extraordinary power. Not Britain, where an act of Parliament binds the courts. Not India, where there is a written constitution and a Supreme Court but where constitutional rights can be suspended by the government's declaration of an emergency. Not even West Germany or Ireland, where the power of judicial review is established but is exercised on a narrower scale.

The President is elected. The Congress is elected. State legislators and Governors are all elected. Supreme Court Justices are not elected; they are appointed for life. So are other federal judges. Yet we give unelected Justices and judges a power—called judicial review—under which they may nullify some acts of an elected President and the elected representatives of the people assembled in Congress or the legislatures of the States. In exercising the power of judicial review the Court answers, case by case, the great questions left open by the Framers concerning both their ingenious plan of government and the guarantees of individual liberty.

How did the Court achieve such power? Why do we approve and, when the role of the Court is attacked, strongly defend it?

I

Great constitutional cases sometimes arise out of the most trivial incidents. Great constitutional issues are often shaped by party politics. Great institutions of government emerge in response to centuries of human needs and aspirations. *Marbury* v. *Madison,*[5] one cornerstone of judicial supremacy in applying the Constitution, illustrates all three propositions.

The election of 1800 had been extraordinarily bitter. The incumbent Federalists were led by President John Adams and Alexander Hamilton. The mainstays of the Federalist Party were the propertied and commercial classes, men who valued order and stability, the security of property, and opportunities for trade. They were frightened by the excesses of the French Revolution. In the early Napoleonic Wars they gave their sympathy, and occasionally more material assistance, to the British. Their heartland was New England.

Opposed to the Federalists were the Jeffersonian Republicans. The backbone of that party was formed from farmers, frontiersmen, and debtor classes, joined in Virginia and to the south by plantation aristocrats and led by Thomas Jefferson, the author of the Declaration of Independence. Today's Democrats claim to be their legitimate heirs. Many had opposed the new Constitution. Associating themselves with the French Revolution, they read Rousseau and preached the "rights of man." They cheered Citizen Genêt, a representative of the revolutionary French government who visited the United States, and occasionally they commissioned privateers to prey on British commerce. Putting their faith in the democratic political process, the Jeffersonian Republicans sought to restrict the powers of the new federal government. Many of them, especially in the South, asserted that even under the Constitution the ultimate sovereignty still lay in the individual States.

The Jeffersonians won sweeping victories in the elections of 1800. Thomas Jefferson would become President. Jeffersonians would command large majorities in the U.S. Senate and House of Representatives. The victors saw the outcome as a second giant democratic stride in a continuing American Revolution. The Federalist newspapers proclaimed the fear that society was disintegrating under the domination of the mob: "We are seeing the general ascendancy of the worthless, the dishonest, the rapacious, the vile, the merciless and the ungodly."[6]

Despite the election Jefferson would not be inaugurated until March 4, 1801. The new Congress would not begin until then. President Adams would remain in office for almost four months, with Federalist majorities in both Senate and House of Representatives. Three events occurred during the interval that would shape the future of the American people.

The seemingly smallest of these was the filling of vacancies in the low-paid, part-time office of Justice of the Peace for the District of Columbia. The appointments went chiefly to Federalists. Among them was a William Marbury. President Adams and his Secretary of State had signed Marbury's commission, along with others, just three days before Jefferson's inauguration, but the Secretary of State had neglected to deliver the signed commissions to the appointees. Four days later, after Jefferson had become President, the commissions were found on the desk of James Madison, the new Secretary of State. Jefferson, offended by the last-minute appointment of so many Federalists, ordered Madison to withhold some of the commissions in order to make room for deserving

Republicans. William Marbury's commission was among those withheld.

Marbury then began against Secretary of State Madison a legal proceeding, known technically as an application for a writ of mandamus, seeking to compel Madison to deliver the commission. Perhaps Marbury sought the job because he really wanted it, although the office was scarcely worth holding. More likely, the suit was a political ploy, brought because the Federalists thought that they could embarrass the new President and score political points with the public by securing a judicial ruling that President Jefferson and Secretary Madison had acted unlawfully in withholding Marbury's commission after the appointment had been made by the President and confirmed by the Senate and the commission had been signed by the President and Secretary of State. The suit was filed in the Supreme Court of the United States. Marbury and his associates must have drawn some encouragement from the fact that the new Chief Justice of that court was John Marshall.

John Marshall was himself a lame-duck appointee. During the dying days of the Adams Administration, he had become Chief Justice of the United States just in time to administer the oath of office to President Jefferson. Oliver Ellsworth had become too old, sick, and tired to continue to serve as Chief Justice. President Adams then nominated Marshall, his Secretary of State, to succeed Ellsworth. The Federalist Senate confirmed the appointment. Marshall stayed on as Secretary of State until just before the inauguration of Thomas Jefferson. If Ellsworth had kept his health just a few months longer, President Jefferson, not John Adams, would have filled the vacancy. Jefferson's choice would have fallen upon a man of a very different political philosophy from Marshall's, probably Spencer Roane, a strong advocate of the ultimate sovereignty of the States.

As Chief Justice, John Marshall was to dominate the Court for thirty-three years, always building the power of the federal government and its supremacy over the States. He was a child of revolutionary Virginia, but more of the rural frontier in the piedmont under the Blue Ridge Mountains than of the tidewater plantations. The eyes of John Marshall first looked west as his father and mother loaded their household goods on a Conestoga wagon to move to "the Hollow" in a Blue Ridge valley. Both father and son looked west again to invest in new land. And John Marshall as Chief

Justice would be moved by the vision of constant growth and expansion to the west with East and West linked by travel and trade, provided that economic unity was allowed to develop.

Life on the frontier engendered the spirit of cooperation that lies next to unity. John Marshall, the child, must have heard constant talk of Braddock's defeat, of the threat of French and Indians, and of the need for some form of colonial union to meet the dangers of invasion. As a young man on General Washington's staff, he saw first hand at Valley Forge the costs of self-interest, selfish pride, and constant rivalry among thirteen sovereign States—costs measured by unfilled quotas, departing militiamen, and half an army in the snow without blankets or shoes. There he also displayed the hearty capacity to rally, persuade, and lead other men that would later win others to his views, even the Justices whom President Jefferson appointed to the Supreme Court. A fellow officer described him at Valley Forge:

> Nothing discouraged, nothing disturbed Mr. Marshall. If he had only bread to eat, it was just as well; if only meat it made no difference. If any of the officers murmured at their deprivations, he would shame them by good-natured railery, or encourage them by his own exuberance of spirits. He was an excellent companion, and idolized by the soldiers and his brother officers, whose gloomy hours were enlivened by his inexhaustible fund of anecdote. John Marshall was the best tempered man I ever knew.[7]

Throughout Marshall's life not a few sophisticated men and women would be initially deceived by the hearty simplicity that won devotion from those who came to know him. (In later years, while Chief Justice of the United States, John Marshall did the family marketing at home in Richmond.) When John Marshall left the army in December 1779, his family was living in Yorktown. Next door lived Jacquelin Ambler and his wife, the Rebecca Burwell whom Thomas Jefferson had loved and courted but to whom he delayed too long in proposing marriage because he had too many ambitions to accomplish. When Marshall arrived at home, the ears of two of Ambler's daughters were ringing with praise for him. Betsy, the older, turned away: "I lost all desire of becoming agreeable in his eyes when I beheld his awkward figure, unpolished manners, and total negligence of person." The younger sister, Polly, set her cap for John and caught him at once, wholly and forever.

From her death in 1827 until his own death eight years later he wore a locket of Polly's hair about his neck day and night. Polly's "superior discernment" had perceived, her sister later wrote, "that under the slouched hat there beamed an eye that penetrated at one glance the inmost recesses of the human character; and beneath the slovenly garb there dwelt a heart replete with every virtue."[8]

The character formed on the frontier and shaped by the Revolutionary War emphasized the need for order as a precondition of both liberty and justice. Perhaps the first source was the rigor of the education imparted first by his father and then by a young Scottish deacon. Before he was twelve years old Marshall had copied in their entirety the disciplined, formal rhyming syllogisms of Alexander Pope's *Essay on Man*.

> All nature is but art unknown to thee,
> All choice, direction which thou canst not see.

Within a few years he had also read Blackstone; but one may surmise that the law's appeal to Marshall lay less in the intellectual challenge than its uses as an instrument for the ordering of human relations.

John Marshall, like the greatest of the Chief Justices who would come after him, enjoyed political experience. His father, a State representative from Fauquier County, often took him to the Virginia House of Burgesses, where he could hear and judge such now-legendary figures as James Madison, Edmund Randolph, and Patrick Henry. Marshall himself served in the Virginia legislature and then took active part, in 1788, in winning Virginia's ratification of the Constitution. Service in the federal House of Representatives and later as President John Adams's Secretary of State completed his years in active politics.

It was strangely ironical that *Marbury* v. *Madison* would be heard by a Court presided over by John Marshall. He was now Chief Justice, but he had been the Secretary of State who forgot to deliver Marbury's commission and thus brought about the lawsuit. Although today's standards of judicial conduct would disqualify a judge from hearing a case arising from his own absent-mindedness, no one thought it odd at the time. All saw the case as extraordinary in other respects. Here in a time of intense party feuding was a disappointed office seeker applying to the Court headed by a prominent Federalist for an order directing the Republican Secretary of State to deliver a commission that the Secretary was withholding on the direct orders of the President of the United States.

The theory of Marbury's case was simple: Marbury's appointment was complete when the commission was signed; Marbury therefore had a legal right to the commission as evidence of his office. Conversely, the delivery of the commission was a purely ministerial act that Madison had no discretion to withhold, and a writ of mandamus was the proper remedy to enforce a ministerial duty. Much would later turn on the fact that the application for mandamus was filed in the Supreme Court of the United States. Apparently counsel chose that course because one section of an early Act of Congress provided that the Supreme Court

> shall have power to issue . . . writs of mandamus, in cases warranted by the principles and usages of law, to any courts appointed, or persons holding office, under the authority of the United States.[9]

Madison, as Secretary of State, held office under the authority of the United States; therefore the statute apparently gave the Supreme Court power to issue a writ of mandamus commanding Madison to give Marbury the commission that was proof of Marbury's right to the office of Justice of the Peace.

One suspects that Chief Justice Marshall would have been happy to embrace Marbury's argument and so to lecture President Jefferson on his legal obligations. Both Jefferson and Marshall were Virginians; both were lawyers; but their personalities were as incompatible as their political philosophies. Personal hatred would grow between them. Yet the Chief Justice must have realized that he faced a dilemma. As an experienced politician he would have asked himself what would happen if the Court accepted Marbury's arguments and issued the writ of mandamus. The Jeffersonians were infuriated by the suit, insofar as they took it seriously. When the Court took the conventional first step in an action for mandamus and entered an order directing Madison to show cause why the writ should not issue, Madison failed to respond. President Jefferson and Secretary Madison ignored the Court throughout the entire proceeding.

At the same time, in the press and in public debate, Administration spokesmen roundly denied the power of any court to issue a judicial order to a Secretary of State acting on the direct instructions of the President of the United States. There was no precedent for judicial interference. Under the theory of the Constitution the Legislative, Executive, and Judicial Branches were to be separate and independent. By what right then would a court interfere with the President and his Secretary of State? Indeed, if one were to have precedence, surely it must be the President, elected by overwhelming popular mandate, and not judges, designated by the party that had just lost a national election. The Jeffersonian fury was the stronger because President Jefferson and his party leaders were engaged in a broad attack upon the Federalist judges, who were often the most visible and hated signs of the new federal establishment.

In this context Chief Justice John Marshall and his Associate Justices could have had little doubt that if they issued a writ of mandamus ordering Secretary Madison to deliver Marbury's commission, President Jefferson would tell the Secretary to ignore the order. Both would get away with the disobedience. Both they and other Republicans would laugh at the Court's pretensions. The danger of political gain to the Jeffersonians must have been obvious. Still worse from John Marshall's viewpoint must have been the danger of weakening the Judiciary by showing its impotence.

Yet the other horn of the dilemma looked equally dangerous. To hold that President Jefferson had acted lawfully would not only be questionable law; it would please the Republicans and embarrass the Federalists. To hold that the Court had no power to issue orders to an official in the Executive Branch would sustain the Jeffersonian position and surrender, perhaps for all time, judicial power to check executive usurpation.

At some point, it must have occurred to the Chief Justice that the Court could escape the dilemma by first declaring that Marbury had a legal right to his commission, a right that a proper court could enforce even against the Executive, and by next declining to issue the writ of mandamus on the ground that Marbury had brought his suit in the wrong court. Marbury had begun his suit in the Supreme Court of the United States, as explained above, thus invoking what is technically known as "original jurisdiction." His lawyers had relied upon the Act of Congress quoted above that seemed to give the Supreme Court this jurisdiction to issue writs of mandamus against any person holding office under the authority of the United States. If the statute governed, Marbury had sued in a proper court. But did the statute govern? What about the Constitution?

The courts in which a legal action may be commenced are said to have original jurisdiction. The courts to which a litigant may appeal for correction of the judgment of another court are said to exercise appellate jurisdiction. Article III of the Constitution establishes the Supreme Court of the United States and empowers Congress to create inferior federal courts. Article III also provides that the Supreme Court may exercise original jurisdiction in cases to which a State or an ambassador or consul is a party; and that in all other cases arising under the Constitution or laws of the United States, the Supreme Court "shall have appellate jurisdiction." These are the words that give the Court the power to hear appeals from both State courts and lower federal courts when the meaning of the Constitution or a federal statute is at issue. In Marbury's case, if the constitutional words "shall have appellate jurisdiction" meant "shall have *only appellate* jurisdiction," and thus excluded original jurisdiction, then the Act of Congress was inconsistent with the Constitution. But suppose that it was inconsistent. Had the Supreme Court the power to go behind the Act of Congress and to disregard the act if it found the act inconsistent with the Constitution? By asserting this power of judicial review in a case brought before it, the Supreme Court could maintain the supremacy of the Constitution, build up its own power, and at the same time avoid a disastrous confrontation with President Jefferson by dismissing Marbury's suit as having been brought in the wrong court.

This escape from their dilemma must have had strong tactical appeal to the Chief Justice and his colleagues. But judges are not free to act simply as politicians. As judges sworn to decide "according to law," John Marshall and his colleagues were obliged to ask whether the Constitution could in good conscience be read to give the Judicial Branch power to review the constitutionality of Acts of Congress.

The Constitution does not say that the Judiciary or the Supreme Court shall have such power, nor does the Constitution deny it. To read the power into the Constitution—to find the power there implicitly as one of the usual responsibilities of courts—would be only to build upon centuries of legal history; one might say, to complete's man's search for some mechanism for putting fundamental human rights beyond the reach of government.

Two threads in that history deserve attention. We may pick up one thread in England, at Runnymede, in 1215. The King was John. Under him came the great Barons, who held fiefdoms in return for which they owed the King specific "aids and reliefs" and other duties. The Barons in turn granted tenure to their tenants in return for the tenants' performance of feudal obligations. In 1215 the Barons revolted, claiming that King John and the royal officers were levying wrongful exactions on them and others of his subjects; that the King was failing to perform his own feudal obligations; and that he and his officers were abusing their feudal rights. The Church and the people of London supported the Barons. At Runnymede King John yielded and signed Magna Carta. Most of the document consists of promises to check specific abuses by the King's officers and to respect the technical feudal rights of the great Barons. One clause grew into a broad and lasting symbol of liberty:

> No freeman shall be taken or imprisoned or disseized or exiled or in any way destroyed, nor will we [King John] go upon nor will we send upon him except by the lawful judgment of his peers or the law of the land.

". . . the law of the land." The words set down the powerful idea of a permanent body of law, existing apart from statute or royal decree, which the King's officers and even the King himself must respect.

About four hundred years later another King confronted the common law. When Queen Elizabeth died, the throne of England passed to James VI of Scotland as King James I. James brought with him the conviction that the King ruled by Divine right and that none might question his will. He turned to the Court of the Star Chamber and other prerogative courts set up by him under judges willing to work the royal will. The new prerogative courts soon came into conflict with the old courts applying the common law. King James I summoned the common law judges before him and ordered their courts to cease interfering with the prerogative courts. The King's will, James asserted, was supreme. Sir Edward Coke, the Chief Justice of the Court of Common Pleas, responded that the judges must follow the common law, to which King James I answered wrathfully, "Then I am to be *under* the law—which it is treason to affirm." Coke replied by quoting Bracton, a medieval

scholar-monk, *"Rex non debet esse sub homine sed sub Deo et
Lege"*—"The King ought not to be under any man, but under God
and the Law."[10] The story of the exchange has echoed down
through the years, even to Watergate and the subpoenas to Richard
Nixon, as a symbol of judicial courage in establishing the principle
that all those who govern are subject to law.

Coke's claims for the common law knew few bounds. In *Dr.
Bonham's Case,* he declared that "when an Act of Parliament is
against common right and reason . . . the common law will control
it and adjudge such act to be void."[11] This was a startling assertion.
It is one thing to say that a hereditary monarch ruling without the
consent of the governed is bound by "law." It is very different to
say that an elected Parliament, a legislature representative of the
people, is subject to law made by unelected judges. The first doctrine limits an outside, imposed power. The second would limit
even the power of the people to govern themselves according to
the will of the majority. For this reason the principle propounded
by Coke in *Dr. Bonham's Case* never took root in Britain, where
Parliamentary supremacy prevails.

But the situation was different in colonial America in the critical
years just prior to the American Revolution. The colonists were
oppressed by a Parliament that they had no voice in choosing.
Coke's writings were the schoolbooks of James Otis, John Adams,
and the other lawyers who stirred the American Revolution. In
1761, a special Act of Parliament applicable to the colonies authorized the issuance of writs of assistance to be used by the King's
agents to rummage about the premises of Boston merchants for
goods escaping taxation. James Otis electrified the colonies by
contending that a law contrary to "natural equity" and the "fundamental principles of laws" was "utterly void." John Adams denied the validity of the Stamp Act on the same principle.

These appeals to "the rights of Englishmen" gained strength in
America from the "natural law" philosophy propounded by the
eighteenth-century Frenchman Jean-Jacques Rousseau. In a state
of nature, Rousseau wrote, men had certain natural rights; rulers
who would deny those rights without the consent of the governed
were illegitimate usurpers. Rousseau was thinking of Kings, nobles,
and inherited titles; but in eighteenth-century America there was
also great fear of legislative despotism and of legislative interference with "natural rights." It was Parliament that adopted the

Stamp Act and authorized the writs of assistance. Rousseau's revolutionary doctrine was easy to proclaim, but it was much harder to define natural rights and give them practical protection.

Here the Founding Fathers turned to another Anglo-American tradition. Beginning with Magna Carta, their English ancestors had wrested from Kings written statements limiting the royal prerogative: Magna Carta in 1215, the Petition of Right in 1628, the Bill of Rights in 1689. Before embarking for the New World, the original colonists had obtained written charters defining their powers and privileges. Some of them had also written down among themselves covenants like the Mayflower Compact, setting forth the terms on which they would conduct their adventure. After Independence, the idea grew that the way to fix the frame of a new government and to protect the natural rights of man was to set those rights down in a written constitution, an American political invention later copied in many parts of the world. State constitutions came first. The United States Constitution followed.

It was harder to know how to enforce a constitution, and how to resolve disputes about its meaning. Many Americans distrusted even legislative power. The influence of Coke and the doctrines proclaimed by James Otis and John Adams led some State courts to rule, even before the U.S. Constitution was adopted, that a court will treat an act of legislature in violation of a written constitution as a nullity. The Virginian George Wythe, America's first law professor and the teacher of both John Marshall and Thomas Jefferson, was one judge to assert the power. Many of the Framers of the U.S. Constitution took it for granted that the courts would void unconstitutional acts of Congress.[12]

The power of judicial review might well have been exercised by the Court and accepted by the people without controversy if questions concerning the proper role of the federal judiciary had not become entangled with both party politics and other constitutional questions.

Early in 1801 the lame-duck Federalist Congress had enacted, and President Adams had signed, a new Judiciary Act. From the standpoint of judicial administration the act was a great improvement upon the earlier act of 1789, but the new act drastically increased the numbers of federal courts and federal judges, thus arousing intense opposition from those distrustful of the new federal establishment and the federal courts. The Jeffersonian oppo-

sition became partisan fury when, in the dying days of his Administration, President Adams gave the new positions to Federalists
who had lost elective office in the election of 1800. The popular
report was that Jefferson's new Attorney General entered the Presidential office after midnight on the day before Jefferson's inauguration and found John Adams still busily signing commissions, even
though his term had technically expired. The story was false, but
the judges became known to history as the Midnight Judges. The
Federalists made no secret of their determination to hold the one
branch of government left to their control. The Republicans were
equally determined to bring the Judicial Branch around to their
political philosophy concerning government generally and, more
specifically, the federal system.

Promptly after taking office, the Republican leaders introduced
a bill to repeal the Judiciary Act of 1801. Knowing that their opponents had the necessary votes, the Federalists in Congress argued that the judges would find the repeal unconstitutional. The
Jeffersonians might have contented themselves with defending the
constitutionality of the repeal, but, fearful of the Federalist judges,
they further responded by denying the power of a court to invalidate an Act of Congress. The response provoked debate on the
central constitutional question: What right has a court to review
the constitutionality of an Act of Congress?

To deny the power of judicial review was naturally congenial to
Jeffersonian Republicans. They were distrustful of the courts. They
controlled both houses of Congress and also the Presidency. The
judges, on the other hand, were Federalists. How dared Federalist
judges stand in the way of the will of the people?

The Jeffersonians' political philosophy supported their partisan
instinct. Judicial review is antimajoritarian; it checks the will of
the people. Jefferson may have been exaggerating somewhat, but
there was an essential core of truth in his later complaint that "[t]o
consider the judges as the ultimate arbiters of all constitutional
questions . . . would place us under the despotism of an oligarchy."[13]

The Jeffersonian Republicans had two further reasons for denying the Judiciary final authority to interpret the Constitution:

1. They looked to a weak federal government with sharply limited powers. The question was debated as early as President Washington's first term, when Alexander Hamilton asserted and Thomas
Jefferson denied that Congress had power to charter the Bank of

the United States. The Federalist judges, if they had the last word on constitutional questions, could be expected to interpret broadly the powers delegated to the federal Congress.

2. Many of the Jeffersonian Republicans, as localists, were deeply committed to the idea of State sovereignty and therefore to the position that the States as the ultimate sovereigns were entitled to the last word on the constitutionality of an Act of Congress. Thomas Jefferson and James Madison had expounded this view in resolutions adopted by the Kentucky and Virginia legislatures, declaring the Sedition Act a nullity because it abridged the freedom of speech guaranteed by the First Amendment. They argued that the federal government, the United States, is simply an agent to which the sovereign States have delegated certain limited powers; and that when the United States, the agent, exercises powers not contained in its instructions (that is, in the Constitution), a State, as the agent's principal, has the right to "interpose" its authority and "nullify" the unauthorized federal law.

It would take the Civil War to obliterate this theory of the nature of American government. Meanwhile, even though the theory of the Kentucky and Virginia resolutions could logically stand alongside judicial review, the reality was that establishing the power of another body to rule on the constitutionality of Acts of Congress would weaken any justification for saying that the same power resided in each and every State. Establishing the authority of the Supreme Court to interpret the Constitution would therefore be a powerful force for national unity.

The congressional battle over repeal of the Judiciary Act of 1801 went to the Jeffersonians, who had the votes. The new courts were abolished before the Supreme Court could hear any question about the constitutionality of the repeal. But it was against the background of this debate and the threads of history reaching back through George Wythe to Otis and Adams and through them to Lord Coke and Jean-Jacques Rousseau that Chief Justice Marshall and the Associate Justices assembled on February 24, 1803, to deliver their judgment in *Marbury* v. *Madison*.

The Chief Justice spoke for the unanimous court. He first expounded the duty of the Executive to obey the laws, and asserted the right of the citizen to judicial redress against executive illegality. He then declared that Madison's refusal to deliver Marbury's commission was unlawful and remediable by mandamus because the signing of the commission had made the appointment complete.

These dicta were to infuriate Thomas Jefferson. They seemed to set the stage for issuance of an order directing Secretary Madison to deliver Marbury's commission, an order that the President and Secretary would have successfully ignored.

But Marshall then turned away from the logical conclusion to inquire whether the Court should not disregard the Act of Congress giving the Court jurisdiction to hear original applications for writs of mandamus, because in such cases the Constitution limits the Supreme Court to appellate jurisdiction. A judge must decide a constitutional question, he declared, when it arises in a case brought before his court in the usual course of judicial business:

> It is emphatically the province and duty of the judicial department to say what the law is. Those who apply the law to particular cases, must of necessity expound and interpret that rule. If two laws conflict with each other, the courts must decide on the operation of each.[14]

After ruling that the Act of Congress giving the Court original jurisdiction was inconsistent with the constitutional provision limiting its jurisdiction to appellate cases, the Chief Justice continued:

> The Constitution is either a superior paramount law, unchangeable by ordinary means, or it is on a level with ordinary legislative acts, and, like other acts, is alterable when the legislature shall please to alter it.
>
> If the former part of the alternative be true, then a legislative act contrary to the Constitution is not law: if the latter part be true, then written constitutions are absurd attempts, on the part of the people, to limit a power in its own nature illimitable.[15]

Between these alternatives, Marshall asserted, "there is no middle ground."[16] He concluded that the case was governed by the Constitution and must, therefore, be dismissed for want of jurisdiction.

The force of Marshall's argument is self-evident, but its logic is not unassailable. Surely Marshall overstates the case when he asserts that there is no middle ground between holding that a legislative act which violates the Constitution is ineffectual and rendering the Constitution a nullity. Legislators might, and I think normally would, feel themselves influenced by their own understanding of a written constitution, even though the only sanctions were those of conscience and political pressure. The unwritten

British constitution has a restraining influence on Parliament despite the lack of judicial review, because members of Parliament are usually careful to observe British constitutional traditions. The irony of Marshall's argument is that the Supreme Court itself is limited in its interpretation of the Constitution only by self-restraint responding to legal tradition and the claims of moral duty. No outside authority can hold the Supreme Court in line.

Looking back, we can also see that the great Chief Justice failed to foresee the full nature of many constitutional questions, and so failed to appreciate some of the most difficult questions concerning judicial review. In arguing that the Court must choose between giving effect to the Constitution and giving effect to inconsistent Acts of Congress, he put simple, clear-cut examples. The Constitution provides that nobody shall be convicted of treason "unless on the testimony of two witnesses to the same overt act."[17] Suppose, Chief Justice Marshall asked, that Congress enacted a statute calling for conviction of treason on the testimony of one witness. In a prosecution for treason, which must the judge obey—the Constitution or the statute? The Constitution says that the Congress shall pass no bill of attainder,[18] a legislative act inflicting a death sentence without a conviction in the usual course of judicial proceedings. If Congress passes a bill of attainder, should a court give effect to it? The cases seem easy. The questions answer themselves. The point that the Chief Justice was making is also important. If the courts lacked the power to give sting to constitutional safeguards in obvious cases, the Legislative and Executive Branches might too often override the Constitution.

But obvious, clear-cut violations have never been the stuff of constitutional adjudication. More often than not, the great constitutional cases involve majestic ideals expressed in broad phrases that give scant guidance to the decision: "freedom of speech," "commerce among the several States," "due process of law," "equal protection of the laws." Interpreting such grand concepts often calls for more than reading the words of the document.

Consider the abortion problem, for example. A State statute makes it a crime for any person, including a doctor, to perform an abortion unless necessary to save the woman's life. A pregnant woman who faces no danger to her life or health but does not wish to have the child challenges the statute, contending that having an abortion is a constitutional right. Her legal claim is that the statute violates the Due Process Clause of the Fourteenth Amendment, which provides:

> [N]or shall any State deprive any person of life, liberty or property without due process of law. . . .

Is a woman's decision to have an abortion an aspect of the constitutional "liberty"? Does the anti-abortion statute deprive the woman of that liberty "without due process of law"? We could study the Due Process Clause for the rest of our lives without finding an answer in the words.

I am not arguing that the decision in *Marbury* v. *Madison* was wrong, only that the Chief Justice's simple absolutes do not present the whole problem and that we now can see that questions concerning the proper relationship between court and legislature are subtler and more complex than the opinion suggests. The ultimate question, which Marshall never discussed, is whether a few judges appointed for life or the elected representatives of the people will exercise more wisely the ultimate, uncontrollable power of determining what rules shall prevail in the areas arguably governed by constitutional law. On that question the wisdom of later experience would offer an answer.

To criticize the logic of the opinion is not to downgrade *Marbury* v. *Madison*. As an act of judicial statesmanship, the opinion was magnificent. First, the declaration that even the highest government officials are subject to judicial correction when they violate a legal obligation is a bulwark of liberty. Richard Nixon would have cause to recall this part of the opinion in *Marbury* v. *Madison* when Judge Sirica directed him to surrender the Watergate Tapes. Second, the decision established the judicial power to rule on the constitutionality of federal laws in the normal course of litigation, thus taking the first step in providing a single authoritative source of constitutional interpretation.

As a political document, the opinion is notable for its craftiness. The Federalist Chief Justice gave the Republican President and Secretary of State a lecture on their legal obligations, and found them in violation. In a direct confrontation, those legal pronouncements would prove hollow against physical and political power. He then escaped the confrontation by asserting the still greater judicial authority to disregard any Act of Congress inconsistent with the Constitution.

By this maneuver a suit about a trivial office, resulting from absent-minded happenstance and perhaps brought as a political ploy, gave the rule of law—the tradition flowing from Magna Carta, Lord Coke, and James Otis's attack on the writs of assistance—a home in the Constitution and Supreme Court of the United States.

Yet many years would pass before the home was secure. Attacks on the Court began as soon as *Marbury* v. *Madison* was decided. President Jefferson led a strong body of opinion insisting that even if the Court had power to interpret the Constitution for the purposes of conducting judicial business, its decisions were not binding elsewhere, neither upon other branches of government nor upon the States. President Jefferson also allowed, and perhaps quietly encouraged, his lieutenants to challenge the independence of the Judiciary. Their philosophy was declared by Senator Giles of Virginia, Jefferson's leader of the Senate: the judges were impeachable for their "assumption of power in issuing their process to the office of Secretary of State, directing the Executive how a law of the United States should be executed, and for the right which the Courts have assumed to themselves of reviewing and passing upon the acts of the legislature."[19] John Quincy Adams confided to his diary that the position for the dominant party was that "[w]e want your offices for the purpose of giving them to those who will fill them better."[20]

The first target was John Pickering, the U.S. District Judge in New Hampshire. His mental instability, perhaps related to alcoholism, made him an easy mark. U.S. Supreme Court Justice Samuel Chase was next. If Chase was convicted, the impeachment of John Marshall would follow. Chase seemed a vulnerable target. A quarrelsome, intemperate, and overbearing man, he had vindictively enforced the Sedition Act against Republican editors and, when sitting on circuit, had used the Bench to deliver diatribes against Republican measures. Chase was impeached by the House of Representatives, but the vote in the Senate fell just short of the two thirds required by the Constitution. Six Republicans broke party ranks. Some were influenced by the excesses of John Randolph, a manager on the part of the House, and some by a local party squabble in Pennsylvania. All were wholly or partly affected by the realization that constitutionalism and the rule of law depend upon the independence of the Judiciary.

There would be later congressional challenges to the Court's independence but none of the scope and depth of the Jefferson Republicans' resort to impeachment.

III

Establishing the independence of the federal Judiciary and the power of federal courts to rule upon the constitutionality of congressional legislation was not enough to provide a single unifying voice to interpret the Constitution. The rub was that in the beginning the federal courts were relatively unimportant. Most personal and property rights were governed by State law. Most litigation would be in State courts. The great constitutional issues whose resolution in the nineteenth century were to shape the destiny of the United States would be litigated and initially decided in cases arising in the State courts. Article VI of the Constitution instructed the State courts to apply the Constitution in appropriate cases:

> This Constitution, and the Laws of the United States which shall be made in Pursuance thereof; and all the Treaties made, or which shall be made under the Authority of the United States, shall be the supreme Law of the Land; and the Judges in every State shall be bound thereby, any Thing in the Constitution or Laws of any State to the Contrary notwithstanding.

But the Supremacy Clause alone could not secure uniformity of interpretation, much less ensure that the grave and hotly debated issues left over from the Philadelphia Convention would be decided in a way that built national unity instead of leaving the United States to become a loose confederation of wrangling, sovereign States. One State court, following Article VI in good conscience, might well interpret the Constitution one way while another State court or the Supreme Court of the United States would give it a different meaning. A contrariety of interpretations would promote disunity. Some State courts would be quick to clip the wings of the federal eagle. A single unifying voice could prevail on constitutional questions only if the Supreme Court of the United States had authority to review and revise the judgments of State courts in cases involving the interpretation of the Constitution or a law of the United States; yet to subject the highest court of a State to the authority of the U.S. Supreme Court would deny the State's ultimate sovereignty and incidentally offend proud and sensitive State judges, who gave their primary loyalty to their States and felt at least equal in importance and dignity to the Justices in Washington. The Constitution itself provided no explicit, specific guidance. We have all become accustomed to the Court's exercise of the power; but in thinking about the Court's role in American history we ought not forget that for decades the outcome was uncertain and the assertion of the power was anathema, sometimes in New England, sometimes in Ohio, and almost always in the South.

Part of the genius of American constitutionalism is that the most basic general issues are developed gradually, case by case, in specific lawsuits growing out of practical disputes between the litigants. Thus it was that the pride of State judges, the States' claim to ultimate sovereignty, the question whether there would be one ultimate voice to interpret the Constitution authoritatively for the whole country, and even the outcome of other constitutional issues, all became bound up in a lawsuit over the ownership of a piece of land in northern Virginia. Oddly, the parcel had been part of the same tract as John Marshall's homestead. The case came to be known as *Martin* v. *Hunter's Lessee*.[21]

Back in the seventeenth century a Lord Fairfax had become the owner of an enormous 300,000-acre tract of Virginia land known as the Northern Neck. His title passed to Denny Martin, a nephew living in England, who thus became an enemy alien during the Revolution. Virginia enacted a statute forfeiting the real estate titles of enemy aliens and vesting ownership of their property in the State. Virginia subsequently conveyed a portion of the tract to David Hunter. In 1794, however, the United States entered into the Jay Treaty with Great Britain, which arguably confirmed the titles of British citizens whose property States had attempted to confiscate during the Revolutionary War. Martin then brought suit against Hunter in an effort to recover the Fairfax land, relying on the constitutional mandate in Article VI that treaties made by the United States shall be part of "the supreme law of the land." The Supreme Court of Virginia ruled against the Fairfax title and in favor of the Hunter claimants.

In 1789, Congress, with very little debate, had enacted Section 25 of the Judiciary Act, giving the U.S. Supreme Court authority to hear an appeal from the highest court of a State when a State court ruled against a claim based upon federal law. Accordingly, Martin carried the question concerning the effect of the Jay Treaty to the U.S. Supreme Court. That Court ruled in favor of the Fairfax title, reversed the decision below, and issued a mandate to the Court of Appeals of Virginia (the State's highest court), commanding it to proceed in accordance with the instructions of the U.S. Supreme Court.

This was too much for the proud and sensitive judges of the Virginia Court of Appeals, especially for Spencer Roane, a State rights extremist and a dominant political force. That court refused to comply with the mandate on the ground that Section 25 of the Judiciary Act was unconstitutional. The Virginia judges conceded that State judges must follow the U.S. Constitution as commanded in the Supremacy Clause but argued that the meaning of the Constitution, laws, and treaties of the United States in cases arising in State courts must be decided finally by the State judges according to their understanding and on their own responsibility. Article III of the Constitution, they continued, gives the U.S. Supreme Court only "appellate jurisdiction," unless a State or a foreign diplomat is a party. The U.S. Supreme Court belongs to one sovereignty, and State tribunals belong to another sovereignty of equal dignity and right. The normal meaning of the words "appellate jurisdiction," the argument ran, does not comprehend appeals from the courts of one sovereign to the courts of another—from a court of Great Britain, for example, to a court of the United States. Between the two sovereigns neither can be superior. Neither can command or instruct the other. Therefore, the Virginia judges concluded, the Supreme Court of the United States can have no appellate jurisdiction over a State court.

State pride was involved as well as political philosophy, and perhaps also the personal pride of State judges. Even today the judges of the highest State courts do not always take kindly to reversal by the Supreme Court of the United States. Behind the pride and even the political philosophy lay very practical differences. The resolution of this question would profoundly influence the outcome of other grave constitutional issues on which the country was divided, such as the power of Congress to establish a national bank, the power of a State to tax federal instrumentalities, the scope of federal power under the Commerce Clause, and the power of a State to apply local laws to vessels engaged in interstate or foreign commerce. So long as John Marshall was Chief Justice of the United States and dominated the Supreme Court, that Court might be expected to decide such questions in favor of federal power and national unity at the expense of the States. On the other hand, if State court decisions were final, State judges would be permitted up to the limits of their judicial consciences to nullify within their State's boundaries federal laws and constitutional guarantees. Later, nearly all the great decisions of the Marshall Court building national unity would be rendered on appeal from State rulings against federal power and in favor of a State.

Back to the U.S. Supreme Court went the losing party. Chief Justice Marshall was disqualified because family lands were part of the huge tract that was the subject of the litigation. Justice Joseph Story held once more that the U.S. Supreme Court was entitled to the final word. To the argument based on the words "appellate jurisdiction," he responded that the power granted the federal courts by Article III is described in terms of kinds of cases, including all "cases arising under the Constitution or laws of the United States"; and that when Article III gives the U.S. Supreme Court original jurisdiction in a few kinds of cases and appellate jurisdiction in "all other cases above mentioned," the words must mean all cases within the judicial power except those of which the Court is given original jurisdiction. To the argument that Virginia was a sovereign State and the courts of one sovereign may not dictate to the courts of another sovereign, Justice Story responded that Virginia had yielded this and other parts of her sovereignty by ratifying the Constitution and joining the Union. When Hunter's lawyers argued that a State cannot irrevocably yield part of its sovereign power, Justice Story pointed out that the preamble to the Constitution recites that it is made by "the people of the United States."

Justice Story's sometimes fine-spun arguments were not the only force behind the decision. Justice Story was an ardent nationalist. Along with the lawyer's reasoning marched the statesman's conviction that the establishment of the U.S. Supreme Court's authority on questions of constitutional interpretation was indispensable to an effective federal union, not only because of the need for a single authoritative voice to provide uniform interpretations, but because the State courts would all too often set State interests above the Nation's.

One decision could not lay to rest such a fundamental question. There was widespread criticism. The question was reargued in

Cohens v. *Virginia*,[22] a criminal case to which the State itself was a party and thus could argue more directly that its sovereignty was impaired by the intervention of a federal court. This time Chief Justice Marshall wrote the opinion upholding the power of the U.S. Supreme Court. Again there was criticism and even talk of secession by such Virginia localists as Spencer Roane and John Tyler of Caroline. But most of Virginia was content; a Virginian was President and federal policies were not unfavorable. South Carolina was not yet disaffected; South Carolina's strongest political figure, John C. Calhoun, was still a nationalist. Secession had not become a serious threat.

Yet the fight to bar appeals from State courts to the U.S. Supreme Court continued. Virginia did not stand alone. The Massachusetts judges had earlier taken the same position. The claim would be asserted in other States. One of the common consequences of our constitutional system is that those who lose a contest in a political forum often can carry on the war in the courts by posing the contest as a constitutional question. The transformation of the country, from a primarily agrarian society into an industrialized and urbanized Nation, beginning in the last quarter of the nineteenth century gave rise to demands for protective social and economic legislation. Financial and industrial entrepreneurs usually lost the battle in State legislatures and at the polls, but they nonetheless succeeded before 1937 in constitutional attacks on important regulatory laws. Similarly, the black victims of race discrimination in the southern States who could find no legislative remedies either in the State capitals or in Congress turned successfully to the Supreme Court of the United States, most notably in *Brown* v. *Board of Education*[23] and subsequent cases.

The system also sometimes permits those who have lost the battle in the judicial forum, in constitutional form, to resume the war in Congress in political terms. In the 1820s and 1830s the opponents of U.S. Supreme Court review of State court decisions on federal constitutional questions sought to circumvent the decisions in *Martin* v. *Hunter's Lessee* and *Cohens* v. *Virginia* by pressing for the repeal of Section 25 of the Judiciary Act. Had they been successful, the Court would have lacked the statutory authority that is probably necessary to implement Article III's grant of potential jurisdiction. The legislative movement met with some success but never enough to accomplish the repeal. The movement would be renewed periodically through American history—even in the 1980s by Senator Jesse Helms and other critics of the modern Supreme Court.

Marbury v. *Madison, Martin* v. *Hunter's Lessee,* and *Cohens* v. *Virginia* taken together provided a single authoritative voice to interpret the Constitution. Without that voice the whole plan of government might well have failed, destroyed by conflict among the many parts into which the power of government was divided. Even with that voice, a civil war was required to establish an indissoluble union. In the long run, the decisions implied still more; they meant that the great unanswered questions which the Framers had left to the future, both those relating to the federal system and those of individual liberty, would be decided by constitutional interpretation—by a court and according to the law.

IV

It is worth pausing near the beginning to reflect on the implications of judicial supremacy and the power of judicial review. The full meaning in all its sophistication and with room for dispute would develop slowly over the years, but much was apparent at the start.

Even in the beginning, judicial review and judicial supremacy meant that the great constitutional issues would be decided by courts when required in ordinary lawsuits. Not every constitutional question may be put to a court for decision. There must be a plaintiff asserting a right or claiming an injury of the kind normally recognized by courts. No court will decide whether a Senator's holding a commission in the U.S. Air Force Reserve violates the constitutional command that "no person holding office under the United States shall be a member of Congress," because no one suffers a legally cognizable injury even if the Senator is in violation.[24]

When a court decides a constitutional question, the decision is technically binding only on the parties to the case before it. All of us fall into the habit of saying that "the Court held the statute unconditional," or that the Court "struck down" or "invalidated" the statute. The shorthand is misleading. The statute remains on the books. Statutes once held unconstitutional have been revived and enforced after a change in constitutional interpretation. When we say that the Court struck down a statute, we can properly mean only three things: (1) that the Court decided that to apply the statute to A in a given situation would violate A's constitutional rights; (2) that A's situation is so typical that the uniformity of decision to be expected of the Court means that the Court would not permit application of the statute in other cases; and (3) that the uniformity of decision to be expected is such that government officials sworn to uphold the Constitution have a moral and political duty to follow the precedent in the absence of reason to believe that the Court will change the rule.

Committing the unanswered questions of federalism and individual rights to the courts also meant that they would be decided by judges reasoning "according to law." The judges were given the security of life tenure and irreducible salaries in order to make them independent—free from the pressures not only of self-interest but of all group and political loyalties. Decision by independent judges excludes both power and politics, always in the ideal and usually in the reality. The simplicity of this statement should not conceal its importance.

It is harder to describe the process of reasoning by which the independent judges decide, yet the process lies at the heart of American constitutionalism. The familiar quip "The Constitution means what the Supreme Court says it means" contains more falsity than truth. The Court is charged with "interpretation" of a written document, not with deciding what is good, or just, or wise with the freedom of a legislature or constitutional convention. When the proper application of the words of the Constitution to a particular situation is plain, it is the Court's duty to give effect to the words. When the bearing of the words is uncertain—for example, when the Court comes to particularize the meaning of our federalism or to apply such majestic ideals as "the freedom of speech," "due process of law," and "the equal protection of the laws"—the words alone may not suffice. Then a reasoned search for the "intent" of the instrument becomes important; but as history demonstrates, "intent" is itself a slippery word as applied to unforeseen future conditions and the evidence of intent is often subject to conflicting interpretations.

In the past, where the words and intent left doubt, it became conventional to follow the Anglo-American common law method by which judges gradually built most of the law defining the mutual rights and duties of individuals and private organizations. Quite likely Chief Justice Marshall and his colleagues foresaw this development. They were trained in the common law. Alexander Hamilton, in Number 78 of *The Federalist,* had foreshadowed John Marshall's reasoning in *Marbury* v. *Madison* and argued that the power of judicial review would not be dangerous, because the courts "should be bound down by strict rules and precedents, which serve to define and point out their duty in every particular case that comes before them." The Anglo-American common law method to which Hamilton referred is best understood when its theoretical logic is stated in a form much more rigid than the actual practice even in the common law's most barren periods. Courts, the theory began, decide one case at a time. The decision would become a binding precedent. The same decision must be rendered in any future case upon facts that were the same in all material respects as in a previous case. Furthermore, any future decisions must be consistent with the reasoning supporting or logically necessary to support the precedents. Over time, therefore, the field that perhaps was once open to discretion is gradually narrowed. Furthermore, as a group of precedents surrounding a particular issue develops, the prospect of extrapolating a broader principle by the inductive method of science develops and that principle can then be applied by deductive reasoning to the new particular. Bit by bit a coherent body of law is formed, capable of continuous growth to meet new instances. The judicial decisions found in the law reports, first kept by individual clerks but later officially published, are the chief source of law, but judges also look to the dicta of other, distinguished judges (observations of lesser weight not required for the decisions), to ancient professional understanding, to general practice, and to the writings of notable legal scholars based upon these sources of law. A legislature may draw arbitrary lines, according to practical politics and the pressures of interest groups. Law implies a generality of principles applied consistently to all persons not only today but yesterday and tomorrow. A legislature is not bound by its predecessors. Law binds the judges as well as the judged.

With time and good fortune the Constitution became the symbol of the traditions, the success, and the ideals of the American people. New questions concerning both individual rights and the distribution of power between the Nation and the States arose to divide powerful interests and arouse strong emotion. By deciding those grave issues as interpretations of the sacred instrument under which the United States had grown and prospered, by demonstrating that its judgments were indeed the authentic voice of a body of principles reaching back through the past, the Court was able to command an authority much greater than the prestige of the Justices' offices or persons could supply.

Yet law cannot be static if it is to meet the needs of men. The common law method could never be applied with all the rigidity of my statement of its logic. Usually the practice was much more creative. Often the practice involved policy choices. New situations continually arise. Some plainly fall outside any precedent. Others call for a choice between opposing precedents, which are somewhat analogous but also distinguishable. In such cases, conscious or inarticulate views of wise policy become decisive. Changes in conditions may rob existing legal concepts, rules, and even principles of their former meaning, so that old ideals and even traditional principles call for new forms of implementation. Better perception of the true meaning of basic ideals may call for new applications. These observations are especially applicable to constitutional cases. The great questions of federalism and of liberty and equality could not always be wisely decided by a Court imprisoned in logical deduction from the formulas of the past. The great constitutional questions of each age must be decided by "interpretation" of the document in accordance with law, but the decision must also face the facts and meet the needs and aspirations of the times.

In short, the obligation to decide "according to law" always has presented an antinomy. The Court must preserve its legitimacy and the ideal of law by invoking a majestic sense of continuity, but it must also discover some composition with the dominant needs and aspirations of the present. Individual Justices and the Court as a whole from time to time have held very different views concerning the weight they should give to each branch of the antinomy. The dilemma was, and is, insoluble by any stated scale of relative values; but by careful attention to the discipline of legal reasoning a great Justice can minimize the danger of writing his personal values and preferences into constitutional decisions while also demonstrating that the new law which his court must make from time to time is linked to the basic ideals of inherited tradition and thus commands the authority of a majestic past.

In the beginning, especially in resolving questions concerning the distribution of power between the federal government and the States, the Court was relatively free, because the words were inconclusive and there were few precedents. Gradually a body of law accumulated, and the story of the Constitution became partly one of how the Justices wrestled with their dilemma as they shaped the growth of the United States.

· 3 ·

Federal Power and Supremacy

RATIFICATION of the Constitution, in 1789, established a new federal government, but the Federalists and Anti-Federalists hotly debated the scope of its powers even before the ink was dry. The question was first raised in dramatic form, after ratification, by Alexander Hamilton's plan for a congressionally chartered Bank of the United States.

Alexander Hamilton was Secretary of the Treasury in President Washington's Cabinet and, like John Marshall, had been one of Washington's military aides during the Revolutionary War. He had also been a driving force in promoting the Philadelphia Constitutional Convention and in securing ratification of the Constitution by New York. Hamilton was little pleased with the new Constitution. He had no faith in democracy and believed the new federal government far too weak, but he was willing to work with what he had and therefore set out to strengthen the new Nation and its government by building up and binding to the support of the federal government the power of the educated and propertied classes, of the old families, and of the men of money, commerce, and affairs. Hamilton therefore proposed that the new federal government not only arrange to pay off at par all the debts incurred under the Continental Congress and Articles of Confederation but that it also assume, fund, and eventually pay off at par all the debts of the individual States. Federal assumption of these debts would require sizable revenue. Hamilton therefore proposed to levy a federal tariff on imports and to use the proceeds to pay the interest and make payments into a sinking fund from which later to pay off the principal. He also proposed, both as part of the plan and for its own sake, that Congress charter a Bank of the United States to act as financial agent of the United States but with power to do a general banking business.

Thomas Jefferson, President Washington's Secretary of State, opposed Hamilton's program, especially the proposed bank. Like other Virginia plantation owners, Jefferson disliked and distrusted all bankers, to whom the Virginians were usually in debt. A believer in sturdy rural democracy, he saw no reason to encourage the growth of cities; indeed, he feared an urban proletariat as much as he feared bankers, merchants, shipowners, and other moneymen. Assumption of the debts would do little for Virginia; the obligations, greatly depreciated, had largely passed into the hands of city speculators. A tariff would injure Virginia, whose planters naturally wished to keep down the cost of imported merchandise. Encouraging commercial activity would build up the political power of States like Massachusetts and New York, where merchants, traders, and shipping interests were fast expanding; they might soon subordinate Virginia and her agricultural neighbors.

Here was a straight-out contest between economic and sectional interests, yet, as would often prove true in America, the contest was framed partly in constitutional terms. The agrarians challenged the constitutionality of the proposed bank. President Washington sought opinions from Jefferson, Hamilton, and Attorney General Edmund Randolph. Randolph set an example too often followed by later Presidential advisers: he played safe by giving two opinions, one pro and the other con. Hamilton argued that the bank was constitutional. Jefferson said that it was not. The divergence opened a constitutional debate central to American life.

Article I, Section 8, does not list issuing bank charters or chartering corporations among the powers granted to Congress; on the contrary, the Philadelphia Convention had rejected a proposal to give Congress very broad powers to charter corporations where the interests of the United States might require. If the proposed bank were constitutional, the grant of the necessary power must be found by implication. Hamilton had no difficulty on this point. The Constitution must be interpreted, he argued, to grant to Congress the "implied powers" to do all those things which are convenient ways of exercising the granted powers or are incidents of their exercise. Here Hamilton could call to his support the last of the express grants:

> To make all laws which may be necessary and proper for carrying into execution the foregoing powers. . . .

Given his premise, it was not hard for Hamilton to show that a national bank was a convenient adjunct to the exercise of the granted powers "to lay and collect taxes," "to raise and support armies," and "to borrow money on the credit of the United States." The bank could support an army by facilitating the transfer of money collected as taxes from one part of the country to another where it was needed to purchase army supplies. The bank could float loans on the credit of the United States. That the bank would become primarily a privately owned financial institution of enormous power did not, in Hamilton's view, undercut the constitutional argument; it would still be a convenient way of pursuing constitutional objectives.

To Jefferson's way of thinking, Hamilton's thesis proved too much. If it were sound, Jefferson argued, there was no effective limit to the powers of Congress, and that would be contrary to the original hypothesis that the United States should be a government of limited powers. A few years later Jefferson wrote, in opposition to a bill to incorporate a mining company:

> Congress are authorized to defend the nation. Ships are necessary for defense; copper is necessary for ships; mines, necessary for copper; a company necessary to work the mines; and who can doubt this reasoning who has ever played at "this is the house that Jack built."[1]

Jefferson concluded that the word "necessary" in the Necessary and Proper Clause must be read to mean "indispensable" or "essential."

Both the policy and the constitutionality of chartering a national bank were first fought out in the political branches. The scope of federal activity is always initially a political question, even though Senators and Representatives may debate its wisdom partly in constitutional terms, just as the British Parliament itself may debate the constitutionality of a bill even though Parliament has the final word. A constitutional question for the courts is presented only when Congress and the President have already pushed federal activity beyond what others contend is the outermost permissible limit. In the case of the Bank of the United States, Congress passed the necessary legislation. The bill was signed by President Washington.

The bank gained acceptance with the passage of time. A new twenty-year charter was approved by Congress in 1816 without a major fight. Nevertheless, strong pockets of resistance remained, especially in the South and the old Northwest. Some opposition came from ideologues. More came from the farming and debtor classes, fearful of monied power and monopoly. After 1816 the opposition grew in both volume and intensity as the bank's policies first encouraged the overexpansion of credit and then turned to a financial stringency that ruined many State banks and caused widespread distress. Illinois and Indiana barred banks chartered outside the State. Five States, including Maryland, imposed heavily discriminatory taxes on the Bank of the United States.

The Maryland statute levied a stamp tax on the notes of any bank that had established a branch in Maryland "without authority from the state." The Bank of the United States had no authority from Maryland. Payment of the tax would drive it out of business, unlike competing banks chartered by the State. The bank therefore continued to circulate its notes in Maryland without payment of the tax. Maryland thereupon sued McCulloch, the cashier of the Baltimore branch, to recover from him personally the heavy penalty the statute imposed on the cashier of any noncomplying bank. After the State courts had decided in favor of the State, the bank sought review by the U.S. Supreme Court.

McCulloch v. *Maryland*[2] was argued for nine days in the room under the Senate Chamber in the Capitol that the Court was to occupy until 1860. A contemporary reporter observed that the apartment

> was not in a style that comports with the dignity of that body. . . .
> In arriving at it, you pass a labyrinth, and almost need the clue of
> Ariadne to guide you to the sanctuary of the blind goddess. A stranger
> might traverse the dark avenues of the Capitol for a week, without
> finding the remote corner in which Justice is administered to the
> American Republic. . . . Owing to the smallness of the room, the
> Judges are compelled to put on their robes in the presence of spec-
> tators, which is an awkward ceremony and destroys the effect in-
> tended to be produced by assuming the gown.[3]

Opposite the bench was a marble bas-relief of figures holding the Constitution and scales of Justice, that was to elicit satirical comment:

> Next him sits Justice, ever broad awake,
>   (For here they have not thought it
>   fit to blind her),
> Who, with an arm too large for weight to
>   break,
> Thrusts the scales forward while she looks
>   behind her.
> Next her, the Nation's Eagle lifts its claws
> And boldly tramples on the prostrate laws.[4]

Daniel Webster opened for the bank. A New Hampshire farm boy, whose path led by way of Phillips Exeter Academy and Dartmouth College to Boston, he became the leading legal and political spokesman for the business and commercial classes. Senator, Secretary of State, and frequent candidate for President, Webster nonetheless found time to argue more cases in the Supreme Court of the United States than any other lawyer has presented. Both as public servant and as advocate, he was a strong nationalist with a vision of a continentwide open economy and one indissoluble political union. In both roles he was a consummate orator, perhaps the greatest of all Supreme Court advocates. Part of Webster's power lay in his appearance, especially his piercing eyes and flowing black locks. Called "the divine Daniel," it was said that "[n]o man can be as great as Daniel Webster looks." (It was also said that he drank a bottle of Madeira wine before each argument. I sometimes wondered whether to try to improve my advocacy by his example, but held back for want of piercing black eyes or flowing black hair.)

Luther Martin, the Attorney General of Maryland, closed the argument for the State. Neither his violent disposition nor excessive drinking kept him from the front rank of American lawyers. He had defended U.S. Supreme Court Justice Samuel Chase in the impeachment trial that secured the independence of the federal Judiciary, and also Aaron Burr when the latter was accused of treason. Earlier, as a delegate to the Philadelphia Convention, he had objected to the Constitution, and in Maryland he had opposed ratification. Now he sought to show by historical proofs that the bank's supporters were denying the strict theories of interpretation that the supporters themselves had advanced to promote ratification: "We are now called upon to apply that theory of interpretation, which was then rejected by the friends of the new constitution, and we are asked to engraft upon it powers of vast extent, which were disclaimed by them, and which if they had been fairly avowed at the time, would have prevented its adoption."[5]

Three days after the close of argument Chief Justice Marshall announced the judgment of the Court in favor of the bank. The opinion ruled, first, that Congress has implied powers in addition to the powers expressly granted, including the power to create a national bank, and, second, that the supremacy of the federal government, when engaging in constitutionally authorized activity, bars a State from taxing an instrumentality of the United States.

The Chief Justice began the portion of the opinion upholding the bank's constitutionality by conceding that the "government of the Union . . . is acknowledged by all to be one of enumerated powers."[6] He acknowledged that establishing a bank is not one of those enumerated powers. But there is no phrase in the instrument, he asserted, "which excludes incidental or implied powers."[7] He then endorsed the theory of implied powers, arguing that the very nature of a constitution "requires that only its great outlines be marked, its important objects designated, and the minor ingredients deduced from the nature of the objects themselves."[8] One should not expect a detailed specification of every particular in a constitution. Then came the famous line "[W]e must never forget that it is *a constitution* we are expounding."[9]

In later years the line would often be quoted out of context to support the conclusion that the meaning of the Constitution may grow and change. The principle is sound, as Marshall might agree; but on this occasion he obviously meant no more than that a basic document written for the future was not to be read as a specification of details.

After giving examples of the need for legislative or executive choice among the various ways of carrying out the specific delegated powers, and also of the need for implementary measures, Marshall turned to the "necessary and proper" clause to show that the grant of implied powers was not left to general reasoning:

Congress shall have power . . . [t]o make all laws which shall be necessary and proper for carrying into execution the foregoing powers.

Maryland had argued, as Jefferson had done, that the clause is restrictive, that Congress may enact only such laws as are strictly necessary, that is, indispensable, to executing the specified powers. Marshall rejected the argument partly by linguistic analysis and partly by demonstrating the inconvenience of thus tying down a government intended to endure for ages. "Necessary," he concluded, means convenient or useful. Then followed the most famous passage:

> Let the end be legitimate, let it be within the scope of the constitution, and all means which are appropriate, which are plainly adapted to that end, which are not prohibited, but consistent with the letter and spirit of the constitution are constitutional.[10]

Having broadly established this predicate, Marshall easily demonstrated that chartering a national bank was a means of exercising the specifically delegated congressional powers "[t]o raise and support Armies" and "[t]o borrow Money on the credit of the United States."

It remained to show that the State of Maryland had no power to levy the tax on the bank. The question touched the most sensitive nerve in the young Republic. Which was sovereign, the federal union or the States? The issue split the political parties and geographical sections for three quarters of a century. Chief Justice Marshall, ever a nationalist, left no room for doubt about the Court's opinion. Referring to the Supremacy Clause of the Constitution, he declared that

> if the right of the States to tax the means employed by the general government be conceded, the declaration that the constitution, and the laws made in pursuance thereof, shall be the supreme law of the land, is empty and unmeaning declamation.[11]

Despite its victory, the bank did not long survive. In the South and old Northwest the Court's opinion evoked violent criticism. Thomas Jefferson, James Madison, and Spencer Roane of Virginia inveighed against it. An editorial in the *Natchez Press* illustrates the newspaper comment:

> The last vestige of the sovereignty and independence of the individual States composing the National Confederacy is obliterated at one fell

swoop. . . . In truth, the idea of any country's long remaining free, that tolerates incorporated banks, in any guise or under any auspices, is altogether delusive.[12]

Ohio officials directly challenged the Court by continuing to levy that State's tax on the bank's notes and specie. Opposition to the bank became the centerpiece of Jacksonian Democracy. President Jackson in 1832 vetoed the bill to renew the bank's charter. The old federal charter was to expire in 1837. In 1833 Jackson completed his attack on the bank by ordering removal of all the deposits of the United States.

Despite the demise of the bank, *McCulloch* v. *Maryland* was a landmark decision with profound impact on the country and of seminal importance in the evolution of our constitutional law. The reasons are three.

First, the ruling that the Supremacy Clause of the Constitution bars a State from taxing or otherwise seeking to control the activities of the federal government was essential to the preservation of that government in a hostile environment. When the case was argued, States were asserting their ultimate sovereignty and were not infrequently seeking to thwart federal laws.

The tax ruling also gave rise to a broad doctrine of intergovernmental immunities that freed the agents of the State and federal governments each from taxation or regulation by the other. Though the doctrine has been greatly modified, its remnants can be found in the exemption from the federal income tax of interest paid on municipal bonds.

Second, in upholding the constitutionality of the bank, the Court, taking up one of the great questions left open by the Philadelphia Convention, expressly adopted the "implied powers" theory espoused by Alexander Hamilton and thus rejected the Jeffersonian theory that the powers delegated to Congress were to be interpreted strictly. The immediate impact of the Court's powerful opinion was to confirm and strengthen the political and philosophical advocates of a broad interpretation of federal power looking toward a tariff that protected infant industries and supplied funds for roads, canals, and the other internal improvements facilitating the movement of people and goods between the eastern seaboard and the new States to the west. In the longer run the reasoning of the opinion would be used to support the vast expansion of federal regulation that presently characterizes the welfare state. For example, even though the production of goods in mines, mills, and factories for later interstate distribution is itself a local activity not part of interstate commerce, Congress may constitutionally regulate the labor-management relations of those enterprises as a means of reducing strikes and thus facilitating commerce among the several States.[13] Similarly, the Prohibition laws enacted following World War I were sustained as means of exercising the granted powers to "raise and support Armies" and to "provide for the common defense," because barring the manufacture of malt and distilled liquors conserved manpower and increased efficiency and production and also helped to husband the supply of grains and cereal depleted by the war effort.[14] Jefferson was not far wrong in arguing that the powers of the federal government could be almost endlessly extended once one embraced the logic of "this is the house that Jack built."

The reasoning of *McCulloch* v. *Maryland* was applied in still other areas in major civil rights cases in the 1960s. Section 1 of the Fifteenth Amendment provides that the right to vote shall not be denied by the United States or by any State "on account of race, color or previous condition of servitude." To require every citizen to demonstrate literacy as a qualification for voting, regardless of race or color, does not violate the Fifteenth Amendment if the literacy test is administered evenhandedly. Prior to 1965 such tests were widely used in the South and Southwest as instruments of racial discrimination to exclude black and Hispanic citizens from participation in democratic government. The discriminatory use did violate the amendment, but proving actual racial discrimination in the administration of literacy tests requires prolonged and expensive investigation and litigation. Years of effort would have been required to realize by this means the promise of the Fifteenth Amendment. Congress therefore outlawed literacy tests in every State or county in which less than half of the adult population voted while such tests were in force, thus dispensing with the need for time-consuming and expensive proof that the tests had been abused. The Voting Rights Act was based on Section 2 of the Fifteenth Amendment, which provides that

> Congress shall have power to enforce this article by appropriate legislation.

South Carolina, in challenging the constitutionality of these provisions of the Voting Rights Act of 1965, argued that the power "to enforce" is the power to prevent or redress State conduct proved actually to violate the prohibition against discrimination, and that there was no proof that South Carolina had actually engaged in violations. In response, the government's brief turned to *McCulloch* v. *Maryland*:

> Congress may employ means which, "although not themselves within the granted power, were nevertheless deemed appropriate aids to the accomplishment of some purpose within an admitted power of the national government."[15]

Prohibition of all literacy tests, the argument continued, is an appropriate means of barring their possible use as engines of racial discrimination—an abuse within the admitted purview of the national government.

The Court accepted this broad interpretation even though Section 2 contains no Necessary and Proper Clause. "The basic test to be applied in a case involving Section 2 of the Fifteenth Amendment," the Chief Justice declared, "is the same as in all cases concerning the express powers of Congress in relation to the reserved powers of the States."[16] Turning to the famous passage in Marshall's opinion quoted above, Chief Justice Earl Warren observed that the end—the elimination of discriminatory denials of voting rights—is a legitimate object of congressional legislation, and that the means—outlawry of literacy tests susceptible of use as engines of discrimination—being plainly adapted to that end, are constitutional too.

The South Carolina case illustrates the genius of American constitutionalism. Denial of voting rights had become a pressing national problem. In order to solve the national problem and eliminate racial injustice, Congress exercised federal power in the area of voting qualifications on an unprecedented scale. In a sense, the constitutional grant of federal power grew to meet a newly recognized national need. At the same time, however, by persuasively linking the decision to *McCulloch* v. *Maryland* and like precedents, the Court was able truthfully to deny that it was simply making new law to suit the occasion, and could invoke the majesty and authority of constitutional tradition.

Third, *McCulloch* v. *Maryland* foreshadows a sophisticated problem of judicial method that we shall later find running through many areas of constitutional law. The constitutionality of a State statute or of an Act of Congress may turn upon some question of fact, upon an appraisal of social or economic conditions, or upon a perception of balance or degree. In such cases, should the fact finding, appraisal, or perception of the Court control the decision, or should the Court leave such questions to Congress?

The problem recurs so often as to deserve concrete illustration. A federal law prohibits campaign contributions in excess of $1000. Another federal law bars independent committees, formed to raise and expend money to support a Presidential candidate without further consultation with the candidate, from spending more than $1000 in a general election in which the candidate's campaign is carried on with public funds. Arguably, both limitations violate the First Amendment, because the ceilings on contributions and independent expenditures tend to curtail the volume of political speeches and advertising. First Amendment rights are not absolute, however, and some limitations are constitutional if they serve a sufficiently important need. Because preventing the corruption of government is such a need, the constitutionality of each of the two restrictions boils down to whether, in fact, large campaign contributions to a candidate or large independent expenditures in support of a candidate induce or appear to induce reciprocal favors from officials after election. Here the problem of judicial method arises. Who is to decide that question of fact, the legislature or the Court? In these two instances the Court treated the question as one for it to decide. It agreed with the Congress that large contributions to a candidate tend to be corrupting, and therefore sustained that limit. But the Court also, in disagreement with the implicit congressional finding, supposed that expenditures of money as small as $1000 raised to support a candidate and spent without consultation with the candidate are not corrupting, and thus found that ceiling unconstitutional.[17]

In *McCulloch* v. *Maryland* the Court seemed to allocate to Congress the primary responsibility for making such determinations of fact and degree. Under the Court's reasoning, the constitutionality of the bank depended on establishing a link between the bank and a legitimate, constitutionally authorized objective. In the first instance, the existence of a link depended on the facts, on the actual conditions. Did the bank in fact aid in supporting an army or in borrowing money on the credit of the United States? But then perceptions become important. The degree of necessity—of need or convenience in achieving the constitutional objective—may be strong or weak. The connection may be proximate or remote. The bank's contribution to maintaining an army or borrowing money on the credit of the United States was trivial in relation to the bank's private financial activities. The nominal objectives might even have been called pretexts. Nevertheless, the Court declined to inquire into such questions, even though, in a broader colloquial sense, the ultimate constitutionality of the bank might be thought to have turned upon them. "[T]he degree of its necessity," the Chief Justice observed, "is to be discussed in another place."

> Where the law is not prohibited and is really calculated to effect any of the objects entrusted to the government, to undertake here to inquire into the degree of its necessity, would be to pass the line which circumscribes the judicial department, and to tread on legislative ground.[18]

The proper application of this self-imposed limitation on the power of judicial review would be much debated in future years. It is worth noting now, however, that when the Court defers, as Marshall did, to congressional determinations concerning facts and their significance, it is allowing the people to govern through their elected representatives, but that when the Court substitutes its own judgment and invalidates the legislation, it is checking majority rule.

· 4 ·

Opening a National Market

THE COMMERCIAL WARFARE among the States during the chaotic times following the Revolutionary War led the Philadelphia Convention readily to agree that the new federal government should have power "[t]o regulate commerce with foreign nations . . . and among the several States," but the delegates left open two key questions stated in Chapter 1:

1. How extensive is the authority thus granted to Congress? What is meant by "commerce . . . among the several States?" *McCulloch* v. *Maryland*[1] suggested that the Court under Chief Justice Marshall would give the Commerce Clause a broad interpretation, but the question was not involved in that ruling.

2. What is the effect of the Commerce Clause on State power to regulate or tax interstate commerce? Presumably any law enacted by Congress pursuant to the power to regulate interstate commerce would control. But suppose that Congress has enacted no relevant legislation. Does the grant to Congress of power to regulate interstate commerce mean that *only* Congress may regulate, thus conferring what lawyers call "exclusive jurisdiction" and barring State legislation? Or are the States free to tax and regulate interstate commerce unless and until Congress ousts State law, thus retaining "concurrent jurisdiction"?

The Supreme Court's answers to these questions would determine how far the local pride and self-interest of individual States would be permitted to hamper the development of one great continentwide, free-trade market on which to build a unified Nation.

The first great test resulted from an event three thousand miles away. On August 9, 1803, a crowd gathered at Quai Chaillot in Paris on the banks of the River Seine. Napoleon sent emissaries. Scientific representatives of the French Academy were also present. One central figure was Robert Fulton, who was about to demonstrate the successful practical operation of a steamboat, an event that Napoleon predicted would change the face of the world. Also present was Robert Livingston, Fulton's chief financial backer and one of the builders of America, both as politician and as entrepreneur.

Livingston saw that a practical steamboat would open up interior America like a ripe fruit. A member of the most powerful political family in New York, he had earlier secured from the legislature a monopoly of the right to operate steamboats on the waters of New York. The grant was conditional upon demonstration of a vessel that could make four miles an hour upstream against the current of the Hudson River. The idea seemed so preposterous to the New York legislators that the bill was enacted in a storm of laughter. After the demonstration on the Seine, the practical operation of the steamboat became reality. So did Livingston's New York monopoly.

Livingston was right in perceiving that the steamboat would open up the North American continent. The Potomac River cut far into the interior. So would the Hudson River when joined to the Erie Canal. The Ohio–Mississippi River system would carry the commerce of those great valleys, as far as New Orleans and from there to foreign shores. Later, the Missouri, the Platte, the Arkansas, and the Red Rivers would open the way to the Rocky Mountains. Waterways had provided the lines of travel even in the days of the flatboat, barge, and canoe. With the coming of swifter means of transportation, the great waterways could become both arteries carrying the life blood of commerce and sinews binding together widely separated and diverse localities across the continent.

If trade can be unifying, it can also be divisive. From the beginning of trade and commerce, those who had sufficient power astride the trade routes exacted tribute from passing merchants. Later, the exactions took the more sophisticated form of tolls, customs, and sundry forms of taxation. Such levies had "Balkanized" the Danube

Valley for centuries. Similar forces were at work in America. Rivalry in exploiting the steamboat by devices like Livingston's New York monopoly could tear States and localities apart in economic warfare. Indeed, rivalry began to tear them apart shortly after both the steamboat and the monopoly became realities. Connecticut passed a law barring vessels of the monopoly from the waters of Connecticut. Ohio and Pennsylvania forbade any of the monopoly's vessels to put down or take off passengers or freight at any of their Lake Erie ports. New Jersey authorized the owner of any vessel seized in New York for violating the monopoly to seize any of the monopoly's vessels found in New Jersey. Imagine what would have happened on the Mississippi and Ohio Rivers if every State with jurisdiction over part of those waterways were to have granted a monopoly to a different entrepreneur. Livingston had already obtained from Louisiana the key monopoly for steamboat traffic entering or leaving the Port of New Orleans. For the steamboat to bring economic unity to the North American continent, the Commerce Clause would have to be made into a vehicle for barring the States from granting such monopolies, and also from erecting the customs barriers, imposts, diverse local regulations, and like instruments of economic rivalry that hampered the Old World. Under *Marbury* v. *Madison,*[2] the task of shaping the Commerce Clause would fall on the courts.

The steamboat was too profitable and too appealing to the imaginative and ambitious for the New York monopoly to go unchallenged. One of the challengers was Thomas Gibbons, who commenced the operation of two ferries across the harbor between New York City and the New Jersey shore. One of Gibbons's captains was Cornelius J. Vanderbilt. Later, Vanderbilt would build the New York Central Railroad into a more modern transportation empire, but even as a steamboat captain Vanderbilt was known as "enormously ambitious and resourceful but not a little ruthless." He built a secret closet on his steamboat in which to hide from thugs hired to enforce the monopoly and from process servers seeking enforcement by legal means.

The effort to enforce the monopoly by legal means gave rise to one of the truly great U.S. Supreme Court cases. Livingston had assigned a portion of his monopoly to Aaron Ogden. Ogden brought suit against Gibbons for an injunction validating Ogden's monopoly and forbidding Gibbons to operate steamboats on the waters of

New York. The New York courts upheld the monopoly, despite Gibbons's claim that the New York statute granting the monopoly was unconstitutional because it was inconsistent with the Constitution and laws of the United States. Gibbons appealed.

In the U.S. Supreme Court Gibbons's chief counsel were William Wirt, then the leader of the Bar, and Daniel Webster, then a rising star, whom Wirt described as "ambitious as Caesar." Wirt and Webster disagreed about the line of argument to be pressed, but in those days there was time for both to be heard. Wirt believed that the strongest argument was that the New York monopoly as applied to Gibbons was unconstitutional under the Supremacy Clause because it conflicted with an Act of Congress under which Gibbons's vessel was licensed to engage in the coastal trade. Webster, who dreamed of an open nationwide economy forming the base of an indissoluble political union, declined to argue "on any other ground than that of . . . the constitutional authority of Congress *exclusively* to regulate commerce in all its forms on all navigable waters of the United States."(Emphasis added.)[3]

In order to reach these points, both Wirt and Webster had to get over two preliminary obstacles. Ogden's lawyers contended that the power to regulate interstate commerce covers only the movement of trade in commodities across State lines. Wirt and Webster first had to persuade the Court that "commerce" included navigation—more broadly, transportation—and even the movement of people and messages. The point could have caused little difficulty even in 1824. In later years the Court would hold that driving a stolen automobile,[4] carrying a bottle of whiskey for personal consumption,[5] and even sending an invitation to dinner across State lines[6] is interstate commerce. So, probably, is the movement of the particles and gases causing acid rain.

The second preliminary step was more difficult. At times Gibbons's ferries were operating wholly upon the waters of New York. Wirt and Webster, in order to prevail, had to show that the Commerce Clause granted the federal government power to reach down into a State and regulate activities wholly within the State when those local activities were part of an interstate movement. The case was much the same as the situation that would arise if Congress were to fix the fares charged by taxi drivers carrying interstate travelers from O'Hare Airport into the City of Chicago, or from Kennedy Airport into New York City.

This interpretation of the Commerce Clause would raise no eye-brows in the current era of extensive federal regulation, but in 1824 it implied a vast expansion of federal authority, highly controversial and anathema to many Southerners and old Jeffersonian Republicans. Only two years earlier, President Monroe had vetoed as unconstitutional an internal improvements bill calling for the expenditure of federal money for a segment of an interstate turnpike located within Indiana. He was following the orthodox Jeffersonian view that Congress may spend federal funds only on what Congress may regulate; that interstate commerce embraces only trade in goods across State lines; and that the granted power of regulation is confined to tariffs, customs, and other measures imposed at interstate boundaries.

In the Steamboat Monopoly Case[7] the Supreme Court rejected these arguments and embraced the broader reading in another of Chief Justice Marshall's great opinions. "Commerce among the States," the Chief Justice wrote, "cannot stop at the external boundary line of each State but may be introduced into the interior."[8] To illustrate the point, he referred to the great rivers that penetrate the country, carrying articles of foreign trade and commerce deep into the interior and passing through several States. Such movement, he reasoned, is part of foreign commerce between the point of destination and the shippers overseas. "If Congress has power to regulate it, that power must be exercised wherever the subject exists. If it exists within the States, if a foreign voyage may commence or terminate at a port within a State, then the power of Congress may be exercised within a State."[9] The same principle, Marshall continued, applies to interstate commerce. This assertion of national power was broad by the standards of the early nineteenth century. The language of the opinion and the vision behind it contained the seeds of the tremendous expansion of the national power in the 1930s.

But these points alone were not enough to invalidate the State monopoly. For Gibbons to prevail, either Webster must convince the Court that the grant of power to Congress "to regulate commerce . . . among the several States" is exclusive, that is, that the words implicitly deny a State any power to regulate the operation of steamboats on its waters when carrying people or goods in interstate commerce, or else Wirt must show that New York's grant of a monopoly was inconsistent with the federal statute pertaining to the coastal trade.

Constitutionalists of the early nineteenth century tended to think in terms of the nature and location of power rather than in terms of the practical consequences of its exercise. Often, under the influence of Newtonian physics, they thought of particular powers as unbreakable integers, like atoms. Upon this reasoning Webster could argue that the words granting Congress the power to regulate interstate commerce logically implied that no part of that power could remain in the States. If the power was in Congress and the power was an integer, it could not be in a State.

Applied to the Steamboat Monopoly Case, the theoretical arguments made good practical sense. The specific example also made plain the broader proposition that the vision of a continentwide open market, binding the diverse peoples and regions of the United States by economic ties, could scarcely be realized if, in the absence of congressional action, the States were free to promote local advantage by selfish regulation or taxation of interstate trade. In theory, Congress could always act to sweep away local obstructions. In practice, there would be delay and difficulty in enacting the necessary legislation.

But would it really make sound policy to deny the States any power to regulate interstate commerce? What about local pilotage laws? Pilotage laws are obviously necessary. Congress would find it hard to write local rules for every port. Thousands of immigrants were flowing into New York City upon trans-Atlantic vessels. Should New York have no power to impose some kind of quarantine in order to protect the health of her residents? Put the problem in modern terms. What about local ordinances fixing the speed at which interstate vehicles may move through villages?

Common sense seemingly required that some State and local regulations of interstate commerce be permitted, but that others be invalid. Yet both the law's need for a rule and the contemporary intellectual mode seemed to dictate an all-or-nothing answer: either the States shared with Congress the power to regulate interstate commerce or they did not.

In the Steamboat Monopoly Case the Supreme Court avoided the dilemma by turning to Wirt's argument and holding that the licenses to enter the coastal trade granted to enrolled American vessels under the Act of Congress conferred a federal right to operate without let or hindrance from any source. Under the Supremacy Clause the federal right prevailed over State law. The decision swept away the steamboat monopolies. Contemporary newspapers reported that the first Connecticut vessel entered the Port of New York "in triumph, with streamers flying, and a large company of passengers exulting in the decision. . . .   She fired a salute which was loudly returned by huzzas from the wharves."[10] Within a year and a half, the number of steamboats plying from New York increased from six to forty-three. The Mississippi and other great rivers of the interior were opened to the free passage of steam vessels.

But the constitutional dilemma remained. For another twenty-five years the Justices wrestled with the question in all-or-nothing terms: either the grant to Congress of power to regulate interstate commerce was exclusive because it took that power away from the States, or the States retained "concurrent jurisdiction" unless and until Congress enacted relevant legislation. Barely below the surface lay two deep differences of political philosophy that, in modified form, still influence the Justices today.

First, the Justices disagreed concerning the relative weights to be assigned, on the one hand, to the national interest in the free movement of persons and goods in an open national economy and, on the other hand, to the power of the States and municipalities to meet local needs. The men of trade and commerce, the nationalists with a vision of a continentwide open market binding together diverse peoples and regions, tended to subordinate the local interests to the national needs. The localists, especially those distrustful of a distant central government, argued for the concurrent jurisdiction of the States.

The second difference, which would grow in importance in later years, lay in the Justices' divergent attitudes toward government regulation. To hold that the power of Congress is exclusive (that is, that the States have no power to regulate interstate commerce), even though Congress has enacted no relevant legislation, tends to free those engaged in interstate commerce from all public regulation. Contrariwise, those who perceive a need for regulation in the public interest would tend to grant the States power to regulate unless and until Congress acts.

The logjam was broken in 1851 in *Cooley* v. *Board of Port Wardens*,[11] another steamboat case. Cooley, the master of a vessel engaged in foreign trade, had violated the local pilotage laws enacted by Pennsylvania for the Port of Philadelphia. The Port Wardens sued to collect a penalty. Cooley argued that Pennsylvania lacked power to regulate interstate or foreign commerce. The U.S. Supreme Court escaped the either/or dilemma that had puzzled it for almost thirty years by asserting:

> The diversities of opinion . . . which have existed on this subject, have arisen from the different views taken of this power [to regulate interstate commerce]. But when the nature of a power like this is spoken of . . . it must be intended to refer to the subjects of this power.[12]

The passage marks a major shift in style of legal analysis. The earlier Justices had not been talking about the "subjects" of regulation but about the seat of an indivisible regulatory power. By pretending otherwise, the Court escaped the supposed dilemma and started down the road toward the much more pragmatic, particularistic, policy-oriented method of decision characteristic of modern legal thinking. "Whatever subjects of this power are in their nature national," the Court ruled, "or admit only of one uniform system or plan of regulation, may be justly said to be of such a nature as to require exclusive legislation by Congress."[13] Where the nature of the subject is such that it admits of diversity of regulation, the Court continued, there the subject is left to regulation by the States, even though it is interstate commerce, unless and until Congress exerts the federal power. Local pilotage laws fell in the second category.

The *Cooley* formula had the enormously important effect of enabling the federal courts thenceforth to strike a balance, case by case, between the competing values of uniformity and diversity, thus keeping the national market free from selfish and seriously obstructive State laws while at the same time permitting the States and localities to deal with truly local problems unsuited to national regulation. Nothing in the Constitution lays down this formula or gives the courts power to apply it when a person engaged in interstate commerce files suit challenging the State or local regulation. By its own invention built upon the bare words of the Framers, the U.S. Supreme Court had made judicial review, step by step, into an instrument for keeping open the national market without unduly sacrificing local interests. The invention assigned to the Judiciary the task of umpiring the federal system, an extraordinary task for a court; but it also satisfied a national need.

II

Even though *Gibbons* v. *Ogden* and *Cooley* v. *Board of Port Wardens* laid the groundwork, much remained to be done to make judicial review of State legislation under the Commerce Clause into an effective mechanism for accommodating the conflicting demands of unity and diversity within the federal system. The verbal formulas in *Cooley*—"subject of regulation," "require uniformity," and "admit of diversity"—quickly break down under careful analysis. When Massachusetts forbade the interstate and local sale of oleomargarine colored to look like butter, the subject of regulation was the sale of oleomargarine. When New Hampshire forbade the interstate and local sale of oleomargarine unless colored pink, the subject of regulation was again the sale of oleomargarine. The Court upheld the Massachusetts law but invalidated the New Hampshire statute.[14] Good sense prevailed in both cases, but obviously the Court was rendering a policy judgment rather than applying abstract legal doctrine. Yet because the policy judgments were and are to be made by judges "according to law," it was and is important to define the manner in which courts go about the task and to develop, if possible, some coherent guiding principles.

The cases in which that work was undertaken lack the drama of the Case of the Steamboat Monopoly. They often descend to details. Yet the cases have a threefold significance. First, they show the Court at work to protect against selfish State legislation the vision of a continentwide open market, a vision turned into reality by the Industrial Revolution, mass production, and modern methods of transportation. Second, the opinions raise continuing problems of judicial method that pervade several areas of constitutional law. Third, the cases illustrate what is still a necessary and major part of the day-to-day work of umpiring the federal system.

Economic Protectionism. State regulation that discriminates against interstate business activities in favor of local interests is now regarded as unconstitutional under the Commerce Clause in the absence of some extraordinary justification. The need for such a check on parochial selfishness became obvious as interstate markets began to develop. In the 1880s, for example, Minnesota prohibited the sale of meat for human consumption unless the live animal was inspected by a Minnesota State inspector within twenty-four hours before slaughter. The Minnesota inspectors were appointed for jurisdictions within the State. In effect, Minnesota slaughterhouses and possibly a few out-of-State slaughterhouses gained a monopoly of the Minnesota market for fresh meat. Because of this discrimination against out-of-State sellers, the Minnesota law was held to be an unconstitutional invasion of the power of Congress to regulate interstate commerce.[15]

As some States have sought to shelter local sellers from out-of-State competition, so other States have sought to give their residents or local businesses preferential access to local resources. The attempts generally run afoul of the Commerce Clause. A Louisiana law of the 1930s offers an amusing example. Vast quantities of shrimp were taken from the waters of Louisiana and carried unshucked to canneries in Biloxi, Mississippi. At that time a State was believed to hold title to wild animals and fish. Louisianians, casting envious eyes at the Mississippi canneries using Louisiana shrimp, secured the enactment of legislation asserting Louisiana's title to the shrimp and barring the out-of-State shipment of unshucked shrimp, on the ground that the heads and tails, unsuitable for food, were needed in Louisiana for fertilizer. The statute, if constitutional, would force the canners to move to Louisiana. The Court held that Louisiana surrendered her title by allowing fishermen to take the shrimp and that the ban on interstate shipment of unshucked shrimp then became an undue burden on interstate commerce.[16] A few years ago the Court similarly invalidated an Oklahoma statute forbidding any person to transport out of Oklahoma minnows taken within the State.[17]

Most of us intuitively condemn such economic protectionism, but occasionally more appealing concerns collide with the principle that the people of one State may not solve their problems by putting the burden on the people of other States. In northeastern New Jersey, behind the cliffs that hold back the Hudson River but readily accessible to the great City of New York, lie the Hackensack meadows, twenty-one thousand acres of saltwater swamps, meadows, and marshes that resisted development because of low elevation, tidal waters, and poor soil composition. At times the meadowlands are a place of strange natural beauty; at times dank, smelly mud flats. One desiring to protect the natural ecology might wish to preserve them. With controlled and wise development they might be a resource of incalculable value for new jobs, home sites, and reclamation.

In 1968 the meadowlands were fast becoming an enormous dump. Each week 300,000 tons of solid waste were dumped there—1.5 million tons a year, of which 200,000 tons came from New York. By 1973 the volume had grown to 42,000 tons a week—2.1 million tons a year, of which almost 20 percent came from New York. Other New Jersey lowlands near metropolitan New York also received "sanitary landfill." Across the State the City of Philadelphia was using New Jersey as a dump for its waste.

In 1974 the New Jersey legislature enacted a statute forbidding any person to bring into the State any solid or liquid waste, except garbage to be fed to swine. A suit to enforce the statute was brought by the New Jersey authorities against the enterprise that accepted much of the waste for dumping on the Hackensack meadows. The defendant answered that the statute was unconstitutional, because it discriminated against interstate commerce while allowing the continued dumping of New Jersey wastes. New Jersey responded that the burden was slight and was amply justified by the need to protect New Jersey's health, resources, and environment against the cascade of rubbish from Philadelphia and New York.

The U.S. Supreme Court held the New Jersey statute unconstitutional by a 6–2 vote.[18] The majority acknowledged the general power of a State to legislate in protection of the local environment, and also the specific power to curtail the dumping of waste; but the Court ruled that New Jersey must choose some method of protecting its meadowlands other than discrimination against the refuse of other States. In effect, the Court was ruling that the great compact drawn up in Philadelphia in 1787 implied a common undertaking that no State would try to solve its problems primarily at the expense of the people of other States.

Evenhanded State Regulation. Striking the balance between the national interest in the free flow of interstate commerce and the State interest in autonomous regulation suited to local needs is much more difficult when the allegedly unconstitutional State regulation applies evenhandedly to both interstate and local activity. The problems are best illustrated by the Court's treatment of State laws regulating railroads and motor trucks.

In the 1930s South Carolina barred from her highways motor trucks whose width exceeded ninety inches or whose weight exceeded twenty thousand pounds. The laws of neighboring States were less stringent. From 85 to 90 percent of all trucks used in interstate commerce were wider and carried heavier loads. Plainly the South Carolina law burdened interstate commerce. In *South Carolina* v. *Barnwell*[19] the Court nevertheless rejected an interstate trucker's challenge to its constitutionality under the Commerce Clause.

> [S]o long as the state action does not discriminate, the burden is one which the Constitution permits because it is an inseparable incident of the exercise of a legislative authority, which, under the Constitution, has been left to the states. . . . [T]he judicial function stops with the inquiry whether the state legislature in adopting regulations such as the present has acted within its province, and whether the means of regulation chosen are reasonably adapted to the end sought. . . . [Courts] cannot act as Congress does when, after weighing all the conflicting interests, state and national, it determines when and how the state regulatory power shall yield to the larger interests of a national commerce.[20]

The lesson to be drawn from this pronouncement seemed plain. If a State regulation operates on local and interstate commerce evenhandedly, it will not be held unconstitutional merely because it imposes what the Court might think to be an undue burden upon interstate commerce. Weighing the relative burdens and benefits is exclusively a legislative function. The courts can intervene only if the legislative finding is irrational.

The *Barnwell* case was decided in 1938, at a time when there was growing recognition of the need for more public regulation of many aspects of industrial and commercial activity. The era was also marked by the narrowing of judicial review that results from extreme judicial deference to legislative findings of fact and legislative judgments of policy. Earlier, in *McCulloch* v. *Maryland,* as we noted in the last chapter, the Court had seemed to allocate to Congress the responsibility for fact finding and policymaking in the federal sphere. Later, we shall encounter like instances of deference to the findings and policy judgments of both Congress and State legislatures when the constitutionality of legislation is challenged as a deprivation of property without due process of law. In *Barnwell,* the Court chose to defer to a State legislature even though the claim was that the State legislature had undervalued the national interest in interstate commerce.

Such choices of judicial method, that is, deciding whether the Court will defer or reach its own findings and conclusions, may seem highly theoretical, but the consequences are both practical and far reaching. Often the choice determines whether a particular statute will be held constitutional or unconstitutional. Cumulatively, the particular choices will determine how large a role the courts will play in the overall government of the country and how much the courts will leave to the elected representatives of the people.

Seven years after *Barnwell,* Chief Justice Harlan Fiske Stone seemed to forget the very limited function that his *Barnwell* opinion allocated to the courts in reviewing State legislation challenged under the Commerce Clause. Arizona had enacted a statute limiting the length of all freight trains to seventy cars. Southern Pacific Railroad violated the statute by operating longer interstate trains. When the State sued to collect penalties, Southern Pacific attacked the train-limit law as an unconstitutional burden on interstate commerce. The trial court heard evidence on the effects of the train-limit law for five and a half months. The court then made findings of fact and concluded that the Arizona law's effects as a safety measure were "so slight or problematical as not to outweigh the national interest in keeping interstate commerce free from interferences that seriously impeded it." In the U.S. Supreme Court, Justice Hugo L. Black bitingly protested putting the State instead of the railroad on trial. But the Chief Justice, speaking for the majority, reviewed the evidence and findings of fact and concluded that "examination of all the relevant factors makes it plain that the state interest is outweighed by the interest of the nation in an adequate economical and efficient transportation service, which must prevail."[21] The observation that States were more involved in regulating motor vehicles and highways than railroads could not hide the truth that in the railroad case the Court engaged in the very process that it had rejected in dealing with trucks: examining all the relevant factors and then striking its own balance of the opposing State and national interests.

Similar litigation is still frequent in both State and federal courts. So long as States respond to the need for public regulation, there will be interstate businesses seeking exemption on the ground that the regulation unduly burdens interstate commerce. The Justices continue to be divided in their basic approach. Both points are illustrated by highway cases. All the Justices joined in striking down an Illinois law requiring trucks to be equipped with contoured rear mud flaps at a time when neighboring States prescribed straight mud flaps.[22] No one could honestly say that the Illinois law was not a safety measure. The Court obviously was striking its own balance between the burden the Illinois statute put on interstate commerce and the contribution, if any, that contoured as opposed to straight mud flaps made to highway safety. A Wisconsin statute barring the thundering "65-foot doubles" from Wisconsin's highways was invalidated by a sharply divided Court.[23] The majority asserted its deference to the judgment of the State but concluded that the statute contributed to safety "so marginally" and interfered with interstate commerce "so substantially" as to be unconstitutional. Later, a divided Court invalidated an Iowa law barring 65-foot doubles. On this occasion Justice Powell explained the Court's failure to defer by suggesting that one function of the Iowa law might be to force doubles using the great east-west routes across Iowa to shift to the highways of other States.[24]

Finding the relevant facts and striking the balance between the gains and costs of a proposed regulation are the essence of the legislative process (when stripped of the elected politician's calculations concerning the effect upon self-interest). Why then should the courts go over the same ground and second-guess the State legislature on a question of purely social and economic policy? Some Justices still say that ordinarily the courts should eschew the task, as Justice Stone ruled in *Barnwell* and Justice Black argued in *Southern Pacific*. Other Justices, usually a majority, give the answer that I find persuasive. Where a balance must be struck between local concerns and the burden that even a nondiscriminatory measure puts on interstate commerce, the State legislature is too likely to be moved by parochial interests to weigh the balance fairly. Justice Oliver Wendell Holmes, Jr., in commenting upon judicial review, observed in 1920:

> I do not think the United States would come to an end if we lost our power to declare an act of Congress unconstitutional. I do think the Union would be imperiled if we could not make that declaration as to the laws of the several states. For one in my place sees how often a local policy prevails with those who are not trained to national views.[25]

One naturally asks next, "Why should the Court decide such questions?" If the State legislatures cannot be trusted to deal fairly with what is partially a national problem, why should not the policy question be left to the Congress, allowing State law to operate without judicial intervention until and unless Congress determines that, from the national point of view, the State law unduly burdens interstate commerce? Congress has now opened the Nation's highways to 65-foot doubles and displaced many State limitations on width and weight.

The explanation for the Court's assumption of the function is partly historical. When the Court first assumed the task, as we have seen, it approached the question in terms of the constitutional division of power: either the Commerce Clause did or did not take away from the States power to tax and regulate interstate commerce. Such true questions of interpretation were plainly for the Court. The shift of intellectual mode that focused attention, first, on the "subject of the regulation" and, later, on its consequences did not occur until the pattern of referring such questions to the courts had been fixed. Furthermore, balancing is required only in cases involving State regulatory laws applied evenhandedly to interstate and intrastate commerce. There is rarely, if ever, room for justification if the State law gives local as opposed to out-of-State sellers a preference in the market, denies out-of-State buyers access to local resources, or otherwise discriminates against interstate commerce.[26]

Relief against selfish State laws, local protectionism, and other obstructions to interstate commerce would be exceedingly slow, even at best, if State measures were allowed to operate until Congress enacted new legislation. Even in the dramatic and urgent instance of the early-nineteenth-century State steamboat monopolies, Congress took no concrete steps to free the channels of interstate commerce. More often, the obstruction is small and local when viewed in isolation, though the cumulative effect of many small obstructions may seriously interfere with the Nation's commerce. It would be hard to get the attention of Congress until much harm had been done. Even then, Congress is ill equipped to examine each particular instance, as a local court may do when a litigant brings the problem to the court's attention. Congress, moreover, is usually more responsive to local pressures than to broad but diffuse national interests. Each Representative is primarily concerned with the demands and welfare of a local constituency. Each knows that he or she will usually gain most by sensitivity to the parochial needs of other Representatives so long as they do not conflict with his own.

A further point is important. The Commerce Clause has long been held to deprive the States of power to levy discriminatory or otherwise unduly burdensome taxes on interstate commerce. The courts perform the same function in this area as in ruling on State and local regulation.[27] Given the natural but selfish wish of every State and local subdivision to raise revenues from outsiders wherever possible, the burdens of State and local taxes in the absence of a constitutional check administered by the judiciary would obstruct interstate trade even more than State and local regulation.

Under the current arrangement Congress still has the last word. The Court's decisions in this area, unlike those with which we shall deal sustaining claims of individual right, do not limit the power of the people ultimately to govern themselves. Even when the courts have held that a nondiscriminatory State law does not burden interstate commerce so unduly as to violate the Commerce Clause in the absence of congressional action, Congress may exercise its power under the Commerce Clause either to substitute its own regulatory measure or to create private rights to engage in interstate commerce free from the State regulation. Congress took that step in authorizing "doubles" on all interstate highways. Conversely, Congress may open the door to State laws that the Court has found to be unconstitutional burdens on interstate commerce. In the nineteenth century, for example, the Court ruled that because of the Commerce Clause, a dry State was powerless to forbid the sale of whiskey or beer brought into the State and sold in its original package.[28] Later, Congress enacted the Webb-Kenyon Act, declaring that such sales should be subject to State regulation or prohibition. When a new seller argued that the State law violated the Constitution and that Congress could not change the Constitution, the Court responded that the first decision had really been an interpretation of "the silence of Congress," not of the Constitution, and that therefore Congress, by speaking, could effectively change the rule.[29]

This pleasant fiction has enabled the Judicial Branch to continue to review from a national viewpoint the effects of State laws regulating interstate commerce, yet to bow to the decision of the national legislative body when the situation is important enough to command the attention of the Congress and Congress decides that the judicial disposition was unwise.

III

National unity requires the free movement of people no less than of goods. Free movement, including opportunities not only to pursue normal occupations anywhere in the United States but to pull up stakes and settle in a new locality, depends upon freedom from discrimination against "outsiders" or "newcomers." The Commerce Clause can be used as one constitutional weapon for attacking divisive State restrictions on the movement of people. The Philadelphia Convention put another safeguard in Article IV, Section 2:

> The Citizens of each State shall be entitled to all Privileges and Immunities of Citizens in the several States.

Two provisions of the Fourteenth Amendment, adopted after the Civil War, are also relevant. One provides:

> No State shall make or enforce any law which shall abridge the privileges or immunities of a citizen of the United States.

The other adds:

> [N]or shall any State . . . deny to any person within its jurisdiction the equal protection of the laws.

Despite these guarantees, parochial pressures on State legislators have often led to attempts at interfering with interstate movement and to discrimination against outsiders or new residents. The most egregious example is a California law enacted during the Great Depression of the 1930s. Poverty-stricken families from the Dust Bowl of Oklahoma began trekking to California in hope of a new life. John Steinbeck vividly portrayed their journey in *Grapes of Wrath*. California sought to check the influx into her relatively healthy economy by making it a crime for any person or corporation to assist in bringing an indigent person into the State. Earl Warren, who later became the most liberal of all our Chief Justices, strongly defended the exclusion. California was for Californians. But once again the Court defended the equal right of all citizens to move and enjoy freely the resources of any part of the country:

> It is frequently the case that a State might gain a momentary respite from the pressure of events by the simple expedient of shutting its gates to the outside world. . . . "The Constitution was framed under the dominion of a political philosophy less parochial in range. It was framed upon the theory that the peoples of the several States must sink or swim together, and that in the long run prosperity and salvation are in union and not division."[30]

That is the dominant principle, but it is not without exceptions. Just as the Commerce Clause bars a State from regulating private business enterprises in a manner that gives preference to the local buyers or sellers, so does the Privileges and Immunities Clause of Article IV bar a State from requiring local businesses, when filling jobs, to give preference to local residents.[31] On the other hand, when municipal jobs or jobs on public works are at stake, the rule may be different. The Commerce Clause is inapplicable.[32] The question is whether the Privileges and Immunities Clause bars the city from giving preference to local residents. In the leading case the Court indicated that a Camden, New Jersey, ordinance, requiring that 40 percent of the labor force on public works projects funded by the city be residents of Camden, would not violate the Privileges and Immunities Clause if Camden could prove that the residency requirement was necessary to counteract spiraling unemployment, "middle-class flight," and an erosion of property values that threatened a financial crisis for the city.[33]

IV

Current litigation under the Commerce and Privileges and Immunities Clauses affecting the free interstate movement of people or goods rarely has the drama of the Case of the Steamboat Monopoly. The institutional framework and main lines of decision were laid down long ago. The vision of John Marshall prevailed, partly because of outside forces more powerful than judicial decisions: the Industrial Revolution, ever-swifter methods of transportation and communication, the Civil War, and the gradual growth of a national tradition. It was the Court, however, that preserved the opportunity for building a continentwide open market, first by catching the essential promise of unity implicit in the work of the Philadelphia Convention and then by converting judicial review into an instrument for accommodating the requirements of both unity and diversity.

The work is no less essential today, even though the legal doctrines have become increasingly sophisticated and the play lies chiefly in the joints. The structure of total government in the United States laid down two hundred years ago in the Miracle at Philadelphia is still extraordinarily complex. Some institution with an overall view is essential to flesh out the structure and determine the interplay between laws purporting to bear upon the same activity but made by different agencies of government. The development of judicial review confided these two functions to the courts, ultimately to the Supreme Court of the United States. The courts' successful performance of these tasks from day to day and year to year remains essential to the effective working of the federal system.

· 5 ·

One Nation Indivisible

AT THE MOMENT crowds on the Bowery in New York were sending up huzzahs to cheer the Supreme Court's ruling in the Case of the Steamboat Monopoly, South Carolina writhed in the grip of fear and resentment, and muttered about resistance. That the powers of the central government should be so pervasive as to permit it to reach down into a State and regulate a portion of a State's internal affairs was anathema. That a State law designed to preserve local institutions might be invalidated by a federal court as an invasion of the exclusive powers of the federal Congress raised in southern emotions the naked issue of State or federal control of slavery. The Court's vision of a vast open economy binding the country together would shape the Constitution into the foundation of one great nation; but in the South the decision, when rendered, was a major force pushing the slave States to press their claim of ultimate sovereignty with renewed vigor, and to test it by nullification and secession. Secession, in turn, brought the Civil War, perceived outside the South as a war to save the Union. At its end, the adoption of Amendments XIII, XIV, and XV increased national authority, especially the authority of the Court, and bound the States more firmly together.

From the beginning the South had been sensitive to any potential threat to State power to deal with its "peculiar institution" and with the risk of a slave rebellion. Nerves were especially raw at the time of the Steamboat Monopoly decision, partly because of

103

recent uprisings in Charleston, South Carolina, and elsewhere across the South, and partly because of a decision by the United States Supreme Court Justice William Johnson while sitting on circuit.

On Saturday night, June 15, 1822, soldiers had swept through black quarters in and near Charleston, rounding up slaves and free blacks accused of plotting rebellion. Thirty-five were hanged within ten days. The leader was Denmark Vesey, a free black with extraordinary intelligence, a self-acquired education, and a compelling oratory that attracted nine thousand followers before the city fathers ordered the arrests. Perhaps because Vesey had come to Charleston with a Danish slave trader when the latter settled there, Charleston adopted the Negro Seaman's Law, which required all black seamen on vessels in Charleston Harbor to be brought ashore and locked in the city jail until their vessels were ready to depart.

In July 1823, after the Steamboat Monopoly Case had been docketed in the U.S. Supreme Court, the sheriff in Charleston boarded a British vessel and led off to the Charleston jail a free black seaman, Henry Elkison, a British subject from Jamaica. When Elkison sought freedom on a writ of habeas corpus, the case came before Justice Johnson, an appointee of President Jefferson and a resident of Charleston. Justice Johnson declared the Negro Seaman's Law unconstitutional, even though he went on to rule, somewhat as the Court had done in *Marbury* v. *Madison,* that he lacked the power to issue a writ releasing Elkison.[1] The issues paralleled those in the Steamboat Monopoly decision. It is scarcely surprising, therefore, that many Southerners reacted to the Steamboat Monopoly decision in the same fashion as Representative Garnett of Virginia:

> Sir, we must look very little to consequences, if we do not perceive in the spirit of this construction, combined with the political fanaticism of the period, reason to anticipate, at no distant day, the usurpation on the part of Congress of the right to legislate on a subject, which, if you once touch it, will inevitably throw this country into revolution—I mean that of slavery.[2]

By 1840 the Court looked less dangerous to the South and its peculiar institution. Five of the seven Justices had been appointed by President Andrew Jackson. President Martin Van Buren named the other two. The death of John Marshall after thirty-four years on the Bench opened the way for President Jackson to appoint as Chief Justice Roger B. Taney, his Secretary of the Treasury, who, after two predecessors refused the President's request, had administered the *coup de grâce* to the Bank of the United States by removing all government deposits. Taney, a very able lawyer, was also a slave-holding, Maryland agrarian.

Viewed in terms of the evolution of modern constitutional law, the years of the Taney Court, 1836 to 1864, were a time of moderation. The Court maintained but did not extend the lines of federal power and supremacy laid down under Marshall. The Court also eschewed the extremes of Federalist doctrine that might have limited the authority of States to regulate corporations. *Cooley* v. *Board of Port Wardens,*[3] discussed in the previous chapter, was the Taney Court's most constructive contribution to the future. The decision also is fairly representative of that Court's middle course. Where strong nationalists like Daniel Webster would have decided that a State has no power to regulate "commerce . . . among the several States" because the power granted to Congress is exclusive, the Taney Court laid one of the foundation stones of modern federalism by rejecting an absolute answer in favor of the rule that the State's power depends upon whether the subject matter of the regulation requires uniformity or permits diversity of treatment.

The Taney years will always be best known for the Court's most colossal blunder—the mistake of attempting to settle by constitutional decision, in the *Dred Scott* case,[4] the highly charged sectional debate over whether slavery should be permitted in the territories of the United States. By that time larger forces may have made the Civil War inevitable, but the tragic conflict was hastened by the passions aroused by the *Dred Scott* ruling and by the subsequent decision in *Ableman* v. *Booth.*[5]

The status of slavery in the territories of the United States had become controversial back in 1819. Spain had permitted slavery in the vast area known as the Louisiana Purchase. Slave holders and their slaves flowed into parts of the area after its acquisition by the United States. In 1819 Missouri's application for admission as a slave State touched off a bitter sectional debate marked by threats of secession. The fight was for power, not moral principle. The slave States and the free States then had equal numbers of Senators in the U.S. Congress. The admission of Missouri would have upset the balance; it would also have set a precedent for carving the Louisiana Purchase into additional slave States. In 1820 the debate ended in the Missouri Compromise. Two new States would be admitted, Missouri and Maine, one slave and the other free. And Congress enacted a law providing that slavery should never exist elsewhere in the Louisiana Purchase above latitude 36°30′.

There the matter of slavery in the territories rested until the close of the Mexican War. Meanwhile slavery became a moral question. The Abolitionist movement grew in strength. The South needed new land for its cotton crops to replace the old, overworked soil. It also needed more slaves. Bootlegging of blacks was rife. Before the end of the 1850s southern politicians and business conventions would call for reopening the slave trade. For the Abolitionists, and even for northern moderates, who, like Abraham Lincoln, condemned slavery as a "moral, social and political wrong" but would leave its correction where it was established to the course of time, the vital question was whether the newly acquired territories would be added to "Freedom's aerie" or become "bigger pens to cram with slaves." In 1850 the men of the passing generation that built the Union patched it together by another compromise, but in 1854 Senator Stephen A. Douglas's Kansas-Nebraska bill effectively undid both that compromise and the Missouri Compromise of 1820 by enacting that as formal territorial governments were organized for Kansas and Nebraska, both lying north of latitude 36°30′, the people of each territory should decide for themselves whether or not to have slavery. The country's eyes turned to Kansas. There the Jayhawkers and other free-soilers, who had been rushed to Kansas by the antislavery Emigrant Aid Company and armed with the new breechloading "Beecher's Bibles" (named for the great Abolitionist preacher Henry Ward Beecher), battled with the Kickapoo Rangers, Doniphan Tigers, and thousands of border ruffians brought into Kansas from the South. "Bleeding Kansas" intensified national passions. The "irrepressible conflict" was coming close.

Sam, a Negro slave who became known to history as Dred Scott, was sold by the Blow family in Virginia to a Dr. John Emerson, a U.S. Army surgeon. Dr. Emerson kept Dred Scott with him during the three years in which he was stationed in Illinois, where slavery was forbidden, and later at Fort Snelling, in the northern part of the Louisiana Purchase, where Congress, in the Missouri Compromise, had said that slavery should never exist. Dr. Emerson afterward took Dred Scott to Missouri, a slave State. On Dr. Emerson's death, Dred Scott first sought to purchase his freedom. When that effort failed, he brought suit to establish his freedom in the Missouri courts, arguing that he had become a free man as a result of residence, with the approval of his "owner," in free territory and a free State.[6]

Dred Scott's suit seems in the beginning to have been neither more nor less than one man's effort to obtain liberty. Such suits were not uncommon. The initial expense was paid by the Blow family, whose members apparently felt an unusual attachment, or at least a duty, to "Sam." When the Missouri suit failed and a new suit was instituted in the U.S. Circuit Court, Abolitionists and friends of the Scotts in Missouri helped bear the expense. When Dred Scott lost again, lack of finance hampered presentation of the appeal to the Supreme Court of the United States. A pamphlet, containing a plea for help and signed with Dred Scott's mark, was circulated:

> While I was in Illinois and Wisconsin I was a free man—just as good as my master—and that I had as much right to make a slave of a white man as a white man to make a slave of me. I was sorry that nobody ever told me that while I was there. . . . But after a little while the judge said that as soon as my master got me back the side of the line of Missouri, my right to be free was gone; and that I and my wife and children became nothing but so many pieces of property. . . . I have no money to pay anybody at Washington to speak for me. My fellow-men, can any of you help me in my day of trial.[7]

In Washington, Montgomery Blair, the son of Francis P. Blair, formerly an ardent Jacksonian, member of the "kitchen cabinet," and editor of the Democratic *Washington Globe* but now a free-soiler in revolt against his party, agreed to argue the appeal without a fee. The Abolitionist, Republican *National Era* agreed to pay court costs. And so the *Dred Scott* case was heard, and then reargued just after the Presidential election of 1856.

By that time, the *Dred Scott* case had become extraordinarily complex. Two issues aroused wide public controversy. One was whether even a free Negro could be a "citizen" within the meaning of the Constitution. That question arose because the U.S. Circuit Court was obliged to dismiss the case for want of jurisdiction unless it was "between Citizens of different States."[8] The second and

greater public issue was whether Dred Scott's claim to have become a free man by virtue of residence in the Louisiana Purchase
above 36°30′ north latitude failed because the Constitution secured
the right to hold slaves in the territories of the United States, thus
rendering the Missouri Compromise unconstitutional.

No law inexorably required a decision on either of those inflam-
matory questions. The first was entangled with technical points of
procedure that strongly argued that the question was not properly
before the Court. As for Dred Scott's claim to have become a free
man, the closest precedent[9] suggested that this was a question to
be decided not by the Constitution and laws of the United States
but by Missouri law—a question on which the Missouri courts
already had ruled against Dred Scott. Discretion argued that the
Court avoid the constitutional questions.

At one point seven of the nine Justices appear to have been
ready to follow that course. Two things apparently intervened. One
was the political ambition of Justice John McLean. The second
may have been the Justices' too-ready acceptance of the belief that
the Court's power and prestige were sufficient for it to put to rest
the debate over slavery in the territories that was rending the
United States. Justice McLean, ever an ambitious politician and
still hoping to become President on a Republican ticket, let it be
known that if the seven Justices avoided the issue, he would deliver
a dissenting opinion upholding the Missouri Compromise and
Scott's claim to have become free. Justice Benjamin Curtis was
prepared to deliver his own dissent. The six proslavery Justices,
including Chief Justice Taney, were unwilling to let those views go
unanswered. In the end, the Chief Justice prepared an opinion for
the Court ruling against Dred Scott on the two main points. In
words degrading Negroes that are almost unimaginable today, Chief
Justice Taney ruled that no black man could be a "citizen" according to the Constitution. Furthermore, Dred Scott had not become
free by virtue of the Missouri Compromise and residence in the
northern part of the Louisiana Purchase, because the Act of Congress would deprive the slave holders of property "without due
process of law," in violation of the Fifth Amendment, if it were
given the effect of freeing slaves taken into the northern part of
the Louisiana Purchase. Other Justices delivered separate opinions,
but only Justices McLean and Curtis dissented.[10]

A firestorm of public criticism raged through the North. Any
sanguine hope that constitutional adjudication might settle the emo-

tional political question of slavery in the territories proved the utmost folly. The basic causes of the Civil War lay deeper, but the *Dred Scott* decision probably accelerated the current of events by speeding the growth of the antislavery Republican Party. Meanwhile, in a single decision the Court had dissipated its prestige and made itself a political football.

New fuel was added to the flames by the decision in *Ableman* v. *Booth*.[11] The Underground Railroad for fugitive slaves and the new, tough, federal Fugitive Slave Law included in the Compromise of 1850 aroused emotions no less feverish than those aroused by slavery in the territories. In 1854 Wisconsin became the scene of a series of events commanding national attention. Joshua Glover, a fugitive slave from Missouri, after living for two years in Racine, was betrayed, then captured by U.S. Deputy Marshals, and held in a jail in Milwaukee for delivery to his owner. A mob of Abolitionists, led by the firebrand editor Sherman M. Booth, battered down the door and freed Glover. Booth was arrested on a federal warrant charging him with violation of the Fugitive Slave Law by aiding the escape of a prisoner. Booth's attorney applied to a judge of the Supreme Court of Wisconsin for a writ of habeas corpus, freeing his client from the custody of the United States Court. The principle of federal supremacy plainly called for denial of the writ on the ground that a State cannot properly interfere with proceedings in a court of the United States; but opposition to the Fugitive Slave Law proved stronger than attachment to the constitutional principles developed under Chief Justice Marshall, and the Wisconsin judge ordered the release of Booth. The U.S. Department of Justice appealed to the Supreme Court of the United States. While the appeal was pending, amid great local furor, Booth was prosecuted in the federal court, convicted, and sentenced to a short term of imprisonment under the Fugitive Slave Law. He was committed to jail. Again, the Wisconsin court ordered Booth's release.[12] Again, the U.S. Department of Justice appealed.

In order to hear and decide an appeal, the U.S. Supreme Court requires the record of the proceedings in the lower court. The normal procedure at that time was for the U.S. Supreme Court to transmit a "writ of error" to the court from which the appeal was taken, ordering it to certify to the U.S. Supreme Court a true record of its proceedings. The Wisconsin court refused to obey the writ.

Here was nullification of a federal law much like Virginia's challenge to the Supreme Court's authority in *Martin* v. *Hunter's Lessee*.[13] Nevertheless, public men throughout the North applauded the leadership of Wisconsin. Senator Charles Sumner sent congratulations on Booth's release: "God grant that Wisconsin may not fail to protect her own rights and the rights of her citizens in the exigency now before her. To her belongs the lead that Massachusetts should have taken."

Foreseeing Wisconsin's defiance of the writ of error, the U.S. Attorney General had previously obtained a transcript of the record in the second habeas corpus proceeding. Both appeals were heard in the Supreme Court of the United States, and a unanimous opinion was issued, denying the State courts power to interfere with the detention of any person held by order of a federal court. The opinion was a powerful restatement of the constitutional principles establishing not only the supremacy of federal law and instrumentalities but also the ultimate authority of the Supreme Court of the United States upon constitutional questions. For modern lawyers, the decision is a major precedent in fixing relationships between State and federal courts. For the northern Abolitionists in 1859 the decision was destined to become quite as infamous as the *Dred Scott* case. In Ohio, as in Wisconsin, State judges resisted conformance to the hated federal law.

It was ironic that Wisconsin and Ohio, with the approval of Abolitionists throughout the North, should be playing the old roles of Virginia and South Carolina, invoking the doctrines of interposition, nullification, and State sovereignty upon which the South relied. But the irony could give little comfort to the South. When slavery was involved, the rule of law—the Fugitive Slave Law, the machinery for enforcing it, and the consistent application of constitutional principles—was overwhelmed by a commanding moral imperative. Where law and government prevailed, the basic constitutional philosophy of the North and old Northwest remained unchanged. The federal government also followed the constitutional philosophy of Alexander Hamilton and John Marshall concerning the scope of federal power, especially on subjects hurtful to the South—on the tariff and expenditures for internal improvements. The States in the Northeast and old Northwest were growing in economic power, prosperity, and population as more and more rich new land was opened and the economic revolution began to take hold. Their expanding populations promised more voting power. The South, with its narrow economic interests, increasingly perceived that it could not hope to prevail against the more populous North as a slave-holding, one-crop economy unless some check was applied to federal power and majority rule.

Nullification failed as a check. As Abolitionism spread and the battle over slavery in the territories intensified, nullification gave way to secession. Secession led to Civil War—and to Gettysburg, Vicksburg, and Appomattox.

II

The Union victory produced a major shift in the distribution of power under the Constitution. The long debate over State sovereignty and the nature of the federal union was closed by force of arms. The United States became one nation indivisible. State rights survived, in a limited form, even as against the federal government, but only because the Constitution preserves those rights and not because of the sometime sovereignty of each of the thirteen original States.

The general opinion that the federal government has only limited powers also was left intact. The great bulk of human affairs remained the exclusive province of State government and State law. But as new forms of transportation and industrialization took hold, pressure to expand the scope of federal power would grow and the country would face new constitutional questions concerning the respective roles of the Nation and the States.

The great difference was that after 1865 all these constitutional questions, left open in 1787, whether of the delegated powers of the federal government or the reserved rights of the States, would be determined finally and authoritatively by national organs, ultimately by the U.S. Supreme Court. The possibility of nullification or secession was gone.

The Civil War also led to three constitutional amendments providing national constitutional guarantees securing fundamental individual rights against aggression by State or local government. They too greatly increased the role of the Supreme Court. Before the Civil War few individual rights had received national protection. The Founding Fathers, as previously noted, were not blind to threats to natural rights, but they saw State Governors and State legislatures as the most likely offenders because human affairs were very largely governed by the States. To protect individual rights against State governments, the Founding Fathers wrote both specific and general guarantees into their State constitutions; and they looked to the State courts for any judicial enforcement. The Bill of Rights, added to the federal Constitution in 1791, protected individual liberty only against abuses by the federal government.[14]

The Thirteenth Amendment, the first of the Civil War amendments, abolished slavery and authorized Congress to enforce the prohibitions by "appropriate legislation." The prohibition is aimed at both government and private persons.

The Fourteenth Amendment is much broader. The first sentence repudiates the *Dred Scott* decision by the declaration:

> All persons born or naturalized in the United States and subject to the jurisdiction thereof are citizens of the United States and of the State in which they reside.

The next sentence has three important clauses, which judges and lawyers put in separate compartments. All three clauses are aimed at the States. The Privileges and Immunities Clause reads:

> No State shall make or enforce any law which abridges the privileges and immunities of citizens of the United States.

The phrase "privileges and immunities" had no settled content when the Fourteenth Amendment was adopted. The words are broad enough to protect almost any right to liberty, human dignity, privacy, or property that the Court might read into them in order to protect individual citizens against governmental action. The present judicial interpretation is too narrow to give the clause substantial importance,[15] but it remains a potential source for judicial enlargement of constitutional rights.

The second clause has become the chief source of national protection of individual rights:

> [N]or shall any State deprive any person of life, liberty or property without due process of law.

The Due Process Clauses of the Fourth and Fourteenth Amendments have always been taken to guarantee procedural fairness in matters affecting life, liberty, or property, and also to safeguard against any Act of Congress or a State legislature held by the judges to be unduly restrictive of the enjoyment of personal liberty, the use of property, or other fundamental rights. Most threats to freedom of speech, freedom of religion, to the rights of the accused in criminal cases, or to other rights of liberty and property still come from the States because the States still are the source of the greater body of criminal law, police regulations, and other regulatory and municipal law. Today, under the Due Process Clause, such threats are central concerns of the U.S. Supreme Court.

The third great clause in the second sentence of the Fourteenth Amendment reads:

> [N]or shall any State . . . deny to any person within its jurisdiction the equal protection of the laws.

The Equal Protection Clause was designed primarily to protect the former slaves. But the clause is broader. It extends not only to other racial and religious minorities but to women and any others whom the Court judges the victims of "arbitrary and capricious" or "invidious" discrimination. It also proscribes some denials of equality in relation to some "fundamental rights." The search for the meaning of "equality," which has been pressed most vigorously since 1950, presents some of the most fascinating questions of constitutional law.[16]

By the Fifteenth Amendment Congress attempted to extend the electoral franchise to the former slaves and their descendants without denying the States the basic power to set voting qualifications:

> The right of citizens to vote shall not be denied or abridged by the United States or by any State on account of race, color, or previous condition of servitude.

The Civil War amendments add new sources of congressional lawmaking power to those in the original Constitution because each provides that Congress shall have power to enforce it by appropriate legislation. All three are also given effect by the federal courts without further legislative implementation whenever the constitutionality of State action that injures a specific person is challenged in an appropriate judicial proceeding.

All three Civil War amendments, especially the Fourteenth Amendment, share a dominant characteristic of the work of the original Philadelphia Convention. The draftsmen made plain the intent to provide national constitutional guarantees for the fundamental rights of individuals when they spoke of "equal protection of the laws," of "life, liberty or property," and of "due process of law," but they left it to the future to particularize those majestic ideals in the course of judicial interpretation. Here again, therefore, the Court, when sufficiently wise, would be enabled by attention to building a continuing body of law to bring to its decisions the authority of the sacred document and national tradition, yet to resolve the questions in the light of the needs and potential of the times.

· PART TWO ·

From Laissez-Faire to the Welfare State

· 6 ·

Economic Liberty

BETWEEN THE CIVIL WAR and World War II the great constitutional questions arose out of the transformation of the United
States from a country of farmers, artisans, and merchants into a
predominantly industrial and urban society characterized by ever-
larger economic units. By 1865 the technological developments of
the Industrial Revolution invited, indeed required, large-scale enterprise. Textiles had been made on a factory basis since the 1820s.
The Bessemer process for making steel became commercially fea-
sible in 1855. Vast natural resources, chiefly in the West, awaited
exploitation: timber, coal, oil, iron ore, copper, and precious met-
als. The expansion and improvement of transportation facilities
opened wider markets. Wartime profits supplied ample capital.
Streams of European immigrants filled the railroad camps, the
mines, and the factories. Gould, Vanderbilt, Harriman, and James
J. Hill built railway empires. Rockefeller organized the Standard
Oil monopoly; the Armours their vast meat-packing houses and
distribution system. Under the guiding hands of Andrew Carnegie
and J. P. Morgan the billion-dollar United States Steel Corporation
was born.

The statistics document the large-scale industrialization that the
names personify. Between 1860 and 1910 the amount of capital
invested in manufacturing increased twelvefold. During the same
fifty years the number of wage earners rose from 1.5 to 5.5 million.

Equally important, industrial establishments whose annual product was valued in excess of $1 million already employed 25 percent of all the nation's wage earners. Just ten years later the proportion employed in such establishments was 35 percent. By 1929 the percentage had risen to 58 percent.

The building of industrial wealth depended on a new transportation system, swift and continental in its scope. The last quarter of the nineteenth century brought the great days of railroading. Stocks were watered; shippers and investors were swindled; wastefully duplicate lines were constructed; ruthless financial battles were waged for control; Chinese coolies and European immigrants were worn out in the construction camps; but with all their sins, the railroad barons built the great bands of steel that carried the country's booming commerce, opened the national markets, supplied the food and raw materials, and welded the bitterly rival, pre–Civil War geographical sections into a continentwide economic unit.

Unlocking vast agricultural, industrial, and financial wealth made for an extremely mobile society. Those near the bottom enjoyed great improvement in their material status, though nowhere near as much as the ever-growing middle classes. An ambitious boy, however low born, could hope to relive the Horatio Alger story unless he was black, Chicano, Chinese, or Native American.

With the riches came rip-offs, hardships, injustice, unemployment and poverty, crowded cities and social upheaval. Vast aggregations of both money and men were needed to develop America's resources and to harness the power unleashed by science and technology. Organized wealth meant gross inequalities of bargaining power—between railroads and shippers, for example, between food processors and farmers, between industrial employers and individual wage earners, and between manufacturers and processors and consumers. Some of the hardships, suffering, and injustice came from problems seemingly inherent in a complex, dynamic, yet tightly articulated economic system. Some resulted from ruthless selfishness on the part of those with preponderant power. The triumph of business enterprise was marked by social and economic convulsions of such violence and magnitude as to threaten the social order: the financial panic of 1873 and great railway strikes of 1877, the Haymarket Square riots in Chicago in 1886, the great Homestead strike against the Carnegie-Illinois Steel Corporation, and the Pullman strike of 1894. Such well-known instances illustrate countless smaller clashes. All resulted from human hardship and suffering. All were ruthlessly suppressed by the forces of law and order, including the United States Army.

Yet the human needs could not be ignored. The disadvantaged and the sympathetic kept pressing for government intervention to allay economic injustice, first on one front and then on another. The political branches of government gradually responded. The farmers sought and obtained protection against the railroads. The industrial workers needed and obtained factory inspection laws, protection for their labor unions, minimum wage and maximum hours laws, and the abolition of child labor. Consumers too began to press for regulation of utilities and insurance companies.

The political pressures were felt first by the State legislatures. In time the pressures would lead to the vast legislative expansion of government regulation and social programs now epitomized as "the welfare state." Because businesses were becoming organized on a national scale and economic interdependence was increasing, the new political pressures also were directed at Congress, and would gradually produce a vast congressional centralization of governmental power, radically altering the balance of the federal system.

The availability of judicial review of the constitutionality of legislation enabled those who lost the battle against change in political forums to carry the war to the Supreme Court of the United States. The great constitutional question of the era was whether the original Constitution, written for a much smaller and simpler society in 1787, was suitable without amendment to the great size and complexity of a modern industrial nation. Would the Court, the ultimate expositor, seek to preserve the small central government and untrammeled economic liberty of the earlier years by invalidating the new legislation? Or would the Court use its power of interpretation to shape the Constitution to the needs of the new age?

The broad underlying question took two specific forms. First, business and financial interests invoked the Fifth Amendment and the new Fourteenth Amendment to attack State and federal laws restricting their freedom of action as deprivations of "life, liberty, or property without due process of law." Second, business and financial interests could attack any regulatory laws enacted by Congress outside the field of interstate transportation as unconstitutional invasions of the powers reserved to the States. The challenges based on the Due Process Clauses came first. The question of congressional power is discussed in the next chapter.

BUSINESSES "AFFECTED WITH A PUBLIC INTEREST"

The question of economic liberty under the Due Process Clause of the Fourteenth Amendment arose first because of the success of the Granger movement among midwestern farmers. In the years following the Civil War the railroads were opening up new parts of the midwest prairies, and also the Great Plains, so suitable to vast acres of wheat. Too much was done by speculation. Every new farm was likely to have a mortgage. Often the farmer borrowed still more money to buy the gangplows and the combines needed to till and harvest fields that seemed boundless to families from New England. Hard times, caused by the weather or the business cycle, often brought ruin. The fate of the hopeful settlers in western Kansas is an example. Virgin soil, peak prices for wheat, and a few lush growing seasons attracted a rush of settlers and wild speculation. A few years later drought withered the crops. Half the people were to leave, their wagons bearing rueful scrawls:

> In God we trusted.
> In Kansas we busted.

The Granger movement was born of such troubles. Because farmers were shippers, railroad rates and a host of piratical railroad practices became the farmers' prime targets for public regulation. So too were the charges and practices of grain elevators, grain and livestock exchanges, and commission men. The farmers also took aim at the "trusts"—a word then used to describe almost any form of actual or alleged corporate or financial monopoly.

The pressure of the farmers was first brought to bear successfully on the State legislatures, partly as a matter of habit because State legislatures were still the predominant lawmaking bodies in the United States and partly because it is a great deal easier to obtain economic legislation favorable to a regional economic interest from a State legislature than it is to persuade a distant national Congress. Beginning in the 1870s the Granger movement pushed bills through the legislatures of a number of farming States to regulate the rates and practices of railroads and grain elevators.

In 1871 the Illinois legislature enacted a statute fixing the maximum charge for storing grain in a public elevator at two cents a bushel for the first thirty days. Charging a higher price became a criminal offense. Munn and Scott, the operators of a Chicago elevator, charged higher rates and were prosecuted for the offense. They admitted the facts but disputed the constitutionality of the statute. After the Illinois courts ruled against them, they carried the case to the Supreme Court of the United States, arguing that for a State to fix the price that the owner of property may charge for its use deprives him of fundamental individual rights to liberty and property in violation of the Constitution of the United States.[1]

The key words of the Fourteenth Amendment, on which Munn pitched his case, deserve renewed attention:

[N]or shall any State deprive any person of life, liberty or property without due process of law.

Several questions leap from the words. Is a corporation a "person" protected by the Fourteenth Amendment? Munn & Scott appears to have been a partnership that would be treated as two individuals, but it is easy to imagine a corporation indicted for the same offense. Although abstractly debatable, history gave short shrift to this question. American law has long personified corporations.

The word "liberty" raises harder questions. Was the freedom of Munn & Scott to charge any price it could get for storing grain a liberty protected by the Fourteenth Amendment? In its narrowest sense the word means freedom from confinement; if this were the meaning, Munn & Scott must lose. In its broadest sense, liberty means freedom to do as one wishes; under this reading Munn & Scott might prevail. Avoiding the extremes, one must ask what particular liberties are encompassed by the abstract word. Economic liberty? Does liberty include freedom to pursue any familiar occupation and to work at whatever wage and for as long hours as one is willing? Does it include the freedom to charge whatever price one can obtain in a free market for the sale or rental of property? Counsel for Munn & Scott argued for affirmative answers to these questions, as would later lawyers for business and financial interests. Decision "according to law" implies decisions based upon

the consistent application of general principles. While pondering
the claims of Munn & Scott, therefore, the Justices had a duty to
consider other specific liberties. Did the liberty protected by the
Fourteenth Amendment include polygamy? Freedom to refuse vac-
cination against smallpox? Freedom of speech? The problem runs
down through the years. A later generation would ask whether the
liberty guaranteed by the Fourteenth Amendment includes freedom
to have an abortion.[2] How should judges go about answering such
questions "according to law"? Could—and can—a consistent principle be developed?

The word "property" raises parallel questions. Munn & Scott
argued that fixing the price that the owner may charge for sale or
rental is a deprivation of property, prohibited by the Fourteenth
Amendment.

Counsel and the Court had to face still another set of questions
raised by the phrase "due process of law." The Fourteenth Amendment is violated only when a State deprives a person of liberty or
property "without due process of law." The quoted words suggest
no more than procedural regularity: any law duly enacted by the
State legislature and enforced by a fair procedure could be consistent with due process of law. If that were their only significance,
Munn & Scott must lose, even if freedom of contract is a liberty
protected by the Fourteenth Amendment. In fact, that never has
been the constitutional meaning of "due process of law." American
jurists, with a few exceptions, have always accepted the view that
the concept of due process of law, like the words "the law of the
Land" in Magna Carta, puts some liberties and some property
interests beyond the power of government, thus embodying in the
Fourteenth Amendment at least a portion of the heritage that we
traced from natural law, Lord Coke, and "the rights of Englishmen."[3] Lawyers call the concept "substantive due process" to
distinguish it from the "procedural due process" also required by
the amendment.

Viewed from one angle, therefore, interpretation of the Due
Process Clause calls upon judges to determine which liberties and
which attributes of the ownership of property are so fundamental—
so valuable—as to be always beyond the reach of government.
Viewed from another angle, the words "life, liberty or property"
are always to be read broadly; but government, by the social compact, has been given power to limit their enjoyment when the needs

of a civilized society justify the regulation, thus making the particular restriction on liberty or property consistent with due process of law. The latter is the conventional approach. The general question then becomes: What is sufficient justification for the limitation? The particular question in Munn's case was whether the stranglehold of grain elevators on the farming regions justified public regulation of their rates.

The wide vistas apparently opened to judicial decision by the generality of the key constitutional phrases recall Thomas Jefferson's protest against the power of judicial review: "To consider the judges as the ultimate arbiters of all constitutional questions would place us under the despotism of an oligarchy." The power to interpret the majestic phrase "life, liberty or property," taken with the power to determine whether and when particular restrictions were so justified by public good as to be consistent with "due process of law," would indeed give rise to judicial despotism if the nine Supreme Court Justices, finding scant guidance in the words, felt free to decide according to their own notions of what is good or just or wise. In fact, most judges, including Supreme Court Justices, have always acknowledged some kinds and degrees of additional constraint, even though largely self-imposed.

One source of constraint is the ancient professional tradition, exemplified in the Anglo-American common law method, that imposes upon all judges an obligation to decide "according to law." The phrase refers to the ideal of a coherent and continuing body of principles found in statutes, judicial precedents, the writings of legal scholars, traditions approved by historic practice, and like sources of law. A legislature may draw arbitrary lines, according to practical politics and the pressures of interest groups. Law implies a generality of principles applied impartially and consistently by disinterested judges to all persons, not only today but yesterday and tomorrow. The legitimacy of a court's judgments, their power to command the uncoerced consent of the people, depends upon the belief that they are indeed the authentic voice of a body of law binding the judges as well as the people. When John Marshall and his successors asserted, and the country accepted, the courts' power of judicial review, they implicitly committed constitutional questions to decision by this judicial method, not to the uncontrolled discretion of those who compose the Court.

Yet the presence of some discretion, as I suggested in discussing

Marbury v. *Madison,* creates the dilemma that gives both vitality and authority to the Constitution. The rule of law leaves some room for choice. Novel situations arise that fall between the lines of precedent. Sometimes there is no precedent. Conditions change dramatically with the passage of time, calling for the reconsideration of old precedents or the evolution of new rules revealing the true application of old ideals to new conditions. The great judge must manage to strike an accommodation between the needs of society in the times in which he lives and the need of a free society at all times for a legal system that binds the judges as well as the litigants. Without the last, judges would indeed be despots. In the end, I think, they would also lose their authority, for the authority rests upon the people's belief that the courts indeed are deciding "according to law."

In constitutional cases the relevant body of law includes the purposes and principles implicit in the basic plan of government. For *Munn* v. *Illinois* and many other cases under the Due Process Clause of the Fourteenth Amendment, those purposes and principles provide two other sources of potential but highly flexible restraint. One is local autonomy. The very existence of a federal system asserts the value of opportunities for diversity according to the needs and wishes of individual States. Any ruling that a State law violates the Fourteenth Amendment imposes a uniform national rule. If the Court sustained the claim of Munn & Scott, no State could regulate the charges of grain elevators or other business enterprises. If the Court rejected the claim, each State could choose for itself whether to impose the regulation. Whenever a State law is challenged under the Fourteenth Amendment, each Justice must ask himself how heavily he should weigh the values of local self-determination in forming his judgment on the constitutionality of the legislation.

History and the Constitution also make it plain that both State and federal governments rest primarily upon the ideal of popular sovereignty. Whenever a court in recognition of individual right invalidates an executive or legislative limitation on liberty or the use of property as unconstitutional, the court limits the power of the people to govern themselves through elected representatives. Conversely, the decision would enlarge the area governed by a national, judge-made rule sometimes only faintly traceable to the Constitution in specific detail. Of course, the very idea of a written constitution given effect by the courts presupposes an intent to put some individual rights beyond the reach of government, but in most instances neither the Constitution nor the rationale for judicial review tells precisely where the line should be drawn. Given the room for choice, the conscientious judge engaged in constitutional adjudication must ask himself how quick or slow he should be to lift a particular subject out of the realm open to representative self-government by upholding the claim of constitutional right. Because the constitutionality of a statute is adjudicated after it becomes effective, the judge, in effect, must decide whether to substitute his judgment, guided and perhaps controlled by the existing body of law, for the judgment already expressed by elected representatives of the people.

I emphasize these problems of judicial philosophy here in connection with Munn & Scott's grain elevators because they run through nearly all cases in which the claim is made that State legislation violates the constitutional right of an individual or organization. The problem of majoritarianism also arises, of course, when an Act of Congress is challenged, not for lack of congressional authority but for violation of individual or corporate rights. As the history unfolds, we shall see that individual Justices have long given widely variant answers to these basic and pervasive questions. Some, perhaps properly, give different answers according to the nature of the case. In current constitutional debate the opposing poles of opinions are often labeled "judicial activism" and "judicial deference" or "judicial self-restraint." Judicial activism enlarges the parts of our lives exclusively ruled by judicial decision in the form of constitutional law. Judicial deference expands the areas open to majority rule. Sometimes the weight of opinion on the Court has fallen on one side; sometimes on the other. It will be the same in the future.

The opinions rendered in *Munn* v. *Illinois* illustrate the two sides of some of the foregoing questions. Chief Justice Morrison R. Waite, speaking for the Court, traced the Due Process Clause to Magna Carta. He implicitly accepted the broad meaning attributed to liberty and property by Munn's attorneys, but he quickly observed that by the social compact the whole people covenants with each citizen, and each citizen covenants with the whole people, that all shall be governed by laws for the common good. For his law the Chief Justice looked to ancient English precedents illus-

trating the right of government to fix the charges of common carriers, wharfingers, ferrymen, and certain other occupations affected
with a public interest. From those precedents the Court derived
the principle that "[w]hen . . . one devotes his property to a use in
which the public has an interest, he, in effect, grants to the public
an interest in that use and must submit to be controlled by the
public for the common good."[4]

The constitutionality of the Illinois rate fixing was thus made to
depend upon matters of fact and degree. What is the relation between grain elevators and the public? How far do grain elevators
affect the common good? The Court noted that the greater part of
the vast grain production of seven or eight States flowed through
the fourteen grain elevators in Chicago, whose operators seemed
to have a "virtual monopoly." It went on to allocate the responsibility for deciding the questions of fact and degree to the legislature,
even though the constitutionality of the statute would depend upon
the legislature's determinations.

> For our purpose we must assume that if a state of facts could exist
> that would justify such legislation, it actually did exist when the
> statute now under consideration was passed. For us [that is, the
> Court] the question is one of power, not of expediency. If no state
> of circumstances could exist to justify such a statute, then we may
> declare this one void, because in excess of the legislative power of
> the State. But if it could, we must presume it did.[5]

On this ground the Court upheld the rate regulation and affirmed
the conviction of Munn & Scott.

The principle of deference stated by Chief Justice Waite—the
"presumption of constitutionality," as it came to be called—allo-
cates vast power to legislative bodies and conversely permits few
judicial restraints under the broadly worded constitutional phrases
guaranteeing rights that in a civilized society can scarcely be absolute. A court could rarely conclude that "no state of facts *could*
exist to justify [a challenged] statute." In dissenting from a later
decision expressly based upon the presumption of constitutionality,
Justice Stephen J. Field protested:

> If the courts could not in such cases examine into the real character
> of the act, but must accept the declaration of the legislature as
> conclusive, the most valued rights of the citizen woud be subject to

the arbitrary control of a temporary majority of such bodies, instead of being protected by the guarantees of the Constitution.[6]

Justice Field also dissented in *Munn* v. *Illinois*. Liberty, he asserted, included a man's freedom "to pursue such callings and avocations as may be most suitable to develop his capacities, and to give them their highest enjoyment."[7] The same broad protection should be extended to property. The right to property includes the owner's untrammeled liberty to determine in a free market the rental that he will charge for the use and the price at which his goods will be sold. Justice Field conceded that both personal liberty and property are subject to regulation where necessary to protect "the peace, good order, morals, and health of the community," but he argued that the police power does not extend to direct interference with the free market:

> I deny the power of any legislature under our government to fix the price which one shall receive for his property of any kind. If the power can be exercised as to one article, it may as to all articles, and the prices of everything, from a calico gown to a city mansion may be the subject of legislative direction.[8]

For the next sixty years this dissent was destined to carry more weight than the opinion of the Court. Stephen J. Field was one of the most powerful minds and personalities ever to shape constitutional law. Appointed by President Lincoln, he served as a Justice for thirty-four years, but his influence lasted for another, equal period. Seemingly, his intelligence and power were in the family genes. His mother, born in Somers, Connecticut, was widely known as "the Somers beauty." His older brother, David Dudley Field, became one of the most successful corporate lawyers in New York. David Dudley Field also left permanent impact upon the procedural law of many States through the reforms embodied in the Field Code. A younger brother, Cyrus J. Field, was the promoter of the first trans-Atlantic cable. Another brother became President of the Massachusetts Senate. A fourth was a prominent engineer. His sister's son, David Brewer, would sit with him on the Supreme Court of the United States.

Late in 1849, after his years of education and legal practice with his brother in New York City, Stephen J. Field joined the Gold Rush to California. By his energy, intelligence, and no small degree of ruthless ambition, Field pushed his way forward in the frontier community. The $10 with which he arrived in California were quickly spent, but he made a fortune. Public order on that turbulent frontier was often maintained only at the point of a gun. Field was disbarred, reinstated, disbarred again, jailed for contempt of court, heavily fined, and threatened with death. He purchased pistols and learned the delicate art of shooting through his pockets. As his importance in the public life grew, Field became counselor, associate, and friend of the railway barons who would dictate large areas of California life. Leland Stanford, President of the Southern Pacific Railroad, was one of the men who successfully pressed President Lincoln to appoint Field a Justice of the U.S. Supreme Court.

The America of Field's day was fertile soil for the social and economic application of Charles Darwin's theory of biological evolution. Its apostle was an Englishman, Herbert Spencer, who rationalized as ordained by natural law the emergence of a rich and powerful class that would preside over any rural poverty or urban squalor. It was Spencer, not Darwin, who coined the phrase "survival of the fittest," a notion quickly picked up by the railroad magnate James J. Hill and by Andrew Carnegie and John D. Rockefeller. Spencer opposed any form of public intervention, even State aid for the most poor. "The whole effect of nature is to get rid of such, to clear the world of them, and make room for the better. If they are sufficiently complete to live, they *do* live. If they are not, they die, and it is best that they should die."[9]

Stephen J. Field's rise to wealth and power in the individualistic competition of early California, blended with the Calvinist teaching of his clerical father that he was one of the appointed, undoubtedly led him to share the opinion that "God intended the great to be great and the little to be little." Field, having subdued mobs in the Sacramento Valley, saw it as the function of the Court to use its "negative power, the power of resistance," to keep the whole mighty fabric of government from rushing to destruction. "The present assault upon capital [the income tax] is but the beginning. It will be but the stepping stone to others, larger and more sweeping, till our political contests will become a war of the poor against the rich."[10]

In *Munn* v. *Illinois* Justice Field lacked the votes. In later cases the broad principle pronounced by Chief Justice Waite would be severely limited; and, for half a century, the constitutional philosophy of Justice Field would profoundly influence the course of constitutional law.

WAGES, HOURS, AND LIBERTY OF CONTRACT

The imbalance of economic bargaining power that led the farmers to seek legislative regulation of railroad and grain elevator rates found parallels in large-scale industry. Industrialization created an ever-growing class of urban wage earners dependent for survival on factory employment and rates of pay. The frontier closed in the 1880s. No longer could a man down on his luck but possessing initiative pull up stakes and start anew on a homestead claim. In the older days even an artisan could fall back on his garden patch and his cow, pigs, and chickens when employment was scarce. Not only was the factory or railroad worker dependent upon his job, but he had no power alone to affect his wages, hours, or other conditions of employment. He could take the job on the terms offered. If he declined, another was waiting in line. Today, it is hard to visualize hundreds of thousands of wage earners utterly without social protection, and factories and factory managers free from any form of regulation. Yet the picture is accurate. In the great Triangle fire in New York City hundreds of young women flung themselves from windows to certain death because the ramshackle wooden building into which they were crowded as clothing workers lacked even fire escapes. In many tenements immigrants rolled cigars on piece rates, day and night, in the rooms in which they ate and slept: parents, grandparents, little children, uncles and aunts. The first need was for factory inspection laws, safety devices, measures protecting health, and some form of insurance against the hardships of industrial accidents. Only slightly less pressing was the need to abolish child labor and sweatshops, and to guarantee a minimum wage for those who had no bargaining power.

Limitation of the number of hours of work for mine, mill, and factory workers also was a pressing need. In 1900 the typical industrial workday was ten hours, six or seven days a week. Steel workers worked twelve hours a day at the blast furnaces, seven days a week. Textile workers put in equally long hours. As early as May Day 1886, tens of thousands of laborers had traveled to

Chicago to parade in a massive show of solidarity for the eight-hour day.

In the baking industry the need for at least a modest limitation on hours of work was linked to the bakery workers' health.

> Bakers, confectioners and pastry cooks represent a body of trades-men exhibiting hygienic conditions of a common character, the principal of which are exposure to heat from ovens, dust, steam, variations of temperature, in too many instances unhealthy bakehouses, fatiguing movements necessitated where kneading is done by hand, disagreeable emanations from materials used, prolonged hours of work, more or less night work and loss of rest. To these evils of their trade the working bakers often add intemperance and irregular living. My own senses also make me conscious of a disagreeable, sickly smell like that of heated bones, superadded to the steam and other fumes. There are, in brief, many incidents in the occupation of baking which reduce vital energy, predispose to lung infections and shorten life.[11]

Medical opinion carried little weight when counsel representing Joseph Lochner, the operator of a small bakery in Utica, New York, asked the U.S. Supreme Court to set aside the $50 fine imposed on him for violating New York's sixty-hour law. Counsel argued that limiting the hours for which workers might agree to labor in a bakery deprived both Lochner and his employees of liberty without due process of law. The composition of the Court had changed since *Munn* v. *Illinois,* and the majority now turned to the ideas so powerfully stated by Justice Field. Lochner's constitutional claim was sustained by a vote of 5–4. Speaking for the Court, Justice Rufus W. Peckham laid down the principle:

> The general right to make a contract in relation to his business is part of the liberty of the individual protected by the Fourteenth Amendment. . . . The right to purchase or sell labor is part of the liberty protected by this amendment, unless there are circumstances which exclude the right.[12]

The right might be limited, Justice Peckham continued, in the legitimate exercise of the State's "police power" to protect the safety, health, and morals of the public. But the sixty-hour week could not be upheld as a legitimate measure for protecting health.

> [T]here can be no fair doubt that the trade of a baker, in and of itself, is not an unhealthy one to that degree which would authorize the

legislature to interfere with the right to labor, and with the right to free contract on the part of the individual, either as employer or employee. . . . Statutes of the nature of that under review, limiting the hours in which grown and intelligent men may labor to earn their living are mere meddlesome interferences with the rights of the individual.[13]

The four dissenting Justices argued in vain that there were substantial reasons for concluding that a ten-hour workday in a bakery would endanger health, and that under *Munn* v. *Illinois* the Court should not reverse the legislature's conclusion.

"Lochnerism" and "Lochnerian" have come to symbolize an era of conservative judicial intervention under the Due Process Clause, seeking to stem the flow of social and economic reform. The trend should not be exaggerated. Many protective measures survived, including statutes limiting hours of work in underground mines.[14] Later, the Court upheld a general limitation on the hours of work of women in factories as a measure related to health.[15] Despite such exceptions, the Court's general stance for the next three decades was unfavorable to legislative interference with the key terms of any bargain that might be struck in the marketplace. *Munn* v. *Illinois* was limited to "businesses affected with a public interest," a closed category meaning chiefly businesses now known as public utilities.[16] All other price or wage regulation was consistently held unconstitutional, even a law guaranteeing women a minimum wage.[17]

UNIONIZATION AND LIBERTY OF CONTRACT

During the 1870s and 1880s increasing numbers of workers, helpless in dealing as individuals with giant corporate employers, began to turn to the formation of labor unions, through which to oppose the bargaining power of their employers with the collective economic power of organized employees. Employers countered by discharging union members, by circulating blacklists of union organizers, by espionage, and by other forms of coercion and restraint. Wage cuts brought a great railroad strike in 1877, during the depression that followed the financial panic of 1873. An army of unemployed and hungry laborers joined the strikers. Commerce through many railway centers was paralyzed. For a time law and order hung in the balance, but with the use of federal troops and federal court injunctions order was restored. The 1880s were marked by more railway strikes. The financial panic of 1893 was followed by another economic depression and the great Pullman strike of 1894, a strike resulting from a 25 percent wage cut imposed by Pullman at a time when the company continued to pay its regular 8 percent dividend to shareholders and refused to lower the rents for the company houses in which employees were expected to live, rents already 25 percent higher than in neighboring communities. George M. Pullman explained that reducing rents proportionately with wages "would have amounted to a gift of money to these men."[18] Railroad workers refused to handle Pullman cars. Again, the commerce of the country was paralyzed. Again, there was violence, even though the leaders of the strike sought to discourage it. Again, the strike was broken by the use of federal troops, the issuance of an injunction, and the arrest of Eugene V. Debs and other strike leaders for contempt of court.[19]

The Pullman strike brought steps toward reform. President Grover Cleveland appointed a commission to inquire into the causes of the strike and make recommendations. The commission laid blame on both sides but strongly criticized the autocratic and paternalistic refusal of the Pullman Company to allow its employees to present their grievances through labor unions. Commenting upon general trends, the commission observed that the "rapid concentration of power and wealth, under stimulating legislative conditions, in persons, corporations, and monopolies has greatly changed the business and industrial situation. . . . While competition among railroad employers of labor is gradually disappearing, competition among those who supply labor goes on with increasing severity. . . . In view of this progressive perversion of the laws of supply and demand by capital and changed conditions, no man can well deny the right or dispute the wisdom of unity for legislative and protective purposes among those who supply labor."[20] The commission accordingly recommended that railway carriers be encouraged to recognize and bargain with labor unions representing their employees, and that a system of conciliation and mediation be established to turn collective bargaining into an instrument of industrial peace.

Congress picked up the theme in the Erdman Act of 1898,[21] an act limited to railroads but nonetheless the legislative ancestor of the present National Labor Relations and Railway Labor Acts.

Section 10 of the Erdman Act made it a criminal offense for a carrier or a carrier's agent to discharge or refuse to hire a worker because of his membership in a labor union. The power of government to provide such protection was tested in litigation growing out of the discharge of O. P. Coppage, a fireman on the Louisville & Nashville Railroad.

Coppage had joined the Brotherhood of Locomotive Firemen. A month or two later, he and another employee were summoned to the office of their supervisor, William Adair. Coppage described the scene:

> He says, "Boys, I have you on the carpet," and we asked what for? He said, "You are members of the Firemen." I says, "Yes." He says, "Don't you know that you cannot belong to the Brotherhood,"—that was the remark that he made—"Don't you know that you cannot belong to the Firemen,"—that is the way he put it—"and work for the Company?" And I says, "No, sir." He says, "You cannot." And of course I was asking him what there was to be done? "Bring me a withdrawal card," he says, "you have got your job." I says, "I can't do it." He says, "You can't work for the L & N." I then asked him, I says, "How is my past record? What has this Company got against me?" He says, "Your past record is clear." I says, "Will you please put on my time check what I am discharged for?" . . . He said he wouldn't do it. I refused to accept my time check and it laid in his office between a week and ten days. I am not positive. Finally, circumstances forced me to go and get my money to keep me on my uppers and I drawed my time.[22]

Coppage's fate was typical of the fate of thousands of employees.

Adair was indicted and convicted of violating Section 10 of the Erdman Act. On appeal to the Supreme Court, the conviction was reversed as an unconstitutional infringement on the railroad's liberty protected by the Due Process Clause of the Fifth Amendment.[23] The opinion tracked the reasoning in *Lochner* v. *New York*. "Such liberty and right [of property] embrace the right to make contracts for the purchase of the labor of others, and equally the right to make contracts for the sale of one's own labor."[24] Such rights might be subject to such restraints as the general welfare required, but

> it is not within the function of government . . . to compel any person, in the course of his business and against his will, to accept or retain the personal services of another, or to compel any person, against his will, to perform personal services for another. . . . The right of

the employé to quit the service of the employer, for whatever reason, is the same as the right of the employer, for whatever reason to dispense with the services of such employé. . . . In all such particulars the employer and employé have equality of right, and any legislation that disturbs that equality is an arbitrary interference with the liberty of contract which no government can legally justify in a free land.[25]

The decision effectively halted legislative efforts to protect the freedom of workers to organize and bargain collectively.

Led by the Supreme Court of the United States, other State and federal courts joined in conservative decisions invalidating many of the regulatory measures that legislatures thought required for the new industrial age. For a time the New York Court of Appeals held even workmen's compensation laws to be unconstitutional, because they imposed liability without proof of fault.[26] When the legislature sought by prohibiting home work to put a stop to the practice of paying tenement dwellers piece rates for the cigars rolled by entire families in crowded living quarters, the same court observed: "It cannot be perceived how the cigar-maker is to be improved in his health or his morals by forcing him from his home and its hallowed associations and beneficent influences to ply his trade elsewhere."[27] It would be easy to multiply examples, but enough have been provided to show that judicial interpretations of the constitutional guarantees of individual liberty during the late nineteenth and early twentieth centuries were major obstructions to the adaptation of law to the needs of the weaker segments of the community in an urban and industrial society.

APPRAISAL OF LOCHNERISM

In earlier chapters I suggested that much of the genius of American constitutionalism lies in the method of interpretation that permits the Court, by building upon a continuing body of law derived from the past, to cloak its decisions with the authority of the sacred document and a majestic past yet also to shape the body of law to the needs of men and women under the changed and changing circumstances of successive generations. The best measures of the Court's performance in any era are, first, the skill and wisdom with which the Justices apply that antinomy and, second, the balances they strike in weighing the importance of judicial safeguards for basic rights against the values of both representative self-government and local autonomy.

The Lochnerian decisions are often characterized as "activist." Plainly the Justices in the majority did not hesitate to substitute judicial opinions for the judgments of elected representatives of the people, not only on such questions of fact as the relation between health and long hours of work in a bakery but also on the relative values of liberty of contract and sundry opposing public interests. The term "activist" is also fairly applicable to some of the Justices in the majority insofar as it implies a self-conscious will to reach a social or political result, giving scant weight to recognized sources of law.

Nineteenth- and early-twentieth-century lawyers lived almost entirely in the world of business, finance, and property. It is unlikely that many of them could as judges wholly slough off the premises of their earlier years of private practice, whatever their effort to achieve detachment. Some frankly acknowledged their purpose to fend off attacks upon business, property, and an open market in which the strong would survive and the weak go under. William Howard Taft, previously a Circuit Judge, Solicitor General, Secretary of War, and President of the United States—and soon to become Chief Justice of the United States—argued during the 1920 election that there was no greater domestic issue than the danger of Democratic appointments that would weaken the protection the Supreme Court should provide against socialistic raids on property rights.

Although the Lochnerian decisions flowed partly from the willful defense of wealth and power in a society in which wealth and power had been achievable by anyone sufficiently strong, intelligent, and energetic, that explanation seems less than complete. It was the gracious Kentuckian Justice John M. Harlan who wrote that "the employer and employé have equality of right," and so concluded that a law prohibiting an employer from discharging an employee because of union membership is an "arbitrary interference with liberty of contract." Yet Justice Harlan was not a conscious defender of wealth and privilege. He argued for interpretations giving the broadest scope to the Sherman Anti-Trust Law and imposing the strictest prohibitions.[28] He alone among the Justices dissented from the "separate but equal" ruling that supplied the constitutional footing for State-enforced racial segregation.[29] His view would eventually prevail in the 1954 decision on school segregation.[30] When a majority of the Justices held that a progressive federal income tax was unconstitutional, Justice Harlan smote the bench and thundered in dissent that by entrenching wealth and property against taxation, the majority were "provoking a contest which in some countries has swept away in a tempest of frenzy and passion existing social organizations, and put in peril all that was dear to friend of the law and order."[31]

The first Justice Harlan was born in 1833 in Boyle County, Kentucky, where he grew up to practice law. It was a time and place of small business units. Skilled labor was in short supply. The individual laborer was not without bargaining power in relation to his employer. I suspect that in 1908, when Justice Harlan was seventy-five years old, his statement that "employer and employé have equality of right" was drawn from the memory of the Kentucky of his youth without sufficient knowledge of the slums of industrial cities or the mines, mills, and factories of the giant corporations.

Similar threads probably ran through the thinking of other Justices at the turn of the century, though they can hardly explain the long life of Lochnerism. All the Supreme Court Justices who participated in the consideration of *Lochner* v. *New York* were born in the 1830s and 1840s. They grew up in an America ignorant of large-scale industrial organization, urban squalor, and the helplessness of the individual in dealing with organized wealth. The ideas they expressed were not unsuited to their early years. Probably most law must lag slightly behind the march of change. Law provides general principles upon which to organize human affairs. A degree of stability is requisite to the performance of that function. But nineteenth- and early-twentieth-century law was extraordinarily rigid. Concepts once well attuned to the reality of human activities dominated judicial reasoning long after relevant human conditions had changed. Lawyers and judges long taught the importance of loyalty to judicial precedent and the resulting body of law continued to apply the concepts with logical consistency but little eye for the underlying facts. With a better understanding of the changes in the world about them, some of them might, like Chief Justice Waite and the majority in *Munn* v. *Illinois,* have shown that decisions rejecting the claims of liberty of contract were consistent with both ancient legal principles and the needs of contemporary times.

In sum, the Court of the *Lochner* era was activist in the sense that in interpreting the Due Process Clauses the majority of the Justices substituted their views of the proper balance between individual liberty and public regulation for the views expressed by the elected representatives of the people. In two other senses the Court was deeply conservative: it took its law from the past, and it sought to preserve quite literally, without examining their new consequences, the liberties of an earlier age that had seen the country grow immeasurably in human freedom as well as wealth and power.

· 7 ·

Dual Federalism

As THE COURT of the *Lochner* era found that the constitutional guarantees of liberty and property raised insuperable obstacles to State or federal regulation of wages, prices, and other key terms of economic bargains, even in the face of gross inequalities of bargaining power, so did a majority of the Justices conclude that the Constitution denies the *federal* government power to reach regulable abuses in the mining, milling, and manufacture of goods by giant multi-State enterprises for regional or national markets.

The pressure for *federal* legislation checking the power and correcting the abuses of organized wealth was a natural response to the economic changes of the last years of the nineteenth and the beginning of the twentieth centuries. The great railroads were protected against State regulation by the negative implications of the Commerce Clause.[1] Swifter communications and improved transportation enabled increasing numbers of industrial concerns to draw their materials from distant areas and to market their goods throughout large regions, even the entire United States. Large corporations not only shipped their goods but operated establishments in many States.

A State that attempted to protect consumers or workers faced serious difficulty. If diseased beef or mislabeled ham packed in Chicago was sold in Georgia, that State could deal with the local retailers, who were usually innocent, but it could not reach the out-of-State packinghouse that was the true source of the harm.

138

Nor could Georgia or any other single State reach a combination of the great packinghouses to fix prices or allocate territory for monopoly control. A producing State that imposed regulations increasing the cost of doing business—a law prohibiting factories from employing twelve- or thirteen-year-old children, for example—risked subjecting its industries to competitive disadvantage, forcing their migration to another State.

In 1887 Congress moved to control railroad rates and bar notorious railroad practices abusive of shippers. The Interstate Commerce Act of 1887[2] is notable as the first major regulatory law enacted by the federal government and also for establishing the first federal administrative agency—a pattern that would be widely followed in the next century. In 1890 Congress enacted the Sherman Anti-Trust Act, declaring unlawful "[e]very contract, combination or conspiracy . . . in restraint of trade or commerce among the several States."[3] Additional measures aimed at protecting workers and consumers—the first Pure Food and Drug Act,[4] for example—were enacted during the Roosevelt and Wilson Administrations.

The new federal legislation revived the old constitutional debates over the scope of the powers delegated to the federal government. In drawing up a federal plan suited to a simpler society, in which travel and transportation were slow and distances were great, the Philadelphia Convention had left to the States the general power to enact laws for the protection of individuals and the welfare of the community. The only relevant exception to this exclusion of the federal government from domestic affairs was the grant of power "to regulate . . . commerce . . . among the several States," perhaps taken in conjunction with the Necessary and Proper Clause as interpreted in *McCulloch* v. *Maryland*. How the Commerce Clause would apply in the new age was one of the great questions left open by the Framers because its conditions far outran their expectations. The constitutionality of the new federal regulatory laws was challenged by business and financial interests whenever applied to mines, mills, or factories, or to local purchases or sales. Regardless of the size of an enterprise or the character of its markets, the business lawyers argued, production could not fairly be characterized as interstate commerce.

In the Case of the Steamboat Monopoly John Marshall had used sweeping words to describe the scope of federal power under the Commerce Clause: "The genius and character of the whole government seem to be that its action is to be applied to all the external concerns of the nation, *and to those internal concerns which affect the States generally; but not to those* which are completely within the particular State, *which do not affect other States*." (Emphasis added.)[5] Marshall's conception, applied to the new industrial economy, seemed broad enough to support federal regulation of the great steel mills, packinghouses, sugar refineries, and like industrial establishments whose activities demonstrably did "affect other States." But the case had actually involved only transportation of travelers or goods on an interstate journey, not activities that might precede or follow the interstate movement or might otherwise affect it. The later cases in which the Court had used the Commerce Clause to prevent the parochial economic selfishness of individual States from clogging the growth of interstate markets had necessitated the drawing of a constitutional boundary between the interstate commerce not subject to State jurisdiction and the local activities subject to State regulation and taxation. Gradually, the Court pricked out a line. The States might tax and regulate activities and goods unless the goods had actually started moving on their interstate journey and had not yet reached their final destinations to be held for processing or retail sale.[6]

By implication the federal sphere was taken as being confined to the interstate travel, transportation, and communication beyond State power to regulate or tax. The implication was hardly a logical necessity, much less one demanded by a practical understanding of the economy. The division of a federal system does not preclude concurrent jurisdiction. Often the powers of the States and the federal government overlap, and both regulate the same subjects unless Congress excludes the States. Today, for example, Congress can and does regulate under the Commerce Clause activities that also are subject to State taxation and regulation, except as Congress otherwise declares. In the nineteenth century a political theory called "dual federalism" prevailed. Dual federalism presupposed two mutually exclusive realms. Specific limited areas of human activity were assigned to the federal government; there, the federal government was sovereign and no State might intrude. Whatever was left was assigned to the States; there, the States were sovereign and the federal government might not intrude. The boundary was not always clear. The broad theory was always subject to exceptions. But in the mid-nineteenth century the line marking the limit of federal power under the Commerce Clause was generally assumed to be that fixed by the judicial precedents dealing with the regulatory and taxing powers of the States.

Whether dual federalism would survive in the new industrial age was first tested in the prosecution of the Sugar Trust under the Sherman Anti-Trust Law. Sugar was obviously a necessity of life. Control of more than 90 percent of the refined sugar in the United States was brought under a monopoly when the American Sugar Refining Company, already the refiner of 65 percent of the national sugar supply, bought the stock of the refiners of another 33 percent. The government's indictment alleged only monopolization of the manufacture of refined sugar, not of sales in interstate commerce. This limitation on the alleged scope of the crime, whether a reflection of the true facts or a mistake in the pleading, enabled John G. Johnson, Esq., to argue that the monopoly was beyond the reach of federal authority because the refining was not part of the interstate commerce. (Johnson, the most powerful Supreme Court advocate of his day, was more than once offered appointment to the Court. He is said to have told a friend who pressed for an explanation of his refusal: "You want to know the *real* reason? I'd rather spend my life talking to one bunch of damned fools than listening to another.")

In *United States* v. *E. C. Knight Co.*[7] the Court accepted Johnson's argument. Commerce succeeds to manufacture, Chief Justice Melville W. Fuller explained; manufacture is not a part of interstate commerce. A monopoly of production would unquestionably affect interstate trade and even the supply available and prices paid by out-of-State consumers; but those would be indirect results bearing "no direct relation to commerce between the States." The result of a contrary conclusion "would be that Congress would be invested, to the exclusion of the States, with the power to regulate, not only manufacturers, but also agriculture, horticulture, stock raising, domestic fisheries, mining—in short, every branch of human industry."[8]

Today one marvels at Chief Justice Fuller's assumption that to permit a broader exercise of congressional authority would mean the exclusion of the States even from areas in which Congress chose not to act. Yet this was the assumption of the prevailing theory of dual federalism. The modern, pragmatic mind also rebels at the Chief Justice's elevation of form, abstractions, and logic over facts and practical consequences. The definition of "manufacture" is constant for some purposes, yet for other purposes the content and significance of the word have greatly changed. Manufacture in the giant steel mills of Pittsburgh and Chicago bears little resemblance to manufacture in the early iron foundry in Saugus, Massachusetts. The practical consequences of what is done today in Pittsburgh and Chicago extend far more widely than the consequences of the early activities at the Saugus ironworks. Similarly, the Court's insistence on the old boundary between local production and interstate transportation could be said to preserve the old balance of power between federal and State governments, provided than one dealt only in general, abstract concepts. On the other hand, if one looked to the practical consequences of the new organization of business and finance, judicial adherence to the old abstractions denied Congress power to enlarge the reach and size of the federal government in order to deal "with those internal concerns which affect the States generally"—a power that John Marshall had perceived as part of "the genius and character of the whole government established by the Constitution." The ultimate question became whether the Court should adhere to the old concepts, forms, and logic unless the Constitution was amended, or whether the new needs should prevail.

For a time, as illustrated by the Case of the Sugar Trust, the old forms and logic did prevail. The *Adair* case, discussed in the preceding chapter, presents another dramatic example. Not content to hold Section 10 of the Erdman Act unconstitutional as an unwarranted interference with liberty of contract, the Court also ruled that the Commerce Clause gives Congress no power to prohibit interstate railroads from discharging train service employees for joining a labor union. "What possible legal or logical connection is there," the Court asked, "between an employee's membership in a labor organization and the carrying on of interstate commerce?"[9] The great railway strikes of 1877 and 1894 provided answer enough for a realist. The Court was looking for a legal or logical connection "important in itself and in the eye of the law."[10]

The course of decision was not altogether uniform. The *Adair* case evoked four dissents, among them an opinion by Justice Holmes, who had taught that the life of the law is not logic but experience. On another occasion Justice Holmes wrote for the Court that "commerce among the States is not a technical legal conception but a practical one, drawn from the course of business."[11] Even more encouraging to progressives, the Lottery Case,[12] decided in 1903, suggested a method by which Congress might possibly circumvent the distinction between production and interstate commerce. In 1895 Congress had made it a federal offense to mail or ship lottery tickets in interstate commerce. A defendant convicted of violation of the act sought his release on the ground that the prohibition could not be supported under any of the enumerated powers of Congress. The tickets themselves were no threat to the conduct of interstate commerce nor to any persons or merchandise moving therein. The only possible reason for congressional exclusion from the pipeline of interstate commerce was that the tickets were used to conduct immoral, and therefore harmful, activities in either the State of origin or the State of receipt. Nevertheless, a majority of the Justices upheld the Act of Congress. The only general principle that could explain the result was that Congress could exclude from interstate commerce things used for undesirable local activities. The implications did not escape the dissenting Justices. Chief Justice Fuller, who had written the opinion in the Case of the Sugar Trust, complained that if Congress could prohibit the interstate transportation of any object, without regard to its intrinsic harmfulness, because of the conditions under which it was made or would be used, then Congress, in effect, could control manufacturing and thus obliterate the distinction made in the Case of the Sugar Trust between the realm of the federal government and the realms of the States. Chief Justice Fuller concluded the dissenting opinion with prophetic foreboding: "Our form of government may remain notwithstanding legislation or decision, but, as long ago observed, it is with governments, as with religions, the form may survive the substance of the faith."[13]

Building on the constitutional theory seemingly implicit in the Lottery Case, progressives persuaded Congress to make it a federal offense to ship in interstate commerce goods made in an establishment in which child labor was employed. In 1918, by a 5–4 vote, this act was held unconstitutional.[14] The Court again declared that the production of articles for interstate commerce is a matter for local regulation. The aim of the act undeniably was to regulate the labor of children in production, throughout the States: "[I]f Congress can thus regulate matters entrusted to local authority by prohibition of the movement of commodities in interstate commerce, all freedom of interstate commerce will be at an end, and the power of the States over local matters may be eliminated, and thus our system of government may be practically destroyed."[15]

Perhaps Chief Justice Fuller mistook form for substance, the continuing substance of American federalism and democracy. I believe that he did. John Marshall's description seems to me to be a truer perception of the essence of the federal plan from the beginning. But more than thirty years were to elapse and a Great Depression occur before Chief Justice Fuller's fears—and the hopes of the progressives—would come to pass.

· 8 ·

*Judicial Self-Restraint
Under the New Deal*

THE YEAR 1937 brought the revolution in constitutional interpretation that proved the Constitution written 150 years earlier to be adaptable without loss of continuity to the highly integrated economy of an urban and industrial society. The revolution altered the interpretation of both the Due Process Clauses and also the Commerce Clause. The impetus came from the shock of the Great Depression.

The shock was the greater because the decade of the 1920s had seemed to many eyes to prove the value of unregulated capitalism protected by constitutional restrictions on the scope of federal power and the Lochnerian interpretation of the Due Process Clause. The 1920s were a time of seemingly unbounded prosperity for all but the farmers, and even the farmers prospered for perhaps half of the decade. Real wages rose markedly. Factory conditions and urban slums were enormously improved. There was an almost unqualified faith in the great industrial and financial magnates. The spirit of the times is revealed by the identity of the two major party candidates in the Presidential election of 1924. The Republican candidate for re-election was Calvin Coolidge, who declared that "the business of America is business." The Democrat was John W. Davis, lawyer for the House of Morgan, at the very peak of financial power. The spirit of liberal and progressive reform, like the labor movement, was almost dead.

Another symbol of the 1920s was the country club. It was the time of Prohibition and bathtub gin, of the new jazz, the flapper, and the beginning of the revolution in sex. Much of the wealth displayed was based on speculation. Yet those features were the froth. America was still a land of villages and towns, of wide lawns and airy houses, of hard work, Puritan values, and self-sufficiency. Sinclair Lewis came closer to portraying the character of mainstream America in *Main Street* and *Babbitt* than did F. Scott Fitzgerald in *The Great Gatsby*. Upton Sinclair's dark descriptions of the cruelty and excesses of the underside of American factories were easily forgotten.

In November 1929 the bubble burst. The collapse of stock market prices measured the collapse of the entire economic structure. In the summer of 1929 the Dow Jones average for industrial stocks had been 381.17. In the summer of 1932 it was 41.22. Ninety percent of the value had disappeared.

The plight of the farmers was worse. Corn sold for seven cents a bushel, sugar for three cents per pound. Twenty-five percent of the land in Mississippi was sold at auction on the foreclosure of mortgages.

The plight of industry was no better. In the three-year period of December 31, 1930 to December 31, 1933, the Gross National Product fell from 194.4 to 56. Bankruptcy liquidation and reorganization were a chief business of the legal profession. The average wage of factory workers was forty cents per hour. Factory payrolls were cut in half. One of every four men available for work was unemployed. There were no labor unions, no unemployment compensation, and no Social Security.

How you were affected depended on who you were. If you were the son of a relatively well-to-do family, the father of one of your friends may have jumped from a twentieth-story window. Another friend would not return to your boarding school or college in the fall. If you were of the middle class, you might sink down to the bottom. In one group of laborers were found clergymen, engineers, a school principal, and a bank president. For factory workers the depression meant unemployment, bread lines, and soup kitchens. Municipal bankruptcies were common. The young hit the road. One young hobo was Eric Severeid, a banker's son, whose face and voice would become familiar to millions on CBS News programs. The estimates of the number of youths who lived as tramps ran up to two million.

Until March 4, 1933, the mood of the country was black. The

depression destroyed faith in industrial magnates and great financiers; they had allowed the collapse, and had no remedy. The misdeeds of some were highly publicized. Samuel Insull, the president of eleven companies and the holder of eighty-five corporate directorships, including the chairmanship of sixty-five boards of directors, fled the country to escape criminal prosecution. Richard Whitney of the House of Morgan, once President of the New York Stock Exchange, was sent to the New York State Penitentiary for embezzlement. The stability of institutions seemed uncertain. One could no longer put faith in the ethic of work and self-reliance.

On March 4, 1933, the country heard the warm and confident voice of the new President, Franklin Delano Roosevelt: "The only thing we have to fear is fear itself." He pledged immediate action. To avoid financial panic he began with the immediate temporary closing of banks. The country responded. Will Rogers, the cowboy humorist read by millions, commented, "Americans have not been as happy in three years as they are today. No money, no banks, no work, no nothing, but they know they got a man who is wise to Congress, wise to our so-called big men. The whole country is with him."

The New Deal produced a new, more active philosophy of government: government should meet the basic need for jobs and, in the case of those who could not work, the need for food, clothing, and shelter. The problems, it was believed, were national in scope, and therefore required national action. At one time the Civil Works Authority had four million men on the payroll. Government, it was also asserted, should prevent the abuse of superior economic power, and should temper the conflicts and help to work out the accommodations and adjustments that a simpler age had supposed could safely be left to individual ability and the free play of impersonal economic forces. For the most part that responsibility would fall upon the federal government as alone adequate to deal with an economy national in scope and complexity.

The new philosophy led the Roosevelt Administration to provide money and jobs for the worst victims of the depression and also to enact the legislation and establish the government agencies upon which national policies would rest for at least half a century; for example, the Agricultural Adjustment Acts, National Labor Relations Act, Fair Labor Standards Act, the Social Security Act, and the Securities and Exchange Act.

Many of the New Deal measures were of doubtful constitutionality. Others, including such key measures as the National Labor Relations and Fair Labor Standards Acts, were plainly unconstitutional under the precedents of the old regime. Lower-court judges rapidly struck down important congressional measures. The constitutional question was whether the Supreme Court would abandon the old religion of Lochnerism and dual federalism or would continue to try to hold back the tide.

At first, the Court seemed to challenge the New Deal by insisting that the old faith in free markets, small government, and dual federalism was embedded in the Constitution. The major New Deal measure for halting the downward spiral in industrial wages and prices was the National Recovery Administration, a federal agency that stimulated the negotiation of industry-by-industry and market-by-market codes of fair competition to be enforced by the government, fixing minimum prices and wages, and outlawing other "destructive" competitive practices. In 1935, upon challenge by a live-poultry dealer that purchased nearly all its poultry from other States but sold only to retailers in New York, the underlying legislation was held unconstitutional, not only on the ground that the act delegated uncanalized legislative power to the Executive and to private persons, but also on the more important ground that the poultry dealer's activities were beyond the power of Congress to regulate because they did not "directly affect" interstate commerce.[1] The major New Deal measure for dealing with the plight of the farmers, the Agricultural Adjustment Act of 1933, attempted to stabilize farm prices by levying a tax on the processing of agricultural commodities with which to pay subsidies to farmers who would agree to reduce the acreage sown to crops. In 1936, in *United States* v. *Butler,* the Court, by a 5–4 vote, held this act unconstitutional as "a statutory plan to regulate and control agricultural production, a matter beyond the powers delegated to the federal government."[2] Here was the dual federalism of the Sugar Trust Case applied to limit government spending. At the same time the four conservative Justices, joined by Justice Owen J. Roberts, affirmed a decision of New York's highest court holding a State law fixing minimum wages for women to be an unconstitutional interference with liberty of contract. Lochnerism too was still alive.[3]

The invalidation of the NRA in *Schechter Poultry Corp.* v. *United States*[4] helped the Roosevelt Administration to free itself from a mismanaged program that would soon have fallen of its own weight, but the reasoning of that and other opinions seemed to presage invalidation of such fundamental New Deal measures as the National Labor Relations Act, the proposed wage and hour law, and even the Social Security Act. *Carter* v. *Carter Coal Co.*[5] deepened the concern. There the Court held that Congress lacked power to legislate concerning the wages and hours of bituminous coal miners, even though coal mining was a major national industry: "[P]roduction is a purely local activity. It follows that none of these essential antecedents of production constitutes a transaction in or forms any part of interstate commerce."[6]

President Roosevelt responded with strong criticism. The *Schechter* ruling, he said, was evidence that the Court was still living "in the horse and buggy age": "[I]t may be the best thing that has happened to the country for a long time . . . because it clarifies the issue."[7] On February 5, 1937, the President launched a direct attack upon the Court. In a special message to Congress he urged the enactment of a bill to create one new judgeship for every judge who was more than seventy years old but had failed to retire. The message spoke of the heavy burden upon the courts, particularly the Supreme Court, of the "delicate subject" of aged or infirm judges, and of the need for "a constant infusion of new blood."[8] No one doubted the true purpose. Six of the nine Supreme Court Justices were older than seventy, including all four conservatives. By appointing six new Justices, President Roosevelt would ensure a majority ready to uphold the constitutionality of New Deal legislation. A month later the President addressed the nation more candidly by acknowledging that he hoped "to bring to the decision of social and economic problems younger men who have had personal experience and contact with modern facts and circumstances under which average men have to live and work."[9]

The Court-packing plan was defeated despite the President's landslide victory at the polls only a few months earlier and despite the overwhelming popular support for New Deal legislation. The President's disingenuous explanation made the plan vulnerable to factual criticism. Justice Louis D. Brandeis, widely known as a progressive dissenter from his colleagues' conservative philosophy, joined Chief Justice Charles Evans Hughes in a letter to the Senate Judiciary Committee, demonstrating that the Court was fully abreast of its docket and would be less efficient if converted into a body of fifteen Justices. Although much of the opposition was partisan, the resistance to the Court-packing plan ran much deeper. At its source lay the American people's well-nigh religious attachment to constitutionalism and the Supreme Court, including their intuitive realization that packing the Court in order to reverse the course of its decisions would not only destroy its independence but erode the essence of constitutionalism in the United States.

Yet there was some truth in the contemporary quip "A stitch in time saves nine." The final defeat of the Court-packing plan did not come until after a revolutionary turning in the Court's interpretation of constitutional limitations. First, under the impact of the lessons taught and pressures generated by the Great Depression, *Lochner* v. *New York* and like decisions securing economic liberty under the Due Process Clauses were overruled. Second, as related in the next chapter, the Court rejected the premise of dual federalism and allowed a vast congressional expansion of federal power.

II

Lochner v. *New York* and like decisions securing liberty of contract for great aggregations of wealth, property, and bargaining power had been under heavy attack from the day the opinions were delivered. The vote in *Lochner* was 5–4. Justice Holmes, dissenting, penned the words that would become the dominant constitutional philosophy in 1937:

> The Fourteenth Amendment does not enact Mr. Herbert Spencer's Social Statics. . . . [A] constitution is not intended to embody a particular economic theory, whether of paternalism and the organic relation of the citizen to the State or of laissez faire. It is made for people of fundamentally differing views, and the accident of our finding certain opinions natural and familiar or novel and even shocking ought not to conclude our judgment upon the question whether statutes embodying them conflict with the Constitution of the United States. . . .
>
> I think that the word liberty in the Fourteenth Amendment is perverted when it is held to prevent the natural outcome of a dominant opinion, unless it can be said that a rational and fair man necessarily would admit that the statute proposed would infringe fundamental principles as they have been understood by the traditions of our people and our law. It does not need research to show

that no such sweeping condemnation can be passed upon the statute before us [limiting the hours of employment in bakeries].[10]

Oliver Wendell Holmes, Jr., profoundly influenced American jurisprudence. As Stephen J. Field embodied in a judge the driving and sometimes ruthless individualism that transformed America in the second half of the nineteenth century, so Holmes, despite his aristocratic personal tastes, became a symbolic leader of the liberal movement of the first half of the twentieth century. Both Field and Holmes came from distinguished New England families. Holmes was the son of Dr. Holmes, the redoubtable Autocrat of the Breakfast Table and the discoverer of the contagiousness of puerperal fever. The son's very presence bespoke aristocracy, not merely of blood but of taste and talent. Acquainted in his youth with his father's lively intellectual circle—Agassiz, Motley, Longfellow, Hawthorne, and Melville, for example—the Justice became the friend both of legal scholars and of a much broader range of leading intellectual figures of his own day. William and Henry James, Charles Peirce, Henry Adams, and George Santayana were among them. Because of Holmes's manifest joy in life and all who lived life to their limits, the marks of Yankee aristocracy inspired rather than offended. For Holmes, the Civil War wounds suffered at Ball's Bluff and the battles at Antietam and Fredericksburg would always mark high moments of existence. He returned to the Harvard Law School and entered the legal profession somewhat reluctantly, doubting whether one could "live greatly" in the law. The outward marks of his later success are many: Professor at the Harvard Law School, Justice of the Supreme Judicial Court of Massachusetts, and Associate Justice of the Supreme Court of the United States. But Holmes did much more and did it in a grand manner. The influence of his writings and judicial opinions, aided by his romantic streak and magnificent presence, would not only shape both law and events but would inspire generations of law students to seek to follow his example.

In 1880, even as the concepts and logic of the law were losing touch with the human condition, Holmes launched a new school of jurisprudence that came to be called "legal realism."

The life of the law has not been logic; it has been experience. The felt necessities of the time, the prevalent moral and political theories, institutions of public policy, avowed or unconscious, even the prejudices which judges share with their fellow-men, have a good deal more to do than the syllogism in determining the rules by which men should be governed.

The words, still valued in intellectual circles, come from a series of lectures known as *The Common Law*.[11]

Holmes was usually a realist in his own judicial opinions. His omnivorous reading and sensitive imagination made him keenly aware of the changes sweeping over America. His dissenting opinions in labor cases in the Supreme Judicial Court of Massachusetts contributed to President Theodore Roosevelt's decision to put Holmes on the U.S. Supreme Court.

> [I]t is plain from the slightest consideration of practical affairs, or the most superficial reading of industrial history, that free competition means combination, and that the organization of the world, now going on so fast, means an ever increasing might and scope of combination. . . . Combination on the one side [of capital] is patent and powerful. Combination [of workers] on the other is the necessary and desirable counterpart, if the battle is to be carried on in a fair and equal way.[12]

In *Adair* v. *United States* Holmes had only scorn for the majority's unrealistic assertion that the "right of a person to sell his labor upon such terms as he deems proper [is] the same as the right of the purchaser to prescribe the conditions on which he will accept such labor." Drawing on the theme expressed in his Massachusetts opinions, Holmes replied, "In present conditions a workman not unnaturally may believe that only by belonging to a union can he secure a contract that shall be fair to him. . . . If that belief, right or wrong, may be held by a reasonable man, it seems to me that it may be enforced by law in order to establish the equality of position between the parties in which liberty of contract begins."[13]

With Holmes's understanding and perhaps a measure of sympathy for the workingman faced by aggregations of capital, there went a note of skepticism: "While I think the strike a lawful instrument in the universal struggle of life, I think it pure phantasy to suppose that there is a body of capital of which labor as a whole secures a larger share by that means. . . . Organization and strikes . . . do not create something out of nothing."[14] Of laws protecting employees against discharge for union membership, he observed, "Whether in the long run it is wise for the workingman to enact legislation of this sort is not my concern, but I am strongly of the opinion that there is nothing in the Constitution of the United States to prevent it."[15]

Holmes's awareness that life is change and that law changes in response to the changes in society, coupled with his philosophic skepticism, made him exceedingly tolerant of legislative measures whose constitutionality was challenged as in excess of legislative power. His views were expressed in a long series of powerful judicial opinions, in which Justices Brandeis and Stone usually joined. When Holmes retired after thirty years as Associate Justice, his place was filled by Benjamin N. Cardozo, who then joined Brandeis and Stone in opposing the invalidation of regulatory laws under the Due Process Clause. Sometimes the liberals could command a majority; but in the key cases—in instances of wage or price regulation, for example—Lochnerism prevailed.[16] The force of the naysaying decisions seemed to peak in the mid-1930s even in the face of a rising political demand for State and national action to halt the Great Depression and adjust the imbalance created by corporate and financial power. In 1936 the majority affirmed the New York decision holding unconstitutional a New York law setting minimum wages for work done by women.[17]

In 1937, in the face of President Roosevelt's Court-packing plan, the Justices retreated on the question of economic liberty, just as they would shortly abandon the old creed of dual federalism. The shift first became manifest in *West Coast Hotel* v. *Parrish,*[18] a 5–4 decision upholding the constitutionality of a statute enacted in the State of Washington authorizing a board to set minimum wages for women in sundry occupations. To the old doctrine confining the permissible justifications of government action to health, safety, and morals, the Court added broadly the "welfare of the people" and "the interests of the community."[19] Where the old opinions declared the conceptual equality of employer and employee, the new majority more realistically asserted that a legislature may consider the "relatively weak bargaining power" of women and may "adopt measures to reduce the evils of the 'sweating system,' and exploiting of workers at wages so low as to be insufficient to meet the bare cost of living, thus making their very helplessness the occasion of a more injurious competition."[20] They bore the stamp of much greater judicial deference to legislative judgments: "[R]egulation which is reasonable in relation to its subject and is adapted to the interests of the community is due process." The old precedents for a contrary decision were overruled.

The *West Coast Hotel* case inaugurated a line of decisions sustaining every piece of economic legislation enacted by a State or by Congress. General minimum wage and maximum hour laws, price regulation, labor relations acts protecting freedom of association and requiring collective bargaining, legislation protecting established methods of distribution against new, cheaper forms of competition, will serve as examples. The trend was strengthened and intensified by the normal replacement of the Justices who had opposed the growth of the welfare state. The philosophy of judicial self-restraint, symbolized by the dissenting opinions of Justice Holmes and associated most closely with Felix Frankfurter, Learned Hand, and their Harvard Law School professor James Bradley Thayer, gradually became dominant on the Court, in the law schools, and throughout the legal profession.

Three components of that philosophy deserve identification, even though their brief statement oversimplifies the judicial process, and no Justice adhered to any, much less to all, the principles absolutely:

1. A judge should be slow to read—or should not read—into such majestic constitutional phrases as "due process of law" and "equal protection of the laws" more particular values based on what some would call "natural law," "fundamental rights," or "the teaching of an inherited constitutional tradition," but which others branded "mere arbitrary personal preferences."

2. A judge should be slow to substitute—or should not substitute—his judgment for the legislature's preference in choosing between opposing values such as economic liberty and the welfare of the wage earners.

3. A judge may not examine too meticulously the facts underlying a constitutional question. He should accept the legislative finding if it could be correct, as ruled more than half a century earlier in *Munn* v. *Illinois*,[21] and should presume the existence of any state of facts that would validate a statute if the existence of such facts is rationally conceivable.

Questions of federalism aside, the troublesome problems of constitutional interpretation call, with rare exceptions, for striking a balance between the opposing ideals of popular sovereignty and the rule of law, between democratic self-government and judicial enforcement of constitutional limitations. In 1940 the philosophy of legislative supremacy and judicial self-restraint was asserted and widely accepted as broadly applicable to all constitutional interpretation except the enforcement of clear and specific verbal commands. Justice Hugo L. Black, President Roosevelt's first appointee, seemed to be writing the epitaph of judicial policymaking in the name of the Constitution when he wrote:

> We have returned to the original constitutional proposition that courts do not substitute their social and economic beliefs for the judgment of legislative bodies, who are elected to pass laws.[22]

· 9 ·

The Expansion of Federal Power

THE REVOLUTIONARY turning point toward modern interpretation of the scope of congressional power to regulate interstate commerce came in a decision known to lawyers as *National Labor Relations Board* v. *Jones & Laughlin Steel Corp.*[1] The case might better be called "The Firing of Harry Phillips, Royal Boyer, and Their Friends." Formal titles make it too easy to forget that great constitutional decisions grow out of common human incidents in the lives of the men and women among whom we live. Human understanding of these incidents and their effect upon the lives of the individuals is the essence of wise decisions and sound law. If the first decisions give rise to precedent-setting general principles, it is because the people involved and the incident are typical of thousands or even millions of other men and women and what is happening or may happen to them in the course of their daily lives. And it is in the later application to individual men and women that the law takes on its real importance.

Harry Phillips was a motor inspector in 1934 in the soaking pits at the Jones & Laughlin steel mill in Aliquippa, Pennsylvania. Working conditions were often harsh. Only a few years earlier, the standard shift had been twelve hours a day, seven days a week. Twice a month, as the shifts swung over, the men worked twenty-four continuous hours. Harry Phillips earned between $100 and $120 a month.

Aliquippa was Jones & Laughlin, and Jones & Laughlin was

Aliquippa. In 1905 Jones & Laughlin had bought up the quiet town of Woodlawn in the Beaver Valley of the Ohio River twenty miles north of Pittsburgh, built a giant steel mill, and renamed the town Aliquippa. In 1934 Jones & Laughlin owned 130 acres in the town itself, seven hundred dwellings occupied by employees, and twelve hundred acres of farmland. Jones & Laughlin owned the street railway, the motor coach franchise, and the waterworks. The police force were the J & L police. Harry Phillips lived in Aliquippa.

Jones & Laughlin was the fourth biggest company in an industry of giants. In 1934 the assets of Jones & Laughlin and its subsidiaries were $181,532,641.36. Iron ore moved to its Pittsburgh and Aliquippa mills from J & L mines in Michigan and Minnesota. Coal and limestone moved in from Pennsylvania and West Virginia. Out to the country—much of it to J & L warehouses in Chicago, Detroit, Cincinnati, Memphis, and New Orleans—flowed steel products: 880,031 tons in 1934 with a value of $47,957,338.36. Harry Phillips was just one of twenty-two thousand J & L employees, ten thousand of them at Aliquippa.

Steel making required huge concentrations of capital and productive capacity, the organization of manpower, vertical integration, and vast, far-flung markets. Even in 1934 it took $100 million to build the most efficient blast furnace.

Combination among the steel workers for collective bargaining had started, moved ahead, sputtered, and failed. By 1891 the Amalgamated Association of Iron and Steel Workers, with 24,068 members, had organized 25 percent of the industry. Pittsburgh was a union town. Andrew Carnegie had been friendly to the union because its minimum wage scale protected him from low-wage competition. In 1892 Carnegie, no longer needing protection, set out to break the union by a lockout at the giant Homestead mills. Three hundred Pinkerton detectives were brought in by boats on the Ohio and Monongahela Rivers. After pitched battles leaving dead and wounded, Carnegie broke the union. It was the age in which federal troops were used to keep order during the great Pullman strike. Other steel masters followed Carnegie's example.

In the industrial boom of World War I, the progressive spirit and wartime labor policies of the Wilson Administration brought to the steel industry a resurgence of union organization. By 1919 the National Committee for Organizing Iron & Steel Workers felt strong enough to challenge the bitterly anti-union leader, United

States Steel Corporation. The union's principal demands were for the right to bargain collectively, overtime pay after eight hours on the standard twelve-hour shift, one day's rest in seven, a wage increase, and the reinstatement of men discharged for union activity. U.S. Steel coldly replied that it did not deal with labor unions. Once again, a strike was broken by the importation of strike breakers and bloodshed. In the 1920s, working conditions in the steel industry improved, employee representation plans carefully controlled by the companies were introduced, but true union organization was virtually dead.

The depression, the New Deal, and the success of John L. Lewis's United Mine Workers in the neighboring coal fields brought new life to the union movement in the industrial regions, particularly in Pennsylvania's steel valleys. The Amalgamated chartered its Beaver Valley Lodge in Aliquippa in August 1934. Harry Phillips became president. Jones & Laughlin countered by systematic intimidation. The important lodge officers were shadowed, day and night, by the J & L police. The financial secretary's home was surrounded by the J & L police, day and night. The lodge could find no space for union meetings in Aliquippa.

As president of the lodge, Harry Phillips began to receive special attention. The day after he and others applied for the union charter, he was approached by the J & L police and offered a job on the police force at a higher wage. The J & L police stopped and questioned him about his union activities when they found him distributing union literature in the streets. One night Phillips was on his way to work when he noticed that he was being followed by a J & L police car. As he walked through the tunnel that led into the mill, he was beaten by men with blackjacks and screwdrivers. After escaping, Phillips ran to the police station and asked for protection. He was told, "Get the hell out of here. You don't deserve protection." Persisting, Phillips continued his union activity. When he sought permission to attend a picnic of the Democratic Social Club, his foreman told him, "If you want off for that picnic, you will have time to go to a lot of picnics in the future." At 4:00 A.M. on the morning of July 20, 1935, Harry Phillips was fired. A whistle had blown, calling him to the scene of a breakdown. He had been working hard, had gone to the washroom, and hadn't heard the whistle. The whistle blew a second time. Phillips looked up and saw a millwright answering the call. Other workers guilty of the same infraction were not seriously penalized, but Phillips was fired: "You fellows coming out at night always want the mill-wrights to do all the work around here. You can get the hell out of here. You are going to have plenty of time to sell papers from now on." Eight other active union organizers suffered the same fate, including Dominic Brandy, who had worked for Jones & Laughlin for twenty-five years but who was also a leader among the Italian workers and had signed 665 employees to union membership.

Royal Boyer, an operator on the nail machine, also lost his job. Boyer, an active union member from the beginning, was a leader among the Aliquippa mill's eight hundred black employees. He signed 250 to membership. He distributed union literature. He served on committees. One of the nail inspectors warned Boyer to pay more attention to work and to leave the union alone and not attend the meetings. The same inspector warned Boyer's wife. Boyer was suspended for the first time as a nail cutter in October 1935, either for making bad nails or for mixing good with bad. The buggy into which he threw his finished nails was shared with another operator. Four days later bad nails were found in the buggy. The other operator had often been charged with the production of bad nails. No action was taken against him, but Boyer was discharged.

In earlier decades Harry Phillips, Royal Boyer, and their fellows would have been out on the street, jobless, without remedy, and unknown to law or history. Such had been the fate of thousands of union men in industrial communities throughout the nation. In 1936, however, the victims of anti-union discrimination could have some hope for a remedy. The Roosevelt Administration strongly supported labor unions. By that time laborers, reformers, and workingmen and -women were not the only ones who perceived the necessity for labor union organization. Even so staunch a conservative as Chief Justice William Howard Taft had written in the 1920s: "A single employee was helpless in dealing with an employer. He was dependent ordinarily on his daily wage for the maintenance of himself and his family. If the employer refused to pay him the wages that he thought fair, he was nonetheless unable to leave the employ and to resist arbitrary and unfair treatment. Union was essential to give laborers opportunity to deal on equality with their employer."[2]

In 1935 Congress had enacted the National Labor Relations Act.[3] The key Section 7 declared the right of employees to form, join, and assist labor organizations and to bargain collectively through representatives of their own choosing. Another section made it an unfair labor practice for an employer to interfere with, restrain, or coerce employees in the exercise of those rights, or to refuse to bargain collectively with a labor union designated by a majority of the employees to represent them. The National Labor Relations Board was established to prevent and remedy unfair labor practices by employers and to conduct elections in order to determine whether the majority of the employees in an appropriate unit had designated a representative.

In January 1936, the Beaver Valley Lodge filed a charge with the National Labor Relations Board (NLRB), asserting that Jones & Laughlin had engaged in unfair labor practices in its union-busting campaign of intimidation, including the discriminatory discharges of Phillips, Boyer, and six other active union members. NLRB issued a complaint against Jones & Laughlin, held a hearing, found the company guilty, and issued an order directing the company not only to cease and desist from unfair labor practices but also to reinstate Phillips, Boyer, and their fellows to their former positions, with back pay. Jones & Laughlin appealed the order to the U.S. Court of Appeals for the Second Circuit, sitting in New York. That court set the order aside on the ground that regulating labor relations in a steel mill is beyond the power of the federal government. As an intermediate court obliged to follow the Supreme Court precedents, the Second Circuit had little choice. The precedents still supported the theory of dual federalism. Only a year earlier, the Supreme Court had reaffirmed the distinction between interstate commerce and production by invalidating federal measures regulating labor relations in the bituminous coal fields and curtailing agricultural production.[4]

Events moved toward a crisis as the government carried the case to the Supreme Court. The political power of President Franklin D. Roosevelt and the New Deal was triumphant. The President had carried all but two states, Maine and Vermont, in the 1936 election. The business and financial community and its spokesman, the American Liberty League, turned to the Court to protect the old regime of economic laissez-faire and small central government. For the most part the Court had stood firm against the New Deal, but the President's Court-packing plan had not yet been defeated. For both sides the constitutionality of the Wagner National Labor

Relations Act had prime importance. The act was anathema to America's giant autocratic, anti-union corporations On the other side, the act was a symbol of the effort to protect the little individual—the Harry Phillipses and the Royal Boyers—and to distribute more fairly both economic and political power. With the *Jones & Laughlin* case the Court would hear cases against other employers testing the range of NLRB jurisdiction: a clothing manufacturer, a producer of truck trailers, an interstate bus line, and the Associated Press.

Argument would be heard in the magnificent marbled courthouse, across from the Capitol, into which the Court had moved in 1935. Georgia marble for the outer walls, Alabama marble for their interior, a thousand freight-car loads from Vermont, and twenty-four massive columns from the Montarrenti quarry in Italy for the Ionic columns that line the courtroom itself. The main west entrance leads to the Great Hall. Ahead, one enters the courtroom facing the bench. Overhead and behind the Justices is a giant frieze, supported by the columns of rare Italian marble. Two central figures portray the Majesty of the Law and the Power of Government, protecting the innocent and the people in their enjoyment of Liberty and the Pursuit of Happiness. The opposing frieze, faced by the Justices, portrays the Powers of Evil confronted by the Powers of Good, with Justice in the center with a sheathed sword, beside Divine Inspiration holding the scales of Justice and flanked by Wisdom and Truth. The great law givers, from Menes, Solomon, and Draco to Chief Justice John Marshall, appear on the friezes on both sides. Deep red in the carpeting and heavy drapes, dark mahogany, and bronze latticework in gates to side corridors give warmth to the austere majesty. Perhaps some of the Justices come to feel easy there. For me, even after some eighty or ninety oral arguments and countless days of attendance, there is always an atmosphere of quiet but tense austerity never quite lifted even by occasional ripples of laughter springing from repartee in argument.

Humanity is also there when counsel and the Justices are at their best. For a moment all this majesty and dignity, all the pages of briefs, and all the learning, energy, and understanding of Court and counsel would be focused upon Harry Phillips, Boyer, and their fellow workers in the mills.

The Labor Board Cases would be argued for three days by a brilliant assemblage of lawyers. Perhaps the old era and the new were symbolized by the identity of counsel in the opening case. John W. Davis, counsel for the Associated Press, represented the old regime. Born in 1873, he was at the peak of a career that had made him Representative in Congress, Solicitor General of the United States, Ambassador to Great Britain, Democratic candidate for President of the United States, and perhaps the ablest Supreme Court advocate of the twentieth century. Opposed was the coming generation: the brilliant Charles E. Wyzanski, Jr., just six years out of law school, and Charles Fahy, General Counsel to the National Labor Relations Board. Neutral observers reported that Wyzanski shredded Davis's arguments. Fahy, who would become Solicitor General of the United States, had a quieter style. He won so many cases by 5–4 votes—his friends would say—only because his voice was too quiet to be heard by more than five Justices.

Charles Evan Hughes had been named Chief Justice of the United States by President Hoover in 1930. His career surpassed Davis's: a reform Governor of New York, Associate Justice of the U.S. Supreme Court, Republican candidate for President in 1916, Secretary of State, a member of the World Court, and, when not in public office, a powerful advocate and leader of the Bar. Hughes's accomplishments, his incisive mind, legal craftsmanship and firm manner, and above all his quiet but radiant integrity made him an ideal Chief Justice. His presence in the courtroom, the white beard, the dignified bearing, the bright eye, and the firm, clear voice, made one think, without irreverence, that Hughes was the image of God—the God of the Old Testament, perhaps, because Hughes would cut a lawyer off in the middle of an "if" when the allotted time for oral argument expired.

Two short months after argument, the Chief Justice delivered the opinion of the Court, sustaining the power of the federal government to protect the Harry Phillipses and the Royal Boyers of the industrial world against an employer's reprisals for their seeking to bargain collectively. The Chief Justice's opinion marched from the words granting Congress power "to regulate commerce . . . among the several States" to the conclusion that the federal government can protect production workers in a steel mill, in five progressive steps reminiscent of the black letter propositions that head each section of a good lawyer's brief.

First, the power to regulate interstate commerce is the power not only to restrain but to "foster, protect, and promote." No one was disposed to question this proposition, even though it gave "regulate" an expanded meaning. Congress had often exercised the power. The Court had often declared it.

Second, "[a]lthough activities may be intrastate in character when separately considered, if they have such a close and substantial relation to interstate commerce that their control is essential or appropriate to protect that commerce from burdens and obstructions, Congress cannot be denied the power to exercise that control."[5]

Here was one of the keys unlocking the door to a vast expansion of federal regulation. Congress, the Court ruled, is not limited to regulating "commerce . . . among the several States." Congress can regulate any other thing if such regulation is "essential or appropriate" to protect commerce among the several States. The proposition was not utterly unprecedented. The Court had ruled back in 1914 that the federal government may raise the local freight rates fixed by a State railroad commission where necessary to protect interstate shippers against unfair local competition.[6] That ruling had been confined to regulation of carriers engaged in interstate transportation. Now the ruling was generalized to wipe out the old boundary stopping federal authority at the line between interstate transportation and production. The result is reminiscent of Chief Justice Marshall's famous exposition in *McCulloch* v. *Maryland*: "Let the end be legitimate, let it be within the scope of the new constitution, and all means which are appropriate, which are plainly adapted to that end, which are not prohibited, but consist with the letter and spirit of the constitution, are constitutional."[7]

Third, as he turned to inquire whether legal protection for the right to organize labor unions and bargain collectively in a steel mill would protect the flow of goods in interstate commerce, Chief Justice Hughes substituted practical observation of contemporary business facts for the conceptualism that perceived no "legal or logical connection" between production and interstate commerce. No one could deny that a lengthy strike at Jones & Laughlin would *in fact* greatly affect the interstate movement of vast quantities of iron ore, limestone, coal, and steel, not to mention the effect of a shortage of steel on the interstate shipments of other manufacturers.

Fourth, the history of labor disturbances abundantly demonstrated that interference with union organization and refusal to bargain collectively were among the prolific causes of strikes. The fact had been noted in government reports and scholarly studies since the great Pullman strike of 1894.

With this fourth proposition, the Chief Justice connected the prohibition against discriminatory discharges and the reinstatement of the victims with the regulation of interstate commerce. The federal government, when Congress chose, could constitutionally protect Harry Phillips, Dominic Brandy, and Royal Boyer in organizing the Beaver Valley Lodge of the Amalgamated Association of Iron and Steel Workers, because the injustices otherwise resulting could produce industrial disturbances disastrous to the national economy.

Eliminating the distinction between production and interstate commerce was itself a revolutionary rejection of the old federalism; but there was more to come. At the time of the *Jones & Laughlin* decision the Court appears to have contemplated the retention of some judicially enforceable constitutional check on the extent of congressional power under the Commerce Clause: "Undoubtedly the scope of this power must be considered in the light of our dual system of government and may not be extended as to embrace effects upon interstate commerce so indirect and remote that to embrace them, in view of our complex society, would effectually obliterate the distinction between what is national and what is local and create a complete centralized government."[8] But the hope of retaining a constitutional check on the scope of federal regulatory power proved illusory. The quoted admonition, though operable as a political principle guiding congressional judgment, yielded no rule of law capable of judicial administration. Once the distinctions between interstate movement and production and between "direct" and "indirect" effects on interstate commerce were rejected, the number of links in the chain of cause and effect became irrelevant. Federal power would reach to the local machine shop that repaired the chain saws that cut the trees that yielded the pulpwood that yielded the pulp that made the paper bought by the publisher to print the newspaper that circulated in interstate commerce. Here was the very "this is the house that Jack built" reasoning that Thomas Jefferson had protested in opposing the Bank of the United States and the Federalists' theory of implied powers.

The size of the particular establishment or transaction also became irrelevant after the *Jones & Laughlin* decision, because the cumulative effect of many small local activities may in fact have major impact on interstate commerce. The most dramatic instance developed in 1941, just after Hughes's retirement, when the Court sustained the federal penalty imposed on a small farmer for growing a few bushels of wheat in excess of his federal quota in order to feed poultry and pigs on his own farm and to make bread for his family.[9] No one could deny that if enough small farmers increased their production by even a few bushels for home consumption in a time of surplus, they would "affect" the price at which wheat was sold in interstate commerce. Were the effects sufficient to make federal regulation "essential or appropriate to protect that commerce"? More than a century earlier, John Marshall, in upholding the power of Congress to charter a national bank, had observed that "to inquire into the degree of its necessity would be to pass the line which circumscribes the judicial department, and to tread upon legislative ground."[10] Similarly, ever since the *Jones & Laughlin* decision, the Court has deferred to Congress on all questions of fact or degree concerning the relationship between a local activity and interstate commerce. On this reasoning, the Court sustained the provisions of the Civil Rights Act of 1964 forbidding racial discrimination by restaurants and other places of public accommodation part of whose supplies are moved in interstate commerce.[11]

A second line of cases also pushed back the limits on the scope of federal regulation of activities theretofore subject exclusively to the control of the States. The Fair Labor Standards Act of 1938 required employers to pay workers engaged in the production of goods for shipment in interstate commerce no less than a specified minimum wage and forbade shipping in interstate commerce any goods in the production of which less than the minimum wage had been paid. The draftsmen had proceeded on the constitutional theory of the Lottery Case, even though the theory had been rejected when Congress sought to prohibit child labor. Congress, the theory asserted, may exclude from the pipeline of interstate commerce things that will, in the judgment of Congress, do harm in the State where received by driving down or holding down wage levels paid in the production of competing local goods, and also do harm to interstate commerce in their competitive effect on shipments from other States. An acknowledged aim of the Fair Labor Standards

Act, like that of the child labor act, was to regulate practices in production. Having rejected dual federalism in the Labor Board Cases, the Court readily upheld the constitutionality of those provisions of the Fair Labor Standards Act prohibiting the shipment of goods in the production of which less than the minimum wage had been paid.[12] The direct prohibition against paying less than the specified minimum wage to employees engaged in the production of goods for interstate shipment was also upheld as a necessary and proper means of preventing goods made under substandard conditions from moving to, and then doing harm in, other States. Years later it was held, apparently on similar reasoning, that under the Commerce Clause Congress may regulate the local possession or use of articles that have moved in interstate commerce.[13]

Needless to say, much more than legal logic lay behind the Court's recognition of virtually unlimited congressional power to regulate business activities under the Commerce Clause. The markets of major firms had become nationwide. The complex and reticulated character of the national economy made widely separated localities interdependent. A century earlier, layoffs at the iron foundry in Saugus, Massachusetts, would have had scant visible effect on other States. During the Great Depression no one could miss the fact that layoffs at the steel mills in Pittsburgh, Pennsylvania, reduced the demand for clothing and so caused more layoffs at the textile mills in Charlotte, North Carolina, and Fall River, Massachusetts. Even as the Hughes Court deliberated the Labor Board Cases, a strike at a General Motors automobile assembly plant in Michigan was injuring automobile sales agencies in cities and towns throughout the United States.

The States were incapable of dealing with the abuses and evils resulting from industrialization. Many States were smaller and less powerful than the giant public utilities and industrial corporations. No State alone could cope with such problems in the face of interstate rivalry to attract industrial establishments. Massachusetts might forbid the employment of child labor or fix a minimum wage if the Due Process Clause permitted, but it could enforce such measures only at the price of watching its industries flee to North Carolina or South Carolina to escape the regulation. New York might seek to ensure the welfare of its dairy farmers by setting minimum prices that handlers must pay for milk, but only at the price of watching the handlers go outside the jurisdiction to Vermont farmers to buy their bulk milk at lower prices than those fixed for New York. The Commerce Clause plainly barred the States from erecting protective barriers against interstate competition.[14]

A shift in intellectual mode was a major influence. We noted a similar shift in the nineteenth century. For thirty years the Court had been trapped by an apparent dilemma: either the States have all power to regulate interstate commerce in the absence of congressional regulation, or they have no power to regulate interstate commerce. Neither rule fitted the needs of the country. The apparent dilemma resulted from the habit of analyzing constitutional questions in terms of the seat of particular powers while also assuming that a power is indivisible, like the Newtonian atom. When the focus of the inquiry was shifted from the seat of the power to the subject of the regulation in *Cooley* v. *Board of Port Wardens*,[15] the Court was freed to permit some State regulation of interstate commerce while invalidating excessive and discriminatory burdens.

A similar change took place in 1937. The Commerce Clause law of the late nineteenth and early twentieth centuries had been highly logical and conceptual, but, as noted in the previous chapter, the new school of jurisprudence, known as "legal realism," began to emerge. Its hero, Justice Oliver Wendell Holmes, Jr., had said of the Commerce Clause: "Commerce among the States is not a technical legal conception, but a practical one, drawn from the course of business."[16] Here was a direct challenge to the older and then still prevailing law that asked rhetorically, "What possible legal or logical connection is there between an employee's membership in a labor organization and the carrying on of interstate commerce?"[17] With the Chief Justice's third key proposition in the *Jones & Laughlin* case, the Court shifted, once and for all time, from the old conceptualism to the practical view.

Finally, legal realism encouraged judicial deference to congressional determinations of fact and degree, and thus led to judicial acquiescence in Acts of Congress vastly expanding the scope of federal regulation. If "law" was truly only a set of determinations based partly on "fact" and partly on the value judgments of those in power, what right had a court to overturn the findings of fact and value judgments of the people's elected representatives? The question had the sharpest point when leveled at Lochnerian inter-

vention under the Due Process Clauses. In the constitutional revolution of 1937, as explained in the last chapter, it led to a new
philosophy of judicial self-restraint so great that Justice Field would
have called it abdication. Even though this new judicial philosophy
was most applicable to the Due Process Clauses, it also had major
influence in the Court's acceptance of congressional expansion of
federal power. If the power of Congress to regulate local activity
depends on its practical effect on interstate commerce and if Congress finds a link, the Court's task is complete and the constitutionality of the legislation must be sustained.

The wise division of regulatory activities between the Nation and
the States is, and may always be, a much-debated question of
constitutional proportions. Congress need not exercise the full
power available; it may choose to leave activities within its power
to State control. Under the two lines of decision laid down by the
Hughes Court interpreting the Commerce Clause, however, the
question is almost exclusively political. The Court has yielded the
final word to Congress.

II

Familiarity with the present size, power, and activities of the federal government makes it easy to forget that practically all result
from vast expansion since 1930. Even the statistics are striking. In
1930 the federal government had 601,319 civilian employees. In
1983 there were 2,754,000, more than a fourfold increase. In 1930
federal expenditures were $3.3 billion. By 1983 they totaled $785.7
billion. Some of the enormous growth results from expansion of
the federal government's regulatory activities under the liberalized
interpretation of the Commerce Clause. Much is attributable to
growth of the defense establishment. No small part, however, is
attributable to spending on domestic programs.

In the beginning, public men and citizens were acutely conscious
of the link between federal spending and the centralization of
power, and they debated the question in constitutional terms. The
argument centered on Article I, Section 8, which grants Congress
the power

[t]o lay and collect Taxes . . . to pay the debts, and provide for the
common Defense and general Welfare of the United States.

Alexander Hamilton, the first Secretary of the Treasury, who
proposed chartering the Bank of the United States, argued that

there is no limit to the objects for which Congress may appropriate money, save that the benefit possibly extend throughout the Union. The Jeffersonians, fearful of the centralization of power, disagreed. Article I, Section 8, after granting the power to tax and spend, lays out in subsequent paragraphs the permissible subjects of federal regulation in relatively specific terms. The Jeffersonians and their ideological descendants argued that the spending power granted in the first paragraph of Article I, Section 8, is limited to the subjects set out in the subsequent paragraphs. On this ground Presidents Madison and Monroe vetoed appropriations for the improvement of the great Cumberland Road, stretching from Maryland across the Appalachian Mountains to the new prairie States and used by tens of thousands both to migrate and to send east the products of the new land. The argument on both sides of the question became more bitter when the Northeast and the old Northwest joined in levying a tariff to protect new industries and finance internal improvements, a program bitterly opposed by the slave-holding South. Spending for internal improvements gradually became accepted practice in the political branches, but the Supreme Court had had no occasion to adjudicate the underlying issue, because no litigant could show that the spending caused such injury to self or property as would sustain a cause of action.

The Roosevelt Administration not only spent federal funds on an unprecedented scale in order to relieve unemployment, it also broke new ground in using subsidies to shape the conduct of both State governments and private persons. In *United States* v. *Butler*,[18] it will be recalled, the Court held the Agricultural Adjustment Act of 1933 unconstitutional because conditioning the payment of a government subsidy to a farmer on the reduction of his planted acreage made the whole "a statutory plan to regulate and control agricultural production, a matter beyond the powers delegated to the federal government."

The decision was a prime target of President Roosevelt's criticism leading to the Court-packing plan. It nullified the Administration's farm program, and it aroused fears that the Court would also invalidate the Social Security Act, a key New Deal measure establishing systems of unemployment and old-age and survivors insurance. Title IX levied a federal payroll tax on all employers of eight or more individuals but gave a credit of up to 90 percent of the federal tax for employer contributions to any State unemployment fund that met federal standards specified in the act. Very few States had previously established unemployment insurance, but the combination of pressure and inducement proved to be sufficient sanction. The combination was attacked as "a coercive, unconstitutional invasion of the realm reserved exclusively to the States by the Tenth Amendment which, if generalized, would enable federal authorities to induce, if not indeed to compel, state enactments for any purpose within the realm of state power, and generally to control state administration of State laws." In the third great set of landmark decisions of 1937 the five-Justice majority answered that offering a choice or even a temptation is not coercion. Spending to relieve the needs of the army of unemployed in a nationwide depression serves the *general* welfare, the majority continued; the spending power knows no other limitation.[19]

With this decision Hamilton's nationalistic theory of the spending power finally prevailed. It has also become plain that attaching regulatory conditions to an offer of federal grants in such areas as housing, highway construction, education, medical care, and local law enforcement raises no constitutional difficulty, even if the subject is otherwise beyond federal control.

In fact, the spending power is often used for regulatory purposes. Conditions may be attached not only to allotments to individuals but also to grants to States and municipalities. Federal aid to primary and secondary schools is tied to the school district's compliance with federal standards. Federal support for unemployment insurance is also tied to minimum standards. The practice is now so familiar that only students of constitutional history raised an eyebrow when Congress forced State legislatures to prohibit the local retail sale of alcoholic beverages to persons under twenty-one years of age by tying federal grants for highway construction to the enactment of such legislation.

III

The constitutional revolution of 1937 erased the limits on the scope of congressional power resulting from the Framers' plan to check the growth of the new federal government by delegating to it specific, limited powers, reserving all the other functions of government to the States. The decisions also wiped out for at least half a century any recourse to the Due Process Clause for check on government regulation of economic activity. Vast changes in government's responsibilities and activities occurred once the constitutional barriers were removed. The changes now seem to have been inevitable. Possibly the Court, by adhering to the past, could have forced constitutional amendment. More likely, to try to cling to the Lochnerian precedents and "dual federalism" precedents would have been to essay the role of King Canute. Yet one who is seeking to understand the genius of American constitutionalism and to define the proper role of the Court is bound to ask whether the Hughes Court simply bowed to the threats of President Roosevelt and other political pressures and thus failed in its duty to fit its decisions into an ever-constant, ever-changing body of law.

Pursuing that question, we should initially note two points. First, the Hughes Court rejected the claims of indistinguishable precedents under both the Commerce Clause and the Due Process Clauses of the Fifth and Fourteenth Amendments. To this extent a majority of the Justices actively made new law.

Second, it must be acknowledged that almost none of the Framers can be supposed to have consciously intended to establish a central government such as now exists and with the present relations between that government and the States. On the contrary, upon any fair appraisal one would have to say that the Framers' specific, conscious intent was that the Congress should not have power to regulate the few manufacturing establishments scattered about the original States, and that, in the unlikely event that regulation were desirable, that regulation should be by the States. By 1937, even the words "manufacture" and "production" had come to embrace technological processes and vast human organizations utterly unknown to the Framers. The nationwide consequences of what was taking place in manufacturing establishments, drawing huge quantities of raw materials from and shipping goods to many States, were beyond the Framers' imagination. Either the Court must say that the same words and concepts used in describing the Framers' particular intent still control, even though the transformation of the economy has changed both their content and the consequences of the rule, or else the Court must say that this form of specific intent is no longer relevant and look elsewhere for its decision. The example is pertinent to our controversies in 1987. Attorney General Edwin Meese III and other conservatives insist that the Court should not go beyond the original intent, by which they usually mean that particular application of broad constitutional commands which the Framers consciously intended.

In 1937, as in both prior and subsequent periods, both country and Court chose to treat the Constitution as a living document adaptable to new conditions, a step at a time, by a process of judicial interpretation that seeks to discern from the Constitution and from previous interpretations identifiable underlying principles and values that reason can project on new and unforeseen conditions. This was the manner in which Chief Justice Marshall approached the interpretation of the Commerce Clause in the Case of the Steamboat Monopoly:

> The genius and character of the whole government seem to be that its action is to be applied to all the external concerns of the nation and to those internal concerns which affect the States generally; but not to those which are completely within a particular State, which do not affect other States, and with which it is not necessary to interfere for the purpose of executing some of the general powers of government.[20]

Given this principle and Marshall's further precept that "the degree of necessity" for the purpose of executing one of the delegated powers of Congress is "to be determined in another place,"[21] the Court's acquiescence in the vast congressional expansion of federal activity seems quite consistent with a proper understanding of the original intent.

My appraisal of the Court's rejection of Lochnerism and acceptance of pervasive interference with liberty of contract follows similar lines. No one can realistically suppose that those who wrote and adopted the Due Process Clauses ever envisioned the kind of government interference with the free market that is accepted today. On the other hand, there is scant reason to suppose that the Framers intended to bar those developments, given national markets, giant business enterprises, an interdependent national economy, mass production, mass consumption, and all the inequalities of bargaining power that would exist in the absence of government regulation in the modern economic world. That might well be reason enough to read no relevant restriction into the Due Process Clauses, but, as the majority opinion demonstrated in *Munn* v. *Illinois*,[22] there was also an ancient principle permitting government interference with market forces where the bargain affected the public interest. Few situations were seen to fall into that category prior to 1870. The broadening of public regulation in the modern

State could at least plausibly be attributed to the much greater number of economic bargains that affect the public interest, rather than to any change of basic principle.

Even more important, the vast changes in law and government involved in the transition from laissez-faire to the welfare state were not primarily the work of judicial hands. The Court's use of constitutional adjudication as an instrument of reform during the third quarter of the present century would raise difficult questions concerning the extent to which the Court may, by new constitutional rulings, ordain profound social change. Then, the area of life governed by the courts as opposed to representative self-government would be importantly enlarged, and questions would be raised concerning the legitimacy of such judicial rule. No such questions were raised by the revolutionary changes of the 1930s. It was an elected Congress that expanded federal activity. It was an elected Congress and elected State legislatures that embarked upon regulatory and welfare programs. It was their action that gave the changes the legitimacy of majoritarianism. The Court can be said to have participated, but only by declining to impose constitutional barriers with scant support in the genius of the original understanding or the earlier ground-breaking interpretations.

Judicial self-restraint, despite some overruling of precedent, had reached its high-water mark.

PART THREE

Constitutional Adjudication as an Instrument of Reform

· 10 ·

The Warren Court

IN 1940 even Thomas Jefferson would have found it hard to say that, by virtue of the Court's power of judicial review, the country was living "under the despotism of an oligarchy." By 1970 the criticism was common. It seems even stronger today.

The 1940s brought a gradual change in the character of constitutional litigation. Between the Civil War and World War II the great constitutional issues, both those of federalism and those involving the constitutional guarantees of liberty and property, grew out of resistance to the expansion of federal power and the development of the regulatory and welfare state. After World War II the Court's responsibility for individual human liberty, dignity, and equality became the predominant theme. The great constitutional issues, not only in the courtroom but for the country, became those of freedom of expression, of political and religious liberty, of civil rights and the meaning of "equality," of the humane administration of criminal justice, and of privacy and individual choice.

As the change progressed, the philosophy of judicial self-restraint began to look less attractive to the so-called liberals—who might better be called "progressives." The recollection of past judicial mistakes and the need for consistency of institutional theory still cautioned against activist judicial ventures, even in so deserving an area as civil liberty. On the other hand, judicial self-restraint would leave much civil liberty at the mercy of the Executive and Legislative Branches; and in the new era the political arms were proving either reactionary or at best resistant to libertarian, egalitarian, and humanitarian impulses. The logical escape from the dilemma was to develop a judicial rationale for elevating civil liberties and civil rights to a preferred position, justifying stricter standards of judicial review than those used in judging economic measures.

The issue was first drawn sharply during World War II in the Flag Salute Cases described in the next chapter.[1] The substantive question was whether a State violated the Due Process Clause of the Fourteenth Amendment by expelling from school and treating as truants the children of Jehovah's Witnesses who refused to salute the United States flag. Justice Felix Frankfurter invoked the then-conventional rationale of judicial self-restraint.[2] National unity and respect for national tradition, he reasoned, are permissible goals of State policy. The compulsory flag salute could *not* be said to be an irrational means of seeking to secure loyalty to those traditional ideals, even though the Court might be convinced that a deeper patriotism would be engendered by refraining from coercing a symbolic gesture. The argument closely paralleled the dissenting opinion of Justice Holmes in the *Lochner* case.

The Court ultimately rejected this plea for consistent application of the philosophy of judicial self-restraint and sustained the claim of freedom to refuse to salute the flag. Justice Jackson explained that the Court owed deference to legislative judgments when legislation is attacked under the vague contours of the Due Process Clause but not when the Court is applying the "specific" provisions of the Bill of Rights. "We cannot, because of modest estimates of our competence in such specialties as public education, withhold the judgment that history authenticates as the function of this Court when liberty is infringed."[3]

Dispute continued, but ultimately the "preferred rights" thesis prevailed. During the following decade it became plain that when freedom of speech and political association were involved, the Court would make its own independent inquiry into the facts said to justify the restriction, and strike its own balance among competing values without deference to a State legislature.[4]

Strict review came next to prevail in the interpretation of the provisions of the Bill of Rights designed to protect the suspected or accused against abuses in law enforcement. The relevant guarantees, the Fourth, Fifth, Sixth, and Eighth Amendments, often afford persons suspected of crime much greater protection than State law. Previously, those guarantees had been applied only to federal cases. Gradually, in the postwar years, they were held to be incorporated into the Fourteenth Amendment and so extended to the courts and law enforcement activities of the States.[5] The School Desegregation Cases of 1954 rest upon extension of the "strict scrutiny" doctrine to the Equal Protection Clause when legislation imposing an "invidious" classification is attacked.[6] During the next two decades strict review and judicial activism expanded to still other areas, not without controversy and setbacks but even, in the Abortion Cases, to the vague contours of the Due Process Clause unaided by the Bill of Rights.[7]

The constitutional theories put forward to support active judicial intervention will require more detailed attention as we examine their development. It is enough for now to say that, at bottom, all the theories assert that the ultimate protection for minorities, for spiritual liberty, for freedom of expression and political activity, and for other personal liberties rightfully comes from the Judiciary. In this realm, the theories assert, the political process too often fails to represent insular minorities, is too filled with arbitrary compromises, and is too responsive, as in some degree it must be, to short-run pressures, and is therefore too often inadequate to enforce the long-range and enduring values that bespeak our true aspirations as a free people instead of reflecting our practical shortcomings. The Warren Court of 1953 to 1969 thus came to be influenced by a conscious sense of judicial responsibility for the open and egalitarian operation of the political system.

Much else in the intellectual and legal climate of the Warren era encouraged judicial activism. In the 1930s a modest view of the judicial function in constitutional interpretation fitted the desire for progressive social and economic reform. The Legislative and Executive Branches were then engaged in the redistribution of power and the protection of the disadvantaged and distressed. In the 1950s, because of the Cold War, increased crime, fear of social disorder, and perhaps entrenched economic and political power, the political process had become resistant to libertarian, humanitarian, and egalitarian impulses. Among those concerned for civil liberties, the multiplication and magnification of government activities and bureaucracy raised fears of disregard for fair procedure and individual justice. Humanitarianism, aided by the prevailing teaching of the psychological and social sciences, cast doubt on the sterner aspects of the criminal law. A wave of egalitarianism stirred by war against Hitler's theories of a master race and by the rise of the peoples of Asia and Africa gave support to the civil rights movement. The ideal of equality once loosed is not easily cabined. Egalitarianism became the hallmark of the Warren Court.

For a time the Court was the branch of government in which these impulses beat the strongest, perhaps by the chance that puts one individual rather than another upon the Court, perhaps because the Justices lived closer to the intellectual than to the political world. In the 1960s, the same impulses inspired dreams of Camelot and President Lyndon B. Johnson's thrust toward "the Great Society." Then the Court and much of the political world marched to the same tune.

At the same time that the Court's sense of responsibility for individuals and minorities was growing, losers in the political process were becoming more conscious of the potentials of constitutional adjudication for achieving goals not attainable through the political process, and they were also becoming better equipped to use them. Constitutional litigation came to be conducted more and more by civil rights and civil liberties organizations, by radical political associations, and later by law offices funded to stimulate community action and provide legal services to the poor.

Two other broad influences encouraged the use of judge-made constitutional law as an instrument of reform. Those born in the United States after 1900 would observe more, greater, and faster changes in science, technology, health, economic organization, and ways of thinking than all the preceding generations. In the midst of philosophical, scientific, technological, and economic revolutions, rapid changes in the law seemed natural, indeed inevitable.

The jurisprudence identified as "legal realism" encouraged the work of reform in the name of the Constitution. The great bulk of the Anglo-American law establishing the rights and duties of property owners, of parties to contracts, and of other persons (including corporations) whose activities impinge on each other is judge-made law built up slowly by centuries of court decisions and only seldom changed by legislation. Our constitutional law was built up in similar fashion, using the document itself as a base. In the late nineteenth century the prevailing tendency was to view the "law" as a static body of rules, the correct application of which could be discovered in any given situation by logical deduction from the body of reports of previous decisions. The legal realists poked fun at those who followed "the law up there," conceiving law to be "a brooding omnipresence in the sky." Their text, as we have noted, became Holmes's observation that "the life of the law has not been logic but experience." Law, he and they asserted, is made by human hands and reflects the judges' morals, policies, and prejudices. This view, when pressed to its logical extreme to the exclusion of other forces in decision making, frees the contemporary judge on a court of last resort to decide as he pleases, writing his own values and social policies into the law whenever he can win the assent of a majority of his colleagues. Law becomes "policy science"; the social good, not adherence to law, becomes the judge's obligation. Few judges accepted the extremes of legal realism. Many were deeply influenced.

Earl Warren, the fourteenth Chief Justice of the United States, not only led the Court but epitomized the spirit of constitutional law during the creative years 1953 to 1969. When he took his seat, his political career gave reason to hope that he would indeed understand and express in public law the long-range needs and aspirations of the American people. Raised in California at a time and place still near the frontier tradition yet Governor of the most rapidly growing of all forty-eight States, he knew the country and the city, the past and the future. Like the great Chief Justices Marshall and Hughes, Earl Warren had been shaped by intimate association with the political process. His politics were not easy to stereotype, unless in terms of Hiram Johnson and the Bull Moose tradition; but he was progressive and a little left of center. That too suggested that the Court's decisions, to the extent that he could influence them, would be in keeping with the idealistic yet pragmatic character of the American people.

Increasingly often during the next sixteen years lawyers at the bar found that arguments based on precedent, accepted legal doctrine, and long-range institutional concepts concerning the proper role of the Judiciary and the distribution of power in a federal system foundered on Chief Justice Warren's persistent questions "Is that fair?" and "Is that what America stands for?" Such questions were profoundly disturbing to those engrossed by the intellectual and institutional side of the law, its history, and sheer professional expertise. No one could successfully argue in simple elemental terms that a poor man charged with crime should not have as much chance to have a lawyer at the preliminary hearing as one who was rich, or that cows and trees should have as much voting power as people. If accepted legal doctrines and institutional concepts called for a different conclusion, was not the fault in the legal and intellectual stratum and in the indifference, blindness, and compromises it reflected rather than in the basic ideal? What the Chief Justice was saying of the legal system parallels the message of the university student of the 1960s explaining his generation with simple honesty: "*We* take seriously the ideals we were taught at home and in Sunday school."

Under the impact of the above forces, constitutional adjudication during the Warren era became an instrument of reform. A judge who believes in progress and in special judicial responsibility for values and groups not adequately represented in the political process will find it natural, if not obligatory, to require the revision of old laws and settled government practices inconsistent with what he sees as national ideals. As a result, where the old activist decisions prior to 1937 merely blocked legislative initiatives in order to maintain the status quo, the decisions of the 1950s and 1960s, discussed below, were to force major changes in the established legal and social order. The constitutional protection for speech and press was vastly expanded. So were procedural safeguards for those accused of crime. The School Desegregation Cases would overturn not only the constitutional precedents built up over three quarters of a century following the Civil War but also the social structure of an entire region. The "one person, one vote" decisions would rule, in effect, that the composition of the legislatures of all but one or two of the fifty states was unconstitutional and had been unconstitutional for fifty or a hundred years. The School Prayer Cases would brand "unconstitutional" a ceremony observed daily by generations of students in the public schools. Not only would the Court initiate changes in the social and political order affecting millions of people in the manner of legislation, but without their votes; the Court's judgments would also, for the first time, mandate affirmative measures often requiring years of judicial planning and oversight, as illustrated by Court-ordered school desegregation.

The use of constitutional adjudication as an instrument of reform made ours a freer, more equal, and more humane society. The strides were long because there was far to go. The creativity was severely criticized by segments of the legal profession even as the decisions were rendered: first, because the Court was sweeping aside established law in order to do good according to its views of policy; second, because the Court was making decisions properly left to Congress, State legislatures, or the people. Segments of the public were aroused by a number of the changes, such as school desegregation, the outlawing of school prayers, and the legalization of abortion. The reforms and reaction, as we shall see, tended to politicize both the law and the courts, and so, to some extent, to impair their legitimacy. We must face the question whether the price paid was too high, but only after looking more closely at the course of development.

· 11 ·

The Nonconformists

Congress shall make no law respecting an establishment of religion, or prohibiting the free exercise thereof; or abridging the freedom of speech, or of the press, or the right of the people peaceably to assemble, and to petition the government for a redress of grievances.

So READS the first Article of Amendment to the United States Constitution—the first in the Federal Bill of Rights. The numerical position is symbolic. Freedom of conscience and expression enjoy primacy in our scale of rights. Yet the words alone cannot convey the true meaning, either the full scope or the limits of the rights. Even as a matter of language there is little merit to Justice Hugo L. Black's insistence that the plain meaning of the words "no law" bars the government from putting any restriction on what may be printed or said. The prohibition is against any law abridging "the freedom of speech, or of the press." History makes it plain that "*the* freedom" was never supposed to include an absolute license to utter *any* words and to publish *any* ideas or information without civil liability for wrongs such as libel or criminal responsibility for offenses such as blasphemy. The words expressed concepts summarizing a philosophy, and thus an aspiration, drawn from experience. Present-day interpretation draws on that philosophy shaped and expanded by new experience and reflection.

The juxtaposition of the key phrases tells a good deal about the chief strains in that philosophy. The Framers put first the prohibition against any law "respecting an establishment of religion, or prohibiting the free exercise thereof." To those guarantees of spiritual liberty they next linked their indispensable prerequisite, "freedom of speech, or of the press." Then, on the far side of the freedoms of expression one finds the political rights of free assembly and free petition for redress of grievances. The progression recalls that the constitutional guarantees of freedom of speech and of the press are also indispensable to self-government. Both aspects of the guarantees seem rooted in a single source. Both the concern for spiritual liberty and the commitment to self-government rest on faith in the potential flowering of the human spirit in a society where the individual is accorded both dignity and the power and responsibility of choice.

It is hardly surprising that the Framers thought first of religious liberty. The American colonists were well acquainted with the costs of religious intolerance. Many of them or their parents or grandparents had fled here to escape religious persecution. As a group they belonged to different churches and held diverse beliefs, yet the range was narrow. Most of them were Protestants. Virtually all of them were Christians. Some were exceedingly intolerant of all but their own orthodoxy. Views concerning the proper relationship between Church and State varied over a wider range. At the time of the Revolution there were established churches in nine States. There were also strong advocates of separation; some because they feared the corruption of the church by dependence upon civil government, others because they feared the hold of the clergy upon the minds and purses of the people.

The movement for rigid separation of Church and State was strongest in Virginia. During the 1780s Virginia was torn by a battle over the proposed revival of the ancient system of tithing. Seeking chiefly to benefit the dominant Anglican Church, the leadership in the Assembly had introduced a bill to levy a small tax for the support of the clergy, giving each taxpayer the privilege of assigning his payment to whatever church he might choose. Thomas Jefferson, the child of the rationalist Enlightenment and its father in America, and James Madison, who would later write the First Amendment, led the opposition. Madison's *Memorial Remonstrance Against Religious Assessments*[1] declared the tax a violation of religious liberty: "That same authority which can force a citizen to contribute three pence only of his property for the support of any one establishment, may force him to conform to any other establishment in all cases whatsoever."[2] The *Remonstrance* also sounded an anticlerical note. What have been the fruits, it asked, of the almost fifteen centuries that the legal establishment of Christianity has been on trial? "More or less in all places, pride and indolence in the clergy, ignorance and servility in the laity; in both superstition, bigotry and persecution."[3] The tax was defeated late in 1785. In 1786, the Virginia Assembly enacted Jefferson's Bill for Establishing Religious Freedom. In 1789 James Madison would be the leading figure in writing the First Amendment. Thomas Jefferson, as President, would later stamp anticlerical overtones on Roger Williams's metaphor:

> I contemplate with solemn reverence that act of the whole American people which declared that their legislature should 'make no law respecting an establishment of religion or prohibiting the free exercise thereof,' thus building a wall of separation between church and state.[4]

The First Amendment is addressed only to Congress. No one then supposed that its restrictions would be applied to the States as they apply today because of the long-subsequent adoption of the Fourteenth Amendment. The Founding Fathers knew that, given the variety of beliefs and practices prevailing in the thirteen States, the coherence of the new federal union could be fixed only if the federal government were required not only to respect the free exercise of religion in States where that freedom prevailed, but also to avoid involvement with religion. The men of South Carolina with their State-established religion and of Massachusetts with religion appurtenant to their government could therefore stand shoulder to shoulder with the deist Thomas Jefferson and other eighteenth-century rationalists in support of a federal prohibition *against any federal establishment* of religion. Most were content to leave any questions concerning the intrusion of a State government into religion to be resolved by the people and laws of that State.

History made it natural for the authors of the amendment to move from freedom of religious belief and worship to "the freedom of speech, or of the press." The one church was breaking up in late-sixteenth- and seventeenth-century Britain. New faiths were emerging, based upon individual study of the Holy Word. The man or woman who has discovered the road to salvation has a need, even feels a duty, to bring the gospel to others. But the goal was not simply the freedom of the speaker. Liberty of expression was essential to all who wished to hear and read the word of God and thus to discover the road to salvation. Modern legal analysis recognizes the importance of the hearers' and readers' access to information and ideas in cases allowing them to bring suits challenging a government restriction on freedom of expression.[5]

Concern for a broader spiritual liberty expanded from the religious core. The thinking man or woman, the man or woman of feeling, the novelist, the poet or dramatist, the artist, like the evangelist, can experience no greater affront to his or her humanity than denial of freedom of expression. The hearer and reader suffer like violation of their spiritual liberty if they are denied access to the ideas of others. The denial thwarts the development of the human potential, the power and responsibility of choice. Although concerned chiefly with religion, John Milton stated the broader concern in his *Areopagitica* (1644), the single most influential plea known to the Framers for unlicensed access to the printing press.

The Enlightenment gave the argument a broader, more rationalistic flavor. Thomas Jefferson and other Founding Fathers who were children of the Enlightenment believed above all else in the power of reason, in the search for truth, in progress and the ultimate perfectibility of man. Freedom of inquiry and liberty of expression were deemed essential to the discovery and spread of truth. Only by endless testing in debate could error be exposed, truth emerge, and men enjoy the opportunities for human progress.

Today, perhaps the compleat liberal would speak only of the ability to progress *toward* truth, and of the value of the process of searching. The compleat liberal posits that he has not reached, and probably can never reach, the ultimate truth. He hopes by constant search—by constant open debate, by trial and error—to do a little better. Meanwhile, he supposes that the process of searching has inestimable value because the lessons of the search—the readiness to learn, the striving to understand the minds and hearts and needs of other men, and the effort to weigh their interests with his own— exemplify the only foundation upon which men can live and grow together.

Despite the eloquence of John Milton and the leaders of the

Enlightenment and despite our own awareness of the many pieces of nonsense formerly accepted as incontrovertible truth, most of us reject the notion that the only test of truth is the ability of an idea to get itself accepted in free competition. Some propositions seem true or false beyond rational debate. The falsity of Hitler's brutal theory of a master race is sufficient example. Some falsities may do inestimable harm before truth prevails. Both we and government must tolerate such foolish and sometimes dangerous appeals not because they may prove true—although some may—but because the freedom of speech is indivisible. The liberty cannot be denied to some persons and extended to others. It cannot be denied to some ideas and saved for others. The reason is plain enough: no man, no committee, and surely no government has the infinite wisdom and disinterestedness accurately and unselfishly to separate what is true from what is debatable, and both from what is false. To license one to impose his truth on dissenters is to give the same license to all others who have, but fear the loss of, power. The risk that harm will occur from the dissemination of false ideas is a lesser danger than the risk that truth will be suppressed by the censor's power.

II

Few of us will ever have occasion to invoke the First Amendment, unless we are reporters, editors, or publishers. Our religious beliefs and practices are so conventional that laws take account of them and elected officials respect them. Our politics are also unlikely to bring us into collision with authority. Generally speaking, it is the "far-out" groups, the unorthodox and dissentient in the worlds of the intellect and the spirit, or of government and policy, who need the protection of the guarantees of religious liberty and the freedom of speech and press. We who live in the mainstream are protected against the imposition of ever-more rigid political and religious orthodoxies because of the protection accorded to them.

Even the unorthodox ordinarily have little need to invoke the First Amendment's guarantees of freedom of expression. Americans have always been an extraordinarily tolerant people, respectful of one another's liberties. Much of the time, in most circles, the First Amendment is useful chiefly as a precept stating our common ideals. But just as officials, in the absence of constitutional guarantees, are tempted to suppress political criticism, so do fierce spasms of intolerant repression sometimes break out against religious and political groups which challenge the established order or otherwise affront right-minded people. The intolerant then use government to silence the nonconformists or otherwise suppress them. The First Amendment is our check upon our aberrations.

The treatment of Eugene Debs and of other "radicals" in the wave of repression during and after World War I is one example.[6] A century earlier the Abolitionist Elijah P. Lovejoy had been driven out of St. Louis to Alton, Illinois, where his printing presses were destroyed again and yet again until the riot in which Lovejoy was shot. Similarly, even though the prevailing spirit of tolerance facilitated the growth of diverse religious sects, the militantly unorthodox sometimes faced persecution. The Mormon Church of the Latter-Day Saints was driven from Independence, Missouri, to Carthage, Illinois, and then to Navoo, Illinois, where the members built a prosperous community, only to watch mobs destroy their town and force them on the long trek to the Utah deserts.

The principal victims of religious persecution in the United States in the twentieth century were the Jehovah's Witnesses. Although founded earlier, they began to attract attention and provoke repression in the 1930s, when their proselytizing and numbers rapidly increased. Drawing on Divine revelation from the Bible, they stood on street corners and canvassed from house to house, offering the tracts of the Watchtower Bible and Tract Society and preaching that the evil triumvirate of organized churches, business, and the State are the instruments of Satan. They seldom hesitated to seek attention from passersby or householders. Their attacks on the Roman Catholic Church were especially vehement:

> All organizations on the earth that are in opposition to God and his kingdom, therefore, necessarily take the name of "Babylon" and "harlot," and those names specifically apply to the leading religious organization, the Roman Catholic church, which claims to be the mother of the so-called Christian religion. That mighty religious organization, foretold in the Scriptures, uses the method of harlots to induce politicians and commercial traffickers and others to fall into her arms and yield to her supposed charms.[7]

Resentment, persecution, and prosecution attached themselves to the Jehovah's Witnesses partly because of the vehemence of their religious attacks on the established order and partly because of the militancy of their proselytizing. Between 1935 and 1945 their attorneys carried fifty cases to the Supreme Court of the United States and won thirty-two. Their willingness to use the courts and Constitution to defend their ways profoundly influenced judicial interpretation of the guarantee of freedom of speech at a critical point in the history of the First and Fourteenth Amendments.

The First Amendment, as we have seen, was directed only to the federal government. The Fourteenth Amendment is addressed to the States, but its majestic generalities forbidding a State to "abridge the privileges or immunities of citizens of the United States" or to "deprive any person of life, liberty or property without due process of law" do not refer specifically to religious liberty or freedom of expression. As late as 1925 the Supreme Court declared that "neither the Fourteenth Amendment nor any other provision of the Constitution of the United States imposes upon the States any restriction about 'freedom of speech.'"[8] Within the next decade it became settled law that the Fourteenth Amendment "incorporates" the First Amendment's guarantees of freedom of speech and thus makes them as applicable to the States as to the federal government. The rule seems in full accordance with what we know about the intent of those who proposed and ratified the Fourteenth Amendment. Plainly, they intended to provide, for the first time, national (that is, federal) constitutional protection against State infringements of individual liberty. Very probably, they also believed, as the Supreme Court quickly held, that the "liberty" protected included individual liberties beyond freedom from confinement. The task of particularizing these two general purposes was left to Congress and the courts. Given the common ancestry and high rank of the freedoms of speech and religion in our inherited hierarchy of values, it seems obvious that anyone who intended to prevent unwarranted State interference with an individual liberty broader than freedom from confinement would, if he thought about particulars, include the freedom of speech and the free exercise of religion.

The long delay in applying the First Amendment to State laws arguably abridging freedom of expression meant that the initial rulings would come when social ferment was strong and the liberal spirit was ascendant in the Court.

Nonconformists seeking to disturb the established order have little access to the conventional channels of effective expression.

For them the best vehicles of expression are the streets and public parks, house-to-house canvassing, picketing, marches, the sound truck, and public demonstrations. Communities that sought to deny unpopular groups access to such forums were plainly told that such exclusion violates the First and Fourteenth Amendments:

> Such use of the streets and public places has, from ancient times, been a part of the privileges, immunities, rights and liberties of citizens. The privilege . . . to use the streets and parks for communication of views on national questions may be regulated in the interest of all . . . but must not in the guise of regulation be abridged or denied.[9]

Another decision invalidated on this ground four city ordinances banning the use of the streets to hand out leaflets.[10] Against that background later Justices would wrestle with the constitutional problems raised by restrictions on the use of other government properties for the purpose of expression.[11] Still another appeal by a Jehovah's Witness led to a ruling that the First Amendment secured the Witnesses' right to engage in house-to-house canvassing.[12] Probably the rule extends to political canvassing but not to salesmen.[13] These decisions were to be of inestimable value to the civil rights movement.

The civil rights movement, labor unions, and other protestors against the established order would also benefit from the Jehovah's Witnesses' challenges to laws that vest wide discretion in local authorities to maintain the peace and public order. Local ordinances often forbade speaking or distributing literature without a license, and gave municipal officials untrammeled discretion to determine whom to license. Such laws had long been used to suppress the unorthodox. When Witness Lovell was convicted of violating such an ordinance in Griffin, Georgia, the Court set the conviction aside, holding that a law requiring a license for the use of the streets or parks for the distribution of leaflets, speeches, parades, or other forms of expression violates the First Amendment unless it confines the licensing authority to considerations of traffic management, crowd control, or other physical inconvenience or menace to the public.[14]

Statutes and ordinances punishing ill-defined crimes such as "breach of the peace" also lend themselves to discrimination against "troublemakers" if extended to words or street demonstrations free from physical violence. When Witness Cantwell was convicted of the ill-defined crime of breach of the peace on proof that he played upon the public streets a gramophone record attacking all organized religions, especially the Roman Catholic Church, in opprobrious words offensive to believers, the Court reversed the conviction because of the danger that Cantwell's arrest and conviction were based on his unorthodox preaching rather than on a fair and narrow judgment of the risk that he would provoke immediate violence.[15] Again, other groups, labor unions, civil rights demonstrators, and opponents of the war in Vietnam were to benefit from the precedent.[16]

III

The most famous of the legal battles fought by the Jehovah's Witnesses raised a question at the very heart of the First Amendment. On October 6, 1935, Judge Joseph F. Rutherford, the leader who revitalized the sect, declared that to engage in a pledge of allegiance or to salute the flag of the United States violates the Second Commandment:

> Thou shalt have no other gods before Me. Thou shalt not make unto thee a graven image, nor any manner of likeness of any thing that is in heaven above or that is in the earth beneath, or that is in the water under the earth; thou shalt not bow down unto them, nor serve them. . . .

Witnesses everywhere in the United States embraced their leader's interpretation of the biblical revelation.

Walter Gobitis and his wife, solid citizens in the little Pennsylvania town of Minersville, were Jehovah's Witnesses. Minersville lies in a depressed coal-mining valley in the mountains, the sort of community in which fundamentalist apocalyptic sects have special appeal; but in this instance most of the residents were Irish Roman Catholics. The superintendent of schools was outraged when the Gobitis children, Lillian and William, refused to join in the customary salute to the flag. The school board promptly adopted a regulation making the salute mandatory for both teachers and students and declaring refusal to be punishable as insubordination. On the day the resolution was adopted, Lillian, William, and a third student, Edmund Wasliewski, were expelled.

For a time the Gobitis children were sent thirty miles to a private school established for children who had been expelled from public schools because of the same act of conscience. The expense proved too great. A suit was brought and carried to the U.S. Supreme Court, charging that the school board was depriving the Gobitis family of rights secured by the Constitution. Judge Rutherford himself took charge of the Witnesses' argument. The conflict, he said, was "the arbitrary totalitarian rule of the State versus full devotion and obedience to the theocratic government or Kingdom of Jehovah God under Jesus Christ his anointed King."[17]

On June 3, 1940, the Court by an 8–1 vote rejected the Jehovah's Witnesses' contention. Religious convictions, the Court declared, do not relieve the individual from compliance with an otherwise valid general regulation of conduct not aimed at the promotion or restriction of religious beliefs. Here the Court could draw for precedent on the decisions sustaining the punishment of Mormons for polygamy.[18] The Constitution does not bar a State legislature or school authorities, the Court concluded, from selecting an appropriate means "to evoke that unifying sentiment without which there can ultimately be no liberties, civil or religious."[19] For Justice Frankfurter, who wrote the opinion of the Court, the need for national unity was overwhelming. Europe was crumbling before Hitler and his storm troopers, the oppressors of Jews and the totalitarian exponents of a master race. Western civilization could be saved only by the active support of the United States.

The sole dissenter was Justice Harlan Fiske Stone. Justice Stone sprang from simple Yankee stock with a conscience strong as the granite of his native New Hampshire. Professor and Dean of the Columbia Law School, a successful practitioner in New York, and Attorney General of the United States when he was named to the Court, he had become a man of wide experience and cultivated tastes. Yet his rugged nature always found both strength and the greatest summer pleasure rowing a dory off the rocky shores of Isle au Haut, Maine. Conservative by nature not only in economics but in judicial philosophy, Justice Stone had regularly joined Justices Holmes and Brandeis in dissenting opinions criticizing the Court for invalidating State and federal laws regulating property and business practices. When Justice Frankfurter learned that Justice Stone planned to dissent in the Flag Salute Case, he wrote him a long personal letter, invoking the principle of judicial self-restraint that Justice Stone had so often endorsed. Justice Stone's reply drew a fundamental issue concerning the Court's role in constitutional interpretation:

> I must distinguish between a vulgar intrusion of law in the domain of conscience and legislation dealing with the control of property. The Court's responsibility is the larger in the domain of conscience.[20]

Justice Frankfurter's opinion for the Court emphasized the duty of judicial deference to democratic judgments. National amity and respect for national traditions, he reasoned, are at the very least permissible goals of legislative action. The compulsory flag salute could not be said to be an irrational means of seeking to secure loyalty to those ideals. To reject the legislative conclusion "would amount to no less than the pronouncement of pedagogical and psychological dogma in a field where courts possess no marked and certainly no controlling competence. . . . To the legislature no less than to courts is committed the guardianship of deeply cherished liberties. . . . Where all the effective means of inducing political changes are left free from interference, education in the abandonment of foolish legislation is itself a training in liberty."[21] Not even Justices Hugo Black and William O. Douglas, reputedly the Court's strongest libertarians, were moved by Justice Stone's reply that this "seems to me to mean no less than the surrender of the constitutional protection of the liberty of small minorities to popular will."[22]

After the *Gobitis* decision, persecution of the Witnesses increased. In some quarters, notably Texas, Witnesses were attacked by mobs for their refusal to salute the flag, and they were sometimes held as "Nazi agents." In Kennebunk, Maine, Witnesses surrounded in the local Kingdom Hall opened fire on the mob stoning them, injuring several people. The hall was burned. The Governor called in the National Guard to restore order. Violence then intensified nationwide. The entire population of Litchfield, Illinois, turned out to attack some sixty Witnesses. The Witnesses were put in jail for their own safety. In Mississippi, a crowd led by the local American Legion descended on Witnesses assembled for a regional convention and drove them to the Louisiana border, where they were turned over to the Louisiana Legionnaires. The Witnesses were then passed from county to county, ending in Dallas, Texas. For the most part, the police stood idly by or actively participated.

By late summer the number of violent acts had diminished, although there were still cases of striking cruelty, including one instance of castration. Often, Witnesses were jailed on sight, "just in case." Witnesses also suffered economically: they were stricken from relief rolls and fired from their jobs.

Persecution could not quiet the Witnesses nor could expulsion from the schools induce their children to salute the flag. A new suit was instituted in West Virginia by the Barnette family. Before the case reached the Supreme Court three new Justices had ascended the Bench.

In the *Barnette* case[23] Justice Stone's philosophy of constitutional adjudication prevailed. The opinion of the Court, delivered by Justice Jackson, distinguished the cases in which the Due Process Clause of the Fourteenth Amendment is "applied for its own sake" from the cases in which it serves as an instrument for applying the First Amendment to a State and local government. He acknowledged that insofar as the Due Process Clause alone is concerned, a State may well be free to regulate conduct in any fashion for which there is a "rational basis." But freedoms of speech, press, assembly, and religion, he asserted, "are susceptible to restriction only to prevent grave and immediate danger to interests that the State may lawfully protect."[24] Determining whether there is a grave and immediate danger to interests the State may lawfully protect is the Court's responsibility:

> We cannot, because of modest estimates of our competence in such specialties as public education, withhold the judgment that history authenticates as the function of this Court when liberty is infringed.[25]

It is important to examine the rationale and implications of this ruling before resuming the story of the second Flag Salute Case. Justice Jackson's opinion marks the Court's first clear-cut commitment to strict review of legislation challenged under the First Amendment, either directly or as incorporated into the Fourteenth Amendment. A regulation of property or economic conduct of business is vulnerable to constitutional attack only if it can be shown to bear no rational relation to any intelligible conception of the general welfare. A law suppressing or punishing the expression of particular information or ideas of possible public concern, on the other hand, will be held unconstitutional only in the rare case in which the government can satisfy the Court that the utterance will give rise to "clear and present danger" of a major evil.[26] A law curtailing opportunities for freedom of speech or association, or other personal liberties, will be sustained only if the government can prove that the limitation is necessary to protect some important public interest not to be secured by less restrictive means.[27] In the latter instances, unlike the first, the Court rarely defers to the judgment of the policymaking branches on the wisdom or need of the measure or even on underlying questions of fact.

Why should the approach be different?

In the second Flag Salute Case, Justice Jackson answered that the deference that courts owe to legislative judgments in applying the Due Process Clause alone is inappropriate when the First Amendment is involved, because "[m]uch of the vagueness of the Due Process Clause disappears when the specific prohibitions of the First became the standard."[28] The difference in specificity is considerable, but its relevance is less obvious. Justice Black stood almost alone in the supposition that the language of the First Amendment could be read literally. The outright suppression of particular ideas is rare. More often, the restriction pertains to time or place or medium of expression, or to an obstacle erected to the gathering or dissemination of information, or to a cost attached to it. In such cases the public purpose served by the constraint must be weighed against the cost in freedom of expression, and the balance depends upon a judgment on a mixture of facts and competing values. For example, when the press claims that the First Amendment gives reporters a constitutional right to refuse to disclose their sources, one must ask how real are the fears of the press that sources of information will dry up if the courts continue to treat reporters like other citizens with information needed in the administration of justice, and if some sources will dry up, whether the losses are justified by the gains of obtaining testimony necessary to the administration of justice.[29] The relative specificity of the First Amendment does not explain why the Justices should resolve such factual issues in First Amendment cases while deferring when property is at stake.

In the most famous footnote in constitutional history, written before the Flag Salute decision, Justice Stone had suggested that a law which distorts the workings of representative government is subject to stricter than usual judicial review because such a law is less open than others to political correction.[30] The Court may step in, he proposed, when necessary to implement the postulate that our political government is open and fairly representative. The explanation justifies some instances of strict scrutiny but not many others. The malapportionment of State legislatures so distorts the political process as to prevent political correction of the evil. Some restrictions on speech or association diminish the usefulness of political remedies, but more often the restrictions are challenged by a press that does not lack opportunity for public hearing. The First Amendment applies, moreover, to literature, entertainment, and the arts with the same force as to political speech. Restrictions in those areas have scant relation to the openness or representativeness of the political process. Justice Stone's rationale seems only partial.

Sometimes a second explanation is put forward. Personal rights are said to be entitled to greater protection than property rights. But the truth of the *ipse dixit* is not self-evident. There is also force to Judge Learned Hand's question "Will someone please tell me why the enjoyment of property is not a personal right?"

In the final analysis the justification for treating First Amendment liberties as "preferred rights" calling for strict judicial scrutiny of any governmental limitation must be found in value judgments distilled from our entire constitutional history, rather than in inferences drawn exclusively from the language or structure of the Constitution. But the document is part of that history. The Framers were seeking to put "natural rights" beyond the reach of government. The specific mention of the freedoms of speech, press, assembly, and religion in the First Amendment shows that the Framers assigned them high value, and probably intended thereby to provide judicial protection against executive or legislative oppression. During the debate in the First Congress, which proposed the Bill of Rights for ratification by the States, James Madison explained:

> If they [the Amendments] are incorporated into the Constitution, independent tribunals of justice will consider themselves in a peculiar manner the guardian of those rights; they will be an impenetrable bulwark against every assumption of power in the Legislative or the Executive.[31]

In the second Flag Salute Case, rejection of the philosophy of judicial self-restraint brought the Court face to face with the substantive question whether the gains in teaching loyalty to the United States and its ideals symbolized by the flag justified the State's requiring all schoolchildren to participate in the flag salute. The majority's answer was unequivocal:

> If there is any fixed star in our constitutional constellation, it is that no official, high or petty, can prescribe what shall be orthodox in politics, nationalism, religion, or other matters of opinion or force citizens to confess by word or act their faith therein.[32]

No other decision recognizes so clearly that the First Amendment protects not only liberty of expression but the freedom of the spirit that leads to expression and that speakers seek to reach.

IV

The offense to the Gobitas and Barnette children was State compulsion to proclaim a political orthodoxy that they did not believe. It was the forced recital that violated the First Amendment. Pennsylvania and West Virginia public school teachers were left free by the *Barnette* decision to lead children in pledging allegiance to the flag. Presumably teachers may also give instruction in the reasons for and values of loyalty to the United States. Thus far the First Amendment has not been applied to restrict nonreligious speech by government officials. But the public school teacher who leads the willing members of a class in the pledge of allegiance may no longer follow the once-settled practice of moving on to lead the class in the recital of a simple ecumenical prayer, even though students who are unwilling to participate are permitted to leave the room. The pledge of allegiance is a secular ceremony. Prayer and readings from the Bible are religious. Hence, the public school teacher's sponsorship of prayer or Bible readings is held to violate the First Amendment's command that "Congress shall make no law respecting an establishment of religion," as applied through the Fourteenth Amendment to the States. The decisions are widely known, but the intense controversy that remains invites a look at their origins, merits, and effect on the Court.

History set the stage for modern controversy over the Establishment Clause, both generally and as applied to school prayers. The very limited role of the federal government in domestic affairs prior to the present century provided little occasion for Congress to enact laws affecting religion, except on such peripheral subjects as appropriations for the Indian tribes. Because the First Amendment applied only to Congress, the States were free to deal with religion as their people wished, even to maintain established churches. The decisions incorporating the First Amendment into the Fourteenth began in the 1920s. Until then and for another two decades the Establishment Clause played little visible part in American life.

Meanwhile, even though the established State churches were disestablished by local action prior to 1830, almost everywhere strands of religious thought, ceremony, and practice continued to run through the law and conduct of governmental activity of both the States and local subdivisions. Church property was usually tax-exempt. Stores were required to close on Sundays. Christmas and Thanksgiving were holidays. State legislatures began each day's session with a prayer. Other examples will quickly come to mind. Justice Douglas was recording a fact when he observed, in a 1952 opinion of the Court, "We are a religious people whose institutions presuppose a Supreme Being."[33]

Even in its application to the federal government, the First Amendment was seldom taken to raise as high and impervious a wall as Thomas Jefferson and James Madison would have built between Church and State. The First and succeeding Congresses opened each day's session with a Christian prayer. The Crier in the Supreme Court still intones, "God save the United States and this honorable Court." The Congress that recommended the First Amendment for ratification by the States adopted, over the protests of some members, a joint resolution to set aside "a day of public Thanksgiving and prayer, to be observed by acknowledging with grateful hearts the many and signal favors of an Almighty God."[34] President George Washington responded with a proclamation calling for "the people of these States" to devote the day "to the services of that great and glorious Being who is the beneficent author of all the good that was, that is, or that will be."[35] The two leading nineteenth-century commentators on the Constitution agreed that, although the First Amendment barred setting up a national ecclesiastical establishment with the exclusive patronage of the federal government and outlawed other forms of favoritism among the Christian sects, it did not bar all favorable treatment of Christianity, which "ought to receive encouragement from the State so far as was not incompatible with the private rights of conscience and the freedom of religious worship."[36] There was never total separation between Church and State.

In this context the practice of beginning the schoolday with religious exercises easily became ingrained in American life: perhaps a reading from the Bible, a prayer, and even a hymn. In New York State, the practice dated back to 1839. In 1951 the New York State Board of Regents drew up a simple prayer that it suggested might well be recited each day as an "act of reverence to God" immediately after the flag salute. The prayer read:

> Almighty God, we acknowledge our dependence upon Thee, and we beg Thy blessings upon us, our parents, our teachers and our Country.

Controversy arose when the Board of Education of the Town of North Hempstead directed the daily recital of the regents' prayer in the North Hempstead public schools. A few parents objected. The board persisted. Apparently, it allowed students to leave the room while the prayer was recited. Admittedly, students were under no compulsion to join in the ceremony. Five parents and taxpayers brought and later carried to the U.S. Supreme Court a suit to halt the practice, alleging that daily use of the prayer "does not protect the rights of nonbelievers or the religious scruples of all of the believers." The plaintiffs included a nonbeliever and also members of the Jewish faith, of the Society for Ethical Culture, and of the Unitarian Church.

The U.S. Supreme Court sustained plaintiffs' claim and entered an order barring continued recital of the regents' prayer in the North Hempstead schools.[37] The opinion declared that whatever the precise contours of the Establishment Clause, "it must at least mean that it is no part of the business of government to compose official prayers for any group of the American people to recite as a part of a religious program carried on by government."[38]

A year later the Court extended the condemnation. A Pennsylvania statute prescribed:

> At least ten verses from the Holy Bible shall be read, without comment, at the opening of each public school on each school day. Any child shall be excused from such Bible reading, or attending such Bible reading, upon written request of his parent or guardian.

In the Abington School District the reading was followed by recital of the Lord's Prayer. Students stood during the ceremony. The Schempps, a family of churchgoing Unitarians, protested the practice, asserting that many of the verses read offended their

religious convictions and violated the constitutional principles requiring the separation of Church and State. Ellory, the oldest child,
manifested his displeasure by reading to himself a copy of the
Koran during the readings from the Bible and by refusing to stand
during the recitation of the Lord's Prayer. Had he wished, he could
have been excused from the room. It is often the odd zealots
seeking to make an issue who best defend the rights of others who
would suffer in silence, even though equally aggrieved. The
Schempps brought suit to enjoin the school authorities from continuing the Bible reading. When the case reached the Supreme
Court, the Court held, 8–1, that in the public schools the ceremony
of regularly reading from the Bible at the start of the day violates
the Establishment Clause as incorporated into the Fourteenth
Amendment.[39]

The decisions shocked many people and surprised many more.
Because they had lived with the ceremony under the Constitution
for many years, most members of most communities all across the
United States took it for granted that the ceremony was constitutional. Resentment, noncompliance, and even resistance still survive. Fundamentalist groups with the support of President Reagan
are intensifying pressure for reversal of the decisions by one or
another means.

The extent of the general shock and surprise was brought home
to me on the afternoon of the June Monday on which one of the
decisions was handed down. I was then Solicitor General of the
United States. As the government's chief lawyer in the Supreme
Court, I followed its proceedings closely, but the United States had
taken no part in that controversy or others under the Establishment
Clause. That summer the student summer interns in Washington
gathered in Constitution Hall on Monday afternoons to hear distinguished figures speak and answer questions. That particular Monday Justice Douglas was scheduled to speak, but he wished to
hurry back to his summer home and therefore asked me to stay
and answer the questions for him. A Solicitor General does not
easily refuse a Supreme Court Justice. The first question concerned
the School Prayer Case. I had never thought much about the issue,
but the decision surprised me. Like millions of children, I had
grown up taking it for granted that school for me and my friends
in other schools would always begin with opening exercises that
included Bible readings or prayer. When I said a few mild words

in defense of the decision, more out of loyalty to the Court and Justice Douglas than out of conviction, the boos lifted the roof off Constitution Hall.

Time and reflection have convinced me that, even though the opinion of the Court in the *Abington* case is not wholly convincing, the decision flows ineluctably from a true understanding of the original intent of the Framers of the First Amendment.

The *Abington* opinion, relying partly on precedents involving financial assistance to education in both secular and sectarian schools, treats the Bible reading as an impermissible State aid to religion. In the first important State case under the Establishment Clause, *Everson* v. *Board of Education,*[40] the question had been whether the Establishment Clause was violated by providing all schoolchildren with free passage to and from school on the public transit lines, regardless of whether they attended public or sectarian schools. Both majority and dissenting opinions rigidly asserted that the Establishment Clause writes into the Constitution Thomas Jefferson's wall of separation between Church and State, though there is scant reason to suppose that his view represented the dominant opinion of those who recommended and adopted the First Amendment. The four dissenting Justices relied on Madison's *Remonstrance* to show the philosophy embodied in the First Amendment as applied to the States. Justice Black, who wrote the opinion of the Court, joined four more conservative Justices in upholding the free public transportation because he perceived no relevant difference between that service and fire and police protection; but Justice Black also drew his law from the Virginians:

> Neither a state nor the Federal Government can set up a church. Neither can pass laws which aid one religion, aid all religions, or prefer one religion over another. . . . No tax in any amount, large or small, can be levied to support any religious activity or institutions, whatever they may be called, or whatever form they may adopt to teach or practice religion.[41]

In speaking of "aid" to religion, Justice Black and like-minded Justices referred not only to financial benefits, large or small, but to every other form of approval or assistance.

To apply that doctrine with full logical rigor would have required the courts to order both State and federal governments to cease giving effect to a wide variety of laws and practices that had been part of our national life for generations under both the original Constitution and the Fourteenth Amendment. Sunday closing laws would be unconstitutional, for example; also the ancient tax exemptions for church property. Logically, even the invocations of Divine blessing and other religious references running through familiar government activities could not survive such judicial scrutiny. Yet Thomas Jefferson was the only early President not to issue a Thanksgiving Day proclamation.

Other Justices, skeptical of their colleagues' reading of the original intent, slower to impose judicial rulings upon the people, and perhaps more attached to the past by personal disposition, have drawn back from the absolutism of *Everson*. They see each question as one of degree, reflecting the tension between the danger of intermixing Church and State and a proper respect for the predominantly religious character of the American people. In the view of the conservative Justices, which now predominates, the balance must be struck case by case. Sunday closing laws are constitutional.[42] Prayer at the start of the legislative day is constitutional,[43] but not teacher-led prayer in the public schools. Public school students may be excused from school to attend religious classes at other locations,[44] but teachers of religion may not be allowed to offer elective religious instruction in the public schools.[45] The State may lend approved textbooks to all schoolchildren, including children in sectarian schools,[46] but it may not supplement all teachers' salaries, including teachers in sectarian schools.[47] Church property may be excepted from the general real estate tax, along with the property of other charitable institutions.[48] Parents may be allowed to deduct tuition paid to sectarian schools in computing their State income tax.[49] But any direct grant to a church school, even as part of a general program of equal aid to all educational institutions, violates the First and Fourteenth Amendments.[50] In deciding specific cases of this character the Court is usually guided by a vague generalization known as the *Lemon*[51] test. To survive challenge under the Establishment Clause a statute or other government activity (1) must have a secular purpose, (2) must have a principal or primary effect that neither advances nor inhibits religion, and (3) must not foster an excessive government entanglement with religion.

In the *Abington* case the Court concluded that readings from the Bible at the start of the schoolday are religious exercises and therefore had neither the required secular purpose nor a primary effect that neither advances nor inhibits religion. The aid to religion seems unimportant until one focuses on the correlative effects on the children in the public schools. When religious exercises are conducted under the official auspices of their teachers, the spiritual freedom of the children, particularly of the dissentient children, is seriously invaded. The central purpose of the First Amendment— the one fixed star by which we can reckon—is to free the minds and spirits of individuals from governmental intrusion. Freedom to avow and spread the truths we have discovered and free access to the ideas and arguments of others are necessary aids to intellectual and spiritual freedom; but that freedom is the core. As the Court said in a passage quoted earlier in this chapter, explaining why requiring public school children to salute the flag violates the First Amendment,

> If there is any fixed star in our constitutional constellation, it is that no official, high or petty, can prescribe what shall be orthodox in politics, nationalism, religion, or other matters of opinion or force citizens to confess by word or act their faith therein.[52]

Public school teachers are the State no less than sheriffs and constables. For school authorities in the schoolroom to lead young pupils in prayer, however ecumenical, or in reading from any Holy Book, is inescapably to prescribe what is orthodox in opinion or belief, even though there is no compulsion to participate. The dissentient who remains silent, like the dissentient who leaves the room, is told, "You are unorthodox. The official view of religion is not your view. Our government is not equally your government." The fatal constitutional wrong, in short, is that the government is teaching its religion.

It is possible to argue that applying the principle of government neutrality so broadly goes beyond the original intent of the Framers of the Establishment Clause. The weight of the historical evidence probably supports the conclusion that for many years the principle of government neutrality was stated and applied only to prevent government from preferring one Christian sect over another Christian sect. Joseph Story, a Justice of the U.S. Supreme Court and Professor of Constitutional Law at the Harvard Law School, wrote that "[t]he real object of the Amendment was not to countenance, much less to advance, Mahometanism, or Judaism, or infidelity, by prostrating Christianity; but to exclude all rivalry among Christian sects."[53] Limiting his findings concerning the original intent to the surface of the statements and practices of the past, Justice William Rehnquist concludes that the "Establishment Clause did not require government neutrality between religion and irreligion."[54]

But the world has broadened, and the diversities of belief and nonbelief among the American people are many times greater than in the little Western world of the eighteenth and early nineteenth centuries. Today, we include many Jews, Buddhists, deists, members of the Ethical Culture Society and other humanistic groups, unbelievers, and disbelievers. All are members of the community. The Constitution is to be interpreted as a continuing charter setting forth basic principles viable in an ever-changing society, but that interpretation must also be guided largely by a wise understanding of the original intent. The key question concerning school prayer becomes whether the original Framers, if brought before us today, would tell us to be guided in today's America by Justice Story's exposition, or would say that underlying their particular manifestations and perhaps not fully appreciated by them because of the limits of their vision lay the broader principle that government should not promote *any* religious orthodoxy, belief or unbelief. This kind of question runs through constitutional interpretation, as we have seen in such diverse fields as interstate commerce and criminal procedure. In the instance of the Establishment Clause, the implications of the Framers' theme seem far broader to me than they do to Justice Rehnquist.

I find it impossible to believe that many of the men who wished to bar government from sponsoring any one set of Protestant tenets as orthodox in their little Christian society would not, given the circumstances of the modern world, actively disapprove government sponsorship of ecumenical Christianity in a society made up not only of Christians but of substantial numbers of Jews, Moslems, deists, and nonbelievers. Government sponsorship of even so broad an orthodoxy makes outcasts of the latter groups in the same fashion and in much the same degree as government sponsorship of the teachings of one Protestant sect would have made outcasts of the others in the earlier world. For this reason, the School Prayer decisions, though novel and reforming in application, seem to me to do little more than extend to new particulars the general principle of religious and ideological tolerance underlying narrower manifestations in the more homogeneous society of the past. That little more is justified, I think, by the Court's duty, even as it is faithful to the inherited body of law, to shape its statement to contemporary reality.

V

The question of school prayer came back before the Court in 1984–1985 because Alabama threw down the gauntlet. In Alabama criticism of the earlier School Prayer decisions was at its height. The Governor had urged disobedience. A statute enacted in 1978 directed teachers to announce at the first class each day that "a period of silence, not to exceed one minute in duration, shall be observed for meditation, and during such period silence shall be maintained." At least twenty-five States have similar laws permitting or requiring public school teachers to lead their students in a moment of silence designated either for meditation alone or, typically, for meditation, prayer, or reflection on the activities of the day. In 1982 the Alabama legislature amended the 1978 legislation by adding after the word "meditation" the words "or voluntary prayer." The acknowledged purpose was to express the State's endorsement of prayer at the start of the schoolday. In 1982 the legislature also enacted that any teacher, "recognizing that the Lord God is one . . . may pray, may lead willing students in the following prayer."

Ishmael Jaffree, the father of three little children in the Mobile public schools, brought suit challenging the constitutionality of the Alabama legislation. On appeal, the U.S. Supreme Court unanimously ruled that the 1982 statute authorizing a public school teacher to lead willing students in prayer violates the Establishment Clause as incorporated in the Fourteenth Amendment. The decision makes it plain that teacher-led prayer in the public schools will remain unconstitutional unless there is radical change in the composition of the Court.[55]

The Court also ruled, 6–3, that the Alabama statute authorizing meditation *or prayer* was unconstitutional, chiefly because the sponsors frankly acknowledged that their subjective purpose was to put the State's imprimatur on individual prayer. The wisdom of placing so much weight on the declared subjective intention of the legislative sponsors of the measure rather than on its actual consequences in the public schools seems open to serious question for reasons too detailed to canvass here. The Court's rationale also raises more questions than it answers concerning the constitutionality of other "moment of silence" statutes whose sponsors were more discreet. Obviously, the three dissenters in *Jaffree* would vote to uphold them.[56] Justices Lewis Powell and Sandra Day O'Connor indicated that they too would regard a "moment of silence" statute as constitutional in the absence of a proven purpose to promote prayer.[57] Even the opinion of the Court can be read to contain that implication. But the outcome seems less certain when one applies the prong of the *Lemon* test requiring a primarily secular effect. The primary effect among the children may well be simply a trivial moment of distraction that allows some adults to get excited about a political ploy and abstract constitutional debate. Surely, if the effects in the classroom are to be presumed to be serious, the resulting encouragement to nonreligious reflection cannot be greater than the encouragement to prayer.

The strongest argument for upholding a "moment of silence" statute may be that it permits the free exercise of religion by allowing the children to follow, if they wish, the ancient practice of commencing any serious and important undertaking by seeking the inner strength that flows from a prayer for Divine assistance. Justice Potter Stewart raised this point in the earlier cases;[58] but where teachers led or supervised the religious exercise, it was enough for the Court to answer that those who wished to pray went far beyond the exercise of their own individual liberty when they used the machinery and endorsement of the State's teachers, classrooms, and educational regime.[59]

Other laws having no purpose other than to allow voluntary performance of the dictates of religion have been held not to violate the Establishment Clause. *Zorach* v. *Clausen*[60] upheld a State statute calling for releasing public school pupils during the school week for a period in which they could go to their churches or parish houses for religious instruction. The Establishment Clause is not violated by opening the sessions of a legislative or executive body with prayer.[61] Familiar laws excuse religious objectors from military service, compulsory inoculation against disease, and carrying a license to operate a motor vehicle bearing the operator's picture. To say that making provision for the free exercise of religion is a "secular" purpose does some violence to the word. Justice O'Connor suggests obviating the difficulty by saying that the purpose is "secular" if the State is merely providing for the free exercise of religion rather than teaching or endorsing prayer. Her criterion seems sound, regardless of whether allowing adherence to the dictates of religion is incorporated within the definition of "secular" or is more candidly substituted in such cases under the *Lemon* test.

The second prong of the *Lemon* test directs the judge to inquire whether the principal or primary effect is one that neither advances nor inhibits religion. Again, we may infer from the precedents that such assistance as flows from allowing the voluntary individual performance of religious obligations is not enough State aid to offend the Establishment Clause. The function of the second prong is to allow the Court to make the inescapable judgments of degree required in cases in which the degree to which the church is using government to finance or otherwise accomplish religious ends must be balanced against the claims of free exercise, historic ceremony, or other secular purposes.

The outcome in any specific case should depend on the way in which the moment of silence is administered. In one school the teacher might introduce the moment of silence by saying, "We will now observe a moment of silence in which everyone may pray." This introduction, coming from a teacher who is a State official, would endorse prayer over other forms of silent reflection, whether thoughtful or trivial. Thus administered, the moment of silence would seem quite plainly to violate the Establishment Clause.

A friend tells me that the Massachusetts "moment of silence" statute has been administered quite differently on at least one occasion in one of the Cambridge public schools. When the students were assembled in their classrooms, announcements were piped from a central office. For example:

- School Bus 42 will leave this afternoon at 2:30 instead of 2:15.

  Students have been observed crossing Elm Street in the middle of the block. This dangerous practice must be stopped.

  We will now observe a moment of silence. . . .

  Tickets for Saturday's football game are available at the athletic office.

Such trivialization serves neither religious nor other purposes. If a suit challenging the practice were not laughed out of court, perhaps it should be treated as if the home room teacher had quietly said, "We will now observe a moment of silence before starting the day's work."

Another home room teacher might say to her junior high school pupils:

> Now we will observe a moment of silence for you to use as you wish. We observe it in order to give you an opportunity to reflect seriously about your life, your studies, and your relation to your fellows, including an opportunity to seek strength from your religion or from other sources inside or outside yourself as may seem best to you.

Neither the last teacher's introduction nor the bare announcement that a moment of silence will be observed teaches an orthodoxy or interferes with intellectual, spiritual, or religious thought or feeling to a degree approaching the effects of the prayers or readings from the Bible in the earlier cases. Yet it seems quite likely that, despite the silence, in strongly religious communities where the moment was treated seriously, the pupils in each grade whose religion or opposition to religion barred orthodox prayer would soon be marked and would then be subjected to some of the same kind of pressure resulting from the old teacher-led prayer.

This danger, coupled with what they see as aid to religion, may well lead Justices who read Jefferson's high wall of separation into the Establishment Clause to hold that all "moment of silence" legislation is unconstitutional. Currently, the majority of the Justices seem more pragmatic. In 1984 the Court held by a 5–4 vote that the City of Pawtucket, Rhode Island, did not violate the Establishment Clause by joining its downtown merchants in sponsoring a Christmas display that included a Nativity scene. The opinion of the Court took as its premise the proposition that

> [i]n every Establishment Clause case, we must reconcile the inescapable tension between the objective of preventing the unnecessary intrusion of either the State or the Church upon the other, and the reality that . . . total separation of the two is not possible.[62]

There the tension was between the degree of official sponsorship of orthodox Christianity implied by the city's participation and the purpose to assist all residents in the celebration of a holiday that had an historic religious origin but had assumed broader seasonal and ceremonial significance. In the "moment of silence" cases the value of accommodating the religious needs of those who wish to pray or humanistically reflect in silence without disturbing their classmates must be balanced against such slight aid to religion and pressure on dissenters as cannot be eliminated if prayer is allowed. It seems likely that the States will be left constitutionally free to decide that in such a case the values of free exercise should prevail.

As we leave the nonconformists, it is worth pausing for reflection. Why should we worry about the spiritual liberty of that tiny minority which refuses to salute the flag? Or about protecting the opportunities of troublemakers like the evangelical Jehovah's Witnesses, who go about attacking the established order, often in a manner offensive and even insulting to responsible citizens? Why should the overwhelming majority in a Christian community worry about the effect of teacher-led prayer on the children of an Ishmael Jaffree? Part of the answer lies in the premise of individual dignity on which our society rests, a dignity belonging to both orthodox and nonconformist. Part lies in the awareness that if the State may silence the speech of Jehovah's Witnesses or violate the spiritual freedom of the Ishmael Jaffrees, our own may be next. And part lies in the awareness that some far-out minority may hit upon the truth—a truth postponed or forever lost by its suppression. The Framers of the First Amendment lived much closer than we to the day when the Inquisition threatened Galileo with the rack and both lay and ecclesiastical rulers sought to control men's minds. They knew from then-recent human experience that rulers could not separate the true from the false, and that rulers who could suppress ideas were all too likely to suppress truths that threatened the rulers' power. Elijah Lovejoy and the early Abolitionists were widely perceived as unorthodox troublemakers. Martin Luther King, Jr., and other civil rights activists challenged the majority. Visionaries like the simple-hearted Gene Debs whose Socialist and pacifist speeches landed him in jail during World War I, as described in the next chapter, may never realize their dreams; but they stand for our liberty and nurture the American spirit.

· 12 ·

National Security and the First Amendment

ON THE NEAR SIDE of the First Amendment's guarantees of the freedom of speech and of press stand the two safeguards of religious liberty. On the far side, one finds the political rights of free assembly and free petition for redress of grievances. The progression recalls that the constitutional guarantees of freedom of speech and of the press have a political as well as an intellectual and spiritual significance. The link was noted in a letter sent by the Continental Congress to the inhabitants of Quebec three years before the Declaration of Independence:

> The last right we shall mention, regards the freedom of the press. The importance of this consists, besides the advancement of truth, science, morality, and arts in general, in its diffusion of liberal sentiments on the administration of Government, its ready communication of thoughts between subjects, and its consequential promotion of union among them, whereby oppressive officers are shamed or intimidated, into more honourable and just modes of conducting affairs.[1]

The opinions of the Supreme Court tend to emphasize the political foundations of the freedom of speech and of the press, perhaps because it is speech of a political nature that government most often seeks to restrict, and therefore the courts most often have occasion to defend.[2]

Alexander Meikeljohn, the foremost modern American philosopher of freedom of expression, was willing to concede that the scholar's freedom to pursue knowledge may be abridged because knowledge may bring irretrievable disaster to mankind, but with respect to speech on issues with which voters have to deal, his views were absolute. While viewing other constitutional guarantees as restrictions protecting the citizens against abuse of the powers delegated to government, Dr. Meikeljohn saw the guarantees of freedom of speech and of the press as measures adopted by the people as the ultimate rulers in order to retain control over government, the people's legislative and executive agents.[3] James Madison, the author of the First Amendment, expressed a similar thought when he wrote, "If we advert to the nature of Republican Government, we shall find that the censorial power is in the people over the Government, and not in the Government over the people."[4]

Only by uninhibited publication can the flow of information be secured and the people informed concerning men, measures, and the conduct of government. Only by freedom of expression can the people voice their grievances and obtain redress. Only by speech and the press can they exercise the power of criticism. Only by freedom of speech, of the press, and of association can people build and assert political power, including the power to change the men who govern them.

Few governments, whether authoritarian or democratic, welcome this kind of criticism. In Britain, at the time of the American Revolution, a too-persistent critic of the government risked prosecution for seditious libel—a false, scandalous, and malicious writing exciting the hatred of the people against the government. Whether the offense of seditious libel could survive in the United States under the First Amendment was uncertain. Blackstone, the best-known legal author of the late seventeenth century, taught that "the freedom of speech, or of the press" is only freedom from previous restraints on publication, such as licensing, and does not bar subsequent liability or punishment for unlawful words, including seditious libel. Dispute arose under President John Adams when Congress enacted a Sedition Act and the Federalist Party, then in office, prosecuted Jeffersonian Republican editors for publishing false, scandalous, and malicious writings exciting the hatred of the people. Thomas Jefferson and James Madison led the attack on the constitutionality of the Sedition Act by drafting resolutions, adopted by the Kentucky and Virginia legislatures, declaring the act to violate the First Amendment. The lower federal courts followed the orthodox teaching of Blackstone, upheld the act, and convicted the Republican editors. Jefferson pardoned them after his election to the Presidency. Still later, Congress appropriated funds to repay their fines. Events thus gave the Speech and Press Clauses an interpretation extending the guarantees beyond mere prohibition of previous restraints. Criminal prosecution for criticism of the government or its officials was consigned to the past.[5]

Civil suits to recover damages for a false and defamatory statement of facts remained open to government officials as they were to private individuals. Liability was usually automatic if the statement was false and defamatory. Damages would usually be presumed. But private suits for libel upon a public official were too infrequent to be perceived as serious threats to press or other public criticism of conduct in office until the civil rights controversies of the 1950s and 1960s.

In 1960 the *New York Times* published a paid political advertisement attacking the conduct of the police during civil rights demonstrations at Alabama State College in Montgomery. The advertisement contained minor misstatements, such as that the police had "ringed" the Alabama State college campus when in fact they were merely deployed near the campus in large numbers. An Alabama jury awarded the Montgomery Commissioner of Public Affairs $500,000 for actual and punitive damages. The Supreme Court unanimously reversed, holding that the First Amendment bars a public official from recovering damages for a defamatory falsehood relating to his official conduct unless the statement was made with knowledge that it was false or with reckless disregard of whether it was true or false.[6] Behind the rule lies the judgment that any risk of uncompensated injury to private reputations resulting from such a rule is outweighed by the benefits to democratic self-government that flow from encouraging public debates about official conduct uninhibited by fear of liability if statements made in honest error turn out to be false. The *New York Times* case is itself a dramatic reminder of the extent to which the ever-present danger of huge judgments for libel might discourage open discussion of vital issues in sections of the country where the local media are closed and popular feeling runs high against criticism of the established order. The rule is now applicable to all statements about public figures, in or out of government.[7]

The American press has also been freed from two other early

rules that sometimes discouraged criticism of government. English law punished comments on pending judicial business as contempt of court.[8] The First Amendment now protects press comment on matters *sub judice* no matter how strident the effort to arouse public pressure to influence the course of justice.[9] Similarly, the press has been freed to publish gory accounts of crime and sensational evidence against the accused prior to trial, even though the consequences must be delay of the trial, change of venue, or possibly dismissal of the indictment on the ground that an untainted jury cannot be assembled.[10]

The Watergate affair illustrates the value of the three modern rules taken together, at least in the case of charges against high government officials. The reporting of Bob Woodward and Carl Bernstein of the *Washington Post* and Seymour Hersh of the *New York Times* built pressure for the appointment of a Special Prosecutor. Their stories might not have been published under risk of libel suits or citation for contempt of court. Later, the wide publicity served the extraordinary purpose of enabling a whole people to sit in judgment on its highest political leaders, to pass judgment on whether they were fit to be leaders, to deliberate on the proper standards of public responsibility, and not merely to decide whether they were guilty or innocent of crime.

II

Constitutional protection for words can never be absolute. Words are too often the triggers of unlawful action. "Hit him, quick" may start or prolong a fight. Plots to rob a bank are laid by spoken words. Here the governing principle may be that words utterly lacking in political content and adding nothing to the wider body of human understanding fall outside the First Amendment.

The problem is different if the spurs to action are political words. A radical speaker from the right or from the left may inflame a mob. "Burn the shanties," "Throw the bomb," or "Kill the cops" may unleash the violence. If a riot follows, may the speaker be punished even though the First Amendment protects political words? What should be the rule if armed police arrive in such overwhelming numbers that fear quells other emotions and no riot occurs? One can vary the case again by supposing that the speaker's political oratory so inflames the crowd's sense of grievance that the riot occurs without his urging. Or that the speaker, a radical critic of the existing economic system, sprinkles his political oratory with calls for revolutionary violence when the time is ripe. To generalize: What relationship between words of political or social advocacy and unlawful acts will deprive the speaker of the protection of the First Amendment?

Such problems arise in many contexts, but the pressures are most intense and the stakes are highest when the criticism is of the Administration's conduct of a war. At such a time the Administration has both good and bad reasons for attempting to silence its most successful critics. National security may be affected because criticism is leading to violation of the Selective Service Act and other wartime measures. The Administration may fear the political consequences of the criticism in terms of public support for the war or in the next election; or it may be yielding to chauvinistic clamor against the dissidents. The War of 1812 and the Civil War brought no important litigation testing the meaning of the First Amendment in such circumstances. Major cases involving Eugene Debs and other left-wing critics did reach the Court toward the close of World War I. The decisions and dissenting opinions by Justices Holmes and Brandeis laid the foundations of the law of the First Amendment.

Eugene Debs had always been a troublemaker. His strong and simple love for his fellow men and women drove him to speak and act with evangelic fervor against every form of cruelty or injustice. His faith in human decency and the power of simple ideas turned him away from violence, even though his belief in human dignity, equality, and economic justice led him to embrace and come to lead the Socialist Party of the United States. Debs's eloquence and talent for organization helped to make him a leader; but men and women loved him most for his sweetness, generosity and kindness, his sensitivity to suffering, and the absolute sincerity in his gray eyes and sad smile. The Hoosier poet James Whitcomb Riley wrote:

> And there's 'Gene Debs, a man 'at stands
> And jest holds out in his two hands
> As warm a heart as ever beat
> Betwixt here and the Judgment Seat.

When fourteen years old, Debs went to work on the railroad at $1.00 a day. Shortly he became a fireman. Labor unions were growing in the railroad industry. Debs rose to leadership in the

American Railway Union. In 1894 he led its successful strike against James J. Hill and the Great Northern Railroad. In the same year the factory employees of the Pullman Company struck in protest at a 25 percent wage cut ordered by the company even though it continued to pay the same dividends to stockholders and to charge the same rent for the houses in which the workers lived. Debs called for the railroad employees to boycott the cars of the Pullman Company. Railroad centers were thrown into turmoil. Traffic halted. Often there was violence. The federal government broke the strike by calling in the army and obtaining an injunction from the federal court. Debs deplored the violence but was held responsible. He was to serve six months in jail for contempt of court. The U.S. Supreme Court affirmed the decision.[11]

Gene Debs came out of jail a hero. In the next four Presidential elections he led the Socialist ticket, a tall, gaunt, earnest but warm-hearted man touring the country on the "Red Special" to shout hoarse-voiced indictments of a selfish, ruthless capitalism. The Socialist vote rose tenfold, from a hundred thousand in 1900 to a million in 1912, 6 percent of the votes cast. Debs and other Socialist leaders, as pacifists, strongly opposed the war in Europe. "I would oppose the war if I stood alone. When I think of a cold, glittering steel bayonet being plunged into the white quivering flesh of a human being I recoil with horror. I have often wondered if I could take the life of my fellow man, even to save my own."[12]

On the eve of America's entry into the European war, President Wilson had rightly predicted that with wartime fervor the very spirit of ruthless brutality would enter into the very fiber of national life, infecting Congress, the courts, the policeman on the beat, the man in the street. The feverish demand for "100 percent Americanism" peaked in 1919–1920. When an enraged sailor shot a spectator who refused to rise for the national anthem, the crowd cheered and applauded. An Indiana jury took two minutes to acquit a man who had killed an alien for yelling, "To hell with the United States." In early 1920 a clothing store salesman was jailed for six months for remarking that Lenin was "one of the brainiest of the world's leaders." The U.S. House of Representatives twice refused to seat Victor Berger, a duly elected, peaceful Milwaukee Socialist. The New York legislature expelled five Socialist members.

The intolerance was fueled by the fears unleashed by turmoil— by racial violence, a wave of strikes, the rise of the Wobblies (the

International Workers of the World), and the occasional bombs of left-wing anarchists. The repressive policies of the Administration peaked in the infamous "Palmer raids," during which thousands of alleged aliens and radicals were rounded up without warrants, held incommunicado, denied the assistance of counsel, and subjected to brutal interrogation. Only a handful of lawyers and scholars objected, including Felix Frankfurter, Zechariah Chafee, Jr., and Roscoe Pound. The *Washington Post* commented, "There is no time to waste hair-splitting over infringement of liberty."

The constitutional safeguards for freedom of speech were first judicially tested in this fevered national mood. The Wilson Administration was intolerant of any criticism of the war. Socialist critics were prosecuted and jailed. Their writings were barred from the mails. Debs and his fellow leaders continued to speak out, confident that they were protected by the First Amendment. When Debs rose to speak to an audience of twelve hundred people in Canton, Ohio, on June 16, 1918, a government stenographer was present to record his words. It was a long speech, lashing out against the "ruling classes" and denouncing the war as their instrument:

> These very gentry, who are today wrapped up in the American flag, who make the claim that they are only patriots, who have their magnifying glasses in hand, who are scanning the country for some evidence of disloyalty, so eager, so ready to apply the brand to the men who dare to even whisper opposition to junker rule in the United States. No wonder Johnson said that "Patriotism is the last refuge of scoundrels." He had the Wall Street gentry in mind, or their prototypes, at least; for in every age it has been the tyrant who has wrapped himself in the cloak of patriotism, or religion, or both.[13]

Debs praised the Socialists who had been jailed for their speeches:

> Why the other day they sent Kate Richard O'Hare to the penitentiary for ten years. Oh, just think of sentencing a woman to the penitentiary for talking. (Laughter) The United States, under the rule of the plutocracy, is the only country that would send a woman to the penitentiary for 10 years for exercising her constitutional right of free speech. (Applause) If this be treason let them make the most of it.[14]

Jail, Debs implied, was preferable to submission to the enemies of socialism. The Socialists would sweep to power in every nation on earth:

Do not worry, please; don't worry over the charges of Treason to your masters, but be concerned about the Treason that involves yourselves. Be true to yourself, and you cannot be a traitor to any cause on earth.[15]

Four days later Debs was arrested, charged with violating Section 3 of the Espionage Act by making the speech in Canton. The act declared guilty of a felony "whoever, when the United States is at war, shall willfully cause or attempt to cause insubordination, disloyalty, mutiny, or refusal of duty in the military or naval forces . . . or shall willfully obstruct the recruiting or enlistment service." At the trial the court instructed the jury that Debs must be acquitted unless the jury was satisfied that the defendant intended, and his words had as their natural tendency and probable effect, the stirring of disloyalty in the armed forces or the obstruction of recruiting. The jury found Debs guilty.

Debs and other Socialists convicted of similar offenses pressed appeals to the Supreme Court of the United States largely in reliance on the First Amendment's mandate that "Congress shall make no law . . . abridging the freedom of speech."

Debs's alleged offense consisted only of political words. Did the First Amendment give immunity to every political utterance? Incitement to riot had always been a crime. Surely an impassioned address inciting soldiers about to board a troopship to mutiny must also be punishable. Why should the law treat differently words inducing young men not to report for Selective Service?

To allow prosecution of political words, it might be answered, is to allow government to suppress opposition to its policies, particularly to bar criticism of its making war. Effective criticism may lead to detestation. Detestation is easily transformed into resistance to authority. If the First Amendment does not protect words having a tendency to encourage resistance to authority, all criticism may be suppressed.

In the most liberal judicial opinion of World War I, Judge Learned Hand attempted to draw a line between direct incitement to unlawful resistance and political agitation that may in fact stimulate men to violation of law. "If one stops short of urging upon others that it is their duty or their interest to resist the law, it seems to me one should not be said to have attempted to cause its violation."[16] Judge Hand's approach leaves room for unlimited criticism, provided that the speaker urges no unlawful acts; but the line that the Judge sought to draw on the question of urging seems fuzzy. Gene Debs urged his listeners that it was their duty to be true to themselves and to the Socialists' pacifist principles, not to the wartime masters. Was this "direct incitement to violent resistance" within Judge Hand's test?

The U.S. Supreme Court took a different tack. The Court affirmed the conviction of Debs and other Socialists in three unanimous opinions delivered in March 1919 by the liberals' hero, Oliver Wendell Holmes, Jr.[17] Words are like acts, Justice Holmes asserted; their status depends on the circumstances under which they are spoken. The Justice then posed the example that would become famous: "The most stringent protection of free speech would not protect a man falsely shouting fire in a theatre and causing a panic." The example led to the general principle:

> The question in every case is whether the words used are in such circumstances as to create a clear and present danger that they will bring about the substantive evils that Congress has a right to prevent.[18]

The "clear and present danger" test was to become synonymous with rigorous, constitutional protection for speech and press. Justice Holmes's example, shouting fire in a crowded theatre, suggested words causing an immediate, unreflecting response, such as the reaction of an angry, inflamed mob to the cry "Burn the shantytown. Drive them out. Do it *now*." But the example is misleading. It was far from "clear" that Debs's words would lead a significant number of listeners to engage in unlawful acts. In any event, the danger was not of immediate violation, still less of spontaneous panic. Nevertheless, the Court held that it was enough to take the speech out of the First Amendment that the "natural tendency and reasonably probable effect"[19] of the words was to obstruct recruiting, and that the speaker intended that effect.

Little constitutional protection was left for wartime critics of government policies. The "natural tendency and reasonably probable effect" of any effective criticism of a war is to encourage some disobedience of the government's wartime measures. A jury stirred by patriotic fervor could all too easily find that the speaker intended that consequence.

Holmes's opinion was strongly criticized not only in public but in private letters and probably in conversations with respected liberal friends. The tone of his subsequent opinion in *Abrams* v. *United States*[20] was markedly different. In August 1918, before the close of the war, Abrams and four other Russian-born immigrants had distributed leaflets, printed in English and Yiddish, abusively attacking the United States for its part in the Allied expedition to Archangel, in northern Russia, in support of the Anti-Bolshevists. The leaflets ended with a call for a general strike. The defendants were indicted and convicted of conspiring to "advocate curtailment of production and ordnance necessary to the prosecution of the war," and of advocating resistance to the United States in its conduct of the war. The Supreme Court affirmed the convictions, but Justices Holmes and Brandeis dissented. The dissent rests on the argument that the government failed to prove a specific, conscious intent to interfere with the war in Germany, but it also contains an eloquent plea for freedom of expression:

> Persecution for the expression of opinions seems to me perfectly logical. If you have no doubt of your premises or your power and want a certain result with all your heart you naturally express your wishes in law and sweep away all opposition. But when men have realized that time has upset many fighting faiths, they may come to believe even more than they believe the very foundations of their own conduct that the ultimate good desired is better reached by free trade in ideas—that the best test of truth is the power of the thought to get itself accepted in the competition of the market, and that truth is the only ground upon which their wishes safely can be carried out. That at any rate is the theory of our Constitution.[21]

Holmes also stiffened the phrasing of his "clear and present danger" test: "It is only the present danger of an immediate evil or an intent to bring it about that warrants Congress in setting a limit to the expression of opinion where private rights are not involved."[22] The word "immediate" is flexible but much more restrictive than "tendency" and "natural effect."

In the 1920s the excesses of wartime patriotism yielded to the "Red scare." Criminal prosecution of alleged Communists and anarchists for conspiring to overthrow the government by force and violence replaced the prosecution of Socialist critics of the war. A Miss Whitney was convicted in the California courts of the crime of "becoming a member of any organization, society, group or assemblage of persons organized or assembled to advocate criminal syndicalism." Criminal syndicalism was defined to include "any doctrine . . . teaching . . . unlawful acts of force and violence . . . as a means of effecting any political change." Miss Whitney was personally opposed to violence, but had remained a member of the Communist Labor Party of California after it adopted a platform abstractly advocating criminal syndicalism. The U.S. Supreme Court affirmed the conviction, citing other decisions of the same years to show that a State may punish "utterances inimical to the public welfare, tending to incite to crime, disturb the public peace, or endanger the foundations of organized government."[23] Teaching the overthrow of the government by force or violence had been held to fall outside the First Amendment because "the spark may kindle a fire that, smoldering for a time, may burst into a sweeping and destructive conflagration."[24]

Justices Holmes and Brandeis had dissented from those rulings. Now, in an eloquent opinion written by Justice Brandeis, they sought to give purpose, and thus meaning, to the "clear and present danger" exception to the general constitutional guarantee of freedom of speech.

> To courageous, self-reliant men, with confidence in the power of free and fearless reasoning applied through the processes of popular government, no danger flowing from speech can be deemed clear and present, unless the incidence of the evil apprehended is so imminent that it may befall before there is opportunity for full discussion. If there be time to expose through discussion the falsehood and fallacies, to avert the evil by the processes of education, the remedy to be applied is more speech, not enforced silence.
>
> Moreover, even imminent danger cannot justify resort to prohibition of these functions essential to effective democracy, unless the evil apprehended is relatively serious. . . . There must be the probability of serious injury to the state.[25]

The 1930s and early 1940s brought a marked change in the national mood and the course of constitutional decisions in cases believed to affect national security. Fear of the Soviet Union abroad and the Communist movement at home diminished. Holmes and Brandeis were the heroes of the generation of lawyers then taking power in the government or seats upon the Bench. The atmosphere of the New Deal encouraged the expansion of civil liberties. Opponents of World War II were fewer and fared better than Eugene Debs and the critics of World War I. Much of the modern law of the First Amendment apart from national security began to develop during the 1930s and early 1940s. Often the Court invoked the "clear and present danger" test, citing with approval the dissenting opinions of Justices Holmes and Brandeis.[26]

The end of World War II brought the Cold War with Soviet Russia abroad and at home fear of the Communist conspiracy and its agent, the Communist Party of the United States. Communists were widely believed to have infiltrated government agencies, notably the State and Treasury Departments and the National Labor Relations Board, as well as labor unions, universities, and the motion picture industry. In the Executive Branch of the federal government loyalty and security investigations became the order of the day. In Congress the Senate Internal Security Committee and the House Un-American Activities Committee exploited television, the newest medium of mass communication. Friendly witnesses listed suspected Communists and Communist sympathizers. Hostile witnesses added to the furor when they refused to answer questions under pleas of the danger of self-incrimination. The Taft-Hartley Act of 1947 barred labor unions from complaining of unfair labor practices and participating in National Labor Relations Board elections unless all their own officers and all the officers of any national or international labor organization with which they were affiliated had filed affidavits denying membership in the Communist Party. Many State legislatures exacted loyalty oaths from teachers at all levels of education, and conducted their own investigations of left-wing organizations. A pervasive fear of being charged as "soft on Communists" hung over members of even slightly liberal organizations. There was equally widespread fear of the taint of association. Student members of the editorial board of *The Harvard Law Review* refused to elect Samuel and Jonathan Lubell to the places on the editorial board that the Lubells had won by their law school grades. The editors feared that their own careers might be tainted by association with the Lubells, who had refused to answer questions about their membership in the Communist Party by pleading the privilege against self-incrimination.

In July 1947 the Department of Justice secured an indictment charging Eugene Dennis and other top members of the Communist Party of the United States with violating the Smith Act by conspiring (1) to advocate the overthrow of the government of the United States by force and violence, and (2) to organize the party as an organization to teach the overthrow. The trial extended over nine months. The evidence tracing the plans, permutations, and doctrinal history of the Communist Party of the United States in meticulous detail was more than sufficient to prove that the party, a tightly disciplined organization adept at infiltration into strategic places by deceit, was dedicated to teaching and planning for the overthrow of the constitutional government by force and violence, not merely as abstract doctrine but as a program of action at some future date. The jury found the defendants guilty. After sentence, an appeal, and affirmance by the circuit court of appeals, the Supreme Court agreed to decide whether the Smith Act, so applied, violated the First Amendment.[27]

It is worth reflecting about the chief arguments for each side, even though the decision is now history. For the defendants it could be said that the conviction was based on words alone, and that mere words, when of political or social consequence, can *never* be punished consistently with the First Amendment. Justice Black sometimes espoused this interpretation, but the precedents, then as now, rejected it. There was more force in the narrower argument that the Communist leaders were protected by the First Amendment and the "clear and present danger" test as developed by Justices Holmes and Brandeis in the *Whitney* case quoted above and endorsed by the Court in other contexts in the liberal decisions of the Roosevelt era. There was not a hint of evidence that violent overthrow or any other unlawful action would begin "before there is opportunity for full discussion."[28] The government's reply was that the Constitution is not a suicide pact formed by a people so blindly dedicated to liberty under the Constitution as to deny themselves the power to protect constitutionalism against forcible destruction by the subversive plots of a monolithic, authoritarian conspiracy. The *Debs* decision, the government argued, is still good law, because the Court has never endorsed the *Whitney* dissent in the context of national security. And the "clear and present danger" test has no relevance, the argument continued, when a State legislature or the Congress, as in the Smith Act, has found a particular class of utterances so dangerous to constitutional government as to require their proscription.

The plurality opinion accepted none of the previous arguments. Purporting to follow Justices Holmes and Brandeis, the plurality endorsed the "clear and present danger" test; but, declaring that "the words cannot mean that before the Government may act, it must wait until the *putsch* is about to be executed," the plurality went on to adopt a new definition of clear and present danger proposed by Judge Learned Hand in the court below:

> In each case, courts must ask whether the gravity of the "evil," discounted by its improbability, justifies such invasion of free speech as is necessary to avoid the danger.[29]

The formulation is manifestly inconsistent with the views of Justices Holmes and Brandeis as expressed in *Whitney.* Justice Black also objected to balancing away the First Amendment.

If one accepts the formula, two procedural questions arise in addition to the ultimate substantive evaluation. Who is to determine the gravity of the evil, the degree of the probability, and how much restriction is necessary—the legislature, the court, or the jury? If the court is to make the determination, may it look only to sworn testimony, or may it draw on wider sources outside the record? Justice Frankfurter, who joined the plurality in voting for affirmance, concluded that the balance had been and should be struck by Congress.[30] His opinion rested on the philosophy of judicial self-restraint in deference to legislative choices among competing interests—the same philosophy that he had pressed to an extreme in the Flag Salute Cases. The plurality ruled that because the Court must apply the First Amendment, the Court itself must determine whether the danger is clear and present.[31] Unfortunately, the Court did not address such questions as where it would get its facts and how it would know the degree of probability that the conspirators, if undeterred, would be successful.

Justice Douglas, who dissented, said that the record contained no evidence on the question and that if he were to decide according to his personal experience, reading, and observation, he would find that there was no risk that the Communist Party could accomplish its purpose.[32] The plurality found the danger sufficient to validate the Smith Act, but it did not explain the factual foundation for that conclusion. I am left with the feeling that differences of temperament, broad impressions concerning the forces at work in the country and the world, and inarticulate hopes and fears played larger parts in these conflicting judgments than hard-headed factual analysis. Perhaps the law can do no better if the *Dennis* calculus of clear and present danger is part of the law of the First Amendment.

In the late 1950s and 1960s the pendulum swung back toward a strict application of the *Whitney* dissent, partly because of changes in personnel and partly because the excesses of Senator Joseph McCarthy and other Communist-baiters came to seem more dangerous than the ebbing influence of Marxists. The Court held, for example, that Congress may not make it a crime for a member of the Communist Party to work in a defense facility[33] or hold office in a labor union.[34] For the Department of State to revoke a passport because the holder was a Communist Party member was likewise held unconstitutional.[35] Finally, in 1969, in *Brandenburg* v. *Ohio,* the Court declared that

> [t]he constitutional guarantees of free speech and free press do not permit a State to forbid or proscribe advocacy of the use of force or of law violation except where such advocacy is directed to inciting or producing imminent lawless action and is likely to incite or produce such action.[36]

The principle thus pronounced seems to go even beyond the formulation of the "clear and present danger" test advanced by Justices Holmes and Brandeis in the *Whitney* case, unless "imminent" in this context does not carry the very high degree of immediacy normally associated with the word. If followed, it is highly protective of the most radical criticism of government up to incitement of immediate lawlessness or mutiny. Yet one seeking to foretell the course of decisions cannot wholly forget that it was easier to write brave words defending speech in 1969 than in time of war. The defendant in *Brandenburg* v. *Ohio* was the leader of only twelve hooded figures who gathered with firearms to burn a cross and hear speeches attacking "niggers" and Jews. There was neither war threatening national security nor fear of internal subversion. The aphorism *Inter arma silent leges* is not wholly true of a people dedicated to constitutionalism and the rule of law. Nor is it absolutely false. Judges and lawyers seek to develop coherent bodies of reasoned principles explicating constitutional guarantees so as to minimize the elements of emotion, personal prejudice, and public passion that might otherwise influence their decisions, but judges also sometimes render decisions under pressures of war that they may come to doubt in calmer years. Today the treatment of Gene Debs seems cruel folly. His simple idealism, though impracticably visionary, nourished the soul of America. The fears of internal subversion that led to the *Dennis* decision now seem excessive. But, being human, judges will always be somewhat influenced by the atmosphere about them if the hopes and fears of the people are pervasive and intense. Legal formulas are subject to interpretation because words lack the precision of mathematical symbols. In the *Brandenburg* formula just quoted, the malleability is in the word "imminent" and in a footnote citing the seemingly inconsistent *Dennis* case as one of the sources of the rule. In a time of apparent crisis ambiguity coupled with the citation might make it all too easy to write an opinion reviving the *Dennis* version of the "clear and present danger" test.

The collision between the values of freedom of expression and of the prevention of lawless action that may carry some threat to national security is inescapable in times of apparent crisis. The judicial pendulum swings, but swings less wildly and in a shorter arc than public or legislative opinion. The judge's duty to reason out his decision within a continuing body of law, when observed, not only sets limits to his action but provides an accumulation of wisdom based upon experience and critical analysis of the past.

II

Until recently constitutional law was seldom concerned with the clash between the claims of the national interest in the preservation of secrecy, on the one side, and, on the other side, the values of publishing information about the conduct and plans of government in a democratic society. The problems are illustrated by the famous case of the Pentagon Papers and subsequent efforts to have the courts bar publication of an issue of *The Progressive* magazine containing an article describing how to build the H-bomb. Leaking stories to the press in violation of confidential relationships appears to be an established method of seeking to shape government policy. The press seems to feel no compunction about encouraging such breaches of confidence. While these trends continue, the government's efforts to suppress publication will occasionally draw in the courts.

The case of the Pentagon Papers involved an elaborate, highly sensitive, and critical study, conducted by the Department of Defense, of the formulation and conduct of U.S. policy and military and diplomatic operations in Southeast Asia before and during the war in Vietnam. The eighteen volumes were classified Secret. Daniel Ellsberg, a consultant to the government, received the highly classified papers, apparently under an express or implied pledge of confidence. Nevertheless, he made copies of all or part and arranged for them to reach the press. The Executive rushed to the courts to enjoin publication, making strong representations that the risk of injury to national interests, if the Pentagon Papers were published, included "the death of soldiers, the destruction of alliances, the greatly increased difficulty of negotiation with our enemies, the inability of our diplomats to negotiate," and the prolongation of the war. The Court ruled, 6–3, that these claims would not support an injunction against publication, even for the period necessary to study how far the fears were justified.[37] The Justices in the majority differed among themselves. Three of the six were heavily influenced by the absence of legislation authorizing the Judiciary to bar the publication of such documents. Two suggested that both leaking and publishing the documents might be punished as criminal offenses. Yet the qualifications ought not to obscure the main point. All the weight of the Executive was insufficient to bar disclosure of highly secret and sensitive documents concerning the earlier conduct of still pressing military and diplomatic affairs. It is unlikely that the information, though clearly relevant to self-government, could have been published anywhere else in the world. In Britain the publication would have been barred by the Official Secrets Act.

The want of a statutory foundation that weakened the government's case against the *New York Times* was not a factor in 1979, when the Carter Administration learned that *The Progressive* magazine planned to publish the article disclosing to laymen the supposedly secret technical information on the design of hydrogen bombs. The Atomic Energy Act of 1954 forbids the disclosure or publication of information that may be useful in the manufacture of nuclear weapons, and it explicitly authorizes enforcement by injunction. There was a rush to the courthouse. Both government officials and some independent and responsible nuclear physicists were convinced that publication of "The H-Bomb Secret" would invite the proliferation of such devices and thus increase the risk of nuclear war. The district court issued an injunction. The case fizzled out when it became apparent that the supposed secret was in truth already available to one and all.[38]

The absurdity of the suit against *The Progressive* underscores two tendencies with broader implications. Control over what information will be released and over the timing of any release has immense political importance both in the competition between political parties and in the formulation and effective implementation of public policy. Accordingly, on hearing that an important supposed secret is about to get out, the executive official's instinctive response is to say "They can't do that" and to demand of the government's lawyers "Can't you do something? Can't you get an injunction?" The lawyer's "lawyerhood" is challenged, and, as in the case of a challenge to a man's manhood, the lawyer can answer only, "We'll give it a good try." This human tendency, present in many kinds of cases, is reinforced by another factor. Given the responsibility of the courts for protecting constitutional rights, the government lawyer tends to ask only whether he can make a responsible argument in support of the government's position. Striking the balance that protects civil liberty is not the lawyer's job but the court's. While this tendency is somewhat less than ideal, it is a natural consequence of the doctrine of judicial review.

In *The Progressive* case the worst fault was in the general failure to realize that the supposed secret was open to anyone who sought to learn it. If the secret had been real, as the district court believed, an extraordinarily difficult constitutional problem would have been presented. Disclosure of some truly important secrets, even in time of peace, would have a tremendously adverse impact on national interests. If the *New York Times* had not voluntarily withheld publication of the CIA plans to overthrow the Castro government by the Bay of Pigs invasion in 1961, could and should publication have been enjoined *in camera*? What about the plans made during President Carter's Administration for the rescue of the hostages held in Tehran? Or the H-bomb secret, assuming that the secrecy was real? Because the plans miscarried in the first two examples, it is easy to say that disclosure would have barred the blunder, but one can scarcely assume that all plans requiring secrecy are blunders or that the press will disclose only the bad.

In the case of the Pentagon Papers, Justices Black and Douglas declared that *ever* to permit any prior restraint on the publication of any news would "make a shambles of the First Amendment."[39] Probably they exaggerated their position. It seems unlikely that they would have ruled during World War II that a newspaper had a constitutional right to publish for British and Nazi eyes the politically important knowledge that, because of the cryptographic work at Bletchley, British authorities were enjoying the extraordinary military advantage of reading every order of the Nazi High Command, yet had taken no special steps to warn the people of Coventry of an air raid that would wreak devastation upon them.

Justice Brennan was slightly less enthusiastic in his Pentagon Papers opinion but still vigorous in condemning prior restraints: "[O]nly governmental allegation and proof that publication must inevitably, directly, and immediately cause the occurrence of an event kindred to imperiling the safety of a transport already at sea can support even the issuance of an interim restraining order."[40] And, in an opinion in which Justice Byron White concurred, Justice Stewart declared that there could be no judicial intervention in the absence of proof that disclosure would "surely result in direct, immediate, and irreparable damage to our Nation or its people."[41]

The Progressive argued that publication of the H-bomb secret would not "inevitably" result in the use of H-bombs by a foreign power, as required by Justice Brennan, nor would it cause "direct" and "immediate" damage, as required by his formulation and also by Justice Stewart's. The argument seems persuasive if the Justices really intended to require proof that the publication would "directly" lead to "immediate" disaster and if their approach is sound. But if one wholeheartedly assumes the truth of the assertion that publication of the information would put awesome, destructive power into the hands of a Kadaffi or an Idi Amin, the validity of the requirement of imminency becomes questionable. The "clear and present danger" test and its several elaborations were formulated to deal with radical political propaganda calling on the audience or the readers to join in overthrow of the government by force and violence or other unlawful action. The underlying rationale, best stated in the words of Justice Brandeis quoted earlier, was that "no danger flowing from speech can be deemed clear and present, unless the incidence of the evil apprehended is so imminent that it may befall before there is opportunity for full discussion."[42] But "confidence in the power of free and fearless reasoning applied through the processes of popular government" has scant relevance where the danger is that a hostile or unfriendly power will use the dangerous information released against the United States. Disclosure of a projected, secret Central Intelligence coup against a Latin American government would frustrate the operation whether the coup was scheduled for immediate execution or planned for the following month. Disclosure of the location of secret ICBMs might bring disaster if war broke out six weeks, six months, or six years into the future. Excepting the cases in which faith is to be put in the efficacy of public debate to produce right action, the immediacy of the harm threatened by the publication seems properly to bear only on the degree of probability that the harm will occur. With imminence put aside, a court would have little choice but to fall back on the *Dennis* formula and ask "whether the gravity of the 'evil,' discounted by its improbability, justifies such invasion of free speech as is necessary to avoid the danger."

Obviously the formula is only the beginning of the difficulties. The next problem would be valuing the speech. At first glance one is tempted to invoke the postulate that a court has no more warrant than other branches of government to pass judgment on the worth of particular information or ideas. On second thought, it seems noteworthy that the most familiar example of an enjoinable publication is the proposed announcement of the sailing date of a troopship in time of war. Other purely military secrets seem to fall in the same category. Perhaps the opinions expressed have been consciously or unconsciously influenced by the fact that the information contributed virtually nothing to political debate on subjects appropriate for democratic decisions. Not all words are within the freedom of speech protected by the First Amendment. Uttering a forged check is indictable even though the check is only words. So is an agreement to commit murder. Some government secrets may fall in that category, and their publication may not be speech protected by the First Amendment. Others obviously involve information relevant to political debate; for example, the publication of a CIA plan for an undercover operation subverting a foreign government. Still other examples fall on the borderline. Learning the H-bomb secret directly adds very little to political debate, but it has larger indirect political relevance. The knowledge explains why Congress makes large annual appropriations for the production of plutonium. The dramatic offer to supply the knowledge attracts readers to the debate over nuclear weapons. The publication raises questions about the policy of seeking to impose secrecy.

Although such questions must be left for case-by-case decisions if and when they arise, it is instructive to approach the clash between democratic debate and secrecy in terms of the other measures available to the Executive Branch. A government agency may impose secrecy on government officials and employees by Presidential or departmental order or by contract. The Central Intelligence Agency, for example, has followed the practice of requiring at least some CIA agents to sign written contracts promising not to "publish . . . any information or material relating to the Agency, its activities or intelligence activities generally, either during or after the term of employment . . . without specific prior approval by the Agency."[43] President Reagan sought unsuccessfully to extend a similar prohibition to thousands of officials and employees having access to a particular form of classified information. As long as the official or employee acquiesces in official policy, no justiciable question is raised. The First Amendment has never yet been held to put the government under an affirmative duty to provide information.

The validity of such agreements can be tested if an employee is in violation and the government takes steps for enforcement, such as discharging the employee or seeking a remedy in court. Frank W. Snepp III signed such a contract on becoming a CIA agent. Later, Snepp deliberately and surreptitiously published an account of CIA activities in South Vietnam, under the title *Decent Interval,* without submitting the manuscript to the CIA for prior approval. Afterward, the United States brought an action to enforce the contract for the future and to recover damages for the past violation, much as one might sue to enforce a contract for the sale of land or a thoroughbred horse. The Supreme Court held the contract enforceable by injunction and required Snepp to account for all the royalties from the sale of *Decent Interval.* The decision may indicate that the First Amendment does not bar the courts from enforcing a pledge of secrecy against a government employee or consultant who gives the pledge in an unusually sensitive position, at least in the case of classified secrets and in other cases for the time required by the government to ascertain whether a proposed publication contains a classified secret. Presumably, Daniel Ellsberg could have been enjoined on this theory from passing the Pentagon Papers along to the press.

The *Snepp* decision leads logically to an inquiry into whether the contract theory extends so far as to permit an injunction against the would-be publisher of material that the government employee has undertaken not to put out without prior censorship. The publisher is knowingly aiding, if not inducing, the unfaithful employee to break the agreement. If the public interest in free access to the information and ideas is insufficient to bring them under the First Amendment when the employee seeks to communicate them, that same interest alone cannot logically be enough when the freedom of the press is at issue. Both the benefit to the public from the knowledge and the harm done by the publication to other interests, whether large or small, would be the same in both cases. The law treats the knowing receiver of stolen goods much like the thief. Is there reason to be more lenient toward the receiver of stolen information?

It seems unlikely that the Court would extend the *Snepp* theory to suppress the publication of news concerning actual or projected government activities having a significant political component. Other decisions allow the government to impose secrecy on juvenile proceedings, certain pretrial hearings in criminal cases, and inquiries into charges of judicial misconduct, yet bar the State from suppressing or punishing publication once the information is obtained.[44] The underlying but unstated theory is probably that a broad prophylactic rule generally barring interference with publication by the press of facts or opinions coming into its possession is necessary to enable the press to function as a fourth estate, informing the people about the conduct of government and serving as vigilant critics. Such a rule undoubtedly requires some exceptions, as in the case of the disclosure of secrets that would truly lead to a national disaster. To increase the exceptions, however, is to increase doubt about freedom to publish in cases near the borderline and thus to curtail the breathing space needed for democratic discussion. Similarly, requiring a check into the source of information would result in uncertainty and delay in publishing protected speech. A rule protecting publication would leave reporters and others subject to prosecution for stealing classified documents or inducing government officials or employees pledged to secrecy to violate the confidence reposed in them.

III

A free, self-governing people needs full information concerning the activities of its government not only to shape views of policy and vote in elections, but also to compel the government, its agent, to act responsively and account for its doings. For most of our history men could be fairly sure of obtaining such facts and of communicating with each other in ways necessary to self-government, provided that government was denied the power of censorship, that the printing presses were open to all to use, and that men could speak, write, and engage in political association without fear of reprisal. Given the scale and complexity of modern society, often only the government has the requisite information, either because it alone has the facilities for gathering the information or because the information pertains to the activities of the government itself. A central problem today, therefore, is how to deal with governmental secrecy and sometimes—to use blunt words—with governmental deception. Even without the *Snepp* case, secrecy imposed by the Executive would generally be observed.

One partial "solution" might be to encourage disclosure by dissidents within the government even though in breach of confidence. The public obtained the Pentagon Papers because a government consultant, whose conscience was shocked by what he read, violated the confidence reposed in him. We regularly read about proposed measures in the morning newspapers because officials fearing to lose the argument in White House or Defense Department deliberations try to influence the decision by taking the issue to the press. Perhaps we have institutionalized the "leak" as one of the checks and balances in a vast modern government. For myself, I cannot help thinking that the leak is both a moral wrong and a slender reed on which to rely for keeping the people informed about the government's conduct of their business.

Conceivably, the First Amendment might be converted by judicial interpretation into the source of a governmental duty to provide the press with access to information. Four Justices have urged the development of such a doctrine.[45] The Court took what is arguably a small step in that direction when it ruled that the First Amendment gives the press and public a right to attend a criminal trial even though the State prosecutor and the defendant agree to close it.[46] Nevertheless, it seems unlikely that the rule barring closure of criminal trials will be built into a general doctrine giving the press and public a right of access to government proceedings and officials whenever the courts think it appropriate. Creation of such a right would stray far from the words and original meaning of the constitutional guarantees. Drawing new lines for the Legislative and Executive Branches between what must be open and what may be closed is unsuited to judicial determination. Even if it were other-wise, lawsuits cannot bring to light activities and information whose very existence is wholly secret.

In the end, therefore, the only protection of the people against excessive government secrecy is the people's own active insistence on disclosure, expressed by their votes and the legislative action of their representatives. The Freedom of Information Act, though subject to many exceptions, is an example. The dangers of exces-sive secrecy are rarely, if ever, important issues in elections, yet self-government is profoundly affected. Unless the people them-selves become concerned, neither Constitution nor Court can as-sure this prerequisite to self-government.

· 13 ·

Protection for the Accused

AS THE SUPREME COURT of the 1950s and 1960s was expanding the constitutional protection for religious liberty and freedom of speech and press, it was also engaged in using constitutional adjudication to reform the administration of criminal justice in both State and federal courts. One consequence was greatly to enlarge the role of the national Judiciary and to reduce correspondingly the autonomy of the States. A second consequence was to check abuses in law enforcement by increasing the procedural safeguards available to persons charged with crime—a change in legal rules that inescapably increased the opportunities for delaying if not avoiding punishment for crime. The best and most controversial example is the development of the so-called exclusionary rule in *Mapp* v. *Ohio*.[1]

In May 1957 the Cleveland, Ohio, police were looking for a fugitive whom they believed to be implicated in a recent bombing. Someone told them that the fugitive was at the home of a Dollree Mapp. Three police officers went there without a search warrant and demanded admission. Apparently Dolly Mapp and the police had had previous encounters, for she refused to open the door, spoke to the officers through a window, and telephoned her attorney. The attorney told her to do nothing until he got there. The officers laid siege to the house, and when the attorney arrived, they barred him from the premises. By this time seven police officers were on the scene. The officers broke through the back door. Mrs. Mapp asked the officers for their search warrant. One held up a paper, falsely saying that it was the warrant. Mrs. Mapp snatched the paper and thrust it into her bosom. The officer, lacking a nice sense of delicacy, "went down after it," and retrieved the paper. He put Mrs. Mapp in handcuffs. The officers then ransacked the house from attic to cellar without finding the fugitive. In the course of the search they came upon obscene books and pictures that one officer said were stored in a trunk. In due course Dolly Mapp was charged in an Ohio court with the possession of "lewd and lascivious" materials, in violation of an Ohio criminal law— four small pamphlets, a couple of photographs, and "a little pencil doodle."

This little drama led in due course to the major U.S. Supreme Court decision in *Mapp* v. *Ohio*. Even though the outcome is widely known, it is instructive to think of the problem facing Mrs. Mapp's attorneys as they planned her defense.

1. Mrs. Mapp would testify that she knew nothing of the trunk or the pornography, which she would say must have been left behind by a former lodger. Would the jury believe her? No lodger would appear and acknowledge ownership of the trunk. To rely solely on Mrs. Mapp's testimony must have seemed from the start to be a risky line of defense.

2. A concurrent line of defense might be to argue that to convict Mrs. Mapp for possession of the books and pictures would violate the freedom of speech guaranteed by both the Ohio Constitution and the Constitution of the United States. The defense would have to be raised in the State court, but if the federal claim was rejected, an appeal would lie to the Supreme Court of the United States. This defense also must have looked like a long shot. Judges and lawyers had long assumed that the guarantees of freedom of speech and press do not include obscene publications. Only a few years earlier, the U.S. Supreme Court had reaffirmed the rule.[2] The Court was engaged in narrowing the definition of obscenity, but hardly enough to help Mrs. Mapp.

Counsel could also contend that even if the First Amendment permits criminal punishment for the sale or distribution of hard-core pornography, still the First Amendment's implicit guarantee of complete freedom of the mind and spirit bars punishment for the mere possession of obscenity in the privacy of one's home for personal use. The prosecution had no evidence that Mrs. Mapp intended to distribute the pornography. A plurality of the Supreme Court Justices would so interpret the amendment a few years later,[3] but in 1958 this defense can hardly have held out much promise.

3. Mrs. Mapp's attorneys might also seek to defeat the indictment by keeping the pamphlets, the photographs, and the little penciled doodle from the jury on the ground that the police obtained them illegally. The search and seizure described above were unquestionably illegal. One of the first grievances of the American people against King George III was that he denied them the protection afforded his subjects in Britain against entry into homes and offices under general warrants instructing royal officers to rummage about for evidence of crime even if there was no reason to believe that the evidence was there. James Otis and John Adams had roused the City of Boston against the searches. After the Revolution both the Fourth Amendment to the U.S. Constitution and many State constitutions, including Ohio's, would state:

> The right of the people to be secure in their persons, houses, papers, and effects, against unreasonable searches and seizures, shall not be violated, and no warrants shall issue, but upon probable cause, supported by oath or affirmation, and particularly describing the place to be searched, and the persons or things to be seized.

Dolly Mapp's attorneys could take it as their premise that this provision of the Ohio Constitution was blatantly violated by the Cleveland police. It was not so clear, however, that the obscene papers and pictures could not be used as evidence. Most State courts, including Ohio's, had allowed relevant and probative evidence to be used in a criminal prosecution even though unlawfully obtained. One of the great American judges, Benjamin Cardozo, then Chief Judge of the New York Court of Appeals, had joined in rejecting a rule barring such evidence because it would mean that

> [t]he criminal is to go free because the constable has blundered. . . .
> A room is searched against the law, and the body of a murdered man is found. . . . The privacy of a home is infringed, and the murderer goes free.[4]

In the federal courts the judge presiding at a criminal trial would exclude from the jury's consideration evidence obtained by a search and seizure conducted by federal officials in violation of the Fourth Amendment. In laying down the rule the Supreme Court reasoned that

[t]he tendency of those who execute the criminal laws of the country to obtain convictions by means of unlawful searches and enforced confessions . . . should find no sanction in the judgment of the courts which are charged at all times with the support of the Constitution and to which people of all conditions have a right to appeal for the maintenance of such fundamental rights. . . . The efforts of the courts and their officials to bring the guilty to punishment . . . are not to be aided by the sacrifice of those great principles established by years of endeavor and suffering which have resulted in their embodiment in the fundamental law of the land.[5]

The Fourth Amendment and the federal exclusionary rule, without more, could give little comfort to Dolly Mapp and her attorneys. They applied only to federal officials and only in the federal courts. Her home had been violated by State officials. She would be tried in a State court, under State rules of evidence, for an alleged violation of State law. She would be entitled to all the federal constitutional guarantees of individual liberty directed to the States, including the Fourteenth Amendment's commands that no State shall abridge the privileges and immunities of citizens of the United States nor shall any State deprive any person of life, liberty, or property without due process of law. The critical legal question for her lawyers, if they pursued this line, would therefore be whether the federal exclusionary rule adopted under the Fourth Amendment could be made applicable to a trial in a State court through the Fourteenth Amendment somewhat as the Fourteenth Amendment had earlier been invoked to apply the First Amendment to the States.

Had Dolly Mapp's counsel analyzed the case in this fashion, they would have come to one of the most fundamental constitutional issues affecting criminal justice in the United States—a question discussed in a number of precedents prior to 1957 and resolved in *Mapp* v. *Ohio,* but one still worth examining as if it were an open question, because, despite the decisions, the debate goes on. To what extent does the Fourteenth Amendment "incorporate" the procedural safeguards that the federal Bill of Rights puts on federal activities in investigation and prosecution of crime, and so make the same restrictions and remedies applicable to the States?

II

The first eight amendments to the Constitution contain a number of specific restrictions on the methods of law enforcement aimed at royal practices experienced by the colonists or by their forebears under the Tudor and Stuart Kings. The Fourth Amendment restricts both arrests and searches and seizures, as described above. The Fifth Amendment requires a grand jury indictment to institute a criminal prosecution; it also gives the accused a privilege against self-incrimination. The Sixth Amendment guarantees trial by jury and the rights to be confronted by witnesses, to have the assistance of counsel, and to obtain compulsory process for the attendance of witnesses for the defense. The Eighth Amendment prohibits cruel and unusual punishment and secures the right to prompt bail, except for capital crimes.

State constitutions vary. A typical State constitution contains some but not all of the federal guarantees. Often the phraseology is different. Still more often State judicial interpretations prior to 1960 differed from federal, nearly always in ways unfavorable to the accused. Because the original federal Bill of Rights was addressed only to Congress, two sets of procedures grew up, one prevailing in State prosecutions and the other only in the federal courts.

The adoption of the Fourteenth Amendment in 1869 brought about a major change, because the oft-quoted words plainly erected national safeguards, enforceable in both State and federal courts, against State violations of some individual rights. The great questions left open concerned the nature and extent of those rights. The struggle over economic liberty first took center stage. Much later, as we have seen, the First Amendment's guarantees of freedom of speech and religious liberty were incorporated into the Fourteenth Amendment. While those issues were being thrashed out, a closely linked, parallel question developed concerning the application of the federal Bill of Rights to State law enforcement. Did the broad phrase "privileges and immunities of citizens of the United States" or the concept of "due process of law" call for precise State compliance with the criminal justice provisions of the federal Bill of Rights? The argument has gone on for a century. Dolly Mapp's case was a major engagement in the long war.

Justice Hugo L. Black, the most vigorous supporter of the incorporation theory in the present century, argued from history that an affirmative answer would carry out the conscious original purpose of those who wrote and adopted the Fourteenth Amendment.[6] Some historians support Justice Black. Others, probably the majority, disagree. Representative John A. Bingham, the chief draftsman, did indeed several times declare that the purpose was to empower Congress to secure the liberties protected by the Bill of Rights against invasion by the States. Senator Jacob M. Howard gave a similar explanation. There is almost no direct evidence, however, to show that the purpose they declared was either shared by other supporters of the amendment or generally understood to be its effect.[7] Anyone who addressed his mind to the subject would have realized that, even in 1868, State criminal procedures would have to be radically altered to conform to the federal Bill of Rights. The total absence of comment on this consequence rather strongly suggests that few supposed that the proposed amendment did incorporate the federal Bill of Rights. Even more striking is the fact that the incorporation theory was advanced by only one of the numerous Justices who lived through the period of debate over the amendment and were presumably familiar with the common understanding of the times; and he did not advance it for a good many years after adoption of the amendment.[8]

By 1937 a long series of case-by-case decisions had developed the rule that the Due Process Clause did not require a State to observe the specific modes of trial derived from Anglo-American common law and made binding in federal criminal cases by the Bill of Rights. It was held or declared that due process was not violated, if the procedure was otherwise fair, by putting a defendant on trial without indictment by a grand jury,[9] by trial to a judge without a jury,[10] by commenting on the defendant's failure to testify in his own defense,[11] or by putting a defendant on trial a second time after a judgment of acquittal was reversed for errors of law on appeal by the State.[12] In each of these instances, if the alleged crime were federal and the trial had been in a federal court, the decision would have gone the other way because of a specific guarantee in the federal Bill of Rights. On the other hand, the Court had held that the want of due process would require setting aside a conviction if the trial was a mockery because the defendants were rushed to judgment before a judge and jury intimidated by a lynch mob,[13] if the judge had a financial stake in conviction,[14] if conviction was based on a confession obtained by torture,[15] or if the defendants were denied time for their counsel to prepare a defense.[16]

The line drawn sometimes seemed thin and wavering. Perhaps it was inescapably so. Mr. Justice Cardozo attempted to articulate the key question in *Palko* v. *Connecticut*. Does denial of the right claimed "violate those 'fundamental principles of liberty and justice which lie at the base of all our civil and political institutions?'" Is the right claimed "of the very essence of a scheme of ordered liberty," so that its denial would invalidate a "principle of justice so rooted in the traditions and conscience of our people as to be ranked as fundamental?"[17] The *Palko* case raised a question of criminal procedure, but Justice Cardozo was also thinking of substantive due process. By the 1930s, as we have seen, the Due Process Clause of the Fourteenth Amendment had been held to incorporate the First Amendment's guarantees of religious liberty and freedom of expression. Justice Cardozo's approach suggested selective incorporation of those Bill of Rights guarantees which were "of the very essence of a scheme of ordered liberty"; but it would neither incorporate all the guarantees nor bar the Court from holding that the Due Process Clause protects some rights not specifically identified in the first ten amendments.

Justice Black took up the fight for the incorporation doctrine in the 1940s. He distrusted judicial use of phrases like "essence of any scheme of ordered liberty," "natural rights," "human rights," and "fundamental principles of liberty and justice." Years later he told me that he would not object to their use by men like Justice Felix Frankfurter—doubtless he would have included Justice Cardozo if we had talked of him—but that he had seen the phrases cause too much damage in the hands of other judges, especially in the lower courts. Justice Black came to the Court in 1937 from the Senate, where he had been an ardent supporter of New Deal measures. Earlier, in Alabama, he had fought for the "little people" against established centers of power and influence, as both lawyer and politician. In those years the Locknerian economic due process decisions had evoked "fundamental principles of liberty and justice" and "fundamental rights" to justify invalidating State and federal laws fixing maximum hours of work and minimum wages and protecting the right to form, join, and assist labor unions. Having ardently supported such laws as a legislator, Justice Black, as a judge, not unnaturally sought to extirpate the doctrine condemning them.

The incorporation doctrine also appealed to Justice Black's desire for certainty and objective standards in constitutional interpretation. It was often said of him that his great talent was a "first-class mind unspoiled by a good legal education." The saying has both the truth and falsity of caricature. Justice Black was far more skillful in handling legal precedents than the saying implies, but it was also true that his greatest gift was the capacity to penetrate to the heart of a problem and state it in simple, human terms. Other judges, long trained in handling legal precedents, doctrines, and logical distinctions, could find sufficient guidance outside themselves in the continuing body of law, and even a degree of certainty. Justice Black's cast of mind was little adapted to those processes of decision. He had promoted radical reforms too long to be much influenced by tradition or *stare decisis*. Somehow he persuaded himself that certainty and objectivity could be achieved in most cases simply by honest reading of the words of the Bill of Rights, and that any ambiguities in the words could be resolved by looking at historical evidence of the sense in which the Framers used them. The approach also fitted his strong views of sound policy. By incorporating the federal guarantees into the Fourteenth Amendment he could secure much wider protection for civil liberties than was available under the "fundamental rights" theory and the laws of the several States. By interpreting the Fourteenth Amendment to do no more, he could also limit the Court's interference with active government regulation.

Strong arguments could be made against the incorporation theory in addition to the historical argument concerning the original intent. The Privileges and Immunities Clause had been authoritatively interpreted not to cover basic human rights but only those rights flowing from the creation of the federal union; for example, the right to petition Congress for the redress of grievances.[18] As for "due process of law," the Bill of Rights contains that guarantee in the very same words as the Fourteenth Amendment. From this, it can be argued that the original authors cannot be supposed to have used the words to signify all the other provisions of the Bill of Rights, and that the authors and supporters of the Fourteenth Amendment who copied the old words must have intended them to have their familiar meaning.

Second, the supporters of the established law illustrated by Justice Cardozo's *Palko* opinion argued that the incorporation doctrine, if consistently applied, would subject the States to outmoded federal rules that are chiefly the product of history. For example, the Fifth Amendment prohibits the federal government from holding a person to answer felony charges without indictment by a grand jury. In Britain, under the Tudor and Stuart monarchs, the grand jury was perceived as a protector of individuals. The dominant perception is different today. There is a large body of opinion that sees grand juries as the prosecutors' instruments of oppression. Total incorporation would nonetheless attach the dubious anachronism to the States. Similarly, the Sixth Amendment guarantee of trial by jury had come to mean a jury of twelve, and a unanimous verdict was required for conviction. History and the words of the Sixth Amendment have probably fastened these rules on the federal courts—the critics of incorporation would say—but they are not required for the fair administration of justice and ought not to be fastened on the State courts.

Finally, the incorporation controversy, like many other constitutional issues, presented questions of federalism. The federal system obviously predicated that criminal justice and the police would be left largely to the States. From this premise it was argued that the Constitution should be read to leave questions of procedure affecting the administration of justice and the conduct of the police to the States, unless a State's rule violated "a principle of justice so rooted in the traditions and conscience of our people" as to be ranked as fundamental. But, again, the argument was not unanswerable. The best way to protect fundamental fairness, it was said, is to adhere literally to the federal Bill of Rights and so to avoid erosion by judges insufficiently sensitive to the requirements of liberty.

The upshot during the years of the Warren Court was to move away from the once-settled view stated in *Palko* toward Justice Black's incorporation doctrine. Justice Cardozo had himself laid the ground. By suggesting that the First Amendment was incorporated into the Fourteenth because the guarantees of religious liberty and freedom of expression are essential parts of any plan of ordered liberty, he seemed to invite the Court to focus on the core of each provision of the Bill of Rights, to ask whether the core was of the essence of ordered liberty, and if the answer was affirmative, to hold the entire provision to be incorporated in the Fourteenth Amendment without regard to whether there was fundamental unfairness in the specific State conduct of which complaint was made. The process gradually led to "selective incorporation" of nearly all the provisions of the Bill of Rights, one at a time.

Mapp v. *Ohio* came before the U.S. Supreme Court after the process of incorporation was well under way, but before it was complete. In 1949 the Court had held that, under the Fourteenth Amendment, the States were bound by the Fourth Amendment's prohibition against unreasonable searches and seizures but not by the federal interpretation barring the use of the fruits of the search as evidence.[19] Dolly Mapp's lawyers disclaimed any intention of asking the Court to overturn the latter ruling. The majority nevertheless overruled the direct precedent and made the federal exclusionary rule binding on the States.

III

The exclusionary rule is still the subject of bitter controversy. Public concern about violence and lawlessness has raised emotion, but the strongest criticism of the rule is that stated by Judge Cardozo: that the police have done wrong is not a good reason to exclude the proof of guilt and set the criminal free. Fairly often, the exclusion results from drawing so fine a constitutional line as to excuse describing it as a technicality. Suppose, for example, that a State trooper observes a motor vehicle being driven erratically. He stops it and asks for the registration and the driver's license. If the trooper sees an unlawful firearm or other contraband while checking the license and registration, he may seize it under what lawyers know as the "plain view" rule. Suppose instead that the trooper, without permission, puts his head inside the car in order to read the vehicle identification number and only then can observe the contraband. Recently a majority held that in this instance too the evidence was admissible, while the dissenters concluded that there had been an unlawful search and seizure, calling for exclusion of the seized contraband and the reversal of the conviction based on it.[20]

Neither the police officer nor anyone else could say in advance which way the Court would rule. At first blush it seems overly technical to have the validity of admission of plainly probative evidence turn on whether the officer guessed correctly about whether the Court would rule that he might lawfully put his head through the automobile's window. On reflection it becomes plain that fine lines are inescapable unless the exclusionary rule is wholly rejected. Some police activities do not require a search warrant. Others do. A line must be drawn between the two categories for each of the numerous borderline situations. Suppose the officer carefully looks into the back seat while his head is in the car to read the identification number? Suppose that he opens the glove compartment? Or that the contraband becomes visible only as the sweater covering it slides to the floor? It has been suggested that the evidence should be admitted whenever the officer acts reasonably and in good faith. The laxer standard would still require fine lines to be drawn as the courts had to rule on what would be reasonable and unreasonable mistakes.

The exclusionary rule rests chiefly upon two considerations. One purpose, explained in the *Mapp* case, "is to deter—to compel respect for the constitutional guaranty [against unreasonable searches and seizures] in the only effectively available way—by removing the incentive to disregard it."[21] Supporters of the rule argue that, without it, law enforcement officials under pressure to solve crimes and obtain convictions all too frequently disregard the constitutional prohibition. The offending officer can feel secure that no superior will discipline him nor jury mulct him in damages if the search produces evidence of guilt or if the person whose rights are violated is an unsavory character. The critics of the rule respond that there is neither empirical proof to support the assertion that the rule reduces the number of unconstitutional searches and seizures nor logic in supposing that the conduct of police officers will be affected by whether the public prosecutor secures a conviction or loses the case. The empirical data consist chiefly of the observations of police officials who support the rule; but the assertion that the conduct of police departments, because they are bureaucratically separated from the office of the prosecutor, is nowise affected by rules pertaining to the admission or exclusion of evidence or by the outcome of trials seems grossly overstated. There is bound to be some relationship. Police departments are not unmoved by the desire to solve crimes and punish criminals. Whether the relationship is close or remote almost surely varies from time to time and place to place.

The other ground of the exclusionary rule has been described by Chief Justice Warren Burger as "the 'sporting contest' thesis that the government must 'play the game fairly' and cannot be allowed to profit from its own illegal acts."[22] The Chief Justice's description seems to me to trivialize a critical inquiry. May not the government's resort to unconstitutional means of obtaining evidence and the introduction of the unlawfully obtained evidence to obtain a conviction do more to undermine the observance of law than to promote it? Justice Brandeis eloquently stated the cause for concern many years ago:

> Decency, security, and liberty alike demand that government officials shall be subject to the same rules of conduct that are commands to the citizen. Our government is the potent, the omnipresent teacher. For good or for ill, it teaches the whole people by its example. If the government becomes a lawbreaker, it breeds contempt for law; it invites every man to become a law unto himself; it invites anarchy.[23]

Most of us have little concern in our daily lives for the Fourth Amendment or other constitutional guarantees designed to check abuses by sheriffs, FBI agents, and the local police. We are rightly confident that today our homes and offices will not be ransacked like Dolly Mapp's. Accordingly, we tend to view the constitutional guarantees as impediments to law enforcement affecting only "the criminal element" and other persons on the fringes of the underworld. We tend to view questions of interpretation in that context. The approach is not wholly wrong. One impact of the exclusionary rule is to make it somewhat more difficult to obtain proof and convict wrongdoers. There are doubtless a fair number of cases in which the police have enough truly persuasive information to indicate that a search would produce proof of guilt but not enough to support issuance of a search warrant.

But the larger concerns ought not to be forgotten. The true character of Dolly Mapp does not appear from the record. It is easy to imagine her as a dubious character well acquainted with the police. Even so, the Dolly Mapps of the world surely should not have to suffer the blockade of their homes by seven police officers, the breaking-down of the doors, and the ransacking of their rooms from floor to cellar, all without a proper warrant.

The Fourth Amendment, moreover, was not written solely for ordinary times, but for periods of intense ferment, when those who control the apparatus of government fear loss of power, and political liberties are at stake. In times of stress only constitutional safeguards, buttressed by effective sanctions, keep the Gestapo and the SS trooper from the dissident's door.

The authors of the Fourth Amendment lived in such a period. Some had watched as the King's men went about Boston with general warrants, searching wherever they pleased for evidence of crime. The authors were also thoroughly familiar with the case of John Wilkes, a turbulent politician and notorious reveler in Rabelaisian orgies, who had bought a seat in Parliament with his wife's money. In 1763 Wilkes was a member of the opposition party. In one of a series of anonymous pamphlets, he violently criticized the conservative ministry and implied that King George III's ministers had induced the King to countenance a lie. The government issued a general warrant requiring strict and diligent search for the authors, printers, and publishers of the "treasonable paper," and the seizure of both them and their papers. Acting on a tip, the King's men seized Wilkes, ransacked his house, and carried away his personal and political papers, stuffed into sacks. The King's agents also broke into the house of Entick, an associate of Wilkes, broke into locked desks and boxes, and seized a variety of papers and charts. Later, the English court held the warrants invalid and awarded Entick damages against an offending official.[24] In the American colonies, the case created a great stir. The stir, coupled with local experience, led to the subsequent adoption of constitutional guarantees not only against unreasonable searches and seizures but also against the issuance of warrants except on probable cause and describing particularly the place to be searched and the things to be seized.

Incidents like the Wilkes case, even though not unknown, have been few in America, partly because of our traditional political tolerance but largely because of the effectiveness of the Fourth and Fourteenth Amendments and corresponding safeguards in State constitutions. The most notable modern example is the burglary of the offices of Dr. Fielding by agents of the Nixon White House, who were hoping to gain copies of the psychiatric files on Daniel Ellsberg with which to destroy his effectiveness as a leader of the movement to stop the war in Vietnam. Checking such abuses is worth more than the cost.

IV

The catalogue of changes in criminal procedure wrought by the Supreme Court in the 1950s and 1960s is too long for detailed examination. The law of confessions was rewritten.[25] Standards governing the admission and exclusion of evidence obtained by wiretapping and other forms of electronic surveillance were developed.[26] There was far closer scrutiny of the observance of constitutional standards relating to the conduct of the prosecutor in using, revealing, or withholding evidence;[27] composition of the jury;[28] the privilege of confronting adverse witnesses;[29] and the right to compulsory process in order to obtain witnesses for the defense.[30] In other cases the Court, again overruling a long line of precedents, extended to State prosecutions the same privilege against self-incrimination that prevails in the federal courts, including freedom from comment on the accused's failure to testify in his own defense.[31] Another precedent-breaking decision assured juveniles many of the safeguards applicable to adult defendants.[32]

The single most important reform was wrought by *Gideon* v. *Wainwright*[33]—a story celebrated in Anthony Lewis's fascinating book, *Gideon's Trumpet*. Throughout our earlier constitutional history men too poor to retain counsel had been put on trial in many States without the assistance of an attorney, even men charged with serious, albeit not capital, crimes. The constitutionality of the practice had been sustained in numerous cases. Now indigents must be supplied with counsel at public expense in all serious criminal cases, whether federal or State. The same rule applies to the provision of transcripts and lawyers for a first appeal.[34] The new rule set in motion countless local reforms, because the activity of counsel brought to the attention of judges practices that had escaped their notice or that they had let slide, such as confining offenders for long periods without arraignment or advice about their legal rights. The spirit engendered by the decision supplied much of the stimulus for broader undertakings, such as the Attorney General's Conference on Bail, the Attorney General's Conference on the Provision of Legal Services to the Indigent, and the work of the President's Commission on Law Enforcement and the Administration of Justice.

Gideon v. *Wainwright*[35] also furnishes another revealing example of the problems raised by Attorney General Meese and other critics of the Warren Court's decisions who allege that the Court erred grievously by creating new constitutional rights not within the "original intent." The first problem, as we observed in studying the Establishment Clause, is to pin down the meaning of "original intent." In the case of criminal prosecutions one can say with justified assurance that the authors and sponsors of the Bill of Rights lacked any specific intent to give indigents charged with crime a constitutional right to counsel at public expense but that they also had a more general conscious intent to guarantee anyone charged with crime a fair trial. Probably the authors and sponsors of the Bill of Rights also believed that in the circumstances then prevailing the provision of counsel at public expense was not necessary to a fair trial, and thus could fairly be said—in one sense of the words—to have intended not to provide this constitutional right. But the circumstances have changed. Both law and life have become vastly more complex than in 1791. The resulting crimes and criminal trials are often correspondingly more complex. Defenses unknown to a lay defendant may be familiar to lawyers. Judges who once had the time and disposition to secure the legitimate interests of a defendant without counsel are now rushed along by overwhelming dockets, the bustling crowds, and dulling tedium of big-city courts. In the circumstances now prevailing, the individual without counsel has much less chance of making a successful defense than the individual who receives sound legal advice. To extend the Founders' original intent not to provide counsel at public expense to altogether different circumstances outside their contemplation is to play games with words ripped from their context. And to force an indigent unaided in a modern courtroom to choose between pleading guilty and defending himself without the assistance of counsel is almost surely to defeat the Framers' more basic intent to guarantee fair trials. The application of old general principles to unforeseen modern particulars is essential if the two-hundred-year-old document is to continue to serve the country's needs. Nor does the process violate the Justices' duty to decide according to a continuing body of inherited law, including the evidence of the original intent, provided that the general principle was present at the start.

School Desegregation

"... all men are created equal"

SO READS the Declaration of Independence. Americans believe its teaching. Yet all individuals are *not* equal. Only a handful are endowed with the talent to quarterback the Dallas Cowboys or to sit as a Justice on the Supreme Court of the United States. What then did the authors of the Declaration of Independence mean by "equality"? What do we mean today?

The Declaration of Independence was a political manifesto—a rallying cry designed to summon support for breaking the link between the colonies and Britain. If its full meaning was uncertain—if, like a plank in a modern political platform, it would mean many things to many people—so much the better. Much of the revolutionary fervor in 1776 flowed from the belief that the colonials were being denied the traditional rights of Englishmen. The declaration asserted equality of political and legal rights as between British and American. The declaration of equality was also leveled at inequalities of status flowing from lineage; there should be no titles or privileges of Dukes, Earls, or other classes of nobility; no King ruling by Divine right. The deeper philosophy was drawn by Thomas Jefferson from the French philosopher Jean-Jacques Rousseau and an Englishman, John Locke. Both taught that in a state of nature men were vested with certain unalienable natural rights, including the rights to life, liberty, and property; and that while men might agree to surrender some authority to a government in order to establish civilized society, they were free to rebel against a government imposed on them without their consent. "Equal" meant equal in the possession of natural rights.

In another sense the America of 1776 was filled with inequalities: political, legal, social, and economic. Probably the Declaration looked to some degree of political equality among those admitted to the political community, but the political community itself was closed. Slaves, free blacks, and women were all excluded. So were the propertyless; they were thought to have too little stake in government to make them responsible members of the political community.

Yet the idea of equality once loosed is not easily cabined. There was enormous generative power in the simple declaration that all men are created equal. If in a state of nature, if in the very beginning the Creator had made all men equal—if existing inequalities of wealth, power, opportunity, or condition have been selfishly imposed by the ruthlessly powerful on the less fortunate—then should not all the unjust differences be eliminated and equality restored? The open lands, rich natural resources, and seemingly endless economic opportunities in a burgeoning society have lent reality to the dream. A boy born in a log cabin could become President. A penniless immigrant could live the Horatio Alger story. The search for "equality"—for its meaning and its realization—became a driving force in American life.

In the beginning neither the Constitution nor the Supreme Court of the United States played much part in the search. The original Constitution contained no assurance of equality. The Constitution did not even assure universal manhood suffrage. All questions of voting rights were left to the States. And even though the contradiction between acceptance of African slavery and their declarations concerning the rights of man troubled the consciences of some of the more sensitive Framers, the Constitution they wrote accepted that most evil of inequalities. Even in the "free States," black men enjoyed few legal or political rights. In the slave States they were chattels.

The *Dred Scott* case[1] accelerated the inevitable conflict between the northern and southern States over the institution of slavery. The Civil War brought the abolition of slavery, first by President Lincoln's Emancipation Proclamation, and later and more permanently by adoption of the Thirteenth Amendment. The Fourteenth Amendment, ratified in 1868, pressed the search for equality a giant step forward. The immediate purpose was to overrule the *Dred Scott* decision and secure the newly freed black men equal civil rights, but the sponsors used much broader words:

> No State . . . shall deprive any person of life, liberty, or property, without due process of law; nor deny to any person within its jurisdiction the equal protection of the laws.

" . . . equal protection of the laws." Coupled with the power and duty of judicial review, this majestic phrase gave the ideal of equality a measure of constitutional sanction and committed the U.S. Supreme Court to participation in the search for its meaning and realization. At first the Court held back. Three quarters of a century later the Equal Protection Clause, in strong judicial hands, would enable the Court to lead a broadly egalitarian movement permeating American society.

RACIAL EQUALITY

Progress was slowest in the very area with which the sponsors of the Fourteenth Amendment were most concerned—equality of civil rights for the former slaves. Two Supreme Court precedents stood in the way.

The first, the *Civil Rights Cases*,[2] held unconstitutional the Civil Rights Act of 1875, which required hotels and other places of public accommodation to grant all persons equal enjoyment of their facilities, regardless of race or color. A theatre, a railroad, and a hotel, prosecuted for continuing racial discrimination, successfully challenged the act's constitutionality. Section 5 of the Fourteenth Amendment gives Congress the power to enact legislation appropriate to the enforcement of the Due Process and Equal Protection Clauses, but the commands in those clauses are addressed only to the States. Although the word "state" covers not only cities, towns, and other governmental subdivisions, but also all agencies, boards, and officials when acting under color of law, private action by individuals or organizations is unaffected. If a State gave a white traveler denied available accommodations a legal remedy against a railroad or innkeeper but withheld the same remedy from a black traveler, then the State would deny the blacks the equal protection of the laws. But in the Civil Rights Cases the indictments alleged only private acts of discrimination. Congress could not punish them, the Court ruled, because there was no showing of State action, no denial of "equal protection *of the laws*."

The general implication of the Civil Rights Cases was plain. The Fourteenth Amendment invalidated State laws imposing special disabilities on the freedmen or otherwise discriminating against them, but it did not reach or authorize Congress to reach the bonds of customary social and economic discrimination that condemned black people to seemingly permanent inferiority under white supremacy. Years later the expansion of federal power under the Commerce Clause would enable Congress to reach the injustice. The equal public accommodations provisions of the Civil Rights Act of 1964 were drawn as an exercise of the federal power to regulate interstate commerce in order to avoid the Civil Rights Cases and the requirement of State action.[3] But before 1937 no one supposed, even in his wildest dreams, that the federal power to regulate commerce among the several States extended to the regulation of restaurants, theatres, and other local places of public accommodation.

Plessy v. *Ferguson*[4] was the second obstacle to blacks' use of the Equal Protection Clause in their search for equality. Louisiana had enacted legislation requiring railroads to provide "equal but separate accommodations for the white and colored races." When the constitutionality of the law was challenged, everyone assumed that the accommodations and service were equal in fact. Possibly so. No one could deny, however, that the major consequence flowing from the State-mandated segregation was to further impress on black people a stamp of caste inferiority: "unfit to mingle with the white race." The Court held that consequence to be irrelevant by an 8–1 vote. "We consider the underlying fallacy of the plaintiff's argument to consist in the assumption that the enforced separation of the two races stamps the colored race with a badge of inferiority. If this be so, it is not by reason of anything found in the act."[5] The Court's concepts of State responsibility and "equal protection of the laws" were obviously narrow.

The "separate but equal" doctrine seemed to make the State laws that provided the legal underpinning for communitywide racial segregation virtually impregnable to constitutional attack. State statutes and municipal ordinances were adopted on a wide scale, requiring segregation in places of public accommodation, upon common carriers, in places of public entertainment, and often in hospitals and cemeteries. State laws and policies mandated segregation in courthouses and public institutions. The intermarriage of whites and blacks was prohibited. Businesses and professional organizations pursued similar practices. The communitywide fabric of white supremacy was thus filled with threads of law and government policy woven through the warp of custom laid down by private prejudice. Black people were condemned to social, political, and economic inequality from the cradle to their segregated graves.

Most rigid and most damaging were the "separate but equal" schools, which marked black boys and girls "inferior" while young enough for the system of segregation to become ingrained in them, and which also denied them the skills necessary to seek advancement.

In theory, the separate black facilities were equal to the white. In fact, they were dramatically inferior. The inferiority in segregated education was the greatest, by any standard of measurement. There lay the chink in the constitutional armor of State-supported white supremacy that would lead to Supreme Court decisions and subsequent federal legislation dismantling the old system. But to exploit the chink there was desperate need for black parents and children courageous enough to go to court as plaintiffs to challenge the system and stubborn enough to persevere in the face of harsh reprisals. There was need, too, for skilled and persevering lawyers to guide them. The Constitution helps those who help themselves.

Harry Briggs, a Navy veteran with five children in Summerton, Clarendon County, South Carolina, was one such parent.[6] He and nineteen others became plaintiffs in a suit, filed in the federal court in November 1949, alleging that the dual school system in Clarendon County violated the Equal Protection Clause. At first Briggs figured that anything to better the children's condition was worthwhile, and there "didn't seem to be much danger to it." He soon learned the dangers. A month later, on the day before Christmas, his boss fired him from his job pumping gas. The motel where his wife worked as chambermaid let her go when she declined to tell Briggs to take his name off the court papers. Their credit was cut off at the Summerton bank. They obtained a loan in Sumter, but that bank too called the loan as soon as it learned the identity of Harry Briggs. Other plaintiffs suffered similar reprisals, but they too persevered.

The black parents in Clarendon County had ample reason to do what they could for their children. The taxpayers of Clarendon County spent $179 on each white child in the public schools in 1949–1950; for each black child, $43. There were twelve white schools for 2375 white pupils, valued at $673,850. The sixty-five buildings for 6531 black pupils were listed as worth $194,675; often they were ramshackle. The teachers' salaries at the black schools were, on the average, only 60 percent of the average salary at white schools. The public paid no other expenses for blacks. Black families were left to find buildings for black schools and to raise money for everything from coal to crayons. Clarendon County had thirty buses for white schoolchildren; it had none for black.

It was the buses that started the ferment in a county that had always prided itself on "good nigras." When black parents in an isolated part of the county asked for a bus to get their children to school, the county refused. When the blacks chipped in together to buy an old bus, the county refused to provide gasoline. With the aid of the National Association for the Advancement of Colored People (NAACP) a suit was brought, challenging the inequality, but it failed on a technical ground.

Stirred by further injustices, the ferment in Clarendon County continued. In March 1949 Thurgood Marshall, NAACP General Counsel, on a visit to South Carolina, had told the county's black leaders that if twenty qualified parents would join as plaintiffs, the NAACP would join in supporting a broad constitutional attack on Clarendon County's dual school system. Given the risk of technical defenses and withdrawals forced by white reprisals, no smaller number of plaintiffs would suffice. It took eight months to gather the necessary number, but by November 1949 Harry Briggs and nineteen others had signed. When the court papers were filed in *Briggs* v. *Elliott,* Thurgood Marshall and Harold R. Boulware, a Columbia, South Carolina, attorney, entered appearances as the plaintiff's attorneys.

Both men were part of the small nucleus of skilled black lawyers, centered on Howard University and the NAACP, who planned and carried forward the legal campaign for racial equality. The leader had been Charles H. Houston, the grandson of Tom Houston, who, according to family legend, served as aide-de-camp to General Ulysses S. Grant and was an honorary pallbearer on the funeral train of Abraham Lincoln. Charles H. Houston, after earning a Phi Beta Kappa key at Amherst College, attended the Harvard Law School, won a place on the prestigious *Harvard Law Review,* and returned to Washington to practice law. In July 1929 he became the Dean of Howard Law School and dedicated himself to teaching and leading the black lawyers who would fight the legal battles of the civil rights movement.

Charles Houston was not an easy man. His law students knew him as "Ironshoes" and "Cement Pants." His favorite precept was "No tea for the feeble, no crepe for the dead." Even though a black lawyer in Virginia's white courtrooms, he won admiration and respect. He remade the Howard Law School by attracting teachers like William Hastie, another Amherst and Harvard Law School graduate, who became the first black judge on a United States Court of Appeals and who might well have become the first black Justice of the Supreme Court of the United States had not Justice William O. Douglas told Attorney General Robert Kennedy that he opposed him as all too likely to be just another vote for Justice Felix Frankfurter.

Thurgood Marshall, the son of a schoolteacher mother and the chief steward at the aristocratic Chesapeake Bay Boat Club, had studied at the Howard Law School. By 1949, when he went down to Clarendon County, his perseverance and successful advocacy had earned him a title as "lawyer for his race."

By 1949 these and other black colleagues had laid the ground-work for an attack on the "separate but equal" doctrine. They wisely perceived not only that the attack upon segregation must be centered on the total school system if black children were ever to have a chance to develop their talents, but also that the fraud inherent in "separate but equal" was most apparent in education for the professions. In a key case they persuaded the Court to rule that Missouri violated the Equal Protection Clause by maintaining an all-white law school at the State university while paying black law students the tuition to attend universities out of state.[7] When the States in the South established separate law schools for black law students, the Court rightly held that a separate black law school, even if properly funded, could not possibly provide equal professional education.

> The law school to which Texas is willing to admit petitioner excludes from its student body members of the racial groups which number 85% of the population of the State and include most of the lawyers, witnesses, jurors, judges and other officials with whom petitioner will inevitably be dealing when he becomes a member of the Texas Bar. With such a substantial and significant segment of society excluded, we cannot conclude that the education offered petitioner is substantially equal to that which he would receive if admitted to the University of Texas Law School.[8]

The campaign peaked when Briggs's Clarendon County case and similar cases from Virginia, Delaware, and Kansas came before the U.S. Supreme Court. In an opinion known everywhere as *Brown* v. *Board of Education*[9] the Court decided for the plaintiffs. Relying on the writings of psychologists and sociologists and the findings of one of the lower courts, the Court declared that segregation of children in public schools solely on the basis of race deprives the children of equal educational opportunities, even where the physical facilities and other tangible factors may be equal, because the separation of black children only because of race narrows opportunities to learn by association with others in the community and also generates a feeling of inferior status that may affect their minds and hearts throughout their lives.[10] Accordingly, the Court unanimously ruled that separate public educational facilities, being inherently unequal, violate the Fourteenth Amendment's guarantee of "equal protection of the laws."

One consequence was a revolution in constitutional law. Subsequent decisions quickly extended the *Brown* principle to other racial segregation laws. State laws enforcing a caste system that segregated black from white from birth through burial were invalidated[11] and enforcement gradually stopped. The command of the Fourteenth Amendment is addressed only to government: "[N]or shall any State deny . . . the equal protection of the laws." But new doctrines were developed extending this constitutional prohibition against racial discrimination to private activities specially encouraged or supported by a State.[12] New federal statutes were enacted in order to deal with acts and practices depriving black citizens of the right to vote, and to secure for them equal treatment in places of public accommodation, equal employment opportunities, and equal access to housing. Constitutional law changed and grew in order to sustain the new federal laws.[13]

The impact of *Brown* and other Desegregation Cases on American constitutional law and society extended far beyond matters of race. Propelled by the decision, the courts began to strike down, as we shall see in Chapter 17, differences in official treatment based on sex, alienage, length of residence, illegitimacy of birth, and sometimes (but less often than one would wish) ability to pay. Emphasis on equality led to the "one person, one vote" rule laid down in the Reapportionment Cases discussed in Chapter 16. The egalitarian influence of *Brown* also ran strong in decisions reforming the administration of criminal law by requiring the State to supply paupers, in both courts and police stations, with the legal assistance others can buy.[14]

The Desegregation Cases had this generative force in other areas because the opinions rejected the presumption of constitutionality and other rules of judicial self-restraint in favor of the principle that "the Equal Protection Clause demands that racial classifications . . . be subjected to the most rigid scrutiny" and were to be upheld, if at all, only when strictly necessary to achieve a "compelling public purpose."[15] The formula obviously envisaged an enlarged judicial role of much the same character as the rigorous judicial scrutiny of laws and government practices said to abridge freedom of expression. So long as race discrimination alone was involved, the more active intervention could be linked to the historic purposes of the Fourteenth Amendment. The new role would become more controversial as other groups seeking equality pressed the Court, with some success, to scrutinize very strictly the State laws subjecting them to disadvantage.

For those concerned about the proper role of the Court and the limits of the judicial function in constitutional adjudication, the *Brown* decision, taken with the subsequent judicial condemnation of all segregation laws, raises suggestive questions. By overruling *Plessy* v. *Ferguson*, the Court rejected a half century of established legal doctrine. Those who defended segregation and encouraged massive resistance were able to say, "The desegregation decision was not law but only the dictate of nine men. In time, with nine different men, the Court will return to its earlier decisions." The departure from established law thus had some tendency to impair the legitimacy and authority of the Court's decision. Those of us who applaud *Brown* and similar decisions can reply that to have adhered to *Plessy* v. *Ferguson* would have ignored the revolution sweeping the world and the emerging moral sense of civilization. We might add that the logical application of precedents and doctrines from the past will not alone provide the legitimacy that evokes public consent. For the law to command consent, the law must deserve it. But unless we can say something more, we should have to admit that sometimes the Court does impose constitutional interpretations supported only by the notions of justice shared by a majority of the Justices. Perhaps it says a little more to point out that the earlier decisions involving professional schools had slightly eroded *Plessy* v. *Ferguson*, but their citation is scarcely a full response.

The most satisfactory response, I think, is that the Desegregation Cases *do* have roots outside the Justices' personal opinions in our inherited constitutional tradition and the basic purpose of the Equal Protection Clause of the Fourteenth Amendment. Surely the proposition that all men are born with equal right to human dignity and to equal standing in the eyes of government regardless of the circumstances of their birth had been a basic American ideal since before the Declaration of Independence. Slavery, its attendant legal disqualifications, and the disparate treatment of even free Negroes had been arbitrary exceptions that had long embarrassed the philosophically inclined. The purpose of the Fourteenth Amendment was to eliminate that excrescence from our law and all other relationships between the individual and the State.

Here it is important to distinguish among the several meanings of "purpose" and "intent." One might ask, "Did the Congress that recommended the Fourteenth Amendment and the State legislators who ratified it consciously and specifically intend to abolish school segregation?" No one has made a persuasive case for an affirmative answer. At least one close student of the history of the Fourteenth Amendment argues strongly that the evidence shows that they specifically and consciously intended *not* to abolish official segregation.[16] Probably the answer nearest the truth is that the sponsors did not specifically and consciously resolve the question one way or the other, even in their own minds, either because they did not focus on the specific question or because they could not agree on an answer.[17] But one charged with applying the Fourteenth Amendment to a statute mandating school desegregation must also ask what was the intent in the sense of the broad purpose or policy, and then must go further and ask how the broad purpose would apply to State-mandated racial segregation with the knowledge and under the circumstances of 1954. The broad intent seems to me to have been the purpose stated above—to secure all individuals a right to human dignity and equal standing before government, without regard to race or color. And even if it were possible in earlier years to view State-mandated segregation on common carriers as imposing no official stamp of inferiority upon black people, that surely could not be said in 1954 of the system of official segregation then pervading the legislation of the States of the old South.

In my view, therefore, the Desegregation Cases of the 1950s faithfully projected the general intent of the sponsors of the Equal Protection Clause upon a more particular set of circumstances as to which the sponsors left no adequate record of their particular intent. In my view, too, a court that on great occasions applies this historically grounded general intent in a manner consistent with traditional national ideals decides in accordance with the judge's antinomous duty to decide in a manner that invokes the authority of an overshadowing past yet discovers some composition with the dominant needs and aspirations of its times. The decision leans toward the creative branch of the antinomy but is in accordance with law even though it requires the overruling of precedent and the abandonment of familiar, specific practices that fail to meet the historical ideal and general constitutional purpose.

SCHOOL DESEGREGATION

The program of school desegregation flowing from Brown v. Board of Education[18] is surely the largest and most difficult venture ever undertaken by the courts in the name of constitutional adjudication: commands to reform established institutions, mandates ordering busing and other affirmative action by school authorities, the directed expenditure of large public funds, and the need not only for continuous judicial resolution of broad questions of policy but also for attention to administrative detail, both outside the realm of constitutional law. Decrees ordering extensive busing added another quasi-legislative quality far removed from typical judicial functions: they required the States, through local school boards, to expend millions of dollars and reorder the lives of hundreds of thousands of parents and children, some pleased but many deeply disappointed, in pursuit of broad social objectives. Today we are all well aware of the busing and like measures, but the evolution from *Brown* was slow and tortuous in both legal theory and practical execution.

Brown made plain that the Fourteenth Amendment required public school authorities to stop assigning children to individual schools on the basis of race and to refrain from other racially motivated measures, such as locating new schools or drawing the boundaries of attendance zones in ways that would promote segregation. Stopping segregative practices, however, would not achieve the movement's goal of winning equal education opportunities for black children then and there. In order to secure further relief, the NAACP and other civil rights organizations could hope to build on two legal doctrines, although neither carried assurance of success.

One theory would invoke the familiar power of a court of equity to order a wrongdoer not only to stop violating the complainants' rights but also to take such further action as would be appropriate to wipe out the effects of past violations. On this theory it could be argued that where all-white and all-black schools resulted from continuing or even past unconstitutional segregation, a federal district court, having the powers of an equity court, should order the School Board to integrate the schools.

The second possible argument was constitutional and had much broader reach. The *Brown* opinion declared that "[s]eparate educational facilities are inherently unequal."[18] The words refer to a condition. Might they not mean that equality under the Fourteenth Amendment requires integrated education in all public schools in districts where there are both black children and white? Perhaps not only in school districts where there had been segregation by force of State law but even where there was "de facto segregation," that is, where racial separation in all-white and all-black schools resulted from residential patterns coupled with a policy of assigning children to the nearest neighborhood school? This second theory would reach beyond the old South to the equally damaging segregation in northern cities even though never explicitly mandated by State law.

At the outset, there was fierce resistance against even the duty to stop making school assignments according to race. The Governor of Virginia led a campaign of massive resistance. Prince Edward County, the defendant in one case, closed its schools rather than halt assignment by race. Governor Orval Faubus of Arkansas attempted to invoke the pre-Civil War doctrine of "interposition" to block what he called unconstitutional interference with local affairs. President Eisenhower was reluctantly forced to use federal troops in 1957 in order to prevent a mob from blocking the admission of black students to a Little Rock, Arkansas, high school. President Kennedy faced the same problem at the University of Mississippi in 1962. In 1965 Governor George Wallace of Alabama "stood in the schoolhouse door" to block the admission of black students to all-white schools; he yielded only to a show of federal force. Hundreds, probably thousands, of lawsuits had to be brought to implement the *Brown* decision.

Fourteen years elapsed between the *Brown* decision and the first Supreme Court ruling on whether either the remedial power of a court of equity or the ideal of racial equality embodied in the Equal Protection Clause requires a school district to do more than stop segregative acts. The question became pressing in its narrowest form when it appeared that stopping the unconstitutional practice and allowing pupils freedom of choice among schools in a district where black and white pupils had long been segregated by law would have scant effect on attendance patterns, and therefore would do very little to provide the "equal education" of which the Supreme Court had spoken.

In Kent County, Virginia, for example, there were two schools, one near either end of the county. For many years segregation was required by Virginia law. Because the area was rural, there was no racial separation by residential neighborhood. Black children were transported to one school and white children to the other. In 1965, after suit had been filed, the School Board installed a plan allowing every student to attend the school of his or her choice. During the next three years no white child chose to attend the "black" school. Only 15 percent of the black children chose to attend the "white" school. The years of segregation by law had taught parents and children that black children go to black schools and white children go to white schools, and the schools were branded accordingly. The momentum of this past teaching could not be stopped—the brands BLACK and WHITE could not be erased from over the schoolhouse door—merely by giving today's pupils freedom of choice. The Supreme Court directed the School Board to "fashion steps which promise realistically to convert promptly to a system without a 'white' school and a Negro school but just schools." The unanimous opinion did not elaborate the underlying reasoning but did assert the duty of any School Boards "operating state-compelled dual systems" promptly to take "whatever steps might be necessary to convert to a unitary system in which racial segregation would be eliminated root and branch."[19]

Eliminating "white" schools and "black" schools in Kent County would be simple. Almost any colorblind method of assignment, including a neighborhood school policy, would achieve that result in most of Kent County and throughout the rural South. Federal courts throughout the area followed the principle, some willingly and others under mandate of the circuit courts of appeals. Freedom-of-choice plans died out. Desegregation gradually became real.

In metropolitan areas the problem was more complex, even in the South. In metropolitan areas social, economic, and legal forces, including School Board policies, had combined to produce segregated housing patterns. Assigning children to the neighborhood school would result in some integration along the fringes, but many schools would remain all black or all white. School Boards might stop actively segregating children by race or color, but segregation as a condition could be eliminated only if many white children were transported to schools in black neighborhoods and vice versa. Beyond the southern cities lay the all-black and all-white northern schools in areas where racial segregation was never mandated by law. Perhaps decrees requiring busing could be obtained as an appropriate remedy for past school segregation laws, but not otherwise, unless the Court had meant to hold that segregation as a condition violated the Equal Protection Clause regardless of its source.

The Charlotte-Mecklenburg School District in North Carolina illustrates the first problem. The 550-square-mile area encompassed the City of Charlotte and its suburbs, with a combined population of 273,000, and also the surrounding rural areas of Mecklenburg County. For many years prior to 1954 all the schools had been segregated, in accordance with the North Carolina statutes. After 1954, the School Board ceased to make racial assignments and substituted attendance zones, assigning each child to a nearby school, regardless of race; but students were allowed some freedom to transfer to other schools. The plan went far to eliminate all-black and all-white schools out in the county, but its remedial effect in the suburbs and core city was limited because there the residential patterns reflected rigid racial separation. In June 1969 the Charlotte-Mecklenburg school system served more than eighty-four thousand pupils in 107 schools. Of the twenty-four thousand black students, over half still attended schools that were more than 99 percent black. Of the sixty thousand white students, three fourths were in schools that were obviously white. The plaintiffs in a pending suit satisfied the U.S. District Court that the School Board had failed to achieve the kind of unitary system required by the *Kent County* case. After careful hearings the court ordered the School Board to institute a new plan of integration that used zoning, pairing, and grouping of zones to distribute students in such a way that the proportion of black students in each of the schools would be not less than 9 percent nor more than 38 percent. The key element was the busing of white students in the suburbs to previously all-black schools in the central city and, conversely, busing black students to the suburban schools. School buses had long been familiar in the Charlotte-Mecklenburg School District, as they were throughout the United States, but under the district court's decree the busing would be greatly expanded. More than thirty-six thousand children would be transported from points near their homes to often-distant schools. The average *one-way trip* would be over fifteen miles and would take an hour and fourteen minutes. The estimates of cost varied widely, but the transportation office of the school system projected a need for 526 buses and a first-year cost of approximately $4.2 million (including the cost of transportation under the old system of school assignment).

The plan was set aside by the circuit court of appeals but reinstated by the U.S. Supreme Court as within the power of a court of equity to provide a remedy adequate to correct past constitutional violations.[20] Its approval of extensive and expensive busing set the pattern for school desegregation in all metropolitan areas in States where racial segregation had previously been mandated by law. The example of Charlotte-Mecklenburg stands for Richmond, Atlanta, Birmingham, Jackson, and other cities throughout the South. The process was slow; the local authorities often dragged their feet; protracted litigation was often necessary to secure full relief; but once the legal points were clear, desegregation went forward in the southern schools.

In many northern cities, where the inequalities were no less damaging to black children, the legal problems proved greater. The *Charlotte-Mecklenburg* opinion strongly indicated that *de facto* segregation is not unconstitutional.[21] In many cities, however, in which residential patterns led to separate "black" and "white" schools—in Boston, Detroit, Denver, and Columbus, Ohio, for example—the School Boards had drawn attendance zones, located new schools, and taken other steps to promote racial separation. The key question became: Under what circumstances should a federal court order integration by busing throughout the district? Each city presented a unique situation. Years of litigation were often required.

The events in Denver, Colorado, illustrate some of the legal and the practical problems. The boundaries of the Denver School District coincided with the city boundaries. In 1969 there were 96,580 pupils at 119 schools. The black and Hispanic populations were heavily concentrated in the core city, where eighteen or nineteen elementary schools, three junior high schools, and three high schools had very few Anglo students, and the education was markedly inferior to the schooling in other parts of the city. The most substantial proof of deliberate racial discrimination, however, was confined to the Park Hill area. During the 1960s the School Board had deliberately fostered racial segregation in its eight schools by gerrymandering attendance zones, building a small school near the black community, creating optional zones, and using mobile classroom units. The discrimination affected about 37 percent of the black pupils in the Denver schools. After numerous hearings the district court ordered citywide desegregation, but the order was reversed by the court of appeals. The U.S. Supreme Court reversed the court of appeals. A majority of the Justices ruled that the finding of purposeful discrimination in the Park Hill area shifted to the School Board the burden of showing that the racial imbalance in the other schools in the Denver School District was not also the result of intentionally segregative actions. If the School Board failed to disprove that presumption, the Court said, the full panoply of remedies illustrated by the *Charlotte-Mecklenburg* case was available to bring about citywide integration. The case was remanded for further proceedings.[22]

In 1985 the Denver School Case was still pending in the U.S. District Court. An order for districtwide integration had been entered, many intermediate steps had been taken, but the court was not satisfied that the integration was complete.

Here again one case must stand as an example of court decrees and social changes across the country. In some cities there was fierce resistance. Here and there schools began to look like armed camps. But progress, though slow and incomplete, was great.

As the decade of the 1980s passes and we enter the 1990s, the courts will be called upon more and more often to decide whether to dissolve busing and other desegregation decrees on the ground that the effects of the old unconstitutional acts that the courts can remedy have been dissipated and any new resegregation will be the result of personal preferences and demographic and economic forces rather than unconstitutional *de jure* discrimination. Changes in the make-up of the Supreme Court are reducing its enthusiasm for school integration. At the October Term 1986, the Court declined to review a lower-court decision governing the Norfolk, Virginia, School District that illustrates the problem and may mark a trend.[23]

In 1954 the Norfolk schools were segregated by Virginia's school segregation law. In 1970, after fourteen years of litigation, the plaintiffs obtained an order requiring the federal district court to formulate a plan for achieving a unitary school system. A year later a plan conforming to the *Charlotte-Mecklenburg* decision was ordered by the district court. The plan used the pairing and clustering of schools, along with crosstown busing, to accomplish desegregation. In 1975 the district court concluded without objection that unconstitutional racial discrimination had ended and a unitary school system had been achieved.

By 1980 large demographic changes had occurred in Norfolk, somewhat typical of changes accompanying desegregation in other cities across the United States. The black population increased slightly but the white population declined 25 percent. In 1969–1970, 57 percent (32,586) of the pupils were white and 43 percent (24,244) were black. By 1980–1981, the white enrollment had dropped more than 50 percent, to only 43 percent of the whole. The race-conscious zoning, pairing of schools, and crosstown busing instituted in 1970 had integrated students so that no school had a black enrollment of more than 70 percent. By 1981 seven elementary schools were more than 70 percent black. The effect on the quality of education is unclear, but the court of appeals thought it significant that parental interest had sharply diminished. PTA membership had dropped more than 75 percent.

After study and hearings the Norfolk School Board adopted a "Proposal for a Voluntary Stably Desegregated School System." The junior high schools would continue fully integrated. Crosstown busing of elementary school pupils would be eliminated, with the result that of the thirty-six elementary schools, six would become 70 to 80 percent white and twelve would become more than 70 percent black, ten of the twelve by more than 95 percent. Roughly five thousand black elementary students would be initially assigned to all-black schools but would be allowed, on request, to transfer to schools where the enrollment was more than 50 percent white.

The plan was challenged by black parents represented by the NAACP. The district court rejected the challenge, and its order was affirmed by the court of appeals chiefly on a finding that "the plaintiffs had not satisfied their burden of proving discriminatory intent."[24] The finding seems heavily influenced by expert testimony that the busing had caused and would continue to cause white pupils to leave the Norfolk public schools and was also responsible for the shocking drop in parental involvement illustrated by the huge decline in PTA membership.

The Norfolk case may well point to the future, but it is not a sure guide. The Supreme Court's denial of *certiorari* does not always signify approval of a decision that it declines to review. (*Certiorari* is a term taken from the ancient form of order by which an inferior tribunal was directed to certify the record of its proceedings to a higher authority.) More could have been done to give black elementary school pupils a desegregated and therefore equal education. An alternative plan offered by the Norfolk School Board would, by busing more students for shorter trips than under the 1971 plan, have ensured that in the absence of further white flight, no school had more than a 25 percent enrollment from one race. And there are ample legal grounds on which to argue that, instead of analyzing the School Board's purposes, the federal courts should have inquired whether the Norfolk School Board was still under a duty to do more than the plan provided to wipe out the consequences of segregating students for decades before *Brown* and of a further fifteen-year delay before adopting a remedy. The narrow consequences of *de jure* segregation had been eliminated by establishing a unitary system, but a decade of desegregation seems hardly enough to offset either the impact on black children or the broader societal consequences of centuries of racial segregation and invidious discrimination.

Whatever the possibility of a better remedy in Norfolk, the example makes it plain that the power of courts to undo the past is limited. The remedies any School Board may be required to adopt are tightly confined to its geographical district by Supreme Court decision[25] and practicability. As white families move out to the suburbs and the population of the central city becomes heavily black, the prospect of integrated and therefore truly equal education inevitably dims. In the end, full equality depends upon equal economic opportunity and the spirit of the people.

To note the limits on judicial power to compel truly equal educational opportunities for all students is not to doubt the vast importance of what has been accomplished by the School Desegregation decrees. The degree of integration is great. The integration is real. In myriad instances both the black vision of opportunity and the white vision of justice have been reborn. We see the consequences in ourselves and all about us. The narrower effects of busing and desegregation on public school education will be widely debated, but for those who embrace the ideal of equality regardless of race or color, as expressed in *Brown* v. *Board of Education*, the decisive factor is that in the face of foot dragging and resistance there simply was no other way in which the Court could say, "And we mean it!"

· 15 ·

Affirmative Action

THE SUPREME COURT DECISIONS under the Equal Protection
Clause gradually halted hostile governmental discrimination against
blacks, Hispanics, and other ethnic minorities. The Civil Rights
Act of 1964 and other State and federal laws then forbade private
discrimination in motels, restaurants, theatres, and other places of
public accommodation, in housing, in employment, and in the administration of any programs, including educational programs, supported by federal funds. Had the ancient goal of "equality" been
achieved? It was clear that these laws and decisions alone could
not quickly bring minorities into the mainstream of American life.
By any measure the economic condition of blacks was far inferior
to that of whites. There were few black business enterprises of
substantial size, and few blacks in the ranks of management in
white businesses. Only a small fraction of the skilled jobs were
open to blacks, virtually none, except as a common laborer, in the
construction industry. The proportion of black students in higher
education was far below the proportion of black people in the whole
population. Relatively few black people made their way into the
professions. One could give endless examples.

Was this "equality"? Would you take a person who, for years,
had been hobbled by chains—President Lyndon B. Johnson asked
in an address at Howard University on June 4, 1965[1]—liberate him,
bring him up to the starting line of a race, and then say, "You are
free to compete with all the others"? Would you believe that you
had been entirely fair?

269

President Johnson's speech sparked a movement for affirmative action by both government and private organizations. An executive order was issued, requiring federal contractors to take affirmative action to recruit and employ racial minorities, even in the absence of a determination that the particular employer had previously engaged in unlawful discrimination.[2] Under that order specific affirmative action plans were developed for the construction industry, area by area, setting percentage targets for the employment of minority journeymen and apprentices in each craft on each job. A federal law, now expired, was enacted requiring that 10 percent of each grant for local public works projects "shall be expended for minority business enterprises."[3] Many cities and towns in all parts of the country had engaged in open or covert racial discrimination in employing firefighters and police officers. Courts, on proof of such violation of the Equal Protection Clause, fixed quotas for minority employment to remedy the wrong.[4] Some fire and police departments acted voluntarily. Colleges and universities adopted various forms of minority admissions plans.

Do such affirmative action plans produce equality? Or are they reverse discrimination, denying equality to the white who might get the job or the place in an entering class but for the preference given to a black because of race or color?

The question divides the American people, with strong emotion on either side. Sometimes the question takes political form; for example, as I write, the Reagan Administration is split over the proposed repeal or modification of the executive order just described. Sometimes the question calls for a judicial ruling on whether an affirmative action plan voluntarily adopted by an employer violates the federal statutory prohibition against discrimination in employment because of race or color.[5] When the racial preference is awarded by an arm of the State—for example, by a municipality or State university—the question will be at least partly constitutional, that is, whether the preference for a member of a minority group denies a competing white applicant the "equal protection of the laws."

II

The situation confronting universities during the past twenty years, particularly medical schools, illustrates in microcosm the problem pervading society. In 1970, there were only 6002 black physicians even though 11.1 percent of the total population was black. There was one black doctor for every 4248 black people. For the population as a whole, the ratio was 1 to 649. Two black medical schools, Howard and Meharry, enrolled 514 students during 1967–1968. The percentage of black students enrolled in all other medical schools collectively was less than 1 percent. In 1969, the Association of American Medical Colleges, disturbed by these figures and the inadequate health care received by black people, adopted a formal recommendation that "[m]edical schools must admit increased numbers of students from geographic areas, economic backgrounds and ethnic groups that are now inadequately represented."

Increased minority enrollment could be achieved only by some form of race-conscious admissions programs. Competition for admission to medical schools was intensifying. In 1960–1961 there were 14,397 applicants for 8560 places. By 1975–1976 there were 42,303 applicants for 15,365 places, roughly three applicants for each available seat. The volume of applications caused admissions committees to put increased emphasis on the Medical College Admission Test (MCAT) and undergraduate college grades, especially grades in the physical sciences. Whatever the explanation, only a tiny number of minority applicants would gain admission to the leading medical schools if judged by these criteria, and only a small number would gain admission to any medical school. In order to remove the barrier, many medical schools, spurred by the need to bring blacks and members of other disadvantaged minorities into the profession, established race-conscious minority admissions programs.

The new School of Medicine of the University of California at Davis was one of these. When the college opened in 1968, the entering class of fifty students contained no blacks and no Mexican-Americans, even though the population of California was 7 percent black and 14 percent Mexican-American. In 1969–1970 the faculty developed a special admissions program that set aside sixteen out of a hundred places in each entering class for disadvantaged members of racial and ethnic minorities, believing that this was the only method that would achieve significant enrollment of minority applicants. Applications from individuals eligible for the sixteen places were first referred to a special subcommittee of the admissions committee, which rated the minority applicants by the same standards applied to the generality of applications but which had priority in filling the sixteen places, provided that the applicants it selected were qualified to do the work. The subcommittee's recommendations for the sixteen places were then reviewed and usually approved by the full admissions committee. The Davis faculty believed that this step would help to eliminate the isolation of minorities from the mainstream of American life, especially by providing role models for grammar school and high school students; that it would improve medical education and the profession by diversifying the student body and members of the profession; and that it would increase the quantity of understanding health services available to underserved minority groups. But giving disadvantaged members of minority groups preference in filling sixteen places in the entering class inevitably excluded white applicants whose ratings by the full admissions committee were not high enough to win admission to one of the eighty-four places for which they were eligible but which were still higher than the ratings of some or all of the applicants accepted for the sixteen seats.

One of those excluded in 1973 and again in 1974 was Allan Bakke, who might well have been accepted in the absence of the Special Admissions Program. Bakke was an engineer who had earned both undergraduate and graduate degrees and then become intensely interested in medicine while working for the National Aeronautics and Space Administration. To fulfill this ambition, Bakke applied for admission to a number of medical schools, including the School of Medicine at Davis. His Davis application was twice rejected because the admissions committee judged that there were better candidates for the eighty-four places for which he was eligible to compete. His applications to other medical schools were also rejected, perhaps because he was in his thirties, an age often deemed too old for entering medical school. Nevertheless, Bakke's credentials, judged by the criteria that prevailed at Davis prior to the establishment of the minority admissions procedure, were superior to those of minority students admitted under the special procedure; but he was not considered for any of the sixteen places because he was white.

Did the Davis School of Medicine grant Bakke an opportunity for admission "equal" to that of the last black or Chicano admitted? On the other hand, did black or Mexican-American boys and girls have an "equal" opportunity for admission in the years before the Special Admissions Program was adopted, when less than 1 percent of the medical students at colleges other than Howard and Meharry were black? Again we are forced to ask what we mean by "equality," or at least to choose among the plausible measures and accommodations of different meanings.

Most Americans, regardless of race, color, religion, or national origin, judge "equality" in terms of the individual rather than the ethnic group. Most Americans also agree that the *ideal* of equality demands that men and women be judged on individual performance—that they be selected for opportunity, if selection is necessary, on individual accomplishment or demonstrated promise—but not on irrelevancies like race, color, national origin, or sex.

Nowhere is this ideal more important than at a university, not only because of the lessons taught by adherence to the ideal but also because adherence measures the institution's dedication to fact and reason. In an ideal world, therefore, neither race nor color would count in admission to a university. Where applications greatly outnumber available places, selection of applicants would be based on tests of promise and accomplishment, not because the tests measure a person's whole worth or even the person's future performance in a profession, but because they eliminate the irrelevant, their use teaches the ideals of equality and objectivity, and, when used with awareness of their limitations, they are the best available objective guides to future academic performance. In an ideal world, free from the practice and consequences of racial discrimination, all ethnic groups would enjoy equal opportunity on the tests.

Is this ideal equality mandated by the Fourteenth Amendment? Before answering, recall Aristotle's advice:

> In the field of moral action truth is judged by the actual facts of life, for it is in them that the decisive element lies. So we must examine the conclusions we have reached so far by applying them to the actual facts of life; if they are in harmony with the facts, we must accept them, and if they clash, we must assume that they are mere words.[6]

One of the actual facts of life is that an ideal, racially blind admissions program based on predictions of academic success would virtually exclude black and Mexican-American applicants from the best American professional schools. Both groups would continue to lack, perhaps for decades, any real access to higher education, the professions, and the major avenues of advancement in American life. The customary predictors of success used in admissions are often poor measures of the ultimate contribution an applicant could make to the profession and the community. Minority students admitted under the Davis program proved unusually good in hospital wards and in encouraging black and Mexican-American boys and girls to think of qualifying for professional education. Given the actual conditions, would continued use of conventional admissions standards be the "equality" guaranteed by the Fourteenth Amendment?

Plainly, equality of opportunity defined in terms of present realities conflicts with the long-range ideal. Affirmative action programs may also be questioned on the pragmatic ground that they create difficulties in persuading all members of society to embrace an ideal. For a State university to make race a factor in its decisions runs the risk of arousing race consciousness in others. To allocate opportunities to some ethnic groups as a matter of group entitlement may encourage all groups to demand their ethnic allocations without regard to individual worth. Should society be permanently organized on such a basis? It hardly needs saying that if you become Number 5490 Black, or Number 1369 Anglo, or Number 888 Italian, or Number 8591 Hindu, you become less human; you lose individuality, and therefore lose both dignity and worth. If you start down this road out of present practicality—if you submerge the ideal—how and when can you stop? Yet to acknowledge the dangers is not to imply that they outweigh the dangers of doing nothing to counteract the present, real inequalities that vex society and do injustice to individuals today because of the pervasive racial discrimination of the past. In the first instance the balance must be struck by each medical school, law school, or like educational authority. If it is struck in favor of affirmative action by a State university, as it was at Davis, then the question arises whether the choice violates the Constitution or some other rule of law.[7]

II

Despite his rejection by Davis and the five or six other medical schools to which he applied, Allan Bakke was determined to study medicine. Lawyers advised him that the race-conscious admissions policy at Davis gave rise to three plausible legal claims against the University of California: (1) of violation of the California Constitution; (2) of violation of Title VI of the U.S. Civil Rights Act of

1964, which prohibits excluding a person from a federally funded program "on the ground of race, color, or national origin"; and (3) of violation of the Fourteenth Amendment's guarantee of "equal protection of the laws." Because the second and third claims would be of wrongs arising under the laws of the United States, Bakke could sue in either an appropriate California court or in the U.S. District Court. The story of what was done illustrates both the constitutional clash over affirmative action and the manner in which cases proceed to and through the United States Supreme Court.

Bakke's lawyers chose to assert his three legal claims beginning in the California Superior Court for Alameda County. All three claims were sustained. The university then carried the case to the California appellate courts. An appellate court sits to decide whether trial courts have erred on some question of law. There are no witnesses. Lawyers for the parties file briefs and argue orally on the printed record of the proceeding in the trial court. The Supreme Court of California ordered the university to admit Bakke as a student at the Davis School of Medicine on the ground that his exclusion under the race-conscious minority admissions program violated the Fourteenth Amendment by denying him the "equal protection of the laws."[8]

The precise ground of the State court's decision was important. If the Supreme Court of California had ruled that the university had violated Bakke's rights under the California Constitution, that would have been the end of the matter. The Supreme Court of the United States has no power to review a State court's decision on a question of State law. But the Court does have the power, which we saw established years earlier in *Martin* v. *Hunter's Lessee*,[9] to review and reverse State court decisions on questions involving the application of the Constitution or laws of the United States. Because nine Justices could not otherwise handle the volume of cases, the Court's jurisdiction is largely discretionary, regardless of whether the case arises in a State or lower federal court. The first step is typically to file a Petition for Certiorari, a summary statement requesting the Court to review the lower court's decision. (In some cases a Jurisdictional Statement takes the place of a Petition for Certiorari.) The respondent (the winning party in the court below) files a short Brief in Opposition, to which the petitioner may reply. The Court then grants or denies *certiorari*. In the *Bakke* case, *certiorari* was granted in February 1977.

Briefs were filed in the late spring and summer of 1977, first by counsel to the university and later by Bakke's lawyers. Early in the spring I had been invited by the university to deliver oral argument on its behalf and to share in the preparation of its briefs. In the nineteenth century briefs were indeed brief. They listed the few main points that counsel intended to present in oral argument, along with a few citations to judicial precedents and other legal authorities. Shorthand, the typewriter, modern methods of printing, and the increased sophistication of legal arguments changed the practice. Our opening brief for the university in the *Bakke* case extended to more than ninety pages. There were twenty briefs *amici curiae,* including a brief filed by the Solicitor General on behalf of the United States, urging reversal of the decision of the California Supreme Court. All told, the briefs covered 750 printed pages. In October 1978 the case was called for oral argument.

For me—I believe for any lawyer—oral argument in the Supreme Court is an indescribable thrill, even in a routine case after long experience. There is always the sleepless night before the argument, the heightening tension, and the joy of a challenge to every capacity. *Bakke* was no ordinary case. The legal issues were difficult but packed with emotion. The case had aroused enormous interest in Congress, in academic circles, and in the press. The courtroom would be crowded by guests of the Justices, members of Congress, lawyers, and those members of the public for whom there was room. In fact, long lines of students hoping to find seats had formed outside the courthouse before dawn.

I myself was up in my hotel room long before dawn, revising and correcting the outline of my argument. It is said that a lawyer makes three arguments in every case: the argument he plans, the argument he makes, and the argument he wishes he had made. I had already written and rewritten the first argument several times. I would neither read nor recite it; but actually writing an oral argument down on paper forces me to discipline my thoughts with a degree of clarity, logic, and precision that I could not otherwise achieve. Rarely does the actual course of argument follow even the general sequence planned. There are too many questions from the Justices, who care little for counsel's planned preparation, and too many occasions on which one cannot foresee which points will seem important to the Justices and which they will take for granted. Yet even in dealing with the partly unexpected, my ideas and the right words to express them seem to flow better if I have labored over a written argument, though I know I will have scant chance to deliver it. And I can never resist that last tense moment for revision.

At ten o'clock the Court came in. The clerk called the *Bakke* case. I rose and went to the lectern. Chief Justice Burger nodded slightly: "Mr. Cox."

> Mr. Chief Justice. May it please the Court.
>
> This case, here on certiorari to the Supreme Court of California, presents a single, vital question:
>
> Whether a State university, which is forced by limited resources to select a relatively small number of students from a much larger number of well-qualified applicants, is free voluntarily to take into account the fact that an applicant is black, Chicano, Asian or Native American in order to increase the number of qualified members of those minority groups trained for the educated professions and participating in them—professions from which the minorities were long excluded because of generations of pervasive racial discrimination.

As I finished outlining three essential points, the Justices began to pepper me with questions. The questions continued without pause. Under such circumstances experienced counsel try to develop the points they wish to argue in the course of answering the questions, but it is hard to present a coherent structure. Forty minutes later, when the white light on the lectern warned me that I had only five minutes left, I had little notion of what ground I had covered. Perhaps it was time to sit down and reflect, and later attempt a coherent summary in rebuttal. I asked leave to reserve the rest of my time for rebuttal. The Chief Justice assented and granted me five additional minutes.

The Honorable Wade H. McCree, Jr., Solicitor General of the United States, then argued as *amicus curiae* that the judgment for Bakke should be reversed. He was followed by Allan Bakke's counsel, Reynold H. Colvin, Esq. After a short rebuttal, the case was submitted. Five days later the Court entered an order directing counsel to file briefs "discussing Title VI of the Civil Rights Act of 1964 as it applies to this case."[10] Title VI, as noted above, enacted that no person "shall, on the ground of race, color, or national origin, be excluded from participation in . . . any activity receiving Federal financial assistance." The Davis School of Medicine received such assistance for the support of medical education. It violated the statute if, but only if, the Special Admissions Program violated Title VI. We had hoped to keep the question out of the

Supreme Court's deliberations, on the ground that Bakke's counsel had never seriously presented it. Now it was in the case.

The *Bakke* case, argued in October 1977, would not be decided until June 28, 1978. The delay was not unusually long for a hard and important case, for there is much the Court must do between argument and announcement of the opinion and decision. Typically, on the Friday of each week of oral arguments the Justices confer alone on the cases heard. No one else—literally no one, not even a messenger—is allowed to enter the conference room. The Chief Justice is said to state each case and present his tentative view of the correct disposition. The Associate Justices follow, in order of seniority. There can scarcely be time in the formal conference for lengthy discussion of even the most important cases, but we know very little of what actually takes place. Typically, a vote is taken at the conference. By tradition, the Justices vote in reverse order of seniority so that the most junior will not feel intimidated. Often, that vote is decisive. Sometimes Justices reserve their votes. Sometimes they change their minds.

After the conference the hard work of preparing opinions begins. When the Chief Justice is in the majority, he selects the Associate Justice to whom he will assign the task of preparing the opinion of the Court. When the Chief is in the minority, the assignment is made by the Senior Associate Justice in the majority. Any Justice may write a separate opinion. Until 1940 separate opinions were relatively infrequent. In recent years hard cases regularly have produced a flurry of opinions, a practice far too likely to weaken the Court's authority and hamper the development of a coherent body of law. Draft opinions are circulated among the Justices for comment and criticism. There are frequent revisions, and occasionally a dramatic shift of votes. In due course, the decision and opinions are handed down.

The *Bakke* case gave rise to six opinions, but several dealt with subsidiary questions.[11] Justice John Paul Stevens, joined by Chief Justice Burger and Justices Stewart and Rehnquist, held that the plain meaning of the words of Title VI of the Civil Rights Act of 1964 forbids making race "the basis for excluding anyone from participation in a federally funded program." Those four Justices, feeling bound by the words, had no need to discuss the underlying philosophical and social issues as questions of constitutional law.

Five Justices concluded that Title VI merely takes up the constitutional standard of the Equal Protection Clause and applies it to all who receive federal grants, whether State agencies or private institutions. All five were therefore required to face the constitutional question. Four of these five, speaking through Justice William Brennan, voted to hold that the setting aside of sixteen places out of a hundred seats for minority applicants in a State medical school is consistent with the Equal Protection Clause because the "articulated purpose of remedying the effects of past societal discrimination [is] sufficiently important to justify the use of race-conscious admissions programs where there is a sound basis for concluding that minority underrepresentation is substantial and chronic, and that the handicap of past discrimination is impeding access of minorities to medical school."[12] Justice Harry Blackmun expressed the theme more simply: "In order to get beyond racism we must first take account of race. . . . And in order to treat some people equally we must first treat them differently."[13]

The view of Justices Brennan, Blackmun, Marshall, and White necessarily embraced three specific propositions that would be sharply contested in later cases: (1) race-conscious affirmative action in awarding access to a future opportunity to redress the pervasive discrimination against blacks that ran through society generally does not violate the Equal Protection Clause, even though the actor has not pursued a discriminatory practice; (2) the beneficiaries of the affirmative action need not be limited to individual victims of identifiable discrimination; and (3) the preference may be extended to a fixed number of opportunities.

The four-to-four split left Justice Powell to cast the deciding vote. He chose a middle course, which he explained in an opinion blending three themes.

Of chief importance was Justice Powell's emphasis on equality of opportunity among individuals and his reciprocal distrust of efforts to measure or achieve equality in terms of ethnic groups. He saw the United States as a country peopled by many distinct racial, national, and other ethnic groups, "most of which can lay claim to a history of prior discrimination at the hands of the state and private individuals."[14] There is no principled basis, the Justice asserted, for determining which groups deserve special solicitude and which do not. He also found "a measure of unfairness" in forcing individuals to suffer burdens in order to enhance the social standing of a particular group.

Being a relativist, Justice Powell left a little room for affirmative action, holding only that

[w]e never had approved a classification that aids persons perceived as members of relatively victimized groups at the expense of other innocent individuals in the absence of judicial, legislative or administrative findings of constitutional or statutory violations.[15]

This emphasis on the need for official judicial, legislative, or administrative findings of previous constitutional or statutory violations as a predicate for affirmative action to remedy the effects of previous injustices is Justice Powell's second pervasive theme. The theme plainly rejects the first proposition implicit in the view of the Brennan four and suggests disagreement with the second.

The third theme was Justice Powell's view of the proper functions of a university. A university should confine itself to educational objectives, Justice Powell seemed to assert, and may not seek to remedy the consequences of past societal discrimination, at least not in the absence of a legislative, executive, or judicial directive identifying the past discrimination. On the other hand, a university may think that a diverse student body, drawing together individuals of many origins, experiences, and talents, has great educational importance. A university that pursues this goal may therefore treat an applicant's origin as a material factor, he explained, as a plus, in selecting students for admission.

Drawing the three themes together, Justice Powell held, on the one hand, that the California program violated both the Equal Protection Clause and the Civil Rights Act of 1964 because it set aside a fixed number of places—sixteen out of a hundred seats—for the minorities that the university characterized as disadvantaged; but he also decided, on the other hand, that universities are free to "make individualized decisions in which ethnic background plays a part," provided that they observe "the constitutional distinction between [California's] preference program and one that assures a measure of competition among all applicants."[16] The critical defect in the California admissions program, he said, was that it "tells applicants who are not Negro, Asian or 'Chicano' that they are totally excluded from a specific percentage of the seats in an entering class."[17] Since Justice Powell cast the deciding vote, his view prevailed as to both what form of minority admissions program is lawful and what is not, even though the four Justices who supported him on one point opposed him on the other.

The *Bakke* decision makes it almost certain that no admissions program can survive judicial scrutiny if it sets aside a fixed number or percentage of places for minority applicants, unless the institution is willing to acknowledge and can prove that it had previously engaged in unlawful discrimination. Looking to the other extreme, a lawyer can say with considerable assurance that a minority admissions program violates neither Title VI nor the Equal Protection Clause if the minority ethnicity of some applicants is given substantial favorable recognition as part of an admissions policy that places major emphasis on attracting a widely diverse body of students. Justice Powell attached a description of the Harvard College undergraduate admissions policy to his opinion as an example of the permissible weighting of minority status. The policy emphasized the inclusion of students from California as well as New York and Massachusetts, city dwellers as well as farm boys, violinists and painters as well as football players, poets as well as scholars, potential stockbrokers as well as potential academics and politicians. Harvard College's concept of diversity included students from disadvantaged economic, racial, and ethnic groups. The description explained that, in practice, the admissions committee had not set target-quotas for the number of blacks but was aware that ten or twenty black students in a class of eleven hundred could not begin to bring to their classmates and to each other the variety of points of view, backgrounds, and experiences of blacks in the United States.

Between the extremes lie undecided questions. Professional schools, especially law schools, tend to give predominant weight to grade point averages, test scores, and other conventional predictors of academic promise. Promise as a musician, painter, novelist, or basketball player, while desirable in an undergraduate body, adds little to legal or medical education. Admissions programs of this type may also posit the value of including in every class not a fixed number but some substantial proportion of students from minorities that have in the past suffered pervasive racial discrimination—approximately 10 or 15 or even 30 percent. Minority applicants with the qualifications to do solid work are thus selected over other applicants with greater promise of academic achievement. Justice Powell's opinion does not speak to this point specifically, but it is worth noting that his emphasis on making individual comparisons as opposed to fixed quotas is satisfied. Many professional schools pursue this form of affirmative action. It has seldom been subjected to legal challenge.

IV

As controversy over affirmative action in admission to higher education quieted, controversy over affirmative action in employment intensified and spread. The Reagan Administration is visibly less interested in civil rights and the elimination of racial inequality than any other Administration in the past fifty years. Edwin Meese, who became the Attorney General of the United States in 1985, and other close advisers to the President pressed for revocation of the executive order requiring government contractors to set targets for increased minority employment. The Department of Justice consistently opposed court decrees giving minority applicants even limited employment preference as a remedy for previous unlawful discrimination unless the beneficiaries could show that they had personally been the victims of specific acts of discrimination. The Department also supported challenges to voluntary affirmative action policies. The justiciable issues were drawn to a head in a series of cases decided by the Supreme Court in 1986.

One key case was *Wygant* v. *Jackson Board of Education*.[18] In the late 1960s and early 1970s there was much racial tension in the Jackson, Michigan, schools. In 1969, when minority representation on the faculty was less than 4 percent, the NAACP filed charges of employment discrimination with the Michigan Civil Rights Commission. The allegation was found to have merit. After conciliation, an order of adjustment was entered. Under the order, the Board of Education agreed to make stronger efforts to recruit, hire, and promote minority group teachers and counselors. In two years the School Board by affirmative action increased the percentage of minority faculty to 8.8 percent. By 1972, however, the decline in enrollment necessitated layoffs. It was a time of increased racial tension, during which the board was seeking full integration of the Jackson public schools. To follow the customary practice of making layoffs in reverse order of seniority in employment would wipe out the increase in the proportion of minority teachers. A proposal to put the burden of layoffs exclusively on whites was rejected by the Jackson Teachers Association, the teachers' representative for the purposes of collective bargaining. The association and the Board of Education then agreed that layoffs should be made in reverse order of seniority, except that the precentage of minority teachers in the system would never be reduced.[19]

The modified seniority clause quickly became a bone of contention. The board refused to lay off tenured white teachers while retaining probationary black teachers in order to comply with the contract. The association brought suit in a federal court, which dismissed the suit as brought in the wrong forum, but the court also concluded that there was insufficient evidence that the board itself had ever been guilty of employment discrimination. When the association sued in a proper State court to enforce the layoff clause, that court held the affirmative action provision to be valid and binding because it was appropriate to redress the racial imbalance among Jackson teachers resulting from "societal discrimination," even though the evidence in the case contained no history of overt discrimination by the Board of Education. Next, after the Jackson board had begun to apply the contract, nonminority teachers commenced a third suit, alleging that the contract and the board's compliance violated the Equal Protection Clause and the provisions of the Civil Rights Act barring discrimination in employment. The U.S. District Court and the U.S. Court of Appeals ruled that the racial preferences were constitutionally permissible as an effort to remedy the effects of societal discrimination by providing role models for black children. The white teachers facing layoff carried the case to the Supreme Court, where the Reagan Administration gave them its support.

Once again the words of the Constitution provided no clear answer. Nor did legal precedents. What would be fair, just, and in accordance with the inherited constitutional ideals? As in the *Bakke* case, one first had to ask whether racial preference granted by the government can ever be constitutional in a country dedicated to the ideal of colorblindness. In *Bakke,* five Justices had said that some forms of racial preference may be permissible if the cause is sufficiently compelling, but not others. In a later case it had been shown that the employer, Kaiser Aluminum, had always hired its skilled employees off the street from among fully qualified journeymen. The practice had in effect barred minorities from skilled jobs at Kaiser, because they could rarely receive the necessary training in the local labor market. Kaiser and the United Steelworkers later agreed that Kaiser should establish its own training program and increase the proportion of blacks among its skilled employees by offering the opportunity for training and promotion to unskilled white employees and unskilled black employees according to seniority among unskilled employees of the same color, even though the white employees had much greater overall seniority. The U.S. Supreme Court held that the racial preference, under these circumstances, did not violate the statutory prohibition against racial discrimination in employment.[20]

Where then to strike the balance in the *Jackson* case? Making exceptions from the strict seniority rule where necessary to preserve a substantial proportion of black teachers would help to eliminate the effects of any past racial discrimination by the Jackson Board of Education by demonstrating that the board in fact now welcomed black teachers. Retaining a significant proportion of black teachers would also show black students and others in the community that the societal discrimination which had long excluded blacks from positions of authority and opportunity in American life had been ended and that they could look forward to the same opportunities as whites. Daily experience in schools where a significant number of black teachers shared opportunities, responsibility, and authority equally with white teachers would also improve the education of all students, including white, by fitting them better to live in a fully integrated society. And surely there was room to argue that no little weight should be given to the judgment of local authorities in solving a racial problem in their community by a voluntary collective bargaining agreement approved by the representative of all the teachers, 90 percent of whom were white.

On the other side of the scales is the burden imposed on the innocent white teachers disadvantaged by the preference. Loss of employment, even when temporary, has severe effects on the psyche and outside life of both employee and family. The practice of making reductions in a faculty or work force in reverse order of seniority is so widespread that accumulated seniority has been described as the worker's "most valuable capital asset." For some teachers the Jackson Board of Education contract would wipe out part of this valuable resource along racial lines. Achieving broad social goals often imposes burdens upon particular individuals or groups. A zoning law protecting land values and the general character of a neighborhood may sharply limit the potential selling price of a particular lot. An urban renewal project may force residents from their homes and neighborhood. Giving minority applicants for admission to a medical school a plus of unspecified weight in order to achieve the educational gains of an integrated student body would impose some disadvantage on competing white applicants. The question in the *Jackson* case, therefore, was not whether any burden upon the white teachers was prohibited but whether the burden of deprivation of some of their seniority rights in making layoffs was excessive in relation to society's gains when imposed along racial lines.

The Supreme Court approached the problem piecemeal, perhaps because the Justices held sharply divergent views. The nine Justices wrote five opinions. Justice Thurgood Marshall, joined by Justices Brennan and Blackmun, voted to uphold the Jackson plan as a means of preserving the integrity of the Education Board's hiring policy.[21] Justice Stevens also voted to affirm, but relied entirely on the public purpose of improving the education of all students for an integrated democratic society by providing an integrated faculty representative of the character of the whole community.[22]

A bare majority of the Court held the plan unconstitutional, but the five Justices delivered three different opinions. Their reasoning emphasizes the narrowness of the decision and the influence of the way in which cases are handled in the lower courts.

Justice O'Connor, for example, held open the possibility that an identical layoff plan might be upheld for the reason given by Justice Stevens, but ruled that the Jackson School Board was barred from urging that justification because its lawyers had not relied on that goal in the lower courts.[23] Justice O'Connor's vote to reverse was necessary to form the majority. She also seemed to leave more room than other Justices in the majority for voluntary plans of affirmative governmental action in situations in which a unit of local government had long had a work force in which the proportion of minority employees was drastically below the minority proportion of the work force in the relevant labor market. Where Justice Powell, joined by Chief Justice Burger and Justice Rehnquist, declared that affirmative action to redress past discrimination in employment can be justified only by proof and a judicial finding that there was strong evidence of the particular employer's having in fact engaged in such discrimination, thus following close to his reasoning in the *Bakke* case,[24] Justice O'Connor reasoned that voluntary local arrangements should be facilitated and therefore seemingly ruled that when an earlier statistical disparity was shown, it would be the duty of those challenging the affirmative action plan to prove that the employer had not been guilty of prior racial discrimination.[25] The plan failed in the *Jackson* case, she concluded, because the proportion of minority faculty to be retained during layoffs was tied to the proportion of minority students in the school system rather than to the proportion of available minority in the relevant work force.[26]

Justice Powell's opinion also appears to have been influenced by the handling of the case in the lower courts. He stressed the absence of any evidence in the record to show that the Jackson Board of Education had previously discriminated against black teachers, and objected to any consideration of the charges or evidence before the Michigan Civil Rights Commission, because they were not parts of the formal record in the case before the U.S. Supreme Court.[27] In the end, perhaps this omission made little difference, because Justice Powell, joined by the Chief Justice and Justices White and Rehnquist, went on to rule that even a government employer that has been guilty of racial discrimination would violate the Equal Protection Clause if it gave minority employees who were not shown to be personally identifiable victims of the discrimination preferential freedom from layoffs at the expense of the seniority rights of some white employees.[28]

Much remains to be litigated before the meaning of "equal protection" of the laws is clarified in the field of affirmative action. We now know from the *Bakke* and *Jackson* cases that a purpose to offset the consequences of past societal discrimination will not justify racial preference even in allocating such new opportunities as admission to a State university or new employment. We know, on the other hand, from other cases, that public employers guilty of gross and persistent racial discrimination may give, and may be required to give, such preferences to members of the minority groups even though the members who benefit have not themselves been victims of identifiable discriminatory acts.[29] But the territory between those bounds is largely uncharted. Specifically, because of the very special grounds relied upon by Justices Stevens and O'Connor in the *Jackson* case, we do not know whether the claims of seniority in retention of employment in a time of forced reduction of the work force can ever be sacrificed to the goal of remedying prior discrimination by the particular employer, and, if so, what evidence of prior discrimination is required to justify either a voluntary or a court-ordered plan. Nor do we know whether a negotiated contract like that in *Jackson* can be justified by evidence that it is purposefully tailored to the goal of improving the education of all students.

The affirmative action cases also have a broader jurisprudential interest. As we have already seen in part, in dealing with human rights the Warren Court gradually developed and expanded the "strict scrutiny" doctrine as a substitute for the "rational basis" formula that had reached its peak as a result of the constitutional revolution of 1937. The principle, that restrictions on speech and certain forms of unequal treatment are to be subjected to the strictest judicial scrutiny and may be held constitutional only if the Court itself is satisfied that they are necessary to secure a compelling public interest and are narrowly tailored to that interest, became the doctrinal foundation of the Court's active use of constitutional adjudication as an instrument of reform. That use has been strongly criticized by those of a conservative disposition, both on and off the Court. Yet in the very recent affirmative action cases it is the more conservative Justices, led by Justice Rehnquist, who have invoked the doctrine to impose their judicial view of "equality" on local government agencies in place of voluntary local solutions to the puzzling search for equality in fact as well as in law. The point must be kept in mind in reflecting on whether the Court will turn away from judicial activism and return closer to the restraint of the previous period as a consequence of conservative appointments.

· 16 ·

Political Equality

THE SILENCE of the Constitution with respect to voting rights contrasts strangely with the traditional American boast of political equality. Even today, the Constitution contains no express guarantee of universal adult suffrage. In the beginning, the Constitution gave no protection to voting rights beyond the stipulation that those persons whom a State allows to vote for members of the State legislature shall be eligible to vote for the State's representatives in Congress.[1] Women could not vote. Slaves and, often, free blacks were barred from the franchise. Property qualifications further narrowed the electorate. The apportionment of seats in the State legislature among geographical districts frequently gave voters in the older settlements much greater representation *per capita* than the districts to the west.

In 1920 the Nineteenth Amendment extended the franchise to women. Earlier, the Fifteenth Amendment had forbidden a State to deny any citizen the right "on account of race, color, or previous condition of servitude." The prohibition was virtually nullified in the old slave States and parts of the Southwest by literacy tests, the poll tax, and their discriminatory and otherwise tricky administration. As Spanish-speaking people moved into eastern cities from Puerto Rico and into the Southwest and West, literacy tests limited their access to the polls. Newcomers to a State often found it hard to satisfy durational residency requirements. Everywhere, the apportionment of seats in State legislatures among geographical

288

districts continued to deny the people of some areas equal *per capita* representation with others.

The civil rights movement and the egalitarian spirit of the third quarter of the present century led to new efforts to achieve greater political equality not only by the exercise of political power but by constitutional interpretation. The Voting Rights Act, first enacted in 1965 and strengthened in later years, removed many of the obstacles to voting by blacks and Hispanic citizens.[2] A series of Supreme Court decisions made the federal courts into new instruments for achieving political equality by invoking the judicial power and responsibility for interpreting the Fourteenth Amendment. The federal government played a major role in the presentation of these questions to the Supreme Court through the Office of the Solicitor General.

Early in 1961, as I was leaving the office of the new Attorney General of the United States, Robert F. Kennedy, I remarked, "Your friend John J. Hooker, Jr., was in my office yesterday. He asked me to give you his best." Hooker had worked closely with Robert Kennedy during the 1960 election campaign.

"That's nice. How is John? What did he want?"

I explained that Hooker had come in with a group of Tennessee attorneys to ask me, as the new Solicitor General, to file a brief *amicus curiae,* on behalf of the United States, supporting an action brought by his friends in the federal court in Tennessee challenging the constitutionality of the existing apportionment of seats in the Tennessee legislature.

"Are you going to file the brief?" asked the Attorney General.

"Yes, unless you object."

"Are you going to win?"

"No, I don't think so," I replied, "but it will be a lot of fun."

No more was said. A large measure of mutual understanding lay behind the seemingly casual conversation. As in many other States, the existing Tennessee apportionment was grossly unfair to the people in urban and suburban legislative districts. It kept the Tennessee legislature under the domination of representatives elected by the rural areas. Both the Attorney General and I knew that President John F. Kennedy was deeply disturbed by the evil of malapportionment. Earlier, as Senator, he had written an article in *The New York Times Magazine,* calling for reform.[3] All three of us were firmly committed to responsible representative government and to political equality for all citizens regardless of race, color, economic status, or geographical district. There was no need for us to recite those fundamental concerns. Such questions as whether the issue was justiciable and whether the Tennessee suit made a good test case were for the Solicitor General. During the Kennedy and Johnson Administrations, unlike the Reagan Administration, the White House and the Attorney General nearly always refrained from interfering in the Solicitor General's conduct of cases before the Supreme Court. At that time, as in earlier years, the federal government rarely participated in litigation to which it was not a formal party; but occasionally the Solicitor General filed briefs *amici curiae* in important cases directly affecting the administration of federal laws or involving civil rights. Voting seemed to have the same national importance.

Despite the casual manner, my conversation with Attorney General Kennedy marked a major commitment. The brief was filed. My forecast proved mistaken. We filed additional briefs in a subsequent series of reapportionment cases that Earl Warren, after retiring as Chief Justice, would say were the most important decisions of the sixteen years that he presided over the Court—even more important, in his opinion, than the School Desegregation Cases. The decision also led to the other, wider uses of the Constitution to protect the voting rights of all people and keep open the channels of political change.

II

At the beginning it was necessary to establish the power of the federal courts to rule on claims that the apportionment of seats in a State legislature violates the U.S. Constitution. My pessimistic answer to the Attorney General resulted from the fear that the Supreme Court would take a narrower view of the judicial function. A Council of Wise Men, charged with doing whatever is good or just or wise, would have found no difficulty in voiding the apportionment of the Tennessee legislature at issue in *Baker* v. *Carr*.[4] The people in some counties had eight, ten, and even thirty times as much representation, meaured *per capita,* as the people in other counties. Malapportionment was great in both Tennessee Senate and House of Representatives. Counties containing more than 60 percent of the population could elect only 35 percent of each house. By failing to make an equal *per capita* apportionment, the Tennessee legislature had been violating an express mandate in Tennessee's own Constitution for sixty years. No one would defend those inequities as a matter of sound government or abstract justice. Other State legislatures under rural domination, as in Tennessee, had failed to adapt themselves to the burgeoning problems of urban, industrial society. There was loss of confidence in local government, coupled with an ever-growing tendency to by-pass State capitals in favor of national solutions. Reapportionment, though not a panacea, might bring new vigor to the State legislatures by making them more responsive to current needs.

But a court is subject to limitations not felt by a Council of Wise Men. The power of judicial review established in *Marbury* v. *Madison* rests on the judicial duty to decide all questions of law, and thus of priority between conflicting laws, when raised in a court in the course of normal judicial business. One cannot simply run to a lawyer and ask her to ask the courts to decide a constitutional question. There are some constitutional questions that no court can decide.

One requirement is that the court's jurisdiction be invoked by a plaintiff who has suffered or is about to suffer not only injury in fact but the kind of injury that a court will redress or prevent. Some constitutional questions cannot be litigated, because there is no one who has suffered the kind of injury that gives "standing" to raise them. Barry Goldwater, like other members of Congress, long held a commission in the U.S. Air Force Reserve while he was also Senator from Arizona. The Constitution forbids any person "holding any office under the United States" to be a member of either House of Congress.[5] Many observers supposed that Senator Goldwater and others were violating this provision. The Senator, in complete good faith, believed that there was no violation, because a reserve commission does not make one the holder of an "office." The constitutional question could not be presented to a court, because the injury is to the body politic—to all people. No one individual can show that he or she suffers the peculiar personal injury required for a judicial ruling.[6] At the time of the Tennessee reapportionment case, it was uncertain whether a voter who claimed to be underrepresented in the legislature because of what he claimed was an unconstitutional apportionment suffered the kind of personal injury that a court will prevent or redress.[7]

The second and major obstacle to obtaining a court decision on the constitutionality of the Tennessee apportionment is the requirement that the constitutional question be justiciable rather than political. The distinction is shadowy, but it had long been clear that there are some constitutional questions of a character that even the Supreme Court will not decide, because they are "political questions." In the nineteenth century the Court had declined to rule on which of two contending State governments was the lawful government of Rhode Island, even though the question was raised in an action to recover damages for trespass.[8] In 1939 the Justices had refused to rule on the effectiveness of the action taken in the Kansas legislature to ratify a proposed child labor amendment to the U.S. Constitution after the lapse of thirteen years and after the legislature had once voted not to ratify the amendment.[9] For many years controversies between the Congress and the President over the constitutional right of the Congress to subpoena, or of the President to withhold, papers in the Executive Branch had been regarded as typical examples of nonjusticiable political questions. Today, there is somewhat more doubt.[10] In 1946 a suit challenging the legality of the congressional districts in Illinois came before the Court. The population of some districts was several times the population of others. Three Justices held in an opinion by Justice Frankfurter that the suit was properly dismissed as presenting a nonjusticiable political question.[11] A fourth Justice, whose vote made a majority because only seven Justices had participated, agreed that the Court should not intervene in questions of legislative apportionment.[12]

One test of a justiciable question is whether reasonably objective standards are available by which the Court may decide. The broad verbal guarantees of "due process of law" and "equal protection of the laws" provided no meaningful standard. There were no judicial precedents. No historic practice supplied a rule of decision. As we wrestled with the problem in preparing the brief for the United States, it occurred to us that perhaps one could fairly argue that the familiar constitutional principle condemning as denials of equal protection differentiations in statutory regulation that lack rational justification could be invoked to invalidate a crazy quilt like Tennessee's apportionment, which lacked both rhyme and reason. But what should be the next step? Equal representation *per capita* would be a readily administrable standard, but it had always been and still was the rare exception, not the general rule, both as State constitutions were written and by historic practice. Possibly, the

Court could attempt to classify permissible and impermissible bases for differentiation. Race, religion, wealth, and occupation could well be said to be irrelevant to any *legitimate* purpose of apportionment, as could any weighting of rural or economic interest. But the very term "legitimate" requires a standard of legitimacy, and such policies as following the lines of political subdivisions, avoiding districts spread over large geographical areas, and even according representation to towns or counties rather than people, could not be described as so irrational in all cases as to fall under the constitutional condemnation of arbitrary action. It would be sufficient in writing the brief, we decided, to say that at a minimum the Constitution condemns an apportionment unexplained by any coherent rule.

Another prime consideration in deciding whether an issue is justiciable is the ability of a court to frame and administer a suitable remedy. Suppose that the Court decided that an existing apportionment was unconstitutional, and, further, that the State legislature afterward failed to make a new apportionment because of recalcitrance or political impasse. What then? How could a court draw the district lines? No one had a good answer to this question in 1961. Hardly anyone was then prepared to answer that the court should indeed draw the district lines. That courts perform the task today, when necessary, measures how far the law has developed.

At bottom, the arguments for treating the apportionment question as nonjusticiable rested on concern for the long-range effectiveness of constitutional adjudication and the rule of law. Malapportionment, though it was growing demonstrably worse, had characterized one or both branches of most State legislatures from colonial times. The federal courts had not even been asked to intervene prior to 1940. Between 1946 and 1962 the Supreme Court had repeatedly declined the invitation. If the Court were suddenly to take jurisdiction, it would sweep old law aside in favor of an entirely novel rule and would intrude into what was historically a partisan political question. As Justice Frankfurter later put it in dissent: "The Court's authority—possessed of neither the purse nor the sword—ultimately rests on sustained public confidence in its moral sanction. Such feeling must be nourished by the Court's complete detachment . . . from political entanglements and by abstention from injecting itself into the clash of political forces in political settlements."[13]

Against those ingrained teachings of the lawyer's profession there stood the stark fact that the cancer of malapportionment would continue to grow unless the Court excised it. It would have been best for the States themselves to act, but most State legislators were more interested in self-perpetuation than electoral reform. No one could realistically suppose that Congress would grasp the nettle. As a practical matter, either the Court must act or nothing would be done.

Ideally, the federal Judicial Branch ought not to enlarge its own jurisdiction simply because Congress and State governments have failed to solve the problems confided to them. Most political wrongs must find their remedies in nonjudicial forums. Not all the business of government is constitutional law. The ideal remedy is to reform the delinquents. But government, even law, is sometimes more pragmatic. In a practical world there is, and I suspect has to be, a good deal of play in the joints. If one arm of government cannot or will not solve an insistent problem, the pressure falls upon another. Constitutional adjudication must recognize that the peculiar nature of the Court's business gives it a governmental function that cannot be perfectly discharged without the simple inquiry "Which decision will be best for the country?" Much of the activism of the Warren Court, not only in reapportionment but in criminal law and race relations, was the consequence of the neglect of other agencies of government.

Two other factors, which operate in a variety of contexts, argued for judicial intervention in the Reapportionment Cases. First, the Court can seldom be wholly neutral on the social, political, or philosophical questions underlying constitutional litigation. Its opinions shape as well as express our national ideals. The School Desegregation decisions, for example, proved to be a tremendous moral force quite apart from the formal decrees. Second, just as a Supreme Court decision commands a measure of obedience because it is the law, so does the Court tend to give legitimacy to practices it leaves undisturbed. The declination of jurisdiction in the Reapportionment Cases could not have been wholly neutral. However skillfully the Court had dressed up in the language of jurisdiction a decision not to deal with malapportionment, the outcome would have put some stamp of legality on the evil in the eyes of laymen and legislators, even if not in the eyes of the judges.

I doubt whether I fully appreciated the importance of the question or the depth and breadth of the arguments on both sides when

I told the Attorney General that I proposed to file a brief on behalf of the United States as *amicus curiae*. They became clearer as we wrote the briefs and prepared for oral argument. They seem still clearer today.

Baker v. *Carr* was first argued in February 1961. On a Monday in May, the Court handed down an order setting the case for reargument at the opening of the next term in October. That evening, the American Bar Association gave its annual dinner in honor of the Chief Justice and Associate Justices of the Supreme Court. The dinner was a grand affair in formal evening dress, held in Anderson House, the home of the Society of Cincinnati. I was seated next to Mrs. Potter Stewart, the wife of Justice Stewart. Mrs. Stewart made some very complimentary remarks about my oral argument in *Baker* v. *Carr*. I thanked her for her generous words, but then launched forth in an effort to be facetiously humorous: "I wish that you would speak to the Justice about that case, Mrs. Stewart. Here we write our briefs and go up and argue the case as best we can in February. Come May, the Court says to come back and do it all over again in October. What kind of a way is that to run the Court?" Across the table cut the loud and familiar voice of my old law school professor. "Archie!" cried Justice Frankfurter. The whole table fell silent. It seemed to me that the entire room listened. "Archie! I will tell you why *Baker* v. *Carr* was set for reargument. When the case was reached in our conference, one of my colleagues said, 'The new Solicitor General doesn't argue very well in February, does he? Let's have him come back and see if he can do better in October.'"

The case was reargued in October and decided in March 1962. Over Justice Frankfurter's dissent, the Court ruled that the federal courts have power to hear and adjudicate questions raised under the Due Process and Equal Protection Clauses concerning the constitutionality of the apportionment of seats in a State legislature. Justice Brennan's opinion for the Court narrowed and attempted to redefine the category of political questions. The opinion left to the future all questions concerning the meaning of the Due Process and Equal Protection Clauses in this context, observing only that they would at least condemn an apportionment that was totally arbitrary and capricious. *Baker* v. *Carr* thus left the consequences uncertain, even as it plunged the Court into the political thicket that a majority had theretofore refused to enter.

III

Plaintiffs and their lawyers were quick to enter the courthouse doors opened by *Baker* v. *Carr*. Suits were brought in Maryland, New York, Alabama, Virginia, and Colorado and twenty-five other States. In *Baker* v. *Carr* the question had been whether a federal court could properly hear and decide on the merits a claim that a State's apportionment of seats in its legislature was so unequal as to violate the Fourteenth Amendment's guarantee of "the equal protection of the laws." Now the questions would be whether the Equal Protection Clause does impose any restrictions on the State's powers of apportionment, and if so, what the restrictions are. The lawyers and judges would all be writing on a clean slate.

At the Department of Justice we faced the problem of proposing a set of criteria by which the Supreme Court should decide the first cases to come before it, and thus establish guidelines for later cases, State legislatures, and all lower courts. Our task was easier than that of the other lawyers in some ways and harder in others. The facts would vary widely from case to case. We would be the only lawyers to file briefs in all the cases. Ours would be the most comprehensive view, but where the attorneys in any case could make whatever arguments seemed likely to win that particular case, we had to think of all the cases and try to be consistent. Furthermore, the Office of the Solicitor General prided itself on a long tradition of professional independence and helpfulness to the Court, even at some cost to the litigating position of the United States or to the political needs of the President. The sense of obligation and restraint was strongest in cases in which the Solicitor General appeared as *amicus curiae*.

The guarantee of "equal protection of the laws" has never been interpreted to require States to treat each individual like every other individual. A blind man may be denied the license to operate motor vehicles that is available to others. The traditional rule under the Equal Protection Clause, as already stated, was that a State may classify persons for differential treatment unless the classification is arbitrary and capricious in the sense that it bears no rational relation to any rational public purpose—a highly permissive test developed in cases involving economic regulation. Conceivably, this standard might apply to legislative apportionment. We had suggested its availability in *Baker* v. *Carr* in arguing that a justiciable question was presented. Nevertheless, there were two strong objections to pressing the Supreme Court to adopt so limited a rule. First, even an apportionment that seemed on the surface to yield to neither rhyme nor reason could arguably be rationalized as the product of compromise among conflicting considerations. Second, the rule seemed too permissive as applied to voting and representation. Many existing plans of apportionment giving small rural minorities control of one or both houses of a State legislature were not irrational; for example, giving each county one representative regardless of population is a "rational" rule even though it may be grossly unfair to give no more representatives to the 6,038,771 people of Los Angeles County, California, than to the 8303 people of Modoc County.

At the other extreme lay the possibility that the Court could be persuaded to rule that the Equal Protection Clause requires the legislative districts from which representatives are elected to be laid out in such a way as to achieve equal *per capita* representation in both houses of the legislature: one person, one vote. Liberals argued for such a rule. Counsel for the plaintiffs in some of the rash of lawsuits following *Baker* v. *Carr* were advocating it. I thought it the fairest and most equitable rule of apportionment, the same that legislatures *should* adopt; but I was strongly inclined to the view that it was much too radical a departure from the country's traditional practices for the Supreme Court suddenly to impose it as an interpretation of the Equal Protection Clause. Each State had two seats in the U.S. Senate, regardless of population. From the beginning, a substantial number of States had followed a similar pattern by assigning each county or town equal representation in one branch of the State legislature. Throughout American history equal *per capita* representation had been the exception rather than the rule. Adoption of a "one person, one vote" rule would amount to a declaration that at least forty-four or forty-five State legislatures were unconstitutionally composed. It seemed to me that even if the Court should adopt a "one person, one vote" rule, the country would not accept it as law.

The Reapportionment Cases are the only instance I can recall in my four and a half years as Solicitor General in which there was frankly political discussion with the White House about the position that the government would take in the Supreme Court.[14] When a group of cases involving New York and Maryland reached the

Supreme Court, a conference was held in the Attorney General's office. Among those present were Lawrence O'Brien, a long-time friend and senior political adviser to the President, Stephen Smith, the President's brother-in-law, and, I think, Theodore Sorensen, Legal Counsel to the President. Larry O'Brien made a very practical forecast of the consequences of invalidating the existing New York and Maryland apportionments, concluding that the Democrats would gain in New York but lose strength in Maryland unless the party improved its organization in the Baltimore suburbs. He then won my admiration by urging us to frame our brief without regard to the political consequences. There was strong sentiment for advocating the "one person, one vote" rule. I objected, both because of the doubts expressed above and because it was not necessary for the Court to rule so broadly in the cases then before it. I spoke of the need to proceed a step at a time. The apportionments challenged in that first set of cases could be held to violate the Equal Protection Clause upon grounds more closely tied to traditional constitutional principles while reserving judgment upon whether the clause mandated absolute *per capita* equality.

We agreed that I would urge the latter course. The briefs and argument for the United States in the New York and Maryland cases attempted to develop from established constitutional principles rules for judging the constitutionality of a legislative apportionment, starting with the familiar proposition that any arbitrary and unreasonable departure from equal representation for each citizen would violate the Equal Protection Clause. The test of "reasonableness," we added, should be much stricter than in judging ordinary State regulatory laws, because voting is a fundamental right at the base of all our civil and political institutions. Here we drew on the analogy of the "strictest scrutiny" test used to judge the constitutionality of State racial discrimination. From these predicates we sought to draw three corollaries and then apply them to the facts of each case. First, as we had suggested in *Baker* v. *Carr*, an apportionment that created gross inequalities in representation, without rhyme or reason, denies equal protection. Second, the Equal Protection Clause is also violated by a denial of *per capita* equality based on criteria that are invidious or irrelevant to the effective functioning of the political system. The desire to give farmers more votes than assembly-line workers, for example, or bankers more votes than seafarers, would be irrelevant; but the policy of following the lines of political subdivisions or of recognizing that towns and counties have each a political life that makes them effective organisms would be proper. Third, the Equal Protection Clause would be violated by an apportionment otherwise valid if it gave power to control the legislature to a small minority of the people. The full meaning of these generalities appeared only as applied to the specific cases pending before the Court and to those which might arise in the future.

New cases reached the Court before decisions could be reached in the New York and Maryland cases. The most difficult case, in my opinion, came from Colorado. Colorado, a large State, has three or four regions that are extraordinarily diverse, each being geographically, economically, and sociologically unlike the others. The sparsely settled eastern plains are given over to farming and ranching. The cities and the bulk of the population all lie at the base of the eastern slope of the Rocky Mountains. The south-central area is a high triangular plateau, relying chiefly on coal mining, livestock, and potato growing, with a distinctly Hispanic heritage. The economy of the thinly populated western slope rests on mines and timber. The lower house of the Colorado legislature was apportioned strictly according to population. A larger proportion of the seats in the Senate was allocated to districts in the three less populous regions than their populations would warrant in order to recognize their distinct economic interests and geographical peculiarities. Most important, the apportionment had been adopted in a Statewide referendum with the approval of a majority of the voters in each and every county. It would be exceedingly hard to hold the Colorado apportionment unconstitutional without imposing the "one person, one vote" rule on the State without regard to the express wish of the majority of its people.

By the time the Colorado case reached the Court, strong sentiment for pressing the Court to adopt the "one person, one vote" rule had developed among all liberals, especially in segments of the press, in the White House, and in the Department of Justice. The harder I worked on the cases, the more convinced I became that, despite the fundamental fairness of that slogan, we could not responsibly press the Court to take so great a leap from traditional practice without first building, piece by piece, a body of precedent linked to established law. Solicitors General had long viewed their obligations to the Court and to proceeding "according to law" as at least equal to their duty to the President. The Solicitor General is responsible for and therefore regularly signs all papers filed in the Supreme Court on behalf of the United States. Nevertheless, Solicitor General Simon Sobeloff had declined to sign a brief for the United States defending the government's power to dismiss an employee as a security risk on the testimony of an unnamed informer, even though the Eisenhower Administration had resolved that the brief should be filed.[15] Solicitor General Erwin N. Griswold would later follow the same course by refusing to defend the Selective Service System's practice of revoking the deferments of students who engaged in demonstrations against conscription for the war in Vietnam.[16] Surely such a step must be accompanied by an offer to resign. I was not quite sure that I ought to follow the course, but I was beginning to dig my heels in. A small conference with Presidential advisers in the Attorney General's office produced no agreement. The Attorney General then scheduled a much larger conference, including the Deputy and all the Assistant Attorneys General, at which the government's position in the Colorado case would be formulated.

On his way to the larger conference, Burke Marshall, the Assistant Attorney General in charge of the Civil Rights Division, stopped by my office. Thirty years earlier, Burke and my younger brother had been intimate boyhood friends. We walked down the long hall leading to the Attorney General's rooms together. "Bob will never file a brief that you won't sign," he said, "but you ought to realize that he really can't turn around now and oppose all those who are arguing for the 'one person, one vote' rule. We've stood together too long. You've got to think of some solution."

"Maybe I have an answer," I replied. "I won't go for 'one person, one vote,' but we can argue that the Colorado apportionment fails to satisfy the standards we've already proposed. That's a stretch and not likely to win, but I'm willing to make the argument. Then, we can argue that if the Court rejects that argument, it should follow the old doctrine that an equity court, unlike a law court, has discretion not to decide a case one way or another if rendering a decision would not be in the public interest. Under the old practice this would be an equity case; there's no claim for damages. We could point to the unanimous popular vote in Colorado ratifying the apportionment, and say that the vote made it unnecessary and unwise to go on to a very close and difficult constitutional question where the apportionment, even if possibly wrong, isn't really grossly unjust."

"I think that will do it," Burke replied. "You can go back to your office. I'll go in and tell Bob that he can call off the conference."

The brief for the United States in the Colorado case followed that line. We argued that Colorado apportionment struck an unreasonable and unconstitutional balance between *per capita* equality and the opposing justifications; but that if the Court rejected that submission, the suit should be dismissed for want of equity without reaching the further and difficult constitutional question whether the Equal Protection Clause requires strict *per capita* representation in both houses of a State legislature.

All six cases before the Court were decided at one time. The major opinion, which came in *Reynolds* v. *Sims*,[17] added voting and apportionment cases to the category in which legislative determinations will be subjected to strict judicial scrutiny: "[T]he right of suffrage is a fundamental matter in a free and democratic society. . . . [A]ny alleged infringement of the right of citizens to vote must be carefully and meticulously scrutinized."[18] The opinion then went on to hold that, as a basic constitutional standard, the Equal Protection Clause requires that the seats in both houses of a bicameral State legislature be apportioned *per capita*. One person, one vote. "Legislatures represent people, not trees or acres. Legislators are elected by voters, not farms or cities or economic interests. . . . The weight of a citizen's vote cannot be made to depend on where he lives."[19] Some slight room was made for exceptions closely related to the effective workings of the political processes. The rule of *Reynolds* v. *Sims* was applied in all the other cases, including Colorado's.[20]

At first the ruling was strongly attacked by professional politicians. In the summer of 1964 only the threat of filibuster blocked legislation to bar its implementation. Senator Everett Dirksen, the Republican leader in the Senate, pressed for a congressional resolution recommending a constitutional amendment. Thirty-two State legislatures, only two less than the required number, requested a constitutional convention. Gradually the attempts to frustrate the constitutional ruling faded away. The decision proved extremely popular among the people. The simple proposition "one person, one vote" had a ringing appeal. More important, it stirred the fundamental political egalitarianism of the Nation.

IV

The decision in *Reynolds* v. *Sims* led quickly to further constitutional developments. Later cases not only made plain that the Court would countenance few exceptions to the "one person, one vote" rule;[21] they also extended the rule to local government and, with some exceptions, to specialized government authorities with elective offices, such as a Board of Education.[22] Eliminating malapportionment did not revitalize State legislatures, as many people had hoped it would. Other methods of skewing representation, such as the party gerrymander, remain.[23] But the Supreme Court's venture into the political thicket did destroy the major device for defeating majority rule, and it gave great impetus to the spirit of equality.

The decision in *Harper* v. *Virginia Board of Elections*,[24] holding that the right to vote may not be conditioned on payment of a poll tax, added to the effect because the opinion flatly pronounced, "Wealth, like race, creed, or color, is not germane to one's ability to participate intelligently in the electoral process. . . . To introduce wealth or the payment of a fee as a measure of a voter's qualifications . . . causes an 'invidious' discrimination [that] runs afoul of the Equal Protection Clause."[25] Later, the Court held unconstitutional a variety of State laws requiring six months' prior residency for eligibility to vote in a Presidential election,[26] prescribing fees to be paid by candidates to get on primary ballots,[27] and setting unduly burdensome requirements obstructing the ballot access of minor parties.[28] The Voting Rights Act of 1965 with later amendments also helped to democratize the electoral process partly because it swept aside all literacy requirements but primarily because it provided means of assuring black citizens effective protection of their right to vote.[29]

V

In *Baker* v. *Carr, Reynolds* v. *Sims,* and the later cases the Court took great strides toward securing opportunities for truly representative government of all the people. My gloomy predictions concerning the effects of supporting a "one person, one vote" rule proved unwarranted. And it is plain, even to me in retrospect, that whatever the intellectual validity of my effort to extrapolate abstract principles from the existing body of law, only a rule of thumb such as *per capita* equality would furnish sufficient guidance to

State legislatures and to the lower courts when litigation was required. Yet one concerned with the Court's long-range effectiveness still must ask whether, from this perspective, it was proper for a Court to make such radical changes, with scarce link to existing law, by constitutional interpretation.

Earlier, in discussing the origins of judicial review, I suggested that the judges' function of deciding "according to law" is best described in terms of an antinomy. On the one hand, the Court must nurture the ideal of a body of law binding the judges no less than the judged by deciding according to a continuity of principle found in the words of the Constitution, in its structure and purposes, and in the judicial precedents, traditional understanding, and historic practices. On the other hand, the Court must meet the enduring human needs and aspirations of its times. These propositions, each pressed to its logical limit, cannot stand together. Somehow over time the Court must strike the right balance and thus resolve the contradiction.

In the reapportionment and voting cases the Court went extraordinarily far in breaking away from established practices, with little apparent support in conventional sources of law. Courts had never adjudicated constitutional claims of malapportionment. The poll tax was an ancient practice. Representatives had never been apportioned to achieve *per capita* equality. Gross malapportionment ran back to colonial times. None of those who put the Equal Protection Clause into the Constitution supposed that it mandated "one person, one vote." It would be intellectually dishonest to argue that the decisions give effect to authors' and supporters' "intent" in any direct sense of the word.

Yet I would deny that the Warren Court simply imposed the Justices' personal theories of representative government upon the country. Beneath the familiar malpractices a deep current of essential political egalitarianism ran through the country's political development. Justice Douglas made the point succinctly:

> The conception of political equality from the Declaration of Independence, to Lincoln's Gettysburg Address, to the Fifteenth, Seventeenth and Nineteenth Amendments, can mean only one thing—one person, one vote.[30]

Even though political perceptions without roots in conventional sources of law are inadequate as a staple diet of constitutional adjudication, important legal principles, both constitutional and other, must occasionally be accomplished by judicial *coup de main*. Then especially, constitutional adjudication depends on a delicate symbiotic relation. The Court must know us better than we know ourselves. Its opinions may, in such cases, be the voice of the spirit, reminding us of our better selves by voicing historic ideals instead of ratifying lesser practices. But while the opinions of the Court can help to shape our national understanding of ourselves, the roots of its decisions must be already in the Nation. The aspirations put into legal form by the Court must be those the community is willing not only to avow but to live by. In such cases the legitimacy of the great strides forward rests on the accuracy of the Court's perception of this kind of common will and on the Court's ability, by expressing its perception in law, to command a genuine consensus.

Viewed by themselves, the apportionment and voting cases meet this test. Whether the Warren Court nonetheless eroded the belief in law that supports the people's belief in constitutionalism by too often going too far too fast remains for later consideration.

· 17 ·

Invidious Distinctions and Fundamental Rights

EQUALITY is a pervasive theme of American history. The Fourteenth Amendment guarantees all persons within a State the "equal protection of the laws." *Unequal* treatment is nonetheless a pervasive and necessary characteristic of laws. A State not only may but must discriminate against blind men and women in granting licenses to operate motor vehicles. It may inspect restaurants but not garages. It may grant financial aid to the blind but not to the deaf. It may tax commercial buildings at a higher rate than residential housing. Perhaps it was the pervasiveness of differential legal treatment that led the Court to say in one of its first rulings on the Equal Protection Clause that "[w]e doubt very much whether any action not directed against the negroes as a class, or on account of their race, will ever be held to come within the purview of this provision."[1] Half a century later Justice Holmes could still disparagingly refer to the Equal Protection Clause as the "usual last resort of constitutional arguments."[2]

In 1940 three rules, closely paralleling the Court's restrained approach to the Due Process Clause, seemed thoroughly settled:

1. Any legislative classification is constitutionally permissible which has *some* rational basis in terms of some rational view of the public interest.

2. If any set of facts could conceivably exist that would render a classification reasonable, its existence must be assumed.
3. Since evils in the same general field may be of different dimensions and proportions—or so a legislature may think—legislation may be addressed to one phase, neglecting the others.

The resulting judicial "hands off" is illustrated by a case from Louisiana. The Louisiana Board of River Pilots, although an official body, practiced unabashed nepotism by confining the training and licensing of apprentice pilots to relatives of licensed pilots. All others were thus excluded by Louisiana law. When the law and official practice were attacked as denials of equal protection, the Court refused to intervene because the legislature *might* rationally have supposed that safer pilotage *might* result from "the benefits to morale and *esprit de corps* which family and neighborly tradition might contribute."[3]

By the mid-1960s the times seemed ripe for a new departure. A growing proportion of all constitutional litigation was being conducted by organized groups seeking to win by constitutional interpretation reforms that they could not win in the political arena. The School Desegregation Cases and the Reapportionment Cases offered not only general encouragement but hope of doctrinal development along two lines.

First, the cases involving segregation and other forms of racial or ethnic discrimination had created a category of "suspect classifications" or "invidious distinctions," requiring "the strictest judicial scrutiny" and constitutional condemnation unless "narrowly tailored to achieve some compelling public interest." Might not the list of "invidious" or "suspect" classifications be expanded to reach all legislation subjecting the members of society's disfavored groups to unequal treatment—aliens, for example, illegitimate children, women, indigents, homosexuals, and perhaps others?

Second, the Reapportionment Cases had required the Court to make another kind of exception to the general rule of judicial tolerance for rational legislative classifications. Any number of relevant considerations could be cited to justify giving some geographical constituencies greater *per capita* representation than others: economic importance, geographical size, offsetting the weight of urban bloc voting, representing political subdivisions as the U.S.

Senate represents States, and so on. Nor could the lines of differentiation be called "invidious." In justifying strict scrutiny, the Court observed:

> Undoubtedly, the right of suffrage is a fundamental matter in a free and democratic society. Especially since the right to exercise the franchise in a free and unimpaired manner is preservative of other basic civil and political rights, any alleged infringement of the right of citizens to vote must be carefully and meticulously scrutinized.[4]

Reform groups began to reason "If strict scrutiny is appropriate for classifications in voting laws because voting is a 'fundamental right,' perhaps we can persuade the Court to apply the strict scrutiny test to laws dealing with public welfare, hospital care, public housing, education, and like necessities, on the ground that they too are 'fundamental rights.'"

"Invidious classification" and "classification affecting access to a fundamental right": here were two doctrinal theories for achieving more social and political reform by constitutional adjudication. For some time longer the search for equality continued to drive the Warren Court. What law professors dubbed the "new Equal Protection Clause" and "two-tiered equal protection" (that is, rationality and strict scrutiny) became for a time the cutting edge of constitutional development.

POVERTY AND FUNDAMENTAL RIGHTS

The next two important cases encouraged the proponents of both doctrinal lines of development. *Harper* v. *Board of Elections*[5] held unconstitutional a Virginia statute making a payment of a modest poll tax a condition of eligibility to vote. "Lines drawn on the basis of wealth or property like those of race are traditionally disfavored."[6] Here was a strong suggestion that differential treatment based on relative wealth is an "invidious classification" requiring strict scrutiny. And, after repeating the earlier assertions that suffrage is fundamental to a free society, the Court went on to say that "[t]o introduce wealth or payment of a fee as a measure of a voter's qualifications is to introduce a capricious or irrelevant factor."[7] Here justification for strict scrutiny was found partly in the effect on access to a fundamental right.

The dissenting opinions revealed growing resistance among the Justices opposed to reading into the open-ended constitutional guarantees judge-made policies unaided by clear historic purpose or the relatively specific provisions of the Bill of Rights. In a biting dissent, Justice Black, who surely thought the poll tax unfair and unwise, protested the tendency of "this Court to use the Equal Protection Clause, as it has today, to write into the Constitution its notions of what it thinks is good governmental policy."[8] Two other Justices dissented. Gradually, the opposition would increase.

Shapiro v. *Thompson*[9] encouraged lawyers to use lawsuits based on the Equal Protection Clause to attack what they saw as inequities in the welfare system. In the classroom a bright and well-prepared law student who was asked to state the holding of *Shapiro* v. *Thompson* might reply that the case decided that State laws requiring one year's immediate prior residency to qualify for welfare payments violates the Equal Protection Clause. The logical precision of the answer could hardly be improved, yet it squeezes the case dry of what Professor Felix Frankfurter called "the vital juices." Behind the generalities and abstractions of statutes and legal doctrines lie the individual men and women whose lives the law poignantly affects. As *NLRB* v. *Jones & Laughlin Steel Corp.*[10] is the case of Harry Phillips, Royal Boyer, and their friends, so *Shapiro* v. *Thompson* is the case of José Foster, Vera Barley, and Juanita Smith, of their children, and of other mothers dependent upon public welfare to keep their families together.

José Foster had lived in Pennsylvania from 1953 to 1965; she was married, had children, and became separated from her husband there. In the summer of 1965 José Foster went to South Carolina to care for an invalid grandmother and a grandfather. When they no longer needed her care, the grandfather because he was permanently hospitalized, José Foster went back to Pennsylvania to rejoin her closest family and friends. She and her four children were forced by poverty to share a three-bedroom house also occupied by her brother-in-law and sister and their six children. Welfare was denied because José Foster and her children had not been residents of Pennsylvania during the immediately preceding year.

In the case of Vera Barley the outcome of the constitutional decision meant—literally—the difference between freedom and confinement. In March 1941 she had moved to the District of Columbia from California. A month later she was committed to St.

Elizabeth's Hospital for mental illness. By 1966 she was competent, and doctors advised her release. But she could not leave St. Elizabeth's without public assistance, because she was sixty-seven years old and had no resources. Under the District of Columbia law her twenty-five years of confinement in St. Elizabeth's Hospital within the District did not count toward residence in the District. To establish residence she must get out of St. Elizabeth's. To get out of St. Elizabeth's she must prove one year's prior residence. Catch-22.

Juanita Smith had lived in Pennsylvania from the time she was one month old until after her marriage. She went to school there and worked there. Her father, mother, brothers, and sisters were all born and raised in Philadelphia and lived there at the time of the litigation. In 1959 Juanita Smith moved with her husband to rural Delaware. In 1966, when her husband left her, she returned to Pennsylvania to rejoin her family, get better education for her children, find better job opportunities for herself. She found no job. She needed medical care but could not obtain it without welfare assistance. Provision could be made for her five children only by breaking up the family and placing the children in centers already overcrowded to 125 percent of capacity. Because of the one-year residence requirement, Juanita Smith and her children were denied public assistance.

Young lawyers in law offices set up as part of President Johnson's war on poverty brought suits on behalf of these and other welfare claimants, alleging that the denial of public assistance to new residents of a State violated the Fourteenth Amendment. They were successful in the lower courts, but the States appealed. After one argument in the U.S. Supreme Court the claimants' lawyers asked me to join them.

On reargument we contended that the legislative classification resulting from the one-year residence requirement violated the Fifth and Fourteenth Amendments because it involved access to fundamental human rights—food, shelter, health, freedom from institutional confinement, and the preservation of family units—and because the differentiation between old residents and newcomers is invidious in that it depends solely on whether the newcomers had chosen to exercise the traditional American privilege of leaving an old and unsatisfactory environment in pursuit of new opportunities for self-preservation or advancement. The argument sought to combine into a single proposition both the "fundamental right" and "invidious classification" grounds for strict judicial scrutiny and invalidation unless the classification was justified by a compelling public interest. The opinion holding the one-year residency requirement unconstitutional put the decision chiefly on the ground that discrimination based on the exercise of the privilege of moving a *bona fide* residence from one State to another is especially invidious, but the majority also intimated that receipt of welfare payments by the indigent might be a fundamental right. José Foster, Juanita Smith, and thousands of other mothers could keep their families together. The Vera Barleys could finish life outside hospitals for the insane.

Shapiro v. *Thompson* encouraged further efforts to use the Equal Protection Clause to reduce the inequalities in access to public services associated with poverty. One reform group attacked the traditional method of financing public education. In most States the cost of primary and secondary school education had traditionally been met chiefly by an *ad valorem* property tax levied by each local school district on the real and personal property within its jurisdiction. In Texas, where the case that went to the Supreme Court arose,[11] about half the cost was thus financed. Enormous disparities developed in both the numbers of children and the taxable value of the property in different districts, and thus in the wealth per pupil. In the Edgewood School District in the old San Antonio central city, there were twenty-two thousand children in the primary and secondary schools, nearly all of them black or Mexican-American. The assessed property value was approximately $131 million—about $5960 per pupil. The Alamo Heights District comprised a wealthy suburb in the same county. The assessed property value was approximately $250 million for five thousand students—more than $49,000 per pupil. Such disparities obviously result in wide variations in expenditures per pupil and in wide but perhaps not proportionate differences in the quality of education. Was it consistent with the dream of equality for the State of Texas to organize a public school system that spends $594 annually for the education of Sammy Smith, the child of wealthy parents in Alamo Heights, while spending only $356 for the education of Demetrio Rodriguez down in Edgewood?

The plaintiffs, who had brought a class action on behalf of children in the disfavored districts, argued that they were being denied the equal protection of the laws because the State was not providing them with education equal to that provided by the State in the wealthier districts. Strict scrutiny, they argued, was warranted not only because the differential was based on relative wealth, an invidious basis for classification under the poll tax case, but also because the differential was in access to education, a fundamental right any discriminatory withholding of which requires strict scrutiny.

In the interval between *Shapiro* v. *Thompson* and the oral argument in the *Rodriguez* case, the composition of the Court had changed. Even in *Shapiro,* four Justices had dissented. In the *Rodriguez* case the four new Justices, joined by Justice Stewart, rejected the constitutional arguments, 5–4. The majority refused to accept either branch of the argument for strict review. Justice Powell, speaking for the Court, reasoned that the differential treatment of children in the poor school districts when compared with those in districts having more valuable property was not "invidious" because there was no discrimination among individuals on the basis of individual wealth. A child of wealthy parents might live in Edgewood; a child of poor parents might live in Alamo Heights. Moreover, the State did provide some education for every child, and no one could fairly conclude that the quality of education in a school is exactly proportionate to the expenditures per pupil. Justice Powell also rejected the "fundamental rights" branch of the argument:

> It is not the province of this Court to create substantive constitutional rights in the name of guaranteeing equal protection of the laws. Thus, the key to discovering whether education is "fundamental" . . . lies in assessing whether there is a right to education explicitly or implied guaranteed by the Constitution. . . . Education, of course, is not among the rights afforded explicit protection under our Federal Constitution. Nor do we find any basis for saying it is implicitly so protected.[12]

The cases did not comfortably fit Justice Powell's Procrustean bed. Not a word in the Constitution other than the guarantees of equal treatment protects the right to vote. The rights to procreation and abortion are protected by the Equal Protection and Due Process Clauses only because the Court chose to characterize them as "fundamental" in the absence of any words directly implying that such protection was intended. Nevertheless, the *Rodriguez* decision seemed to nip in the bud the "fundamental rights" branch of strict judicial review under the Equal Protection Clause.[13]

Other efforts to use the "new Equal Protection Clause" to attack inequalities resulting from differences in wealth bore little fruit. Prior to *Rodriguez* the Court had ruled that an indigent person charged with crime in a State court has, on conviction, a constitutional right to a transcript of the trial record and an attorney at State expense in order to enjoy the same opportunities for an appeal as a wealthier person could buy.[14] The Court did not explain whether these constitutional rights arose because the State's failure to provide the indigent defendant with the transcript and legal representation that others could buy would be a violation of the Equal Protection Clause or because convicting a person without the means of appeal available to others is a deprivation of liberty without due process of law. If the earlier decisions rested on the Equal Protection Clause, then the State might have a like duty to provide indigents with the means of access to the civil courts—a fundamental right—in order to avoid invidious discrimination. The argument was turned back in a series of decisions in the early 1970s.[15]

In the same vein the Court held that it was not unconstitutional discrimination along lines of wealth to require that any municipal ordinance providing for the construction of public housing be submitted to a popular referendum, even though ordinances satisfying the needs of other identifiable groups were immediately effective.[16] Some years later the Court held that neither a State nor Congress has a constitutional obligation to provide funds to pay for an abortion for an indigent woman, even though a woman with the necessary funds could have an abortion without State interference as a constitutional right. And *Dandridge* v. *Williams*[17] ruled that classifications affecting the size of grants of public assistance were generally subject only to the same "minimum rationality" scrutiny as statutes regulating business practices. The constitutional attack on inequalities resulting from poverty was brought to an end.

Two circumstances explain the change in the prevailing approach. Racial discrimination aside, a strong minority of the Justices opposed extending strict judicial review from the Bill of Rights to the Equal Protection Clause. The dissenters continued to emphasize judicial deference to political decisions on matters of social and economic policy, and to the values of local autonomy. The rationale used to develop the preferred rights thesis under the First and Fourteenth Amendments was inapplicable. There was no closing of normal political processes, no genuine insular minority, and no relatively specific guarantee. There was too much danger that the Court, cast loose from precedent, would simply read the personal ideals of individual Justices into the open-ended phrase "equal protection of the laws." The original dissenters were strengthened by the changes in personnel when Chief Justice Burger replaced Chief Justice Warren, and Justices Black, Harlan, and Abe Fortas were replaced by Justices Blackmun, Powell, and Rehnquist. The four new Justices as a group were more conservative than their predecessors in both social and judicial philosophy.

In dealing with inequalities resulting from distinctions in wealth, the natural judicial caution of the new majority was doubtless enhanced by awareness of the relative unsuitability of judicial tools. Reducing such inequalities requires public expenditures. Expenditures require legislative appropriations. Appropriations must be balanced by taxes. All these typically lie outside the judicial realm.

The difficulties have not always deterred the Court from placing affirmative duties on governments, as we noted in Chapter 14 in connection with school desegregation; but it seems highly probable that the decisive factor in rejecting efforts to use the Equal Protection Clause to reduce inequalities resulting from differences in wealth was often the practical difficulty of laying on communities essentially affirmative, on-going obligations for the benefit of disadvantaged groups.

The *Rodriguez* case furnishes a useful example. Suppose that the Court had held that Texas was denying children in the Edgewood and other relatively poor school districts the equal protection of the laws? Similar decrees would have to be rendered in many other States. What would happen next? Ideally, the legislatures would promptly set up new methods of financing primary and secondary education. Each would face extraordinarily difficult questions of tax and fiscal policy. Should public school education be centrally financed from State revenues? Or should the State adopt the ingenious "district power equalization" scheme, under which a district with a tax base per pupil above the Statewide average would contribute part of the school revenues it chose to raise to districts whose tax base per pupil was below the Statewide average? A third possibility might be to redraw school district lines to equalize the tax bases. A fourth would be to remove commercial, industrial, and mineral property from the local tax rolls, tax this property Statewide, and use the proceeds to eliminate inequalities resulting from the disparities in the remaining local tax bases. From a constitutional standpoint it would not matter what choice was made. The only question the Court need worry about would be: Will the judicial mandate impel the legislatures of forty-nine States to appropriate action?

Perhaps a judicial mandate would have been sufficient, but surely the strain on the authority of the Court is greater than that created by the traditional decree forbidding a named official from interfering with private individuals or businesses in a specified manner. It would be hardly surprising if some legislature failed to act out of stubbornness, inability to reach a consensus among its members, or a despairing willingness, as in some reapportionment cases, to dump its problems on the court. Surely the risk was sufficient for the Supreme Court to ask itself "If some legislature fails to act, what happens next?"

What *would* happen next? Should federal courts all over the country decide the policy questions, levy the taxes, and distribute the revenues? Not to act would be to acknowledge judicial futility. To act would be to adopt a tax and fiscal policy for the State. It might even become necessary for the courts to set up the machinery to make the policy effective. In addition to questions of competency, those of legitimacy would surely arise. Even in the case of legislative default, does a federal court—usually a single judge—have legitimate power to levy taxes on a people without their consent, and to decide where and how public money shall be spent? Nor would this be the end of the road. For the court to act would risk a collision between the court and the political authorities at some subsequent date if the court is forced to act and the legislature afterward chooses a different program.

An alternative might be to forbid the continued operation of the public schools under the system held unconstitutional, thus seeking to force the legislature to do its duty. The Supreme Court of New Jersey followed that course. In an opinion handed down on April 3, 1973, the court undertook to particularize the broad ideal of equality guaranteed by the New Jersey Constitution into a ruling that the number of dollars spent on a child's education in the public schools may not be dependent on the value of the taxable property in each local school district.[18] After further argument the court gave the legislature eight months—until December 31, 1973—to comply by enacting appropriate legislation.[19] The legislature failed to act. On May 23, 1975, the court entered a decree that required executive officials to divert appropriations for State education away from the legislatively prescribed purposes to achieve a degree of equalization.[20] The court intended this decree to be only a partial remedy, and retained jurisdiction. During 1975 the legislature enacted a new program that would have satisfied the judicial mandate if, but only if, the plan were funded by taxation and appropriation. The legislature failed to provide either. In January 1976 the court upheld the program, if funded, and gave the legislature until April 6—a little over two months—to provide the funding.[21] The legislature again failed to act. On May 13 the court tightened the screw by issuing an injunction against any expediture of funds on public education after June 30, unless the legislature provided equalized funding.[22] Now the court and the legislature "stood eyeball to eyeball." The legislature blinked.

In New Jersey the court had the strong support of the Governor. Without it, I suspect, the necessary legislation would not have been adopted. What would have happened? Perhaps the schools would have been closed for the summer; the timing of the decree shows that judges do not lack for political skill. Could the judges have kept the schools closed into the fall and winter? I wonder. If not, the judicial ruling would stand *brutum fulmen*—a revelation with the same potential as the mythical child's observation that the emperor hailed for magnificent raiment wore no clothes.

These and like dangers should not always deter judicial intervention. Questions expressing similar fears of ultimate judicial impotence were put to me from the bench in *Baker* v. *Carr,* the first Reapportionment Case, and again in the case of the Watergate Tapes. In each instance I urged the Court to press on. But when *San Antonio School District* v. *Rodriguez* came on for decision, the lower federal courts were widely engaged in the difficult and controversial process of securing desegregation of the schools. It is hardly surprising that a majority of the Justices held back from simultaneously mandating another, even broader program of reform in school finance. The example also underscores the difficulty of applying constitutional guarantees on a wide scale to the conduct of affirmative governmental programs and institutions.

The *Rodriguez* case also marked the end of doctrinal success in expanding the "access to a fundamental right" branch of strict judicial scrutiny under the Equal Protection Clause. At the same time, the Court was growing more cautious in applying the concept of "suspect" or "invidious" classification. In the latter area, however, one more great judicial step in the search for equality still lay ahead.

SEX AND OTHER INVIDIOUS CLASSIFICATIONS

From the beginning, American laws and social customs discriminated against women no less than those of the Old World. The principal author of the Declaration of Independence wrote: "Were our state a pure democracy there would still be excluded from our deliberations women, who, to prevent deprivation of morals and ambiguity of issues, should not mix promiscuously in gatherings of men."[23] Alexis de Tocqueville, in his commentaries on the United States of the 1830s, observed that in no country had such constant care been taken to mark out separate pathways for men and women: "American women never manage the outward concerns of the family, or conduct a business, or take a part in political life."[24] Despite its verbal guarantee of equal protection of the laws for every "person," the Fourteenth Amendment adopted in 1869 neither had nor was intended to have any effect on the great mass of laws discriminating against women.

The Court proceeded on this view for more than a century. In 1948 the Court upheld a State statute prohibiting women from tending bar except when the woman was the wife or daughter of a male owner of the bar. Justice Frankfurter, speaking for the Court, took note of the increasing liberation of women, but ruled, "The fact that women may now have achieved the virtues that men have long claimed as their prerogatives and now indulge in vices that men have long practiced does not preclude the States from drawing a sharp line between the sexes. . . . The Constitution does not require legislatures to reflect sociological insight or shifting social standards."[25]

Customs, standards, and even statutory law were indeed changing. After 1954, as the drive for equality for women was aided by the civil rights movement, so did the lawyers framing constitutional attacks on official sex discrimination gain a powerful weapon in *Brown* v. *Board of Education*.[26] That decision and related cases, as we have seen, substituted for the rule of "minimum rationality" the strictest judicial scrutiny and a presumption of unconstitutionality, which can be overcome only by proof that the discrimination is narrowly tailored to serve a compelling public purpose. Judges and lawyers reason by analogy. The logic of a ground-breaking decision is often pressed out toward broader generalizations by discounting some of the facts, emphasizing a smaller number, and thus enlarging the class that fits within the rule. Lawyers representing not only women but also aliens, illegitimate children, indigents, homosexuals, and other groups argued that the critical fact in cases like *Brown* v. *Board of Education* was not race or color but membership in a class victimized by arbitrary prejudice. Arguing that their classes of clients were likewise the victims of arbitrary prejudice, they then sought the greater constitutional protection of the strict scrutiny rule.

Other precedents added force to the argument. Despite its initial prediction that only legislation directed against Negroes as a class would run afoul of the Fourteenth Amendment, the Court soon after ratification of the amendment struck down laws and official practices discriminating against persons of Chinese, Japanese, or Mexican-American origin.[27] By 1967 the Reapportionment, Voting Rights, and Poll Tax Cases had shown that racial and national minorities were not the only groups entitled to strict judicial scrutiny.[28] The movements seeking extension to all cases involving "suspect" or "invidious" classifications were given further encouragement in 1968, when the Court set aside a Louisiana statute denying unacknowledged illegitimate children the right to recover damages from one who wrongfully caused the death of their mother,[29] and again in 1971, when the Court voided State laws denying resident aliens welfare benefits,[30] civil service jobs,[31] and admission to the Bar.[32] *Shapiro* v. *Thompson*,[33] discussed above, had applied the strict scrutiny test to State laws denying welfare benefits to a State's new but nonetheless *bona fide* residents.

The stage thus seemed set for a broad ruling extending the "invidious classification" and "strict scrutiny" principles to women. *Reed* v. *Reed*[34] then brought before the Court an Idaho statute which provided that when two relatives of a decedent in the same degree both sought to be appointed the administrator of the decedent's estate, the male should be preferred over the female. Counsel for the woman seeking appointment were joined by Ruth Bader Ginsburg, a Harvard Law School graduate then teaching at Rutgers Law School, and now a judge on the U.S. Court of Appeals. Their powerful brief argued that any sex-based statutory classification unrelated to biological differences is a "suspect classification," proscribed by the Fourteenth Amendment. The Court held that the statute violated the Equal Protection Clause because there was no rational basis for the discrimination against women.

The purported ground for the decision is manifestly unacceptable. It may be unfair and unwise, but it is not irrational to provide a workable rule of thumb for resolving such disputes, provided that the rule may be expected to lead to a sound result in a sizable proportion of the cases to which it applies; and in Idaho, in the 1960s, one could rationally presume that men would have had more experience in managing businesses and other property than women. Quite plainly, the Court was applying a stricter standard but was reluctant to acknowledge it.

Ms. Ginsburg and her colleagues scored a second success in *Frontiero* v. *Richardson*,[35] but once again the Court failed to enunciate a clear-cut rule. Sharron Frontiero had joined the U.S. Air Force in 1968. A physical therapist and first lieutenant assigned to Maxwell Field, Alabama, she married Joseph Frontiero, a full-time college student, late in 1969. Sharron supported the couple, except for Joseph's slender part-time earnings and G.I. educational allowance. Federal legislation provided for automatic dependency allowances to the spouses of male members of the armed forces but withheld the allowances from the spouse of a female unless he was proved to draw more than half his support from his wife. Joseph drew slightly less than half his support from Sharron. Accordingly, when their request for the allowances automatically available to male members of the armed forces and their spouses was denied, Sharron and Joseph brought suit, claiming that the sex-based discrimination violated the Fifth Amendment. The U.S. District Court dismissed the action.

On appeal Justice Brennan, joined by Justices Douglas, White, and Marshall, reasoned that "classifications based upon sex, like classifications based upon race, alienage, or national origin, are inherently suspect, and must therefore be subjected to strict judicial

scrutiny."[36] Much of the opinion is devoted to the "long and un-
fortunate history of sex discrimination."[37] The recital, far from
showing that the decision was based upon law, goes a long way to
show that the four Justices were reading new values into the Constitution without support in the original intent or traditional ideals
of the American people. If that were all, the ruling would indeed
seem open to the charge that the Court was improperly substituting
a new social vision for the original intent and the rule of law. The
more persuasive part of the opinion reasons by analogy. It de-
duces—from the decisions holding that classifications based on
race, national origin, and legitimacy of birth require strict judicial
scrutiny—the broader general proposition that a legislative classification is suspect if it is at war with "the basic concept of our
system that legal burdens should bear some relationship to individual responsibility."[38] The underlying principle has strong support
in our legal inheritance, even though it, like the egalitarian premise
of our political philosophy, had long been violated in some particulars. Differentiations based on sex fell within the suspect class
because "the sex characteristic frequently bears no relation to ability to perform or contribute to society."[39]

Only Justice Rehnquist dissented, but four more Justices refrained from joining Justice Brennan and his three colleagues in
ranking statutory differentiations according to sex as suspect classifications calling for strict judicial scrutiny. The most plausible
explanation is that they felt, or were coming to feel, increasing
doubt about building a structure of legal analysis that subjected
some regulatory distinctions to a test of "minimum rationality" but
a growing number to "strict scrutiny," with the result that the latter
were almost automatically branded unconstitutional because their
justification could rarely be characterized as a "compelling public
interest." The misgivings had become evident in the decisions discussed above in which the Court refused to extend strict scrutiny
to classifications differentiating the poor from the well-to-do in
access to fundamental rights. The doubts and opposition would
soon carry the day in upholding laws denying aliens appointment
to a State police force or to the teaching staff of a public school
even though the justifications were less than compelling.[40]

Three years later a majority of the Justices were able to agree
on a new formula for judging the constitutionality of laws discriminating against women. "Sex" gave way to "gender." The two
standards of judicial review, the "minimum rationality" and "strict

scrutiny" tests, became three. "[C]lassifications by gender must serve important governmental objectives and must be substantially related to achievement of those objectives."[41] The new intermediate standard was announced in a decision holding that an Oklahoma statute forbidding the sale of 3.2 percent beer to young men under twenty-one years old while allowing sales to young women over eighteen violated the Fourteenth Amendment by denying the young men equal protection of the laws. Justice O'Connor elaborated the underlying rationale in the opinion of the Court, holding it unconstitutional for the Mississippi University for Women to deny men admission to its all-female School of Nursing. The "important governmental objectives test" must be applied, she explained, "free of fixed notions concerning the roles and abilities of males and females. Thus, if the statutory objective is to exclude or 'protect' members of one gender because they are presumed to suffer from an inherent handicap or to be innately inferior, the objective itself is illegitimate. The validity of a classification is to be determined by reasoned analysis rather than through the mechanical application of traditional, often inaccurate, assumptions about the proper roles of men and women."[42]

Perhaps it is ironic that the great progress made by the advocates of women's rights under the Fourteenth Amendment was a substantial cause of the failure of enough States to ratify the proposed Equal Rights Amendment. Apart from symbolism, there was little need for ERA. Few, if any, remnants of the once-pervasive discrimination against women could any longer survive attack under the Equal Protection Clause. Perhaps some women view reaffirmation of the federal government's power to register young men for military service while passing over young women as an example of injustice that has survived.[43] Judicial scrutiny of laws favoring women over men is somewhat less exacting,[44] but even this form of classification by sex seldom survives constitutional attack. The expansion of the idea of "equality" to include equal treatment of the sexes ranks second only to the civil rights revolution among the judicial accomplishments of the Warren and Burger Courts.

CONCLUDING OBSERVATIONS

In the areas of race and color, women's rights, voting rights, and legislative representation, the substitution of strict judicial scrutiny for judicial self-restraint under the Equal Protection Clause brought massive changes expanding the ideal of equality and enlarging the role of the courts. Egalitarian ideals also infused other developments, particularly in the reform of criminal procedure. On the other hand, the Court refused to expand either the "suspect classification" or "access to a fundamental right" basis for strict scrutiny to its full logical potential.

In the middle ground confusion reigns. The original doctrinal purity of the "strict scrutiny–compelling public purpose" and "minimum rationality" tests has yielded to three formulations. All three have surrendered even the pretense of precision; and at least two Justices—Justices Marshall and Stevens—insist that in every case the process of decision calls for *ad hoc* balancing of what they perceive as the particular degree of unfairness resulting from disadvantage imposed on some persons by the challenged statute against what they perceive as the worth of the statute in promoting public interests.

The net effect in the middle ground has been ten or twelve years of highly particularistic decisions resulting from shifting alliances among the Justices. On the whole, judicial review has been considerably stricter than that under the "rational basis" test in the era of judicial self-restraint. For example, when Texas denied public education to school-age children living in the State whose parents were not legally admitted aliens, the Court ruled, 5–4, that the Texas statute violated the Equal Protection Clause even though undocumented aliens could not be treated as a suspect class and education is not a fundamental right. Any detached observer is likely to agree that the Texas law was peculiarly harsh and shortsighted; but it is hard to fault on grounds of logic the four dissenting Justices' contention that it was no more irrational than many laws previously sustained by the Court. The line of equal protection decisions is bound to waver so long as the individual Justices hold widely varying views concerning the nature of their function. And one both hopes and suspects that even if the "rational basis" test comes to prevail in all but a narrow class of cases, the sense of justice will remain strong enough to stretch the rule and invalidate injustices such as that involved in the alien children's case.

· 18 ·

Abortion

DURING THE WARREN YEARS, 1953–1969, the U.S. Supreme Court had vigorously expanded its role in American government. Appeals for judicial deference to legislative fact finding and policymaking, like appeals to State autonomy, lost force. Strict scrutiny rather than judicial self-restraint became the guiding principle in interpreting the First Amendment, the procedural guarantees of the Bill of Rights incorporated into the Fourteenth Amendment, and some applications of the Equal Protection Clause. But the area of "substantive due process," where the doctrines of judicial self-restraint developed, had not been directly affected. The appeals to specificity and historic purpose that rationalized the activist decisions under the Bill of Rights and Equal Protection Clause did not logically apply to the Due Process Clause. Nevertheless, that bastion fell under Chief Justice Burger, when the Court held in *Roe* v. *Wade*[1] that the Due Process Clause of the Fourteenth Amendment bars a State from prohibiting abortion.

Many constitutional decisions have had more immediate direct effects on American society than *Roe* v. *Wade*. None except the *Dred Scott* case[2] has aroused as intense popular emotion. Few have raised more profound questions concerning the role of the Supreme Court of the United States in American government.

We learn little about "Jane Roe" from the court records. The pseudonym was used to cloak her true identity. Her affidavit filed in her lawsuit tells us that she was a single woman more than twenty-one years old, living in Dallas County, Texas. She was pregnant on March 3, 1970, and still pregnant on May 21, 1970, when her affidavit was filed. She had had a tenth-grade education. She swore that her pregnancy made it difficult to find or keep employment, and that she was "barely able to make ends meet." She "wanted to terminate my pregnancy because of the economic hardship that pregnancy entailed and because of the social stigma of bearing illegitimate children in our society."[3] Jane Roe could not secure a legal abortion in Texas because a Texas statute made performing an abortion a crime, except when necessary to save the woman's life. She could not afford to travel to a more liberal jurisdiction. Accordingly, she asked a District Court of the United States in Texas to issue a declaratory judgment holding the Texas anti-abortion statute unconstitutional and thus removing the obstacle to her exercising her constitutional right to freedom of choice. The Texas law enforcement officials acknowledged these facts but defended the statute's constitutionality.

Jane Roe prevailed in the U.S. Supreme Court, as we all know. The 7–2 decision held that the Fourteenth Amendment secures an adult woman the right to seek a termination of her pregnancy during the first three months without any interference by government, and that during the second three months—until the unborn child could live outside its mother—the State may limit the right only to safeguard the woman's health. But although we know this, it will be useful to try to put out of our minds for a moment not only familiarity with the actual decision but any prejudices and preconceptions concerning the proper result. Suppose that we were the Justices of the U.S. Supreme Court charged with deciding the case of Jane Roe. What would we decide? How would we, and each of us, as conscientious judges work our way to a decision?

As Justices, our position would be quite different from that of a pregnant woman faced with an undesired pregnancy. In deciding as a personal matter whether to have an abortion, the pregnant woman must consider among other concerns her religion and the personal morality instilled by upbringing, reading, and reflection. The Justice must put aside many of the concerns that would shape her personal conduct. The devout Roman Catholic, for example, may feel bound in his personal life by his Church's condemnation of abortion. A Roman Catholic Justice could not properly allow his religious faith to determine his judicial ruling.

Our position as Justices is also distinct from that of legislators. Whether a State legislature should forbid abortion is quite different from the question whether the Constitution allows a State legislature to forbid abortion. Also, different factors enter into the decision. The knowledge that illicit abortion mills would flourish and that the well-to-do could circumvent the law by visiting more permissive jurisdictions might persuade a legislator that an anti-abortion law would be unwise. Such concerns would have little bearing on whether an anti-abortion law is an unconstitutional interference with personal liberty.

As Justices, then, we must decide "according to law." The question becomes: Where do we find our law? Probably we should all agree that, because our task is limited to interpretation, we must look first to its words. Jane Roe's claim is that Texas, by enforcing its anti-abortion law, is depriving her of "liberty" without due process of law. What then is the meaning of "liberty" as used in the Fourteenth Amendment? Jane Roe's claim that "liberty" includes the specific freedom to have an abortion recalls Munn's assertion that "liberty" includes the specific freedom to choose the price at which one will rent space in his grain elevator; and also the *Lochner* argument that "liberty" includes the specific freedom of an employer and employee to decide by mutual agreement for how long the employee will work and at what wages. The cases are different in many important respects, but all raise the common question: How should a judge go about deciding what particular activities are comprehended within the general word "liberty" when used in the Fourteenth Amendment?

Where the correct application of a written instrument to a particular situation is not clear from the words, courts customarily look to the intent. The principle applies in constitutional interpretation, but when applied to an instrument written two hundred years ago the very word "intent" gives difficulty. Are the majestic phrases guaranteeing individual rights to apply only to the particulars that the Framers consciously and specifically intended? Or does the search for intent call for asking what underlying ideals and values of an enduring character must have moved the Framers, for applying the latter to current conditions, and even for new applications of old ideals and values whose full meaning the past had scarcely perceived? There is no evidence that in 1791 the Framers believed abortion to be an aspect of the "liberty" guaranteed by the Due Process Clause of the Fifth Amendment even though prior to quickening, and perhaps after quickening, it was not a crime. By 1869, when the Fourteenth Amendment was ratified, a number of States had enacted statutes making abortion a crime. Quite surely there was no specific intent to render them unconstitutional.

Justice Hugo L. Black would have had no difficulty in concluding that Jane Roe had no constitutional right. His judicial philosophy, developed during the era of resistance to Lochnerism, called for active judicial intervention to promote freedom of speech and press, the privilege against self-incrimination, jury trials, and other liberties identified in the relatively specific provisions of the Bill of Rights, but for virtually total judicial restraint in applying the Due Process Clause unaided by incorporation of the Bill of Rights. In an opinion explaining why he would not join in the Court in holding unconstitutional a statute forbidding the use of contraceptives, Justice Black wrote:

> I do not believe that we are granted power by the Due Process Clause or any other constitutional provision or provisions to measure constitutionality by our belief that legislation is arbitrary, capricious or unreasonable, or accomplishes no justifiable purpose, or is offensive to our own notions of "civilized standards of conduct." . . . The use by federal courts of such formula or doctrine or whatnot to veto federal or state laws simply takes away from Congress and States the power to make laws based upon their own judgment of fairness and wisdom and transfers the power to this Court for ultimate determination.[4]

Justice Black's approach, which constitutional scholars currently call "interpretivism," has never commanded many adherents. Similarly, the Court has very rarely specifically confined general constitutional phrases to the particular applications that the Framers had consciously in mind. The view prevailing almost from the beginning, as we noted in discussing Munn's grain elevator, allowed judges to draw upon the tradition of natural law and read the words "life, liberty or property" very broadly. The question would then be whether the State could justify the deprivation as consistent with "due process of law" by showing that the restriction on individual rights contributed to a broader public interest. Some justification could almost always be put forward. When a representative legislature restricted a person's freedom to engage in a particular activity for reasons the legislators deemed sufficient, the key question of judicial method became: How far may the judge go in second-guessing the legislature and perhaps substituting his judicial judgment for that of the legislature on whether the justification is sufficient? The question grows out of the collision between the ideal of representative self-government, on the one hand, and, on the other hand, the ancient yearning for protection against government intrusion on fundamental human rights. By the early 1940s, as we noted in Chapter 8, a broad philosophy of judicial deference to legislative judgments had developed. The Court repeatedly proclaimed that a State or federal law will not be held unconstitutional under the Due Process Clause unless the restriction on liberty or property bears no rational relation to any rational view of the public interest: "We refuse to sit as a 'super legislature' to review the wisdom of legislation."[5]

If any of us, as a Justice, was to accept the philosophy of judicial self-restraint as an unexceptionable general principle in all cases arising under the Due Process Clause unaided by the Bill of Rights, he or she would be obliged to refuse Jane Roe's claim without further argument. It may be wrong, but it is not irrational to suppose that anti-abortion laws discourage sexual promiscuity and protect the public morals. For more than a century a majority of reasonable persons in every State had deemed laws against abortion to serve the public interest. (In *Roe* v. *Wade* Justices White and Rehnquist took this ground in dissenting opinions.[6])

There is much to be said for this judicial philosophy as a check on excessive judicial intervention in areas where neither the words of the Constitution nor the record of history provides pretty firm evidence of an intent to limit the people's powers of self-government through elections and majority rule. Representative self-government is the basic principle. When the Court resolves a debatable question such as abortion by recognizing a constitutional right, it lifts the question out of the realm open to self-government and imposes its answer upon the people. Granted that one purpose of a Constitution guaranteeing individual rights enforceable by the judiciary is to limit majority rule; still, it can be argued effectively that the individual should carry the burden of demonstrating the applicability of the exception.

But for open-minded judges developing their philosophies of constitutional interpretation for the first time in the abortion case, the "rational basis" test need not be the end of the matter. Neither scale nor yardstick is available for measuring the degree of deference that a court of last resort ought to yield to legislative expression of the will of the people. As Justice Stephen J. Field foresaw, the deferential philosophy set out by the Court in dealing with Munn's grain elevator and revived as orthodoxy during the New Deal revolution would virtually eliminate judicial protection for individual rights under the broad Due Process and Equal Protection Clauses and would severely curtail such protection even under the other, relatively specific guarantees found in the Bill of Rights. The very notion of constitutional guarantees in favor of individuals presupposes some limits to majority rule. By 1973 judicial self-restraint had yielded to strict scrutiny in the areas of speech, political association, and criminal procedure. The opinions in those cases explained that they dealt with specific rights guaranteed by the Bill of Rights and incorporated into the Fourteenth Amendment, but the true explanation might be thought to be that they dealt with "fundamental rights." Specificity had ceased to be decisive when the general words of the Equal Protection Clause were read to prohibit legislation resulting in unequal access to a fundamental right unless shown on strict judicial scrutiny to be necessary to achieve some compelling public purpose not attainable by other means. If the "strict scrutiny" and "compelling purpose" test applies to cases invoking speech, association, and equal access to fundamental rights, why should we not adopt it for alleged deprivations of a "fundamental right" under the Due Process Clause of the Fourteenth Amendment?

The earlier "due process" cases dealt with the regulation of property and other economic activity. A number of opinions stressing deference to the political process and the values of decentralization in the federal system, while upholding the regulation of property and economic conduct against attack under the Due Process Clause, had reserved judgment on a case in which the liberty asserted by the individual is so "fundamental as to come to this court with a momentum of respect lacking when appeal is made to liberties which derive merely from shifting economic arrangements."[7]

Logic will not supply an answer. As conscientious, open-minded judges, we have to reason it out as far as we can, and then decide intuitively where to strike the balance between the values of representative self-government and State autonomy, on the one side, and, on the other side, the values of national protection for individual human rights. One of our dominant concerns might well be for the long-range effect of judicial activism on the institution of judicial review and the respect of the people for constitutionalism and the rule of law.

Still another set of questions will confront any judge who decides to extend the "strict scrutiny–compelling public purpose" test to legislation alleged to interfere with the exercise of a fundamental right. If as judges we are bound to decide "according to law," where do we find the law that tells us what rights are "fundamental," and, particularly, whether terminating a pregnancy by abortion is a "fundamental right"? How are we to know what is a "compelling public purpose" sufficient to justify State interference with the exercise of a fundamental right?

The great body of Anglo-American common law defining both crimes and rights and liabilities among private persons was built up by judges deciding one specific case at a time. In theory, each decision became a binding precedent. Each subsequent case was to be decided in a way that was logically consistent with the previous decisions. Much precedential weight was given to the reasons advanced by the judges in the previous cases, but logical consistency of result was supposed to be essential. Gradually, as a body of decisions developed, judges could reason by analogy. If A was pressing a claim against B, the court could ask whether A's claim against B was the more like C's claim against D, which was upheld, or the more like E's claim against F, which had been denied. Given a body of more or less relevant decisions, it was often possible to draw from them some broader general principle that could then be applied by deductive logic to the case awaiting decision. The decisions and opinions were reported. Legal treatises gradually came to be written, analyzing the reports and recording the customs and general understanding of the Bar. It was "to these books about us"—these sources of law—that judges turned.

In America, in constitutional cases, lawyers and judges apparently assumed that they were to follow this common law method in interpreting the broad and general constitutional phrases whose correct meaning cannot be derived from the words. The method is especially well suited to the interpretation of open-ended phrases like the Due Process Clause.

In *Roe* v. *Wade* it was argued that by pursuing the common law method the Court should derive from its own precedents the generalization that the Constitution protects a fundamental "right of privacy," broad enough to encompass a woman's decision whether or not to terminate her pregnancy.

Prior cases had upheld constitutional claims to be free from specific instances of State interference with aspects of marriage, procreation, contraception, and the rearing and education of children, but the generalization sought to be drawn from them seems tenuous. Three of the seven closest cases dealt with spiritual or intellectual freedom secured by the First Amendment: teaching the German language,[8] attending a parochial school,[9] and looking at pornographic materials in the privacy of one's home.[10] A fourth case held unconstitutional a Virginia statute prohibiting interracial marriage, a plain violation of the Equal Protection Clause.[11] A fifth case struck down as a violation of the Equal Protection Clause an Oklahoma statute mandating the sterilization of "habitual criminals" and defining the term in a manner that included such crimes as stealing chickens but excluded embezzlement.[12] The opinion spoke of procreation as a "fundamental right." In deciding whether the case is a precedent on abortion, a judge would have to consider whether the compulsory physical invasion of a person's body in order to destroy the power of procreation is not a significantly greater deprivation of liberty than forbidding the performance of an abortion. The two closest cases dealt with birth control. One struck down, as an undue invasion of marital privacy, an old Connecticut statute making it criminal to use artificial methods of birth control.[13] The other held that it would violate the Equal Protection Clause for Massachusetts to enforce a statute prohibiting the distribution of contraceptives to the unmarried.[14]

If *Roe* v. *Wade* were before us as independent judges, we would have to decide whether these precedents were so analogous as to show that values previously recognized by the law lead to the conclusion that terminating a pregnancy is a fundamental right. Seven of the nine Justices thought the precedents sufficient.[15] My own view is that all except the two birth control cases are quite different and that even the birth control cases are distinguishable.

Even if one rejects the analogies and misleading use of "privacy," still it is hard to think of a more fundamental invasion of personal liberty than to tell a woman that she must or may not bear a child. Her whole life—physical, psychological, spiritual, familial, and economic—will be profoundly affected. Would not just about everyone agree that this aspect of personal liberty is fundamental?

To tell a woman that she must bear a child conceived as a consequence of voluntary intercourse may possibly be a little less intrusive, but it is still a major interference with freedom to shape one's own life. Here, perhaps, no precedent is needed to show the values of our civilization.

But no liberty is absolute; and the question remains whether the invasion is justified by a "compelling public purpose." Sometimes it is asserted that the unborn child is a "person"; that its life begins on conception; and that protecting that person's life is a compelling public purpose. The argument depends upon the meaning of "person" and of "life." It is important not to tuck the conclusion into the definition. The biological and medical sciences can detail the manifold steps in the long progression from impregnation in the beginning to the emergence of the being we all recognize as a living man or woman, and they can then follow the progression to its end in the body's utter decay. But if we ask the scientists exactly when that life began or ended, they must ask, in turn, "What do you mean by life?" Is there "life" if the brain is utterly dead but the body can continue to perform some physiological functions with the aid of complex life-support equipment? If the brain is dead but the body will function in part if fed artificially? If senility has progressed to a catatonic state, but the body functions? Similar questions can be asked about each step in the progression from intercourse to childbirth. To say that life begins at one particular stage in the process or ends at another is not simply to state a biological fact; it is to supply a legal, moral, or philosophical standard asserting that the actual factual condition should be treated as if there were present what we all recognize as "life."

In *Roe* v. *Wade* the Court found it unnecessary to decide when "life" begins. As independent judges making up our own minds, we might well reach the same conclusion. Respect for the paramount sanctity of human life lies at the center of Western civilization. However narrowly one defines life itself—however uncertain one may be about the correct definition—protecting the penumbra, "near-life" or "life becoming," would seem to promote that central public purpose. The precedents available in *Roe* v. *Wade* did nothing to affirm or deny that the purpose in protecting "near-life" or "becoming life" is "compelling" when measured against the value of the woman's freedom of choice.

Where else might we as judges look for our law? To our personal philosophies? The devout Roman Catholic to the teaching of his religion? The descendant of Puritans to his Victorian ancestors? The sensualists to youthful experience? The ideal of law would require us to search outside ourselves in both history and contemporary life for expressions of the basic ideals and values of the American people. Sometimes the values are revealed in legislation, both past and current; sometimes in the prevailing moral code. Often they are found in the expression of leaders whose judgments have been accepted over time. Practice is revealing; but it is the values, if any, behind the practices that are important. The standards and values of other free and civilized people are also relevant. In pressing such inquiries it will always be hard for the individual judge to separate his own views from what he finds to be those of the people, but the goal of submerging the personal is not wholly beyond the grasp of a disciplined mind.

The first stage of such a search in the Abortion Case would lead me to the conclusion that the basic values of our society have not given the woman an absolute right to freedom of choice ranking above the interests served by anti-abortion laws. Sustaining the claim would override the laws of all fifty States, some more than a century old, others quite recently liberalized and re-enacted. Sustaining the claim would also run counter to the moral code prevailing for the previous century.

A judge with a conservative view of the nature of the judicial function would typically stop at this stage of the inquiry. Judge Robert Bork, a leading prospect to fill any new vacancy on the Supreme Court under President Reagan, stated the conservative judge's reasons clearly and persuasively in a decision holding that the Due Process Clause does not secure freedom to engage in private, consensual homosexual conduct.

> [This court is] asked to protect from regulation a form of behavior never before protected and indeed traditionally condemned. . . . If the resolution in sexual mores that the petty officer proclaims is to arrive, it must arrive through the moral choices of the people and their elected representatives, not through the ukase of this court. . . . The Constitution creates specific rights. A court that refuses to create a new constitutional right to protect homosexual conduct does not thereby destroy established rights that are solidly based in constitutional text and history.[16]

My own view would give the Court a somewhat larger and more creative role. Law is a human instrument designed for human needs and aspirations, all subject to change and growth. The judge is bound by law no less than the litigants, but he must also make law upon some occasions, in some ways, and to some degree. The School Desegregation Cases and Reapportionment Cases both illustrate the paradox. Both sets of cases created new rights, yet both had strong roots in older principles underlying our constitutional traditions.

When *Brown* v. *Board of Education* was argued, the "separate but equal" standard was plainly written into established law. Racial segregation was a fixed way of life, both by law and in fact, in the South and in parts of the Southwest. Although the lines were blurred and there were marked exceptions, racial discrimination was a fact throughout the country. Nevertheless, the Court made new law; and we applaud it. Suppose that a judge was overwhelmingly convinced that just as equality required freedom from official racial segregation, so liberty for a woman implies freedom of choice. Should that judge have the same freedom to write the latter view into the Due Process Clause?

In the Reapportionment Cases, it was clear that precedent cautioned against judicial intervention; that a "one person, one vote" rule would invalidate the existing apportionments in well over four fifths of the States; and that widespread departure from *per capita* equality of representation had been established practice through the country from colonial times to the day of decision. Nevertheless, the Court laid down the "one person, one vote" rule in one of its most successful decisions.

In the School Desegregation and Reapportionment Cases the Court went behind the past practices and the immediately applicable existing law (the statutes and the closest precedents) to ask whether they were consistent with the long-range and more fundamental ideals embraced by the American people. To have reaffirmed the "separate but equal" doctrine would have ignored not only the revolution sweeping the world but the growing moral sense of civilization. It would have also ignored the pronounced ideals and painfully slow progress of our own society since the Declaration of Independence. Similarly, I think that the "one person, one vote" rulings caught the deep-underlying current of essentially egalitarian history of our political development. Creative continuity characterized the rulings; the rulings changed the law, but they had strong links to the past.

This kind of inquiry is dangerous and subtle. The judge who makes it is in constant danger of confusing his personal values with the ethos of America. Yet if the School Desegregation and Reapportionment Cases were rightly decided, there are times when constitutional decisions may be made to embody what the perceptive judge, still submerging his personal preferences, finds to be the teaching of our national ideals despite our inconsistent practices. And if this be sound, then we, as open-minded judges forced to work out our general constitutional philosophy in the Abortion Case, would have to ask whether Jane Roe's suit presented a similar occasion.

Perhaps the case can be made with respect to the importance of the woman's liberty. History suggests that at least the seed of the ideal of equal freedom and equal opportunity for women was implicit from the beginning and has been growing in much the same way as equality for individuals of differing color. There was a gap between our ideals and practices in both cases. In the major series of decisions during the 1960s and 1970s holding that laws discriminating on the basis of sex violate the Equal Protection Clause unless justified by some truly important public interest, the Court looked to the longer-range ideal rather than direct precedent and historical practices.

Any law requiring a woman who has conceived to carry the unborn to birth denies her equal liberty and opportunity with men. Could conscientious and open-minded judges conclude with equal assurance either that the anti-abortion laws were all too easily enacted, without compelling or even important justification, because of indifference to the resulting inequalities of liberty and opportunity? Or did the nearly unanimous acceptance of such laws for many decades rest to an important degree on the belief that they helped to preserve the special sanctity of human life (however broadly or narrowly the word be defined)? If the latter, can we as judges say with assurance that modern science and medicine have undermined the old reasons for confidently believing that the prohibition does help to preserve the special sanctity of a human life? The right answer is far from obvious. My own judgment is that the people's belief in anti-abortion laws rested for the most part on belief in their role in preserving our respect for the special sanctity of human life, and that the people ranked that interest as compelling. And even though science and technology have dispelled much of the mystery of creation and birth, just as they have clouded the line and protracted the time between life and death, I cannot say that prohibiting abortions can no longer be said to serve the compelling public purpose once underlying the anti-abortion laws.

If these perceptions are fairly accurate, the actual decision in *Roe* v. *Wade* can be supported only upon an exceedingly broad view of the creative, lawmaking aspect of the Court's role in constitutional interpretation. The ruling swept aside the anti-abortion laws of all fifty States, some of them only recently revised and reenacted. It ran contrary to the moral code prevailing for at least a century. It lacked significant support in conventional sources of law. And while the basic theme can be traced to ancient ideals of human dignity and equality, the connection seems more attenuated and the opposing traditional values seem much more important than in any of the previous ground-breaking decisions. Conversely, the Court acted very little like the traditional courts of law charged with responsibility "to these books about us" and almost wholly like a body of Platonic Guardians, charged with bringing the Constitution up to date by deciding, according to the circumstances of our times, without regard to the past or the long-run sentiment of the people, whether a free and humane society should respect a woman's freedom of choice as fundamental.

That nine individuals appointed for life should play such a role in government, either sometimes or regularly, is not inconceivable. Such questions as whether that role is consistent with other parts of our basic political philosophy and whether in the long run it would dangerously erode our constitutionalism are better examined in long-range institutional terms and after reviewing the reaction to the Warren Court's use of constitutional adjudication as an instrument of reform.

II

Roe v. *Wade* and later decisions on abortion stirred such intense and widespread public debate as to suggest that the Court, far from putting the question to rest, had raised it to new heights of public attention. Advocates of both "freedom of choice" and the "right to life" pursued every legitimate form of political activism—speeches, tracts, marches, and other public demonstrations—and also some forms that were plainly criminal, such as blowing up abortion clinics. Prior to *Roe* v. *Wade,* political pressure looking to legislative repeal or relaxation of State anti-abortion laws had been growing. The decision made pursuit of that avenue wholly unnecessary; it also made abortion a very much larger factor in elections than ever before, because enough groups had or seemed to have sufficiently intense feelings on the subject to swing decisive votes. Legislative battles were also fought. A number of States enacted legislation seeking by sundry devices to increase the expense and difficulty of obtaining an abortion, and sometimes by presenting arguments designed to dissuade the woman from making that choice. Congress enacted the Hyde Amendment, which prohibits the federal government from reimbursing a State for monies disbursed to the needy for medical care in connection with an abortion.[17] President Reagan has frequently stirred the issue not only by attacks on the Court but by seeking out nominees for judicial appointment who are openly critical of *Roe* v. *Wade*.

In 1986, through the Solicitor General of the United States, the Reagan Administration argued that *Roe* v. *Wade* should be overruled. The effort fanned emotions and political debate but was unsuccessful. The Court had reaffirmed *Roe* v. *Wade* in 1985 in an opinion joined by six Justices.[18] In 1986 five Justices adhered to the precedent.[19] All five Justices are still on the Court.

Another decision handed down in 1986 presents a fascinating counterpoint to the Abortion Case.[20] On August 3, 1982, police officers lawfully entered the home of Michael Hardwick in Atlanta, Georgia, pursuant to a search warrant. The police did not find the reputed objects of the search, but when they pressed the search to Hardwick's bedroom, they at once arrested him on the charge of committing sodomy with another adult man, in violation of the Georgia criminal code. Hardwick was bound over for the grand jury, but the District Attorney decided not to seek an indictment. Hardwick, instead of letting the matter drop, brought his own suit against Georgia law enforcement officials, alleging that he was a practicing homosexual, that he desired to engage in sodomy with another consenting male, and that enforcement of the Georgia statute criminalizing all acts of sodomy would violate his constitutional rights secured by the Due Process Clause of the Fourteenth Amendment. Accordingly, he asked that enforcement be enjoined.

The federal district court upheld the constitutionality of the Georgia sodomy law and denied an injunction. The court of appeals reversed, holding that Hardwick had made out a *prima facie* case that engaging in sodomy in one's own bedroom with another consenting adult, whether male or female, is an aspect of privacy and is therefore a "fundamental right." The court of appeals then remanded the case to the trial court in order that Georgia be given an opportunity to prove that the invasion of the fundamental right is justified by a "compelling public interest." The U.S. Supreme Court granted *certiorari*.

Analysis of the Sodomy Case raises questions closely paralleling the questions in the Abortion Case. Both call for interpreting the words "liberty" and "due process of law." Neither could be decided by resort to the plain meaning of the words. Under the prevailing approach to the Due Process Clause, both cases called for deciding whether the activity prohibited by the State involved a "fundamental right," any invasion of which was subject to strict judicial scrutiny. Both cases fell in an area in which the Court has traditionally pursued the common law method of elaborating the open-ended constitutional guarantee. Both called for examining the same set of precedents with a view to determining whether they rested on a general principle embracing the case before the Court. Both Jane Roe and Hardwick were asking the Court to recognize as the exercise of a fundamental right conduct that not only had never been regarded as a right but that had long been forbidden by both the criminal law and the established moral code. But the parallel is incomplete. In the Abortion Case the State could refer to its interest in protecting the unborn child—the life-about-to-be, whether fertilized egg, embryo, or fetus. At some time during pregnancy it becomes plausible to speak of the interest of the unborn and of the societal interest in human life as competing values to be balanced against the interest of the woman in freedom of choice. In the Sodomy Case there was no similar offsetting interest. Finally, for the Justice who thought both sets of laws ill advised, both cases raised the question: How free is the Court to break new constitutional ground?

By a 5–4 vote the Supreme Court upheld the Georgia sodomy law. Only three weeks earlier the Court, by another 5–4 vote, had reaffirmed *Roe* v. *Wade* and struck down a Pennsylvania statute that would have discouraged abortion. The four dissenting Justices in the Sodomy Case were all in the majority in the Abortion Case. The four dissenters in the Abortion Case were all in the majority in the Sodomy Case. Only Justice Powell perceived a difference sufficient to make him anti-sodomy but pro-abortion.

Justice Blackmun, who had delivered the opinion of the Court in *Roe* v. *Wade,* wrote an eloquent dissent in *Hardwick*. He found private homosexual sodomy between consenting adults to be an aspect of the fundamental right "all adults have in controlling the nature of their intimate associations with others"—a right that is secured by the Fourteenth Amendment because it is "central to any concept of liberty."

> Only the most willful blindness could obscure the fact that sexual intimacy is "a sensitive key relationship of human existence, central to family life, community welfare and the development of human personality." [M]uch of the richness of a relationship will come from the freedom an individual has to choose the form and nature of these intensely personal bonds.[21]

Justice Blackmun cited *Roe* v. *Wade* and the precedents from which he derived the woman's right to have an abortion as examples of the more encompassing right to engage in any form of intimate sexual relations in private when there could be no injury to others. He sought to draw further support from the Fourth Amendment's guarantee of the right of the people "to be secure in their persons, houses, papers and effects against unreasonable searches and seizures." The central purpose of that guarantee, he reasoned, is to protect "the right of the individual to conduct intimate relationships," developing one's personality, and experiencing one's emotions in one's own way "in the intimacy of his or her own home."[22]

Justice White, who had dissented in the Abortion Case, spoke for the majority in rejecting the broad fundamental right identified by Justice Blackmun. None of the earlier cases, the Justice wrote, "bears any resemblance to the claimed constitutional right of homosexuals to engage in acts of sodomy. . . . No connection between family, marriage, or procreation on the one hand and homosexual activity on the other has been demonstrated."[23] It seems fair to say that the law, the general moral code of society, and custom had long put sodomy in a separate class, but one must add almost in the same breath that the earlier decisions expanding constitutional protection had been rendered despite the fact that the law, the general moral code, and custom had also long put abortion and heterosexual relationships outside marriage in special classes for condemnation.

The critical difference between the majority and dissent came on the same underlying question of judicial philosophy that divided the Justices in *Roe* v. *Wade*. Assume that Justice Blackmun identified a fundamental right that any philosopher-king would decree and that a wise legislature would recognize by repeal of the restrictive statutes. Under what circumstances may the Court read that right into the constitutional guarantees of liberty in the face of the fact that the conduct claimed to be constitutionally protected has never before been regarded as the exercise of a fundamental right by any organ of society but, on the contrary, has been continuously forbidden for over a century not only by statute in a large majority of the States but by the prevailing moral code? Justice White gave a firm answer:

> Nor are we inclined to take a more expansive view of our authority to discover new fundamental rights imbedded in the Due Process Clause. The Court is most vulnerable and comes nearest to illegitimacy when it deals with judge-made constitutional law having little or no cognizable roles in the language or design of the Constitution. . . . There should be therefore great resistance to expanding the substantive reach of those Clauses, particularly if it requires redefining the category of rights deemed to be fundamental. Otherwise the Judiciary necessarily takes to itself further authority to govern the country without express constitutional authority.[24]

The dissenters barely touched this question. Justice Blackmun was content to observe "I cannot agree that either the length of time a majority has held its conviction, or the passions with which it defends them, can withdraw legislation from this Court's scrutiny."[25] The *Hardwick* case therefore points to the somewhat broader conclusion that the Court as presently constituted is strongly inclined to be less vigorous than in the past three decades in the use of constitutional adjudication as an instrument of reform. The shift goes to the heart of the current debate over the proper role of the Supreme Court of the United States in American society, a debate vigorously pressed not only among the Justices but throughout the legal profession, in the other branches of government, and among the public at large. Its outcome—if it has an outcome—will profoundly influence the future of judicial review.

PART FOUR

Constitutionalism and the Rule of Law

· 19 ·

The Future of
Judicial Review

THE EXTENSIVE USE of constitutional adjudication as an instrument of reform aroused intense legal and political controversy. Much of the criticism flowed from opposition to the changes mandated by the Court. The desegregation cases reordered society throughout large regions. *Brown* v. *Board of Education*[1] initially set off cries of "massive resistance." The resistance gradually yielded to acceptance; but the acceptance is not everywhere wholehearted, and busing to achieve integration still faces strong though diminishing opposition. The School Prayer Cases came as a shock, upsetting established ways.[2] Probably most of the country now accepts the ruling as inevitable or desirable protection for the liberty of the unorthodox, but in many areas the emotional demand for returning an orthodox God to the classroom remains intense. *Roe* v. *Wade*[3] deeply offended strong religious and moral convictions; it also became an identifiable target on which to focus the unease aroused by changing moral standards, life styles, and social institutions. Expanded protection for persons accused of crime ran against a growing demand for law and order.

Other critics, led by dissenting Justices and an important part of the legal profession, were deeply disturbed by the Court's vigorous expansion of its role in society and its near-abandonment of the orthodox principles of judicial self-restraint. Even so progressive

341

an egalitarian as Justice Hugo Black had taxed the majority of his fellow Justices with using the Equal Protection Clause "to write into the Constitution its notions of what it thinks is good governmental policy."[4]

The storm produced by the use of constitutional adjudication as an instrument of reform intensified during the 1980s as the national political mood grew increasingly conservative and extremists on the right became more vocal. The President and Attorney General Meese lambaste the Court for disregarding the intent of the Framers of the Constitution in order to impose on the country what they charge are social experiments flowing from the Justices' personal values. They often speak and have sometimes acted as if they intend to fill the federal Bench with judges whose political philosophy is far to the right. From the liberals comes loud reaction, charging the Attorney General with planning to use the courts to carry out the fundamentalist program of the Moral Majority. Senator Jesse Helms gathered substantial support for bills seeking to strip the Court of power to hear cases involving school prayer or abortion. Senator David Boren has proposed a constitutional amendment to deprive federal judges of life tenure. The Court's opinions show the Justices to be deeply divided in judicial philosophy. At least two of them, Justices Brennan and Stevens, have made speeches seeming to enter into political debate with the Attorney General. Judges, practicing lawyers, and law professors debate the standards that should guide the Court in reaching its decisions.

In appraising both action and reaction, we should remember that storms of controversy have always swirled about the Supreme Court. The Jeffersonian Republicans accused Chief Justice Marshall of usurping power and sought to dominate the Court by impeachment. In the 1820s the advocates of State sovereignty sought to clip the Court's wings by congressional legislation depriving the Court of the jurisdiction to review the decisions of State courts interpreting the Constitution. The *Dred Scott* case led to repudiation and resistance. President Franklin D. Roosevelt was so frustrated by the Court's decisions that he proposed to increase the size of the Court in order to pack it with supporters of the New Deal. Judicial review nonetheless retained wide popular support. General attacks on the Court's independence or jurisdiction invariably fell short. Yet today's debate seems sharper than in the past, and the questions raised cut closer to the heart of our constitutionalism. A lover of the Court and the rule of law can scarcely avoid worrying that progressive politicization is endangering their historic role.

The future of judicial review—of "constitutional adjudication," as I prefer to call it—will be molded in unpredictable ways by many hands: by the Justices of the U.S. Supreme Court; by professional criticism; by the Presidents who select the Justices and the Senate that must confirm each nomination; by the Congress that has an uncertain measure of control over the Court's jurisdiction; and, most influential of all in the long run, by our own collective expectations as citizens. In a free, democratic society the Court can never break very far away for very long from the dominant long-range will of the people.

What then do *we* expect of the Court? What *should* we expect? How should the Justices go about their work? What should the President expect of a new Justice when the President makes his selection? In the final analysis, what's the Supreme Court for?

The Subject Matter of
Future Constitutional Decisions

The subject matter with which the Court is to deal is easily identifiable. By resolving the constitutional controversies that may be raised by lawsuit,[5] the Court, aided by lower courts, serves two principal functions:

1. The Court provides a final resolution of some but not all disputes over the constitutional division of power among the parts of our extraordinarily complex system of government; first, of disputes over the division between federal authority and the States, and, second, of disputes within the federal share among the Legislative, Executive, and Judicial Branches.

2. The Court protects the civil liberties and other rights of persons against government and government officials, whether federal or State.

I.

For almost a century and a half the first function was dominant, but after 1937 the Court ruled that an Act of Congress would be held to exceed federal power only if it were demonstrated that the activities regulated could not rationally be found to affect interstate commerce even in their cumulative effects.[6] In the modern economy almost all activities can rationally be found to have such an effect. The distribution of power in the federal system has therefore become largely a legislative or political question—an issue of still high national significance but not for the Court.

Umpiring other aspects of the federal system remains a routine part of the Court's function. Some final arbiter is needed to resolve the innumerable disputes that arise concerning the interplay between State and federal courts[7] and State and federal laws operating in the same territory and often addressed to the same activities.[8]

Questions involving the division of power between the Judiciary, on the one hand, and the Legislative and Executive Branches, on the other hand, pervade the entire process of constitutional interpretation. Under *Marbury* v. *Madison*[9] the Judiciary has the final word, but both history and reason make plain that the courts themselves must decide when and how far the constitutional constraints on courts require them to defer to Legislative or Executive Branch determinations. (The institutional constraints—the ways in which courts, as distinguished from political bodies, decide constitutional controversies—are considered below.)

Justiciable questions concerning the division of power between the Legislative and Executive Branches arise less frequently, but occasionally the issues are both dramatic and important. Under the New Deal, for example, and again during World War II, the Court was required to decide on several occasions whether and under what conditions Congress may delegate to the President or some other agency very wide discretion to frame regulations or issue decisions having the force of law.[10] The decisions ultimately upheld very broad delegations of legislative power,[11] and thus opened the door to great masses of regulation by executive and administrative agencies that Congress itself could never prepare and enact. In 1952, during the Korean War, the Court was called upon to decide whether the President, in the absence of statutory authority, has constitutional power to seize and operate the properties of a basic industry as a way of terminating a strike that threatens to halt the flow of arms and military equipment needed to prosecute a war.[12]

In 1986 a constitutional attack on the Gramm-Rudman Act once again turned the spotlight at least briefly upon the separation of powers. Simply stated, the Gramm-Rudman Act provides that each year, after the revenue laws and appropriations for the next fiscal year have been enacted, the Comptroller General shall estimate the government's revenues and disbursements for the next fiscal year, and if his estimates show a deficit in excess of a prescribed sum, then he shall order that expenditures be reduced, according to a prescribed allocation, by the percentages that he deems necessary to yield no more than the prescribed deficit.[13] Two lines of attack were leveled at the constitutionality of vesting this power in the Comptroller General. One started from a major premise having considerable support in precedent: because Congress may make law only by the concurrent action of both Senate and House of Representatives, it may not confer the power to make law on one chamber, a committee, or any other congressional instrument.[14] The minor premise asserted that the Comptroller General is a congressional instrument within the meaning of the major premise, not only because the General Accounting Office, which he heads, continually performs services for Congress but also because Congress shares in his appointment and may remove him for misconduct, without the assent of the President, by a two-thirds vote of both houses.

The second of the two arguments would impose stricter limitations on the ability of Congress to delegate legislative power. All the powers of government—the argument ran—are divided among the three branches and, under the Constitution, must be exercised by one of them and then only in the manner that the Constitution prescribes for that branch. Legislative power can therefore be delegated only to the President or to an officer of the United States who is in the Executive Branch. No officer can be part of the Executive Branch who is not subject to removal at the will of the President. Because the Comptroller General is not removable at the will of the President, the Gramm-Rudman delegation of authority is unconstitutional.[15]

The Supreme Court held the delegation unconstitutional on the first ground.[16] The opinion may be thought to disapprove the second line of reasoning, because it cites the precedents opposed to the reasoning;[17] it neither accepts the reasoning nor rejects it expressly. The argument has strong support in parts of the Reagan Administration.

The implications of the second line of argument carry enormous consequences. Nearly all the members of the independent regulatory agencies first created by the Interstate Commerce and Federal Trade Commission Acts[18] and proliferated by the New Deal and later Democratic Administrations hold office for fixed terms and are removable only for misconduct. Because acceptance of the second line of attack on Gramm-Rudman might instantly nullify the regulatory laws administered by independent agencies, it offers a mighty weapon against big government and the regulation of private enterprise. The Court might accept the argument but strike down only the prohibition against removal.[19] In that event, acceptance of the argument would result in an enormous increase in Presidential power. Today the President is not free to work his will with the policies and regulations of independent agencies, either by removal and appointment or by direct command. Most Presidents have felt great constraint in using other pressures to influence agency decisions. Both the barriers and the constraints would be removed if the argument prevails that regulatory power can be delegated only to the Executive Branch.

The turn of events could also bring to the Court major issues concerning the use of the United States Armed Forces in military or naval operations short of war. The Constitution makes the President Commander-in-Chief of the Armed Forces and vests in him wide responsibility for the conduct of international relations. But it gives to Congress the only express power "to declare war." The location of the dividing line first became a matter of grave concern when President Jefferson sent naval vessels to punish Libyan President Kadaffi's piratical predecessors in Tripoli almost two centuries ago. Debate intensified during and after the Korean War and the extensive military operations conducted in Vietnam without a declaration of war or other express authority of Congress. In 1973 Congress passed over President Nixon's veto a War Powers Resolution, attempting to clarify the limits of Presidential power and require express congressional approval of future hostilities like those in Vietnam.[20] Two key provisions are illustrative. Section 4 enacts that the President "in every possible instance shall consult with Congress before introducing the United States Armed Forces into hostilities, or into situations where imminent involvement is clearly indicated by the circumstances." Section 5 requires the President to terminate such use within sixty days unless Congress has declared war, granted express authority, or extended the sixty-day limit.

Successive administrations have asserted the unconstitutionality of the War Powers Resolution but have also grudgingly taken steps that could be called compliance. Thus far the debate over both constitutionality and compliance has been primarily political. The "standing" and "political question" doctrines invoked in Reapportionment Cases make it exceedingly difficult to invoke judicial remedies for any violations of the War Powers Resolution. Sufficient standing to maintain a lawsuit challenging the President's authority might be alleged by a member of the armed forces if ordered to the scene of hostilities conducted by the President without congressional authority for more than sixty days in, for example, Nicaragua; but no one can reliably predict whether the Court would treat the question as political or how it would decide the constitutional question.

2.

Today the major function of the Court as the voice of the Constitution centers on the protection of individual rights against governmental aggression.

The dramatic shift in emphasis occurred during and after World War II, even though it began fifty years earlier. The multiplication and magnification of government activities increased sensitivity to threats to civil liberty. Humanitarianism, aided by the prevailing teachings of the psychological and social sciences, cast doubt on the sterner aspects of criminal law. Barring some cataclysmic development, like a worldwide nuclear holocaust, the forces that brought government and private rights into conflict during the past half century seem likely to continue to operate, and unless there is a marked resurgence of the free market philosophy at the center of the major constitutional battles between the Civil War and World War II, the key issues will continue to be of personal and political liberty.

Often the familiar conflict between the individual and organized society will take new form because of startling developments in medical science and technology. Already claims are made of a "right to die." The claim could have constitutional dimensions if a State law abridged the alleged right or if a State institution were keeping the individual alive.[21] The conflict might take other new forms by the government's use of drugs or other advanced techniques to shape the conduct of "dangerous" individuals. And the spread of terrorism into the United States would raise enormous pressure to elevate security above the customary safeguards of liberty and privacy. But even though its forms will often be novel, the essential character of the conflict will remain the same.

The Method of Constitutional Adjudication

The critical aspects of the question "What's the Supreme Court for?" are institutional in the sense that they concern the limits on the manner in which the Court deals with the subject matter confided to it. A superficial answer to this aspect of the question would therefore be: "The Supreme Court is for judicial interpretation of the Constitution in justiciable cases and controversies." A more complete answer must explore the meaning of "*judicial* interpretation" even though the distinctions are subtle and the process is complex.

The range of current thinking about this function of the Supreme Court can best be pictured by imagining two lines drawn horizontally from left to right across a piece of graph paper, each linking two magnetic poles pulling Justices and observers in opposite directions.

One line marks the range of fundamental differences of temperament and philosophy that divide us all in greater or lesser degree throughout the whole realm of politics and government. The division is suggested by the loose terms "conservative" at the right-hand pole and "liberal" at the left. The liberals tend in varying degree to see the proper role of all branches of government as the active promotion of human freedom and equality. Extending from the center toward the conservative pole are those who, again in varying degree, are attached by temperament and philosophy to settled ways and institutions, who place great stress on government authority to preserve security and order, but who insist that the proper role of government is confined to the preservation of public order, health, safety, and morality, leaving the opportunities for human development to individual initiative in the private sector, controlled only by the forces of a free market.

So simple a description is manifestly incomplete. Individuals may be conservative on some issues and liberal on others. The degree of their conservatism or liberalism may vary from issue to issue.

Other factors are often relevant. Yet, while too simple for some purposes, for the present the classification captures the essence.

The second line on my graph paper runs between the two poles of opinion concerning the proper institutional role of the Court and the process of constitutional interpretation. Here again the differences are often more subtle, but their essence is best described in caricature. One extreme views the Court as a political body actually and properly engaged in pursuing policy goals, even though somewhat limited by jurisdictional rules and by the tradition of cloaking judicial policymaking in the concepts of the legal profession. This is often described as an "activist" view of the judicial function; it can be said to "politicize" the process of constitutional interpretation. Extending toward the other pole are those who feel the pull of the activist pole less strongly and who are attracted in varying degrees toward the pole of "judicial self-restraint" or "judicial conservatism"—not political conservatism, but a conservative view of the nature of the judicial process. Those who feel the need for judicial self-restraint stress four considerations.

First, the values of representative self-government and majority rule—of government by consent of the governed—require the Court, which is oligarchical, to go slow in imposing its social, economic, or political views on the country under vague constitutional phrases such as "due process" and "the equal protection of the laws."

Second, the values of a federal system that provides for decentralized decision making through State and local government require the Court, which is a national body, to go slow in using vague constitutional phrases to set aside State laws or local ordinances in favor of national rules.

Third, an accumulated body of wisdom expressed in the precedents and other sources of law built up by judges and constitutional custom step by step is a better guide to the wise resolution of constitutional questions than the individual views of one judge or a majority of nine Justices.

Fourth and most important is the need to ensure the effectiveness of the rulings of an institution charged with enforcing constitutional limitations against the popularly elected Executive and Legislative Branches, even in times of crisis and even though the Judiciary has the power of neither the purse nor the sword.

On the extreme right along this second line on our graph paper fall those who see law as a static set of rules derived by logical deduction, with scant attention to the underlying social and economic conditions, from the concepts found in precedents and secondary sources of law. In constitutional interpretation they are likely to call for "strict construction," thus implying that the Court should recognize no constitutional rights not plainly required by the words, and that when the words are general, the Court should confine them to those particular applications which the Framers specifically intended. The speeches of Attorney General Meese exemplify the argument.

To complete the figure one must imagine the two lines lying close enough together for the fields of force to overlap. The judge or observer who is strongly attracted toward either the conservative or liberal pole on the political axis will be pulled back toward a more moderate net position if he also feels strongly attracted toward the pole of judicial restraint along the institutional axis. Conversely, the judge or observer who believes that law is chiefly policy that courts enforce, and that the Supreme Court is, within its jurisdiction, essentially a political instrument, will feel relatively free to decide or appraise a decision according to his place on the political axis. The dilemma or antinomy to which I have often referred seeks to describe the position of the judge near the center who feels the pull of both the poles of the institutional axis; it says nothing of his place in the range of political views.

Historic Interplay of Political and Judicial Philosophies

The story of the Court and the Constitution illustrates the complex interplay of these forces. It also reveals that during the years 1950 to 1975 the Court moved farther toward the liberal and political poles than ever before, thereby stimulating the strong reaction that threatens still further to politicize the whole process of constitutional adjudication, and thus perhaps to erode the force of law.

From 1789 until 1865, in dealing with the then-critical questions concerning the nature of the new federal system, the Court saw its task as limited to interpretation of the words of a written document, but the style of interpretation, especially under Chief Justice Marshall, was active and creative. When the text was inconclusive, the

Justices searched for the "intent" revealed by the underlying purposes after the traditional manner of courts in reading other ambiguously written instruments. Both the words and the intent were to be read broadly: "[W]e must never forget that it is *a constitution* we are expounding."[22] The honest search for the Founders' purposes and their conscientious particularization in the case at hand imposed limits, but because the purposes were general and the Founders were not wholly of one mind, the identification and particularization required the Justices to make conscious choices, influenced by their own vision of the country's needs and potential. In this sense, they made new policy even though they confined themselves within limits set by the past. Unburdened by further restraints, the Court—an instrument of national government—established itself as the final authoritative voice of the Constitution. It construed liberally the grants of specified powers to the federal government, and affirmed that government's supremacy over the States within its assigned realm. The Court's creative interpretation of the Commerce Clause, beginning in the Case of the Steamboat Monopoly and *Cooley* v. *Board of Port Wardens,* enabled it to keep the channels of interstate migration and trade free from the kinds of State taxation and regulation that would lead to economic warfare rather than the growth of a continentwide open market.[23]

There were few precedents either to help or to limit the Court in dealing with the constitutional structure of government; but as decisions were rendered, they were treated as binding precedents, and later decisions were linked to a continuing body of law. Even before *Marbury* v. *Madison,* Alexander Hamilton had written in *The Federalist* papers that in exercising the essential power of judicial review, the federal courts would "be bound down by the strict rules and precedents."[24]

John Marshall's vision shaped the early decisions, but the vision was not his or the Court's alone. In expanding national power, the Court was moving in step with the dominant trend in the political branches, and therefore rarely had need to face the institutional problem of majoritarianism. Most of the decisions denying the effectiveness of State laws flowed from the Court's interpretation of the constitutional allocation of power between the Nation and the States; they did not deny the power of a majority to work its will through the appropriate governmental unit. The *Dred Scott* decision,[25] holding that the Due Process Clause gave slave owners a private constitutional right to extend slavery to the territories marked "free" in the Missouri Compromise, is the single notable instance of a pre–Civil War decision attempting to impose a judge-made set of policies on the country under an open-ended constitutional guarantee in the face of a contrary determination by the political process. The *Dred Scott* case shook the Court's legitimacy; it has long been seen as a tragic judicial blunder into the political realm.

After 1870, the pressing constitutional issues began to involve questions of political and institutional philosophy somewhat more like those on the current political scene. America was changing from a land of frontiersmen, farmers, small merchants, and artisans into an enormously complex, reticulated economy, industrialized, largely urbanized, and filled with large aggregations of people and property. The regulatory and welfare state began to emerge in response to the pressure for government to redress imbalances of private power and thus protect the health, safety, and welfare, and so the liberty, of those unable to protect themselves in unremitting contest for economic power.

At first the Court asserted that the Constitution forbade the change, forbade not only federal regulation of the production and local distribution of goods but also any governmental interference, either State or federal,[26] with the essentials of liberty of contract.[27] On the political line running from a strongly conservative political philosophy on the right to strong liberalism on the left, the decisions fell well to the conservative side.

It is harder to grade the decisions on the judicial and institutional line. They are usually presented as examples of misplaced judicial activism, and are often invoked as arguments against the activism of the Warren and Burger Courts. In invalidating a federal income tax[28] and also protecting liberty and property under the Due Process Clauses the Court did indeed go far to impose uniform judge-made rules on the country in place of determinations made through representative government by majority rule. The decisions were countermajoritarian both in frustrating legislation enacted by the Congress and in overturning as invasions of private rights State laws on subjects otherwise within the State's jurisdiction. Scant weight was given to the values of State and local autonomy. Arguably, the Court's ruling that freedom of contract is a fundamental aspect of the liberty secured by the Fifth and Fourteenth Amendments abused judicial power by creating new rights in the same fashion as later Justices would do in the Abortion Cases. The charge of politicization is also supported by evidence that at least some of the Justices of the *Lochner* era viewed the courts and judicial review as the last bastion against the socialist temper of political forces.

The decisions of the era can be seen, however, as examples of the harm done by a highly verbal and conceptual, and therefore static, jurisprudence rather than as arguments for strict construction and total judicial self-restraint. The decisions adhering to the doctrine of dual federalism in the face of vast economic changes pursued a policy of strict construction by denying Congress power not plainly granted by the words and by adhering to the almost certain supposition of the Framers that they had withheld from Congress the power to regulate "production" as they knew it and its effects on the economy. It was "strict construction" that failed to meet the country's needs. Similarly, in protecting economic liberty and property the Court was applying words and concepts that were familiar parts of the American legal and political tradition. In both instances, the fault—it can be argued—lay not in excessive activism but in applying the old words and concepts too woodenly, without regard to the differences in the underlying realities. The economy had changed. Local production had marked effects upon the national economy quite different from any effects in 1787. Liberty of contract in an artisan's negotiations with prospective employers in the cities and towns of 1800 had strikingly different practical human significance from an immigrant steel worker's negotiations with U.S. Steel Corporation a century later.

Whether the mistake was politicization of the judicial process or unimaginative emphasis on the logic of the law stated "in these books about us" at the expense of "an accommodation with the dominant needs of [the] times,"[29] the decisions of the *Lochner* era damaged the Court's powers of legitimacy and led, first, to efforts to still further politicize the law and, later, to the era of judicial self-restraint.

In the era of judicial self-restraint that began in 1937 the Court greatly diminished its own role in government by assuming a posture of extreme deference to the political process and to the values of State and local autonomy. The Court would decide a constitutional question only if presented in a justiciable controversy narrowly defined and only if there was no other way of deciding the case.[30] An Act of Congress would be held to exceed federal power, as we have seen, only if it was demonstrated that the activities regulated could not rationally be found to affect interstate commerce even in their cumulative effect. A State or federal law would be held to violate the Due Process Clause only if the challengers demonstrated that the measure bore no rational relation to any rational view of the public interest. In 1937 and for the next few years the pull of the liberal pole of the political axis reinforced the pull of forces counseling judicial conservatism in defining the role of the Court. A liberal judge or observer who might be impatient in different times with the notion that the freedom of the Court to make sound policy is limited by the duty to decide "according to law" had scant occasion to disagree with the dominant jurisprudence so long as the Court was dealing with economic regulation, because at that time the dominant political philosophy in the Executive and Legislative Branches, and in the industrial States, was much more liberal than in the Judicial Branch.

The years following World War II brought the realignment of forces described in Part Three. The great cases, not only in the courtroom but for the country, came to be those of freedom of speech, of political and religious liberty, of civil rights and the meaning of "equality," of the humane administration of criminal justice, and of privacy and individual choice. The Court came to be, for much of the time, the branch of government in which the libertarian, egalitarian, and humanitarian impulses beat the strongest. In the new milieu the polar forces of liberal political philosophy and institutional restraint pulled in opposite directions, just as a strongly conservative political philosophy had generally pulled against some claims of institutional restraint in the period of dual federalism and liberty of contract. At the same time, the pull of judicial activism was growing more powerful because more and more members of the legal profession, especially professors and law students, came to question the reality of the old ideal of law. The forces of liberalism, aided by the new belief that law is only policy, proved the stronger, and thus led to the active use of constitutional adjudication as an instrument of reform.

Judged by political criteria, the decisions made ours a freer and more equal society, more humane and more respectful of human dignity. Their general direction seems in keeping with dominant trends of American history. Each of the major decisions except the abortion rulings can, for reasons stated in Part Three, be viewed as a projection of fundamental ideals running through our constitutional history, even though not actually reflected in the actual practices of earlier American life. In each important instance—I incline to think, again excepting *Roe* v. *Wade*[31]—the Court kept within the banks marked by the basic antinomy; but it openly pressed to the political side farther and more often than ever before in history. Six dominant and partly novel characteristics of the course of decision fed a strong political and professional reaction. The dangers created by that reaction lead me to go back and ask whether, taking the Warren and Burger Courts' decisions as a whole rather than bit by bit, the Court too often went too far too fast, and so endangered its own legitimacy.

First, invoking the doctrine of "strict scrutiny," the Court often substituted judicial rules, resting on judicially determined values, for the values determined and rules laid down by elected representatives of the people. The most dramatic examples are the Reapportionment and Abortion Cases. The laws held unconstitutional were sometimes old and arguably outmoded, but they were nonetheless the work of elected legislatures whose successors had left the laws untouched.

Judicial enforcement of constitutional limitations designed to protect individual liberty is necessarily countermajoritarian, but the Court's history demonstrates that whenever interpretation of one of the majestic but vaguely worded guarantees turns on appraisal of facts or competing values, Justices have a wide range of choice in deciding whether to defer to the actual or presumed judgments of the legislature or to substitute their own conclusions. The vigorous use of the doctrine of "strict scrutiny" during the Warren years contrasted so sharply with the preceding philosophy of judicial self-restraint as to lend weight to the charge that in this respect the Court was repeatedly overstepping the Judiciary's proper bounds.

Second, in protecting individual rights the Court repeatedly substituted national rules—held to be derived from the Constitution—in the place of local determinations in the form of State law and for the decisions of local authorities like School Boards.

Again, the change was of degree. Such substitution occurs whenever a State law is held unconstitutional because it conflicts with the Constitution or a legitimate exercise of congressional power. In the early history of the Court such substitutions usually resulted from rulings on the distribution of power in the federal system rather than from the Court's national ruling on the limits to which government may intrude on individual rights. The Lochnerian decisions of the years 1885 to 1937 fall in the latter category, but their thoroughgoing repudiation rested in considerable part on the view that allowing States to pursue varied paths in formulating public policy is one of the chief values of federalism. Here again, therefore, the course of decisions in the third quarter of the century ran contrary to the orthodox constitutional philosophy of the immediately preceding years.

In a broad sense the trend toward nationalization of legal rules under the aegis of the Constitution was part of a longer and very much wider drift toward the nationalization of American life. The underlying causes run deeper than law, but their impact is evident in the Court's validation of the vast expansion of congressional power under the Commerce and Spending Clauses and in indirect federal regulation even of such seemingly local matters as the age at which individuals may be served alcoholic beverages. But while lessened deference to the States in constitutional adjudication was in keeping with the larger trends in American life, it also added the conservatives who favor a small federal government to the critics of the Court.

Third, the decisions made new law on an extensive scale, broadening the protection of familiar constitutional rights, such as the freedom of speech and press, and creating under the long-familiar guarantees of liberty and equal protection new particular rights, such as abortion and freedom from racial segregation and sex discrimination. Sometimes, once-settled precedents were directly overruled. More often, the new decisions ran counter to widespread legal practice or assumptions generally accepted, although never squarely embedded, in Supreme Court precedents. In both cases, the decisions were open to the charge that the Court was no longer deciding "according to law."

Similar charges had been leveled at the Hughes Court in 1937, when it overruled the precedents establishing a constitutionally protected liberty of contract and denying Congress the power to regulate industrial production. In those instances, however, the "new" constitutional law did no more than validate the legislation already enacted by the representatives of the people. The new law made in the Warren years and in the Abortion Cases rarely had a legislative base. Often it ran contrary to the legislative enactments of the chosen representatives of the people.

Fourth, the new decisions mandated major institutional changes not only in the administration of justice but in the larger society. Previously, the Court's constitutional decisions invalidating executive or legislative measures had done no more than uphold or block legislative or executive initiatives. The Constitution was invoked by the Court as an instrument of continuity. From 1950 to 1974 the Court used the Constitution to mandate change, without legislative support. The Desegregation Cases reordered society throughout large regions. The Reapportionment Cases upset ancient political arrangements. The School Prayer Cases banished a practice familiar to generations of Americans. The Constitution was being used as an instrument of massive reforms.

Fifth, effectuation of such reforms required the courts to prescribe remedies with many of the characteristics of legislation and executive administration. The School Desegregation decrees are the best example. Each decree affects thousands, even millions, of people. Each looks to future conduct. Each disappoints some people and benefits others in order to achieve broad social objectives. Each decree may, and many do, require the appropriation of large sums of money.

In some communities the cumulative effect of the court decrees in a variety of contexts precipitated charges that the courts were taking over the business of government. A few years ago, for example, federal judges in Boston were, at the same time, superintending public school administration, reforming the care of retarded and emotionally disturbed young people, and attempting to correct defects in prison administration by forcing the construction of new facilities. Concurrently, a State court receiver was supervising the Boston Housing Authority.[32]

Sixth, the Supreme Court encouraged constitutional litigation by easing access to the federal courts in constitutional cases, and also by loosening the rules determining whether, when, and on whose complaint a court will decide a constitutional question. Even though the specific rulings are individually too small and too technical for discussion in these pages, the trend is illustrated by the broadening of the rules of standing and the narrowing of the political question doctrine in *Baker* v. *Carr*,[33] which together opened the door to applying the Equal Protection Clause to legislative apportionment. The overall shift in attitude significantly affected both the Court's role in American government and the country's response.

The Movement for Counterreform

Such active and expansive use of judicial power to mandate societal reforms was bound to arouse intense political and professional reaction in the conservative political mood of the 1970s and 1980s. Political cleavages widened and intensified, even though there were more crosscurrents, because many advocates of individual freedom seemed to many conservatives to be attacking the family, the church, and the fundamentals of morality. For the critics of the Court, the pull of conservatism on the political axis coincided with the pull toward judicial self-restraint. Against the background of very active judicial policymaking, even the most narrow view of the judicial function appeared plausible, and support could be mustered for the proposition that a court acts illegitimately if it gives constitutional protection to any aspect of "liberty" or "equality" not consciously and particularly intended by the Framers.

The forces driving for counterreform are currently led by extreme political conservatives, but the ranks of the critics and the doubters were broader. Not a few liberals on the political scale who would wholeheartedly support the results of the reforming decisions if expressed in legislation or constitutional amendment were pulled into positions on the institutional scale ranging from doubt to criticism by the fear that excessive politicization of the process of constitutional adjudication was threatening long-range institutional values, including the independence of the Judiciary and the legitimacy of judicial review. So long as counterreformers stress the faults of judicial activism, they can draw strength from the critics and doubters moved by institutional concerns. When they propose to overturn what is now settled law, the counterreformers lose much of that support because the critics and doubters fear that such a judicial counterrevolution would accelerate the process of politicization and thus further erode the base of our traditional constitutionalism.

The counterreform program has taken two forms. The earlier shape was pressure for legislation stripping the Supreme Court and lower federal courts of jurisdiction to hear cases involving abortion or school prayer. The later and current movement looks to reversing the course of decision by the careful selection of new judges and new Justices of a strongly conservative political philosophy who have been highly critical of the most controversial decisions of the Warren and Burger eras.

WITHDRAWAL OF JURISDICTION

From time to time throughout our history, especially when the ear of the Court seemed ill tuned to the will of the people, critics have attacked its independence and power to protect constitutional rights. The Jeffersonian Republicans tried to politicize the Judiciary by impeachment. Even during the present century the Progressive movement sought to reduce the power of judges, partly by requiring more than a simple majority vote of the Justices to invalidate legislation and partly by providing for the election and recall of judges. Criticism reached a new peak in the mid-1930s, when President Franklin D. Roosevelt proposed to pack the Supreme Court.

More often the political attack has taken the form of a congressional effort to deprive the federal courts of jurisdiction to hear some or all claims of constitutional right. In the 1820s, following the decisions in *Martin* v. *Hunter's Lessee*[34] and *Cohens* v. *Virginia*,[35] the proponents of State sovereignty sought to take away the Supreme Court's jurisdiction to review State court decisions on constitutional questions. After the Civil War, the radical Republicans, fearful that the Supreme Court would find the Reconstruction Acts unconstitutional, revoked the Court's authority to hear a Mississippi newspaper editor's appeal of the denial of his habeas corpus petition,[36] and considered other methods of barring judicial review. The McCarthyites of the 1950s unsuccessfully sought to persuade Congress to limit Supreme Court jurisdiction over unconstitutional federal and State programs aimed at alleged subversives. In 1964 Senator Dirksen led an attempt to deprive the federal courts of jurisdiction to give effect to the "one person, one vote" rule regarding legislative apportionment.

As the storm of controversy aroused by the School Prayer, Abortion, and School Busing decisions intensified during the late 1970s and early 1980s, a group of Senators, led by Senators Jesse Helms and John East of North Carolina, pressed bills to withdraw from the federal courts jurisdiction to hear cases involving school prayer or abortion. Had the measures been enacted and found constitutional, any person asserting a claim of constitutional right in these areas would have been limited to a suit in a State court without the right of appeal to the Supreme Court of the United States as the one final arbiter. The sponsors obviously hoped that some or all of the State courts would refuse to follow the Supreme Court's decisions. Other Senators pressed to limit judicial power to order school busing in order to achieve the racial integration that courts deemed necessary to remedy past violations of the Equal Protection Clause.[37]

The constitutional foundation invoked to support withdrawing jurisdiction from the U.S. Supreme Court is the language of Article III, Section 2, giving the Court "appellate jurisdiction, both as to Law and Fact," over all cases arising under the Constitution, laws, and treaties of the United States "with such exceptions, and under such regulations as the Congress shall make." The scope of this "Exceptions Clause" is still debatable. The sponsors of the measure emphasize the unqualified scope of the words. Legal scholars have long been divided. Some would give the words their full literal meaning. Others, relying on early history, argue that the Exceptions Clause relates only to review of questions of fact. Still others argue that the clause does not permit stripping the Court of its "essential constitutional functions of maintaining the uniformity and supremacy of federal law," and that denying all power of review "in every case involving a particular subject" is to strip away an essential function.[38] And a fourth group, with whom I incline to agree, submits that even if the power to make exceptions is complete under Article III, Section 2, any legislation limiting the Court's jurisdiction must still pass muster under the Bill of Rights, which contains an implied guarantee of "equal protection of the laws."[39] Denying access to the Supreme Court to those who assert constitutional rights in particular areas—school prayer or abortion, for example—while allowing appeals by those who assert other constitutional rights, would seem to deny the first group the equal protection of the laws.

Such measures, even if technically constitutional, are fundamentally inconsistent with the basic principle upon which American constitutionalism has been based since the decisions in *Marbury* v. *Madison* and *Martin* v. *Hunter's Lessee*—that when the application of power by one of the many branches of government is challenged in a case suitable for judicial cognizance as in excess of its authority under the Constitution or as a violation of constitutionally guaranteed private rights, then it is for the Judicial Branch to determine the meaning of the Constitution, and that in order to achieve uniformity and finality the U.S. Supreme Court shall be the court of last resort. Although it was a Senate filibuster that blocked passage of the East and Helms bills, it seems unlikely that public confidence in the Court had declined to the point at which an attack on such basic principles could muster majorities in both Senate and House of Representatives.

JUDICIAL COUNTERREFORMATION

Judicial Selection

When it became evident that the East and Helms bills could not be passed in the face of constitutional doubts and widespread recognition of their challenge to the independence of the Judiciary, the extreme conservative right turned to an effort to control the future and undo a wide range of decisions by carefully tailoring appointments to the federal Bench, including the Supreme Court of the United States, to a strongly conservative political ideology. Attorney General Meese and his aides in the Department of Justice concerned with judicial selection have been spearheading the drive, with the apparent encouragement of President Reagan. The opportunity to shape the course of decisions in the lower courts is greater than under any President since George Washington, because an increasing flood of litigation requires many new judges. By mid-1986, President Reagan had also had the opportunity to make Associate Justice Rehnquist Chief Justice and to name two new Justices, Sandra Day O'Connor and Antonin Scalia, to the Supreme Court. He is likely to have one or two more opportunities.

Even though many of President Reagan's nominees for positions on the lower courts do not conform to the ideological pattern and are highly qualified, by politically neutral, professional standards, it seems fair to say that a fixed political ideology has played a larger part in President Reagan's judicial selections than either a strictly liberal or strictly conservative political ideology has ever played before. A larger proportion than ever before has been found only minimally qualified by the American Bar Association. In the selection of Justices for the Supreme Court, party politics and party loyalty as well as personal connections have historically been the most important factors. Often those factors carry some assurance of loose philosophical compatibility. The number of Presidents who consciously sought and also succeeded in picking Justices who would follow a predetermined line of decision is relatively small. Many Presidents did not try. Others misjudged their choices. Still others failed to foresee the dominant constitutional questions of the succeeding decade.

To pack the Bench with men and women of a single, narrow political ideology has a tendency to erode long-range public confidence in judicial institutions. If the legitimacy of judicial decrees depends, as I believe, in considerable part on public confidence that the judges are predominantly engaged not in making personal political judgments but in applying a body of law, then the farther a President goes in proclaiming an intent to predetermine the course of decisions, the more he will undercut the foundations of legitimacy. Similarly, the avowed selection of judges whose minds are already closed on the cases that may come before them in the future, such as abortion or school prayer, erodes the respect and support for judicial rulings that flow from public confidence that the cases submitted for adjudication are being decided by individuals with open minds as free as humanly possible from political or economic self-interest, from the obligations of loyalty to a political party or other organization, and from most forms of ambition. That neither belief is entirely true, even when the ideal is earnestly sought, does not destroy their significance so long as the ideal is sincerely pursued and a critical degree of achievement is present.

Judicial Decision

Whether the politicization of our constitutionalism accelerates dangerously will chiefly depend upon how the new Justices regard the institutional constraints on constitutional adjudication when they come to render decisions. So long as one is attacking major reforming decisions as driven by personal social or political philosophy, it is unnecessary to distinguish between conservatism on the political axis and conservatism with respect to the nature of the judicial function. But in the process of reaching decisions there are times when, as in the *Lochner* era, the pull of strong political conservatism conflicts with the pull of some or all the components of a cautious institutional philosophy. Chief Justice Rehnquist, Justices O'Connor and Scalia, and any other new Justice of a strongly conservative political bent, if named by President Reagan or his successor, will face that tension if they become part of a controlling majority. Each will then have to choose between institutional restraint and a form of judicial activism not very different from the activism of their immediate predecessors, albeit in pursuit of conservative rather than liberal policy goals.

The necessity for choice will arise because the constitutional rights to which strong political conservatives object are now part of the fabric of existing law. The most publicized targets of counterreformation are the Abortion and School Prayer decisions. *Roe v. Wade,* the first of the Abortion rulings, was decided in 1971. For sixteen years the decision has been followed and reaffirmed. The first School Prayer decision of the U.S. Supreme Court was handed down twenty-five years ago, and its roots go back to the 1940s.[40] The counterreformists' major goals apparently also include reducing present constitutional protection for persons accused of crimes, some return of power to the States, and cutting back on school busing, affirmative action, and other measures to remedy the long years of racial segregation. One school of thought on the right seeks to sweep away all the New Deal and regulatory agencies whose members serve for fixed terms beyond the President's discretionary power of removal, on the ground that the Constitution bars Congress from delegating power to any official other than the President or an "officer of the United States" whom the President has discretion both to choose and to remove.

As illustrated by the tale of Dolly Mapp in Chapter 13, the constitutional restrictions on State police and prosecutorial practices to which strong political conservatives object rest on the doctrine that the Fourteenth Amendment incorporates the federal Bill of Rights. The attack is on that principle of interpretation. The first of those rights, freedom of speech, was initially held to be incorporated into the Fourteenth Amendment as long ago as 1925.[41] The Court began to extend the doctrine to guarantees of fair criminal procedure in the 1950s and 1960s.[42] A vast body of law has been built upon that foundation. School desegregation, by busing if necessary, became the standard judicial remedy for unconstitutional school segregation in the 1960s. The Reagan Administration's position on affirmative action has already been at least partly rejected.[43] The constitutionality of denying the President discretionary power to remove the members of independent agencies to which Congress had delegated mixtures of quasi-legislative and quasi-judicial power was upheld in 1935.[44] The congressional practice of giving the members of administrative agencies fixed terms of office dates back to 1887,[45] however, and since the New Deal a large part of the business of the federal government has been conducted upon this foundation.

The overruling of even the shortest of these lines of settled law—the Abortion Cases—would carry some suggestion that constitutional rights depend on the vagaries of individual Justices and the politics of the President who appoints them. The message would become louder and clearer if the reversals spread. The example, moreover, would go far to encourage a swing back to the law as it stands today if a second new majority should result from a second wave of new appointments, that time by a more liberal President. Constitutionalism as practiced in the past could not survive if, as a result of a succession of carefully chosen Presidential appointments, the sentiment of a majority of the Justices shifted back and forth at five- or ten-year intervals, so that the rights to freedom of choice, freedom from State-mandated prayer, and the use of unconstitutionally seized evidence were alternately recognized and denied.

Some overruling of precedent is nonetheless part of our constitutional tradition. The step, when taken with discretion, is essential to the correction of errors. The constitutional revolution of 1937 offers the closest example of successful large-scale repudiation of existing law.[46] In upholding sweeping assertions of federal regulatory and spending power and also State regulation of wages and prices, the Hughes Court overruled long lines of precedent with little observable cost to its legitimacy or to the ideal of decision according to law. Its success seems largely attributable to three causes. One was the great legal skill and moral force of Chief Justice Hughes. Second, the new rulings yielded to both majoritarianism and State rights. The Justices merely refused to block the administration of regulatory laws that the chosen representatives of the people had enacted. Third, in opening the way to an expansion of federal power and in removing obstacles to positive government intervention to redress imbalances of private power, the Court was shaping the Constitution to changes in the economy without sacrifice of human liberty and thus touched a responsive chord in the American people.

The experience of the Hughes era also suggests that the costs are lowest when precedent is overturned because of changes in the realities behind legal concepts and doctrines used by the Court in reasoning out and explaining the earlier decisions. To say that the Commerce Clause gives Congress no power to regulate production within the borders of a single State had a different meaning in 1800 from the meaning the statement would have today, even though the words were the same, because the ways of doing business and interstate ramifications are radically different. Similarly, the operative meaning of "liberty of contract" in twentieth-century industrial communities is altogether different from the human and social significance of the concept in rural America. Abandoning the old verbal formulas was hardly a change in underlying goals. The currently projected conservative counterreformation cannot offer this kind of explanation, however, because there have been no changes in societal conditions altering the operative significance of the individual rights recognized by the Warren and Burger Courts.

It can be argued that overruling *Roe* v. *Wade* and the School Prayer decisions would fit the pattern of the Hughes years insofar as reversal would defer to both majoritarianism and local autonomy and would be more responsive to our long-range American values. The argument has considerable force, but the fit is not exact. *Roe* v. *Wade* did indeed invalidate legislation on the statute books of every State, but much of it had been enacted so long ago that a judge with intellectual honesty could doubt whether the anti-abortion laws still represented the values of the people. The School Prayer decisions are not demonstrably inconsistent with majoritarianism except in a few localities. Only time could tell whether the overruling of the Abortion and School Prayer decisions would shape the future to the tide of events and touch responsive chords in the American people in the same way as the revolutionary decisions of 1937. For a State through its public schools to teach children who reject the orthodox religion that they must conform or be outsiders seems fundamentally inconsistent with our historic religious tolerance. Even in the case of abortion the Burger Court may have read the future right, like the Warren Court in its reforming decisions on race, sex, and political equality.

Overruling the incorporation doctrine as applied in criminal cases can perhaps be fairly described as a return to judicial self-restraint in the form of deference to State rights. Other targets of conservative counterreform call for a larger degree of reverse judicial activism. To achieve them, the Court, in addition to rejecting existing law, would have to substitute its new judicial judgments for majoritarianism and local self-rule. For example, for the Court to accept the conservative argument that Article II of the Constitution bars Congress from restricting the President's power to remove the members of administrative agencies would require not only overruling the fifty-year-old precedent,[47] but also rejecting judgments implicit in the consistent action of Presidents and both Houses of Congress for a like number of years.

Obviously the process of overruling need not extend so far, either in the breadth of the counterreforms or in the wild cycle of action and reaction. The members of any new conservative majority among the Justices will almost surely come from the ranks of dissenting Justices or critics who charged the Warren and Burger Courts with excessive activism. Again, the upshot will depend upon whether their institutional philosophy as lawyers and judges is conservative enough and strong enough to restrain their political bent. Self-restraint should prevail if the charges flowed from a deeply held judicial philosophy and not predominantly from political conservatism.

The opinions of Justices of a conservative outlook in recent Affirmative Action Cases raise some doubt, however, about the breadth and depth of their commitment to a philosophy of judicial deference to majoritarianism and State rights when it conflicts with political views.

In the *Jackson* case described in Chapter 15 the question was whether performance of a contract voluntarily negotiated by the Board of Education and the teachers' representative for the purposes of collective bargaining violated the Equal Protection Clause because the contract provided that in making layoffs, in accordance with prescribed seniority rules, the Education Board should not reduce the proportion of black teachers in the Jackson schools below the proportion of black students. The race-conscious departure from strict seniority was said to serve a number of important public interests: (1) the need to open the teaching profession to minorities excluded by years of societal discrimination; (2) the educational goal of providing encouraging role models for black students; and (3) the further educational goal of introducing all students, both white and black, to an adult world in which whites and blacks play important roles without regard to color. The values of majoritarianism and State and local autonomy argued for the balance struck by the Jackson Board of Education, much as they do for allowing a local School Board to instruct teachers to start the day with a prayer. So do the values of voluntarism and decentralized private initiative in seeking to solve wrenching social problems. The words of the Equal Protection Clause, however strictly construed, do not require government always to be colorblind in pursuing compelling public interests. Nevertheless, a bare majority composed of Justices usually labeled conservative, including Justices Rehnquist and O'Connor, substituted their view of the balance to be struck for that of the representatives chosen by majorities of the people affected.[48]

Similarly, in an earlier Affirmative Action Case Justice Rehnquist took a strongly countermajoritarian position as one of two dissenting Justices who argued that the Fifth Amendment bars Congress from requiring that a stated percentage of money granted to State, county, and municipal governments for public works be set aside for minority contractors in order to ensure that the racist practices well known in the past would not be used to deny them equality of opportunity.[49] In both instances the new Chief Justice's political conservatism overcame any belief in institutional self-restraint.

A generally conservative philosophy has also proved consistent with strict judicial review in dealing with Acts of Congress regulating political campaign contributions and expenditures. The Federal Election Campaign Act amendments of 1974 prohibited any person from contributing more than $1000 to a candidate for federal office in any one election, and also prohibited the expenditure of more than $1000 in support of any such candidate for election. The prohibitions obviously rested on implicit congressional findings that both large contributions and large expenditures in support of a clearly identified candidate have the actual and apparent tendency to corrupt the conduct of government. The Court, by a divided vote, accepted the implicit legislative view with respect to contributions but rejected it with respect to expenditures.[50] Later, the Court also struck down as a violation of the First Amendment another congressional enactment that prohibited a "political committee" from expending more than $1000 in support of a Presidential candidate who has barred himself from lawfully accepting private contributions by agreeing to campaign exclusively with money allocated by the U.S. Treasury from a fund built up by taxpayers who check off the $1.00 on their federal income tax returns.[51] The second decision may turn out to rest exclusively on the ground that the expenditure of a little more than the $1000 ceiling is too small to corrupt, but the general thrust of the opinion was to reject at all levels of expenditure the congressional view that "independent spending" yields corrupting influence.

Chief Justice Rehnquist, as an Associate Justice, wrote the opinion of the Court in the later case, joined by Justice O'Connor. Justice Rehnquist joined in the earlier ruling holding the expenditures limit unconstitutional and also delivered a dissenting opinion arguing that the provisions for public funding of Presidential elections were partially invalid.[52] In both instances he was following the principle that legislation restricting freedom of speech is to be subjected to the "strictest judicial scrutiny"—an approach that traces back at least to the early 1940s and was fully developed and often used by the Warren and Burger Courts. Justice Brennan joined the opinions holding the bans on expenditures unconstitutional. The cases and opinions are nonetheless important reminders that dissent from previous liberal reforming decisions is not always inconsistent with later activism in the judicial promotion of conservative political views.

There is no serious foundation for Attorney General Meese's argument that overruling the "wrong" decisions is not inconsistent with a judge's traditional duty to decide "according to law" when those decisions mistakenly created new constitutional rights beyond the original intent of the Framers. The superficial plausibility rests upon the implicit assumption that the "original intent" of the Framers was to confine the guarantees of individual rights to the particular instances foreseen by the Framers or the sponsors of the pertinent provision. The truth of that assumption cannot be either proved or disproved by reference to recorded history, but it seems unlikely that men writing a charter for the future, with the Founders' sense of history, would have expected to limit to the narrow instances that they knew the broad and majestic guarantees of liberty that they chose to write.

For example, when the Framers wrote the Bill of Rights, they had consciously in mind particular abuses practiced in Tudor and

Stuart England or in the American colonies. The Fourth Admendment guarantee against "unreasonable searches and seizures" was aimed consciously at the government's practice of sending its agents to break into houses, offices, and like private places to seize alleged contraband or to obtain evidence. There was invariably some kind of trespass, a physical invasion of private property. The specific, conscious intent of the Framers went no further. Obviously they had no specific, conscious intent to prevent government agents from using electronic eavesdropping equipment to pick up a personal conversation without entering the premises, or from using cameras to photograph papers on a desk through the office window from the roof of a building across the street. If the Court were held to exceed its power whenever it went beyond the demonstrable conscious, specific intent of the Framers, it could not protect individuals against either camera or bugging. Behind the particular applications that the Framers intended quite obviously lay a broader policy or principle—the intent to secure the privacy of office papers against the government's making copies without either a search warrant or consent, and the privacy of household conversations against eavesdropping by government agents without a warrant, whether accomplished by hiding under a bed or any other means. The decisions holding the electronic eavesdropping to violate the Fourth Amendment are consistent with this kind of intent.[53]

The constitutional history related in earlier chapters affords many other examples of this fundamental principle. The Court has never strictly confined the guarantees of individual rights to the particular claims and situations that the Founders or the sponsors of an amendment had foreseen. Except in seeking to preserve dual federalism, the Court has normally been creative at least to the point where it treated the Constitution as a living instrument whose purposes and values are to be applied to activities and situations that the Framers could not possibly have foreseen. The unworkability of the strict constructionists' approach is demonstrated by their inability to apply their own rule with logical consistency. Attorney General Meese approves the desegregation decisions even though the history of the Fourteenth Amendment shows that its supporters had no specific intent to forbid segregation by State law.[54] Segregation by law was widely practiced for eighty-five years after the adoption of that amendment.

The Constitution could not have served so well for two hundred years, with rare amendments, under the strict constructionists' view; the social, economic, scientific, and technological changes were too revolutionary. This observation is no less true of the threats to liberty than of the federal system. To search for and apply, with human understanding but intellectual honesty, the general principles underlying the specific manifestations in the constitutional text and subsequent precedents may also be more truly conservative than blind imposition of particular rules. The method preserves and develops the important essence while acknowledging the inevitability of outward change. It also enables the Court to demonstrate the legitimacy of its decisions by linking them to the sacred inheritance.

THE VALUES OF CONSTITUTIONALISM

The style of constitutional interpretation and the traditional independence of the Judiciary from political pressures and responsibility are interrelated. If the process of decision making is excessively politicized, there will be additional pressure to choose judges who will cast their votes on grounds of policy. Such choices, in turn, would make the style of decision making still more political, in both fact and public perception. The heightened perception would fuel still further demand. The cycle would inevitably lead to demands for the election of Justices and judges. If the key court decisions are little different from the determinations of policy by other branches of government, why should not the voters elect the Justices and judges for terms of years?

The cause for worry is real. In the summer of 1986 an opinion poll reported that a majority of the respondents expressed the belief that the Justices of the U.S. Supreme Court should be elected.[55]

Earlier periods in which the Supreme Court Justices and other federal judges were perceived as most political were marked by efforts to subject them to political control. The drive of the Jeffersonian Republicans to win control of the federal courts by impeachment and removal of the Federalist judges resulted from fear that the Federalist judges, some of whom had used their positions for political purposes, would frustrate the democratic revolution of 1800. Early in the present century, as we have seen, the Court's decisions invalidating regulatory laws interfering with liberty of contract and the uninhibited use of property led Progressives and liberal Democrats to put forward such measures as the election and recall of judges by popular vote. The apparent politicization of constitutional decisions peaked in the constitutional invalidation of early New Deal measures. The reaction reached its new peak in President Franklin D. Roosevelt's Court-packing plan.

There are also early signs of a possible trend toward increasing politicization in States in which Judges are elected or, although initially appointed, must submit to periodic popular referenda on continuance in office. The election of State judges is not new, but, for the most part, informal arrangements between the major political parties, custom, and the professional standards of judges have blunted the reciprocal dangers that, on the one hand, elections involving a sitting judge will be fought out between organized special interest groups favoring or opposing the judge's past decisions and that, on the other hand, judges will come to decide cases with an eye on the electorate and perhaps on campaign contributions. A few years ago, however, the Arkansas Supreme Court interpreted banking legislation in a way that limited the interest rates on credit extended on consumers' purchases and thus offended major retailers and Arkansas banks. The banks and retailers announced that they would form a political action committee to which they would contribute the funds necessary to defeat those judges in the majority who would have to stand for re-election, in the hope of bringing the question before the court for a new ruling by a friendlier majority. Apparently the threat died out.

Just such a campaign was waged in California in 1985–1986 to recall the Chief Justice of the Supreme Court, Rose Bird, because she was "soft on criminals" and insufficiently pro-business. Several million dollars was spent to defeat her. The Governor and other candidates campaigned against her. One of the organized groups taking a vigorous part in the campaign was an association of prosecuting attorneys. To the charge that they were politicizing the administration of justice, the groups seeking recall of Chief Justice Bird could reply, possibly with some measure of accuracy, that her judicial activism had already politicized her decisions. The danger is that giving tit for tat will simply accelerate the process at the ultimate expense of the rule of law.

A few years ago Senator Sam Ervin of Watergate fame wrote, "To my mind an independent judiciary is perhaps the most essential characteristic of a free society."[56] The Founding Fathers held the same view. James Madison, in proposing the Bill of Rights, emphasized that "*independent* tribunals of Justice will consider themselves in a peculiar manner the guardian of those rights." (Emphasis added.)[57] Thomas Jefferson expressed a similar thought to a French correspondent, before he clashed with and came to hate John Marshall, by explaining that in the United States "the laws of the land, administered by upright judges, would protect you from any exercise of power unauthorized by the Constitution of the United States."[58] In order to ensure the independence of federal judges, Article III of the Constitution provides life tenure and a guarantee against reduction of compensation.

The loss of independence would endanger the basic values of constitutionalism. The very purpose of written constitutions containing Bills of Rights and guaranteeing judicial independence was to put some rights beyond the reach of government policy, even beyond the power of a majority of the people. Judicial interpretation gives better protection than the political branches to unpopular individuals and minorities shut out of, or inadequately represented in, the political process. It was the Court that spoke for the national conscience in *Brown* v. *Board of Education* while Congress and the President were silent.

Similarly, judicial review provides better protection for the enduring values that politicians too often neglect and of which the people too often lose sight in the emotional intensity and maneuvering of political conflict, especially in national crises. Individual liberties such as freedom of speech and guarantees of privacy are often in this character. It was the Court that protected unorthodox "troublemakers," such as the Jehovah's Witnesses and truly peaceful civil rights demonstrators, against harassment by local ordinances and officials. It was the Court that excised the cancer of legislative malapportionment when incumbent legislators were perpetuating themselves by refusing to act. The full impact of statutes on individual and minority rights often comes to light only through experience. Judicial review in the years following legislative or executive action provides what Justice Stone called "the sober second thought of the community."

There is value in all these cases in having them decided by men and women as free as any individual can become from political or economic self-interest, from most forms of ambition, and from the obligations of loyalty to political parties or other organizations.

Only independent judges have the necessary security. There is even greater value, I think, in having the questions adjudicated according to a continuing body of law that guides the understanding and judgments of those who render the decision. For while the personal qualities and preferences of the Justices who hear the current case neither can nor should be wholly eliminated, the law provides both a steadying influence and a source of accumulated wisdom likely to be greater than that of any individual.

Nor should our personal good fortune in experiencing unbroken liberty lead us to forget that the Dolly Mapps, Jehovah's Witnesses, and Ishmael Jaffrees are fighting our battles, not because we expect our homes to be invaded or our children to refuse to salute the flag and join in prayer but because the constitutional safeguards and judicial assistance that they invoke are our own bulwarks against the imposition of strict orthodoxy, conformity, and suppression of political dissent. Both the English history known to the Framers and later experience in many other lands convincingly demonstrate that when a popular leader seizes power and moves to suppress dissent, an independent Judiciary affords the best, and perhaps the only, protection against such threats to truly fundamental liberties as arbitrary arrest and detention without trial, the invasion of homes by security forces without judicial warrants, and the suppression of political opposition, including all freedom of expression. In countries with written constitutions and other democratic forms of government, the switch to a dictatorship or another form of authoritarian rule has usually been accomplished by declaration of an emergency suspending the constitution and the customary powers of independent courts.

The Sources of Legitimacy

As we look on the Court as the ultimate guardian of liberty, equality, and property against oppression by the Executive and Legislative Branches or by the States, not merely in ordinary times when the threats are few and seem trivial to conventional eyes but in times of crisis and high emotion when the threat may have the backing of the dominant part of the people, we are bound to return to some hard questions akin to those raised in the Prologue. What has enabled the Court for two hundred years to withstand repeated attacks upon its independence? What then is the source of the Court's power, both in ordinary times and in times of stress?

Constitutionalism would prove an ineffective safeguard of liberty without an extraordinary measure of voluntary compliance with Supreme Court rulings by officials and private citizens far beyond the reach of the courts. What is it that causes these hundreds and often thousands of government officials to comply with the Constitution as the Court interprets it, even though, because they were not parties to the litigation, disobedience would not bring punishment for contempt of court?

The Court controls neither the purse nor the sword. What caused President Truman, who seized the basic steel mills in time of war in order to halt a strike threatening essential military supplies, to return the mills to the owners in accordance with a Supreme Court decision, despite his own furious personal resentment and his conviction that both the long- and short-range public consequences of the decision would be against the public interest?

When voluntary compliance fails, the courts must look to others to require obedience. What impelled President Eisenhower in such a case to send troops to Little Rock to prevent crowds of angry citizens from barring desegregation of the high school in accordance with a court decree, even though Governor Faubus of Arkansas objected and President Eisenhower himself did not wish to see desegregation forced? What caused the public outcry when President Nixon announced his intent to disobey the court order requiring him to produce the Watergate Tapes?

We may call the capacity of constitutional rulings to evoke assent and support "the power of legitimacy." The power has many springs. One source in the beginning was a link between law and Divine command or "natural law." Later, after experience under royal despots, came the practical judgment that courts and law were the best safeguard against executive or legislative violations of liberty. As Walter Bagehot wrote, because of "the dull traditional habit of mankind," yesterday's institutions tend to be accepted as the best for today and are "the most easy to get obeyed, the most likely to retain the reverence which they alone inherit, and which every other must win."[59] The wisdom and moral force of great judges, past and present, make their contribution. Procedural fairness and regularity are also essential to legitimacy. In the constitutional sphere law has long drawn strength from traditional and evocative precepts that symbolize the historic struggles for freedom from government oppression: "Liberty under Law," for example, and "A government of laws, not of men."

The principal source of legitimacy, I believe, is the all-important but fragile faith that the courts apply to current constitutional controversies a continuing body of "law" finding symbolic expression in, but also derived from, the agreement worked out at the Philadelphia Convention in the summer of 1787 and later approved at State conventions by the people of the United States. By "law" I mean a set of governing principles—call them "values," "policies," or "standards," if you prefer—that have a separate existence and command an allegiance greater than that due any individual merely by virtue of office or personal prestige, however strong or wise. The link to the Constitution is important, perhaps because it suggests a delegated authority but especially because it evokes an historic sense of the common ideals, common success, and common purposes of the American people—a people made up not only of ourselves today but of those who went before and will come after us.

But the historic link alone is not enough. The essence of law is that it binds everyone. Constitutionalism and judicial review would never have achieved success and could not long survive if Charles Evans Hughes's statement that the Constitution means whatever the judges say it means expressed a general truth.[60] To command an uncoerced allegiance while lacking the sanction of majoritarianism, law must not only apply to all people equally; it must apply not just today but yesterday and tomorrow; and, above all, it must bind the judges as well as the judged. As Judge Learned Hand reminded us:

> [The judge's] authority and immunity depend upon the assumption that he speaks with the mouth of others: The momentum of his utterance must be greater than any which his personal reputation and character can command, if it is to stand against the passionate resentments arising out of the interests he must frustrate.[61]

Much law, in this sense of the word, is inherited and is therefore found, as Judge Hand used to say, "in these books about us." But the books are not to be followed, as happened in some arid periods of legal history, simply by logical application of the words, concepts, and precepts found on their pages. Rather, the books, like the Constitution itself, must be read with understanding of the changes in the human condition. New conditions may rob old legal concepts, rules, and even principles of their former meaning, so that the underlying ideals call for new application. Better perception of the true meaning of basic ideals may call for new developments. An entirely static body of law is unworkable, because sooner or later it fails to meet human needs.

A wooden reading of the law in these books about us would also cut against the second essential quality of any body of law rising above legislative or administrative fiat. The law, even as it honors the past, must reach for justice of a kind not measured by force, by the pressures of interest groups, nor even by votes, but only by what reason and a sense of justice say is right. *Brown* v. *Board of Education*, not *Plessy* v. *Ferguson*, was "law" in 1954, even though the "separate but equal" doctrine had half a century of precedent and practice behind it. Continuity is essential to law as a whole, but the continuity must be creative.

The tendency in academic circles today is to decry the ideal of law as an independent force, and to emphasize the judges' role as the makers and re-makers of social policy. O.W. Holmes, Jr., in criticizing the arid logic chopping of much late-nineteenth-century jurisprudence, poked fun at the notion of law as a "brooding omnipresence in the sky."[62] Extreme legal realists often call upon the metaphor to assert that the very idea of a body of law binding the judges as well as the judged is nonsense—a step that Holmes would not have taken. They can readily demonstrate that the books about them often leave judges important opportunities for choice. Most of the great cases described in this book are examples; they are great cases because there was opportunity for choice. It is also easy to show that judges change the law from time to time, not only superficially, as when new conditions require the formal restatement of an old rule, but fundamentally, as the ideals of the society evolve. The growth of legal realism was a major influence in expanding the use of constitutional adjudication as an instrument of reform. Similar policy-based reforms were taking place without legislation in other fields of law.

In my view, the easy and convincing proof that the Court can, does, and should make law in constitutional adjudication falls short of demonstrating that the Justices are in nowise limited by law. Proof that resort to the words of the Constitution sometimes provides scant guidance fails to demonstrate that the Justices are free to interpolate whatever they will. Similarly, judges can feel, and therefore be, limited by law even though there is room for choice. The task calls for judgments of balance and degree mindful of both branches of the basic antinomy. That the questions of degree cannot be resolved nor the balance struck with certainty does not disprove the value of the effort. Dedicated pursuit of an ideal is a legitimating reality, even though the reach exceeds the grasp, provided that the people know that the effort is undertaken.

The future of judicial review probably depends in good measure on whether the view that law is only policy made by courts carries the day in the legal profession, or whether room is left for the older belief that judges are truly bound by law both as a confining force and as an ideal search for reasoned justice detached so far as humanly possible from the interests and predilections of the individual judge. The heavily policy-oriented view not only carries the dangers of the "despotism of an oligarchy" of which Thomas Jefferson spoke, but it cuts off the taproots of judicial independence and legitimacy. The older view, I believe, also conforms more closely to the people's expectations. Surely, if the people could be asked whether judges should decide without restraint, a heavy majority would reply, "No, they should follow the law." But if asked whether precedent should always be binding, surely the majority would reply, "No, precedent should not always be binding. Sometimes past law was unjust."

In its creative aspects, wise constitutional adjudication seems to me to draw additional legitimacy from, and is limited by, a delicate symbiotic relationship. The great opinions of the past shaped the Nation's understanding of itself. They told the people what they were by reminding them of what they might be. But while the opinions of the Court can sometimes be the voice of the spirit reminding us of our better selves, the roots of such decisions must be already in the people. The aspirations voiced by the Court must be those that the community is willing not only to avow but in the end to live by. The legitimacy of the great creative decisions of the past flowed in large measure from the accuracy of the Court's perception of this kind of common will and from the Court's ability, by expressing the perception, to strike a responsive chord equivalent to the consent of the governed. To go further—to impose the Court's own wiser choice—is illegitimate.

The Constitution has served so well for two hundred years because the genius of the Framers was partly a talent for saying enough but not too much. They outlined a unique federal form of government. Shortly later, by amendments to the Constitution, they identified the basic individual rights they wished to guarantee against government oppression. In both areas important questions were left open, questions that the Framers could not foresee and questions on which they could not agree. They left those questions to be decided as they came to a head in accordance with the dominant needs of each generation. Yet they also said enough to provide points of reference. The great unanswered questions fell to the Judiciary to be decided "according to law." As the plan outlined in the Constitutional Convention succeeded, as the country grew and prospered both materially and in the realization of ideals, the Constitution gained a majesty and authority far greater than those of any individual or body of men. Because enough was written in the document and because decision "according to law" calls *both* for meeting the contemporary needs of the people *and* for building upon a continuity of principle found in the instrument, its structure and purposes, and in judicial precedents, traditional understanding, and historic practices, the Court, by always referring through the continuing body of law to the sacred document, could bring to its resolution of the new and often divisive constitutional issues of each generation the momentum and authority of an overshadowing past, yet it also had leeway to accommodate the dominant needs of the times.

In the end, among a free people, both constitutionalism and the belief in law require an extraordinary degree of tolerance and cooperation—the instincts to which the British philosopher Alfred North Whitehead attributed the extraordinary success of the American people. Tolerance and the will to cooperate flow from a larger belief in the worthwhileness of the common enterprise—despite its faults, despite our selfishness, and despite our dim perception of the goal. For me, belief in the value of the enterprise is an article of faith. Whether enough of us still have enough belief in the worthwhileness of our common fate for the spirit of tolerance and cooperation to prevail, and whether we share sufficient common ideals with sufficient confidence, along with the extent of belief in the rule of law, will determine the survival of constitutionalism.

Notes

Index

Notes

PROLOGUE

1. Brown v. Board of Education, 347 U.S. 483 (1954).
2. Engel v. Vitale, 370 U.S. 421 (1962); Abington School District v. Schempp, 374 U.S. 203 (1963).
3. NLRB v. Jones & Laughlin Steel Corp., 301 U.S. 1 (1937).
4. 1 Cranch 137 (1803).
5. U.S. v. Burr, Fed. Cas. No. 14, 692d (1807).
6. Dumas Malone, *Jefferson the President: Second Term* (Boston: Little, Brown, 1974), p. 320.
7. 1 Cranch 137 (1803).
8. *Id.* at 149.
9. Mississippi v. Johnson, 4 Wall. 475, 484 (1867).
10. 1 Cranch at 166.
11. *E.g.,* Kendall v. U.S. *ex rel.* Stokes, 12 Pet. 524 (1838); Land v. Dollar, 190 F. 2d 623 (D.C. Cir. 1951, vacated as moot, 344 U.S. 806 (1952).
12. Youngstown Sheet and Tube Co. v. Sawyer, 343 U.S. 579 (1952).
13. *Id.* at 655.
14. *In re* Grand Jury Subpoena Duces Tecum to Nixon, 360 F. Supp. 1 (D.D.C. 1973).
15. Nixon v. Sirica, 487 F. 2d 700 (D.C. Circ. 1973).
16. U.S. v. Nixon, 418 U.S. 683 (1974).
17. Worcester v. Georgia, 6 Pet. 515 (1832).
18. Abington School District v. Schempp, 374 U.S. 203 (1963).
19. L. Hand, *Mr. Justice Cardozo,* 52 Harv. L. Rev. 361 (1939).

CHAPTER I

1. 1 Annals of Cong. 439 (1789).
2. Both George Washington and James Madison used the word "miracle"

in letters describing the Philadelphia Convention. Catherine Drinker Bowen drew upon them for the title to the most fascinating readable account of the proceedings, *Miracle at Philadelphia* (Boston: Little, Brown, 1966)—a title that I also presume to use for the present chapter.

CHAPTER 2

1. *The Federalist Papers,* No. 78 (New York: Modern Library), p. 510.
2. Brown v. Board of Education, 349 U.S. 294 (1955).
3. Engel v. Vitale, 370 U.S. 421 (1962); Abington School District v. Schempp, 374 U.S. 203 (1963).
4. Roe v. Wade, 410 U.S. 113 (1973).
5. 1 Cranch 137 (1803).
6. Communication, "To the Public," reprinted in *Columbia Sentinal,* Jan. 21, 1801, from *Gazette of the U.S.,* Jan 10, 1801.
7. Albert J. Beveridge, *The Life of John Marshall* (Boston: Houghton Mifflin, 1916), vol. 1, p. 118.
8. The letters are quoted in Leonard Baker, *John Marshall: A Life in Law* (New York; Macmillan, 1974), p. 59.
9. Section 13 of the Judiciary Act of 1789, 1 Stat. 73.
10. 12 Coke 65, in John Campbell, *The Lives of the Chief Justices of England* (London: John Murray, 1849), vol. 1, p. 272.
11. 8 Rep. 118a (Common Pleas 1610).
12. For one of the many reviews of the spotty State precedents and the evidence in Madison's notes on the Constitutional Convention, see Raoul Berger, *Congress v. The Supreme Court* (Cambridge, MA: Harvard University Press, 1969).
13. Letter to William C. Jarvis, Sept. 28, 1820, *The Writings of Thomas Jefferson,* Paul L. Ford, ed. (New York: Putnam, 1892–1899), vol. 10, p. 160.
14. 1 Cranch at 177.
15. *Ibid.*
16. *Ibid.*
17. Article III, Section 3.
18. Article I, Section 9.
19. *Baltimore Federal Gazette,* Jan. 3, 1805, quoted in Charles Warren, *The Supreme Court in United States History* (Boston: Little, Brown, 2nd ed., 1926), vol. 1, p. 294.
20. *Diary of John Quincy Adams,* entry of Dec. 21, 1804, in David Grayson Allen et al., eds. (Cambridge, MA: Belknap Press of Harvard University Press, 1981).
21. 7 Cranch 603 (1813); 1 Wheat. 304 (1816).
22. 6 Wheat. 264 (1821).

23. 347 U.S. 483 (1955).
24. Schlesinger v. Reservists to Stop the War, 418 U.S. 208 (1974).

CHAPTER 3

1. Quoted in Gerald Gunther and Noel Dowling, *Cases and Materials on Constitutional Law* (Mineola, NY: Foundation Press, 11th ed., 1985), p. 87.
2. 4 Wheat. 316 (1819).
3. *New York Statesman,* Feb. 7 and 24, 1824, quoted in Charles Warren, *The Supreme Court in United States History* (Boston: Little, Brown, 2nd ed., 1926), vol. 1, pp. 460–461.
4. *Ibid.*
5. 4 Wheat. at 373.
6. *Id.* at 404–405.
7. *Id.* at 406.
8. *Id.* at 407.
9. *Ibid.*
10. *Id.* at 421.
11. *Id.* at 433.
12. *Natchez Press,* quoted in *Niles Register,* May 22, 1819.
13. See Chapter 9.
14. Hamilton v. Kentucky Distilleries Co., 251 U.S. 146 (1919).
15. Brief for the Respondent in South Carolina v. Katzenbach, 383 U.S. 301 (1966), p. 75.
16. South Carolina v. Katzenbach, 383 U.S. 301, 326 (1966).
17. Buckley v. Valeo, 424 U.S. 1 (1976). The Court has kept open the question whether a higher ceiling on independent expenditures would be constitutional.
18. 4 Wheat. at 423.

CHAPTER 4

1. 4 Wheat. 316 (1819).
2. 1 Cranch 137 (1803).
3. *Reminiscences and Anecdotes of Daniel Webster* (1877), by Peter Harvey, quoted in Charles Warren, *The Supreme Court in United States History* (Boston: Little, Brown, 2nd ed., 1926), vol. 1, pp. 601–602.
4. Brooks v. U.S., 267 U.S. 124 (1925).
5. U.S. v. Simpson, 252 U.S. 465 (1920).
6. See Lottery Case (*Champion* v. *Ames*), 188 U.S. 321 (1903).
7. Gibbons v. Ogden, 9 Wheat. 1 (1824).
8. *Id.* at 194.
9. *Id.* at 195.
10. Quoted in Warren, *op.cit.,* p. 615.

11. 12 How. 299 (1851).
12. *Id.* at 319.
13. *Ibid.*
14. Compare Plumley v. Massachusetts, 155 U.S. 461 (1894) with Collins v. New Hampshire, 171 U.S. 30 (1898).
15. Minnesota v. Barber, 136 U.S. 313 (1890).
16. Foster-Fountain Packing Co. v. Haydel, 278 U.S. 1 (1928).
17. Hughes v. Oklahoma, 441 U.S. 322 (1979).
18. Philadelphia v. New Jersey, 437 U.S. 617 (1978).
19. 303 U.S. 177 (1938).
20. *Id.* at 189–190.
21. South Pacific Co. v. Arizona, 325 U.S. 761, 783–784 (1945).
22. Bibb v. Navajo Freight Lines, Inc., 359 U.S. 520 (1959).
23. Raymond Motor Transportation, Inc. v. Rice, 434 U.S. 429 (1978).
24. Kassel v. Consolidated Freightways, Inc., 450 U.S. 662 (1981).
25. Oliver Wendell Holmes, Jr., *Collected Legal Papers* (New York: Peter Smith, 1952, originally printed c. 1920), p. 295.
26. For the rare exception, see Maine v. Taylor, 86 S. Ct. 477 (1986).
27. *E.g.,* Welton v. Missouri, 91 U.S. 275 (1876); Robbins v. Shelby County, 120 U.S. 489 (1887); Complete Auto Transit, Inc. v. Brady, 430 U.S. 274 (1977).
28. Leisy v. Hardin, 135 U.S. 100 (1890).
29. *In re* Rahrer, 140 U.S. 545 (1891).
30. Edwards v. California, 314 U.S. 160, 173–174 (1941).
31. Hicklin v. Orbek, 437 U.S. 518 (1978).
32. White v. Massachusetts Council of Construction Employers, 460 U.S. 204 (1983).
33. United Building and Construction Trades v. Camden, 465 U.S. 208 (1984).

CHAPTER 5

1. Elkisin v. Deliesseline, 8 Fed. Cas. 493 No. 4366 (1823).
2. Speech delivered in the House of Representatives on April 2, 1824, and quoted in Charles Warren, *The Supreme Court in United States History* (Boston: Little, Brown, 2nd ed., 1926), p. 622.
3. 12 How. 290 (1851).
4. 19 How. 393 (1857).
5. 21 How. 506 (1859).
6. Scott v. Emerson, 15 Mo. 193 (1852).
7. John D. Lawson, ed., *American State Trials* (St. Louis: Thomas Law Books, 1914–1936), vol. 13, n. pp. 243–245.
8. At that time the only basis for invoking the jurisdiction out of the U.S. Circuit was that the suit was "between Citizens of different

States." Actions arising under the laws of the United States could not be brought in the federal courts in the first instance until 1875.

9. Strader v. Graham, 10 How. 82 (1851).
10. Dred Scott v. Sanford, 19 How. 393 (1857).
11. 21 How. 506 (1859).
12. *In re* Booth, 3 Wisc. 1 (1855).
13. 1 Wheat. 304 (1816), discussed in Chapter 2.
14. Barron v. Baltimore, 7 Pet. 243 (1833).
15. See, *e.g.,* Slaughterhouse Cases, 16 Wall. 36 (1873), wherein the court ruled that most of the basic civil liberties are privileges and immunities of State citizenship and limited the privileges and immunities of citizens of the United States to those specifically granted to U.S. citizens by the Constitution plus those arising from the creation of the federal union.
16. See Chapters 14 to 17.

CHAPTER 6

1. Munn v. Illinois, 94 U.S. 113 (1877).
2. See Chapter 18.
3. For a broad treatment of the history of substantive due process, see Edward S. Corwin, *Liberty Against Government* (Baton Rouge: Louisiana State University Press, 1948).
4. Munn v. Illinois 94 U.S. 113, 126 (1877).
5. *Id.* at 132.
6. Powell v. Pennsylvania, 127 U.S. 678, 696–697 (1888).
7. Munn v. Illinois 94 U.S. 113, 126, 142 (1877).
8. *Id.* at 152.
9. Herbert Spencer, *Social Statics* (New York: Robert Schalkenbach Foundation, 1954, 1969, reprint of original edition), p. 380.
10. Pollock v. Farmers Loan & Trust Co., 157 U.S. 429, 586, 607 (1895) (Field, J., concurring).
11. John T. Arlidge, *The Hygiene, Diseases and Mortality of Occupations* (London: Percival, 1892), p. 225.
12. Lochner v. New York, 198 U.S. 45, 53 (1905).
13. *Id.* at 59–61.
14. Holden v. Hardy, 169 U.S. 366 (1898).
15. Mueller v. Oregon, 208 U.S. 412 (1908).
16. See, *e.g.,* Ribnik v. McBride, 277 U.S. 350 (1928) (State regulation of employment agency fees).
17. Adkins v. Children's Hospital, 261 U.S. 525 (1923).
18. U.S. Strike Comm., Report on the Chicago Strike (Washington, DC: Government Printing Office, 1895), pp. 554–557.
19. *In re* Debs, 158 U.S. 564 (1895).
20. U.S. Strike Comm., Report on the Chicago Strike, p. xlviii.
21. 30 Stat. 424 (1898).

22. Transcript of Record in Adair v. United States, No. 293, October Term 1907, p. 42.
23. Adair v. United States, 208 U.S. 161 (1908).
24. *Id.* at 170.
25. *Id.* at 174.
26. Ives v. South Buffalo Ry., 201 N.Y. 271 (1911).
27. Matter of Jacobs, 98 N.Y. 98, 113 (1884).
28. *E.g.,* Northern Securities Co. v. United States, 193 U.S. 197 (1903).
29. Plessy v. Ferguson, 163 U.S. 537 (1896).
30. Brown v. Board of Education 347 U.S. 483 (1954).
31. Pollock v. Farmers Loan & Trust Co., 158 U.S. 601, 638, 672 (1895).

CHAPTER 7

1. Wabash, St. Louis & P. Ry. v. Illinois, 118 U.S. 557 (1886).
2. 24 Stat. 379 (1887).
3. 26 Stat. 109 (1890).
4. 34 Stat. 768 (1906).
5. Gibbons v. Ogden, 9 Wheat. 1, 195 (1824).
6. Coe v. Errol, 116 U.S. 517 (1886) (State may tax logs resting upon frozen river which, without further human intervention, will float downstream during spring freshet to sawmill in neighboring State); Kidd v. Pearson, 128 U.S. 1 (1888) (State may prohibit manufacture of intoxicating liquor for sale in other States); Brown v. Houston, 114 U.S. 622 (1885) (State may tax coal resting in flatboats on which it was carried from Pittsburgh to New Orleans, where it is awaiting sale).
7. 156 U.S. 1 (1895).
8. *Id.* at 14.
9. Adair v. United States, 208 U.S. 161, 178 (1908).
10. *Ibid.*
11. Swift & Co. v. United States, 196 U.S. 375, 398 (1905).
12. 188 U.S. 321 (1903).
13. *Id.* at 364, 375.
14. Hammer v. Dagenhart, 247 U.S. 251 (1918).
15. *Id.* at 276.

CHAPTER 8

1. Schechter Poultry Corp. v. United States, 295 U.S. 495 (1935).
2. United States v. Butler, 297 U.S. 1, 68 (1936).
3. Morehead v. New York *ex rel.* Tipaldo, 298 U.S. 587 (1936).
4. 295 U.S. 495 (1935).
5. 298 U.S. 238 (1936).
6. *Id.* at 304.

7. *The Public Papers and Addresses of Franklin D. Roosevelt,* Samuel I. Rosenman, ed. (New York: Random House, 1938–1941), 1935 volume, p. 219.

8. *Ibid.,* 1937 volume, p. 55.

9. *Ibid.,* p. 128.

10. Lochner v. New York, 198 U.S. 45, 74, 75–76 (1905).

11. Oliver Wendell Holmes, Jr., *The Common Law,* Mark Howe, ed. (London: Macmillan, 1968), p. 5.

12. Vegelahn v. Guntner, 167 Mass. 92, 108 (1896).

13. Coppage v. Kansas, 236 U.S. 1, 26, 27 (1915).

14. Plant v. Woods, 176 Mass. 492, 505 (1900).

15. Coppage v. Kansas, 236 U.S. 1, 26, 27 (1915).

16. *E.g.,* Ribnik v. McBride, 277 U.S. 350 (1928) (employment agency fees); Adkins v. Children's Hospital, 261 U.S. 525 (1923) (minimum wages for women).

17. Morehead v. New York *ex rel.* Tipaldo, 298 U.S. 587 (1936).

18. West Coast Hotel v. Parrish, 300 U.S. 379 (1937).

19. *Id.* at 391.

20. *Id.* at 398–399.

21. 94 U.S. 113, 132 (1877).

22. Ferguson v. Skrupa, 372 U.S. 726, 730 (1963).

CHAPTER 9

1. 301 U.S. 1 (1937). The facts concerning Jones & Laughlin stated in the text are taken from the record on which the case was decided in the U.S. Supreme Court.

2. American Steel Foundries v. Tri-City Metal Trades Council, 257 U.S. 184, 209 (1921).

3. 49 Stat. 449 (1935).

4. Carter v. Carter Coal Co., 298 U.S. 238 (1936).

5. 301 U.S. at 37.

6. Shreveport Case, 234 U.S. 342 (1914).

7. 4 Wheat. 316, 421 (1819).

8. 301 U.S. at 37.

9. Wickard v. Filburn, 317 U.S. 111 (1942).

10. McCulloch v. Maryland, 4 Wheat. 316, 423 (1819).

11. Katzenbach v. McClung, 379 U.S. 294 (1964).

12. U.S. v. Darby, 312 U.S. 100 (1941).

13. Scarborough v. U.S., 43 U.S. 563 (1977); cf. U.S. v. Sullivan, 332 U.S. 689 (1948).

14. See, *e.g.,* Baldwin v. Seelig, 294 U.S. 511 (1935).

15. 12 How. 290 (1851).

16. Swift & Co. v. U.S., 196 U.S. 375, 398 (1905).

17. Adair v. U.S., 208 U.S. 161 (1908).
18. 297 U.S. 1 (1936).
19. Steward Machine Co. v. Davis, 301 U.S. 548 (1937).
20. Gibbons v. Ogden, 9 Wheat. 1, 195 (1824).
21. McCulloch v. Maryland, 4 Wheat. 316, 423 (1819).
22. Munn v. Illinois, 94 U.S. 113 (1877).

CHAPTER 10

1. Minersville School District v. Gobitis, 310 U.S. 586 (1940); overruled by Board of Education v. Barnette, 319 U.S. 624 (1943).
2. Minersville School District v. Gobitis, 310 U.S. 586 (1940) (opinion of the Court); Board of Education v. Barnette, 319 U.S. 624, 646–671 (1943).
3. 319 U.S. at 640.
4. *E.g.,* Virginia Pharmacy Board v. Virginia Consumer Council, 425 U.S. 748 (1976); Landmark Communications, Inc. v. Virginia, 435 U.S. 829 (1978).
5. *E.g.,* Malloy v. Hogan, 378 U.S. 1 (1964); Duncan v. Louisiana, 391 U.S. 145 (1968).
6. Brown v. Board of Education, 347 U.S. 483 (1954).
7. Roe v. Wade, 410 U.S. 113 (1973); *cf.* Moore v. East Cleveland, 431 U.S. 494 (1977).

CHAPTER 11

1. *The Writings of James Madison,* Gaillard Hunt, ed. (New York: Putnam, 1900–1910), vol. 2, p. 183.
2. *Ibid.*
3. *Ibid.*
4. Andrew A. Lipscomb, editor in chief, *The Writings of Thomas Jefferson* (Washington: Thomas Jefferson Memorial Association, 1903), vol. 16, pp. 281–282.
5. Lamont v. Postmaster General, 381 U.S. 301 (1965); Kleindienst v. Mandel, 408 U.S. 753 (1972).
6. See Chapter 12.
7. Cantwell v. Connecticut, 310 U.S. 296 (1940), Transcript of Record, p. 48.
8. Prudential Insurance Co. v. Cheek, 259 U.S. 530, 543 (1922).
9. Hague v. CIO, 307 U.S. 496, 515–516 (1939).
10. Schneider v. State, 308 U.S. 147 (1939).
11. Martin v. Struthers, 319 U.S. 141 (1943).
12. *E.g.,* Adderley v. Florida, 385 U.S. 39 (1966); Greer v. Spock, 424 U.S. 828 (1976).
13. Breard v. City of Alexandria, 341 U.S. 622 (1951).

14. Lovell v. City of Griffin, 303 U.S. 444 (1938).

15. Cantwell v. Connecticut, 310 U.S. 296 (1940).

16. *E.g.,* Cox v. Louisiana, 379 U.S. 559 (1965); Shuttlesworth v. Birmingham, 394 U.S. 137 (1969).

17. Minersville School District v. Gobitis, 310 U.S. 586 (1940).

18. Reynolds v. United States, 98 U.S. 145 (1878).

19. Minersville School District v. Gobitis, 310 U.S. 586, 597 (1940).

20. Harlan F. Stone to Felix Frankfurter, quoted in Alpheus T. Mason, *Harlan Fiske Stone: Pillar of the Law* (New York: Viking, 1956), p. 527.

21. 310 U.S. at 599–600.

22. *Id.* at 606.

23. 319 U.S. 624 (1943).

24. *Id.* at 639.

25. *Id.* at 624.

26. See Chapter 12.

27. United States v. O'Brien, 391 U.S. 367 (1968).

28. 319 U.S. at 639.

29. See, *e.g.,* Branzburg v. Hayes, 408 U.S. 665 (1972) (rejected a broad claim of First Amendment privilege).

30. United States v. Carolene Products Co., 304 U.S. 144, 152, n. 4 (1938).

31. 1 Annals of Congress 439 (1789).

32. 319 U.S. at 642.

33. Zorach v. Clauson, 343 U.S. 306, 313 (1952).

34. I Annals of Cong. 914 (1789).

35. *Messages and Papers of the Presidents, 1789–1897,* James D. Richardson (Washington, DC: Government Printing Office, 1896–1899), vol. 1, p. 64.

36. Joseph Story, *Commentaries on the Constitution of the United States* (Boston: Little, Brown, 5th ed., by Melville Bigelow, 1891), vol. 2, p. 630. See also *A Treatise on the Constitutional Limitations Which Rest Upon the Legislative Power of the States of the American Union,* Thomas M. Cooley (Boston: Little, Brown, 1868), pp. 470–471.

37. Engel v. Vitale, 370 U.S. 421 (1962).

38. *Id.* at 425.

39. Abington School District v. Schempp, 374 U.S. 203 (1963).

40. 330 U.S. 1 (1947).

41. *Id.* at 15–16.

42. McGowan v. Maryland, 366 U.S. 420 (1961).

43. Marsh v. Chambers, 463 U.S. 783 (1983).

44. Zorach v. Clauson, 343 U.S. 306 (1952).

45. McCollum v. Board of Education, 333 U.S. 203 (1948).

46. Board of Education v. Allen, 392 U.S. 236 (1968).

47. Lemon v. Kurtzman, 403 U.S. 602 (1971).
48. Walz v. Tax Comm., 397 U.S. 664 (1970).
49. Mueller v. Allen, 463 U.S. 388 (1983).
50. Levitt v. Committee for Public Education, 413 U.S. 472 (1973).
51. Lemon v. Kurtzman, 403 U.S. 602 (1971).
52. Board of Education v. Barnette, 316 U.S. 624, 642 (1943).
53. Joseph Story, *op. cit.*, vol. 2, pp. 470–471.
54. Wallace v. Jaffree, 105 S.Ct. 2479, 2508, 2520 (1985).
55. Wallace v. Jaffree, 105 S.Ct. 2479 (1985).
56. Chief Justice Burger and Justices White and Rehnquist.
57. 105 S.Ct. at 2493 and 2496–2501.
58. Abington School District v. Schempp, 374 U.S. 203, 308 (1963).
59. *Id.* at 225–226.
60. 343 U.S. 306 (1952).
61. Marsh v. Chambers, 363 U.S. 783 (1983).
62. Lynch v. Donnelly, 465 U.S. 668, 672 (1984).

CHAPTER 12

1. *Journals of the Continental Congress, 1774–1789,* Worthington C. Ford, ed. (Washington, DC: Government Printing Office, 1904), vol. 1, p. 108.
2. See, *e.g.,* Garrison v. Louisiana, 379 U.S. 64, 74–75 (1964), where the Court observed that "speech concerning public affairs is more than self-expression; it is the essence of self-government."
3. Alexander Meiklejohn, *Free Speech and Its Relation to Self-Government* (New York: Harper & Brothers, 1948).
4. 4 Annals of Congress 934 (1794).
5. The history is summarized with references in Leonard W. Levy, *Legacy of Suppression* (Cambridge, MA: Harvard University Press, 1960), p. 258 *et seq.*
6. New York Times v. Sullivan, 376 U.S. 254 (1964).
7. *E.g.,* Curtis Publishing Co. v. Butts, 388 U.S. 130 (1967) (prominent football coach a public figure).
8. Goodhardt, *Newspapers and Contempt of Court in English Law,* 48 Harv. L. Rev. 885 (1935).
9. Bridges v. California, 314 U.S. 252 (1941); Wood v. Georgia, 370 U.S. 375 (1962).
10. Nebraska Press Ass'n. v. Stuart, 427 U.S. 539 (1979).
11. *In re* Debs, 158 U.S. 564 (1895).
12. Transcript of record in Debs v. United States, 249 U.S. 211 (1919), p. 239.
13. *Id.* at 199.
14. *Id.* at 200–201.
15. *Id.* at 214–215.

16. Masses Pub. Co. v. Patten, 244 Fed. 535 (S.D.N.Y. 1917).
17. Schenck v. United States, 249 U.S. 47 (1919); Frohwerk v. United States, 249 U.S. 204 (1919); Debs v. United States, 249 U.S. 211 (1919).
18. Schenck v. United States, 249 U.S. 47, 52 (1919).
19. *Ibid.*
20. 250 U.S. 616 (1919).
21. *Id.* at 630.
22. *Id.* at 628.
23. Whitney v. California, 274 U.S. 357, 371 (1927).
24. Gitlow v. New York, 268 U.S. 652, 669 (1925).
25. Whitney v. California, 274 U.S. 357, 372, 376 (1927).
26. *E.g.,* Bridges v. California, 314 U.S. 252 (1941); Thornhill v. Alabama, 310 U.S. 88 (1940).
27. Dennis v. United States, 341 U.S. 494 (1951).
28. Brandeis and Holmes, J. J., concurring in Whitney v. California, 274 U.S. 357, 372, 378 (1927).
29. 341 U.S. at 510.
30. *Id.* at 517–556.
31. *Id.* at 513–515.
32. *Id.* at 588.
33. United States v. Robel, 389 U.S. 258 (1967).
34. United States v. Brown, 381 U.S. 437 (1965).
35. Aptheker v. Secretary of State, 378 U.S. 500 (1964).
36. Brandenburg v. Ohio, 395 U.S. 444, 447 (1969).
37. New York Times Co. v. United States, 403 U.S. 713 (1971).
38. United States v. Progressive, Inc., 467 F. Supp. 990 (W.D. Wis.), appeal dismissed, 610 F. 2d 819 (7th Cir. 1979).
39. 403 U.S. at 715.
40. *Id.* at 726–727.
41. *Id.* at 730.
42. See note 25.
43. The contract is quoted in Snepp v. United States, 444 U.S. 507 (1980).
44. Landmark Communications v. Virginia, 435 U.S. 829 (1978); *cf.* Smith v. Daily Mail, 443 U.S. 97 (1979).
45. See the dissenting opinions Pell v. Procunier, 417 U.S. 817 (1974), and Washington Post v. Saxby, 417 U.S. 843 (1974).
46. Richmond Newspaper, Inc. v. Virginia, 448 U.S. 555 (1980). See especially the concurring opinions of Justices Brennan and Stevens.

CHAPTER 13

1. 367 U.S. 643 (1961).
2. Roth v. United States, 354 U.S. 476 (1957).
3. Stanley v. Georgia, 394 U.S. 557 (1969).

4. People v. Defore, 242 N.Y. 13, 23–24, 150 N.E. 585 (1926), cert. denied, 270 U.S. 657 (1926).
5. Weeks v. United States, 232 U.S. 383, 393 (1914).
6. Adamson v. California, 332 U.S. 46, 68–123 (1947) (Black, J., dissenting).
7. Compare Fairman, *Does the Fourteenth Amendment Incorporate the Bill of Rights? The Original Understanding,* Stan. L. Rev. 5 (1949), with Crosskey, Charles Fairman, *Legislative History and the Constitutional Limitations on State Authority,* 22 Uni. Chi. L. Rev. 1 (1954).
8. The first Justice Harlan advanced the theory in Twining v. New Jersey, 211 U.S. a dissenting opinion in 78, 114–127 (1908).
9. Hurtado v. California, 110 U.S. 516 (1884).
10. Maxwell v. Dow, 176 U.S. 581 (1900).
11. Adamson v. California, 332 U.S. 46 (1947).
12. Palko v. Connecticut, 302 U.S. 319 (1937).
13. Moore v. Dempsey, 261 U.S. 86 (1923).
14. Tumey v. Ohio, 273 U.S. 510 (1927).
15. Chambers v. Florida, 309 U.S. 227 (1940).
16. Powell v. Alabama, 287 U.S. 45 (1932).
17. 302 U.S. at 328.
18. Slaughterhouse Cases, 16 Wall. 36 (1873).
19. Wolf v. Colorado, 338 U.S. 25 (1949).
20. New York v. Class, 106 S.Ct. 960 (1986).
21. 367 U.S. at 656.
22. Bivens v. Six Unknown Named Federal Agents, 403 U.S. 388, 414 (1971) (Burger, Ch. J., dissenting).
23. Olmstead v. United States, 277 U.S. 438, 485 (1928) (dissenting opinion).
24. Entick v. Carrington, 19 Howell State Trials 1029 (1765).
25. *E.g.,* Miranda v. Arizona, 384 U.S. 436 (1966).
26. Katz v. United States, 389 U.S. 347 (1967).
27. Brady v. Maryland, 373 U.S. 83 (1963); but cf. Moore v. Illinois, 408 U.S. 786 (1972).
28. Duncan v. Louisiana, 391 U.S. 145 (1968).
29. Pointer v. Texas, 380 U.S. 400 (1965).
30. Washington v. Texas, 388 U.S. 14 (1967).
31. Malloy v. Hogan 378 U.S. 1 (1964); Griffin v. California 380 U.S. 609 (1965).
32. *In re* Gault, 387 U.S. 1 (1967).
33. 372 U.S. 335 (1963).
34. Griffin v. Illinois, 351 U.S. 12 (1956); Douglas v. California, 372 U.S. 353 (1963).
35. 372 U.S. 335 (1963).

CHAPTER 14

1. Dred Scott v. Sanford, 19 How. 393 (1857).
2. 109 U.S. 3 (1883).
3. Katzenbach v. McClung, 379 U.S. 294 (1964).
4. 163 U.S. 537 (1896).
5. *Id.* at 551.
6. The story of the School Desegregation Cases is admirably told in Richard Kluger's *Simple Justice: The History of Brown v. Board of Education and Black America's Struggle for Equality* (New York: Knopf, 1976), with attention to both the human drama and the professional work of legal counsel.
7. Missouri *ex rel.* Gaines v. Canada, 305 U.S. 337 (1938).
8. Sweatt v. Painter, 339 U.S. 629, 634 (1950).
9. 347 U.S. 483 (1954).
10. *Id.* at 493–495.
11. *E.g.,* Mayor and City Council of Baltimore v. Dawson, 350 U.S. 877 (1955) (municipal beaches); Johnson v. Virginia, 373 U.S. 61 (1963) (seating in courtroom).
12. *E.g.,* Burton v. Wilmington Parking Authority, 365 U.S. 715 (1961); Reitman v. Mulkey, 387 U.S. 369 (1967).
13. *E.g.,* Katzenbach v. McClung, 379 U.S. 294 (1964); South Carolina v. Katzenbach, 383 U.S. 301 (1966); Jones v. A. H. Mayer Co., 392 U.S. 409 (1968).
14. Gideon v. Wainwright, 372 U.S. 335 (1963); Douglas v. California, 372 U.S. 353 (1963).
15. The only measures disadvantaging an ethnic minority ever found to be constitutional by the U.S. Supreme Court were directed against Japanese living in the United States at the outbreak of war between the United States and Japan on December 7, 1941. Korematsu v. United States, 323 U.S. 214 (1944). The decision is widely regarded as an aberrational product of wartime pressures.
16. Raoul Berger, *Government by Judiciary* (Cambridge, MA: Harvard University Press, 1977), pp. 117–134.
17. Bickel, *The Original Understanding and the Segregation Decision,* 69 Harv. L. Rev. 1 (1955).
18. 347 U.S. 483, 495 (1954).
19. Green v. County School, 391 U.S. 430, 437–438, 442 (1968).
20. Swann v. Charlotte-Mecklenburg School District, 402 U.S. 1 (1971).
21. Key passages read (402 U.S. 24, 26):

    The constitutional command to desegregate schools does not mean that every school in every community must always reflect the racial composition of the school system as a whole. . . .

> Absent a constitutional violation there would be no basis for judicially ordering assignment of students on a racial basis. All things being equal, with no history of discrimination, it might well be desirable to assign pupils to schools nearest their homes.

22. Keyes v. School District No. 1, 413 U.S. 189 (1973).
23. Riddick by Riddick v. School Board of City of Norfolk, 784 F.2d 521 (1986), cert. denied, Nov. 3, 1986, 55 U.S. Law Wk. 3311.
24. *Id.* at 528.
25. Milliken v. Bradley, 418 U.S. 717 (1974).

CHAPTER 15

1. *Public Papers of the Presidents of the United States: Lyndon B. Johnson—1965,* book 2 (Washington, DC: Government Printing Office, 1966), p. 636.
2. Executive Order 11, 246, 30 Fed. Reg. 12319, amended 32 Fed. Reg. 14, 303, 34 Fed. Reg. 12, 985.
3. Public Works Employment Act of 1977, Section 103(f)(2), 91 Stat. 116 (1977).
4. *E.g.,* Bridgeport Guardians v. Bridgeport Civil Service Comm., 482 F.2d, 1333 (2d Cir. 1973); Contractors Ass'n. of Eastern Pennsylvania v. Secretary of Labor, 442 F.2d 159 (3rd Cir. 1971), cert. denied, 404 U.S. 854 (1971).
5. *E.g.,* United Steelworkers v. Weber, 443 U.S. 193 (1979).
6. *Nichomachean Ethics,* book 10, chapter 8.
7. The Equal Protection Clause applies only to "State action." Civil Rights Cases, 109 U.S. 3 (1883).
8. University of California Regents v. Bakke, 18 Cal. 3rd 34, 553 P.2d 1/ 52 (1977).
9. 1 Wheat. 304 (1816).
10. 434 U.S. 900 (1977).
11. 438 U.S. 265 (1978).
12. *Id.* at 362.
13. *Id.* at 407.
14. *Id.* at 295.
15. *Id.* at 307.
16. *Id.* at 319, n. 53.
17. *Id.* at 319.
18. 106 S.Ct. 1842 (1986).
19. The text summarizes the pertinent provision of the collective bargaining agreement. Justice O'Connor concluded that the percentage of minority teachers in the system had been purposefully tied to the percentage of minority pupils. 106 S.Ct. at 1857.
20. United Steelworkers v. Weber, 443 U.S. 193 (1979).

21. 106 S.Ct. at 1858–1867.
22. *Id.* at 1867–1870.
23. *Id.* at 1854, fn.
24. *Id.* at 1848.
25. *Id.* at 1855–1857.
26. *Id.* at 1857.
27. *Id.*at 1848–1849.
28. Justice Powell sought to explain this holding by asserting that a less discriminatory method was available for eliminating the consequences of the past violations, giving the example of preferential hiring. Preferential hiring in a time of layoffs!
29. Local 28 of Sheet Metal Workers v. EEOC, 106 S.Ct. 3019 (1986); Local 93, Firefighters v. City of Cleveland, 106 S.Ct. 3063 (1963).

CHAPTER 16

1. Article I, Section 2.
2. 42 U.S.C. §1971 *et seq.*
3. "The Shame of the States," by John F. Kennedy, *New York Times Magazine,* May 18, 1958, p. 18.
4. 369 U.S. 186 (1962).
5. Article I, Section 4.
6. Schlesinger v. Reservists to Stop the War, 418 U.S. 208 (1974).
7. Nixon v. Herndon, 273 U.S. 536 (1932), had held that an action would lie in complaining of denial of the right to vote.
8. Luther v. Borden, 7 How. 1 (1849).
9. Coleman v. Miller, 307 U.S. 433 (1939).
10. The doubt arises because the Court has ruled on claims of executive privilege when presented in resistance to a judicial subpoena. United States v. Nixon, 418 U.S. 683 (1974).
11. Colegrove v. Green, 328 U.S. 549 (1946).
12. *Id.* at 564.
13. 369 U.S.at 267.
14. Only three other instances of any form of White House intervention come to mind:
    1. In a group of cases reported as *Griffin* v. *Maryland,* 378 U.S. 130 (1965) and *Bell* v. *Maryland,* 378 U.S. 226 (1965) Attorney General Nicholas Katzenbach notified President Johnson that we proposed to file a brief *amicus curiae* urging that the prosecution of sit-in demonstrators for criminal trespass violated the Fourteenth Amendment. The aim was to give President Johnson a chance to object, but the President indicated his approval.
    2. When *United States* v. *Atlas Life Ins. Co.,* 381 U.S. 233 (1965) was before the Court, President Johnson sent word that he wished the Solicitor General to argue the case personally because the extraor-

dinarily large volume of tax receipts in issue was sufficient to result in a budget deficit if the government lost the case.

3. In 1962, a group of cases decided as *McCulloch* v. *Sociedad Nacional de Marineros de Hondura,* 372 U.S. 10 (1963) brought before the Court the question whether the National Labor Relations Board has jurisdiction over vessels owned by Panamanian, Liberian, or Honduran corporations and registered under the flags of those nations when the beneficial ownership and control is in domestic corporations doing business in the United States. In the particular case, the vessels flew the Honduran flag, carried Honduran products, and were manned by Honduran nationals, at least in part. The issue went to the White House because the Defense Department deemed it to be of prime importance to keep the vessels sailing under flags of convenience, which were nearly all tankers carrying oil, subject to the control of the United States. The Defense Department feared that if the seamen were organized by the National Maritime Union and other U.S. labor unions, wages would be raised so high that vessels would be transferred to foreign registry so that the owners might remain competitive by reducing wages. The Department of Labor took the opposite view. The Shipping Board, the Department of Commerce, and the Bureau of the Budget were all drawn into the controversy, the last because one possible solution was to expand the subsidy paid to vessels under U.S. registry sufficiently to ensure that the tankers would not be transferred to other flags.

The problem was handled in textbook fashion. President Kennedy appointed a Cabinet committee; the committee appointed a subcommittee, which in turn named working groups. In due course papers passed up to the Cabinet committee. All but the Secretary of Labor agreed that the Solicitor General should urge upon the Supreme Court that the National Labor Relations Board had no jurisdiction over vessels flying the so-called flags of convenience. The committee assembled in the Cabinet Room. President Kennedy walked in and said, "I understand that the Secretary of Defense tells me that keeping these vessels out from under NLRB jurisdiction is essential to our national security. If he tells me that, I haven't any choice." The President paused and then went on: "But before you fellows make up your minds, I wish that you would consider this." He walked over to the bookcase and pulled out a Senate document containing all the speeches, letters, and other campaign papers that either he or Richard Nixon had used during the 1960 election campaign. Then he read a telegram to Joseph Curran, President of the National Maritime Union, expressing his conviction that vessels flying flags of convenience should be under NLRB jurisdiction.

I was aghast. Under the normal allocation of responsibility among members of the Kennedy campaign nothing pertaining to labor policy should have gone out without my approval. Perhaps I had even sent the telegram, although I could not remember it.

The President left the room. The meeting broke up. My Harvard Law School classmate W. Willard Wirtz, then Acting Secretary of Labor, offered me a ride back to the Department of Justice in his Cabinet automobile. "You and I have got to get the President out of this jam," he said. I suggested that we might do it by confining the government's argument to the vessels under the Honduran flag, manned by Honduran seamen, and carrying in large part Honduran bananas. We would leave open the question whether NLRB had jurisdiction over the Liberian and Panamanian tankers, the real bone of contention. This course was followed in the briefs and argument in the Supreme Court of the United States. The Court then rendered a much broader decision, holding that NLRB does not have jurisdiction over any vessels flying flags of convenience.

15. Peters v. Hobby, 349 U.S. 331 (1955).
16. Breen v. Selective Service Local Bd. No. 16, Bridgeport, Conn., 396 U.S. 460 (1970).
17. 377 U.S. 533 (1964).
18. *Id.* at 561–562.
19. *Id.* at 562–567.
20. WMCA Inc. v. Lomenzo, 377 U.S. 633 (1964); Maryland Committee v. Tawes, 377 U.S. 656 (1964); Davis v. Mann, 377 U.S. 678 (1964); Roman v. Sincock, 377 U.S. 695 (1964); Lucas v. Colorado General Assembly, 377 U.S. 713 (1964).
21. *E.g.,* White v. Register, 412 U.S. 755 (1973); Brown v. Thompson, 463 U.S. 835 (1983).
22. Avery v. Midland County, 390 U.S. 474 (1968); Hadley v. Junior College District, 397 U.S. 50 (1970).
23. Whether a partisan gerrymander is a purposeful denial of equal access to the political process violating the Fourteenth Amendment rights of members of the opposing party has been held to be a justiciable question, but the Court set the requirements of proof of purposeful discrimination so high as to lead most observers to believe that constitutional challenges to party gerrymanders will rarely succeed. Davis v. Bandemer, 106 S.Ct. 2797 (1986).
24. 383 U.S. 663 (1966).
25. *Id.* at 668.
26. Dunn v. Blumstein, 405 U.S. 330 (1972).
27. Bullock v. Carter, 405 U.S. 134 (1972).
28. Illinois Elections Board v. Socialist Workers Party, 440 U.S. 173 (1979).
29. The constitutionality of the key provisions was first established in

South Carolina v. Katzenbach, 383 U.S. 301 (1966). See also Oregon v. Mitchell, 400 U.S. 112 (1970), upholding a nationwide ban on literacy tests but invalidating a congressional effort to reduce the voting age to 18 years in State as well as federal elections.

30. Gray v. Sanders, 372 U.S. 368, 381 (1962).

CHAPTER 17

1. Slaughterhouse Cases, 16 Wall. 36, 81 (1873).
2. Buck v. Bell, 274 U.S. 200, 208 (1927).
3. Kotch v. Board of River Pilot Commissioners, 330 U.S. 552, 563 (1947).
4. Reynolds v. Sims, 377 U.S. 533, 561–562 (1964).
5. 383 U.S. 663 (1966).
6. *Id*. at 668.
7. *Ibid*.
8. *Id*. at 670, 676.
9. 394 U.S. 618 (1969).
10. 301 U.S. 1 (1937).
11. San Antonio School District v. Rodriguez, 411 U.S. 1 (1973).
12. *Id*. at 33–35.
13. Litigation in State courts invoking State constitutions proved more successful in attacking inequalities in primary and secondary education. See, *e.g.*, Serrano v. Priest, 5 Cal. 2d 584, 487 P. 2d 1241 (1971), cert. denied 432 U.S. 907; Robinson v. Cahill, 70 N.J. 155, 358 A. 2d 457, cert. denied, 426 U.S. 931 (1976).
14. Griffin v. Illinois, 351 U.S. 12 (1956); Douglas v. California, 372 U.S. 353 (1963).
15. United States v. Kras, 409 U.S. 434 (1973); Ortwein v. Schwab, 410 U.S. 656 (1973). But *cf*. Boddie v. Connecticut, 401 U.S. 371 (1971), holding that a pauper must be given access to a divorce court even though too poor to pay the filing fee.
16. James v. Valtierra, 402 U.S. 137 (1971).
17. 397 U.S. 471 (1970).
18. Robinson v. Cahill, 62 N.J. 473, 303 A.2d 273, cert. denied, 414 U.S. 976 (1973).
19. Robinson v. Cahill, 63 N.J. 196, 306 A.2d 65 (1973).
20. Robinson v. Cahill, 67 N.J. 333, 339 A.2d 193 (1975).
21. Robinson v. Cahill, 69 N.J. 449, 355 A.2d 129 (1976).
22. Robinson v. Cahill, 70 N.J. 155, 358 A.2d 457, cert. denied, 426 U.S. 931 (1976).
23. Quoted in Martin Gruberg, *Women in American Politics: An Assessment and Sourcebook* (Oshkosh: Academia Press, 1968), p. 4.
25. Goesaert v. Cleary, 335 U.S. 464, 465–466 (1948).

26. 347 U.S. 483 (1954).
27. *E.g.,* Yick Wo v. Hopkins, 118 U.S. 356 (1886); Takahashi v. Fish and Game Commission, 334 U.S. 410 (1943); Hernandez v. Texas, 347 U.S. 475 (1954).
28. See Chapter 16.
29. Levy v. Louisiana, 391 U.S. 68 (1968). Later cases follow a wavering line. See, *e.g.,* Labine v. Vincent, 401 U.S. 532 (1971); Weber v. Aetna Cas. & Sur. Co., 406 U.S. 64 (1972); Mathews v. Lucas, 427 U.S. 495 (1976); Lalli v. Lalli, 439 U.S. 259 (1978).
30. Graham v. Richardson, 403 U.S. 365 (1971).
31. Sugarman v. Dougall, 413 U.S. 634 (1973).
32. *In re* Griffiths, 413 U.S. 717 (1973).
33. 394 U.S. 618 (1969).
34. 404 U.S. 71 (1971).
35. 411 U.S. 677 (1973).
36. *Id.* at 682.
37. *Id.* at 684.
38. *Id.* at 686.
39. *Ibid.*
40. Foley v. Connelie, 435 U.S. 291 (1978); Ambach v. Norwick, 441 U.S. 68 (1979).
41. Craig v. Boren, 429 U.S. 190, 197 (1976).
42. Mississippi University for Women v. Hogan, 458 U.S. 718 (1982).
43. Rostker v. Goldberg, 453 U.S. 57 (1981). See also Michael M. v. Superior Court, 450 U.S. 464 (1981) (a 5–4 decision permitting a State to punish as criminal young men under 18 years old who have extra-marital intercourse with young women under 18, even though the young woman's participation is not a crime.)
44. Plyler v. Doe, 457 U.S. 202 (1982).

CHAPTER 18

1. 410 U.S. 113 (1973).
2. Dred Scott v. Sandford, 19 How. 393 (1857).
3. Transcript of Record in Roe v. Wade, 410 U.S. 113 (1973), pp. 56–57.
4. Griswold v. Connecticut, 381 U.S. 479, 513 (1965).
5. Ferguson v. Skrupa, 372 U.S. 726, 730 (1963).
6. 410 U.S. at 171. See also Doe v. Bolton, 410 U.S. 179, 221 (1973).
7. See, *e.g.,* Kovaacs v. Cooper, 336 U.S. 77, 95 (1949).
8. Meyer v. Nebraska, 262 U.S. 390 (1923).
9. Pierce v. Society of Sisters, 268 U.S. 510 (1925).
10. Stanley v. Georgia, 394 U.S. 557 (1969).
11. Loving v. Virginia, 388 U.S. 1 (1967).
12. Skinner v. Oklahoma, 316 U.S. 535 (1942).

13. Griswold v. Connecticut, 381 U.S. 479, 513 (1965).
14. Eisenstadt v. Baird, 405 U.S. 438 (1972).
15. 410 U.S. at 153.
16. Dronenburg v. Zech, 741 F.2d 1388, 1396–1397 (D.C. Cir. 1984). Judge Bork was speaking as a judge of an intermediate appellate court, but he also acknowledges that he held a similar view about the proper role of the Supreme Court of the United States.
17. The constitutionality of the Hyde Amendment was upheld in Harris v. McCrae, 448 U.S. 297 (1980).
18. Akron Center for Reproductive Health v. City of Akron, 462 U.S. 416 (1983).
19. Thornburg v. American College of Obstetricians, 106 S.Ct. 2169 (1986).
20. Bowers v. Hardwick, 106 S.Ct. 2841 (1986).
21. *Id.* at 2851.
22. *Id.* at 2853.
23. *Id.* at 2844.
24. *Id.* at 2846.
25. *Id.* at 2854.

CHAPTER 19

1. 347 U.S. 483 (1954).
2. Engel v. Vitale, 370 U.S. 421 (1962); Abington School District v. Schempp, 374 U.S. 203 (1963).
3. 410 U.S. 113 (1973).
4. Harper v. Virginia Board of Elections, 383 U.S. 663, 676 (1966).
5. Some constitutional questions are not justiciable. See Chapter 16.
6. See Chapter 16.
7. The problems include such questions as whether a particular action is removable from the State court to a federal court, whether the federal court may review a State criminal conviction by habeas corpus, whether a federal court may interpret a State statute or must wait for a State decision, etc.
8. Where State and federal laws overlap, the central question is often whether the federal law "pre-empts" the field so as to exclude State regulation or, contrariwise, permits concurrent regulation. For example, the provisions of the National Labor Relations Act prohibiting organizational picketing are held to exclude State restrictions in situations affecting interstate commerce, but a State may deal with violence on the picket line even when it constitutes a federal unfair labor practice. Compare San Diego Blg. Trades Council v. Garmon, 359 U.S. 236 (1959), with International Union, UAW v. Wisconsin E.R. Bd., 351 U.S. 266 (1959).

9. 1 Cranch 137 (1803).
10. See, *e.g.,* Panama Refining Co. v. Ryan, 293 U.S. 388 (1935); Schechter Poultry Corp. v. United States, 295 U.S. 495 (1935).
11. See, *e.g.,* Yakus v. United States, 321 U.S. 414 (1944).
12. Youngstown Sheet & Tube Co. v. Sawyer, 343 U.S. 579 (1952).
13. Balanced Budget and Emergency Deficit Control Act of 1985, 99 Stat. 1038, 2 U.S.C.A. 901 *et seq.* (Supp. 1986).
14. INS v. Chadha, 462 U.S. 919 (1983).
15. Judge (now Justice) Scalia outlined the argument with overtones of approval in the lower court opinion in Bowsher v. Synar, but he did not base the decision upon it or expressly approve it. See 626 F. Supp. 1374, 1391–1399 (1986).
16. 106 S.Ct. 3181 (1986).
17. Humphrey's Executor v. United States, 295 U.S. 602 (1935); Weiner v. United States, 357 U.S. 349 (1958).
18. Act of Feb. 4, 1887, §11, 24 Stat. 383, 49 U.S.C. §10301 (1986). Act of 1914, §1, 38 Stat. 717, 15 U.S.C. §41 (1982).
19. The disposition would turn upon whether the provision for fixed terms of office, and thus for agency independence, was thought to be so integral a part of the congressional scheme that Congress would not have intended the rest to survive if it were invalid. Many such laws carry separability clauses.
20. 87 Stat. 555 (1974); 50 U.S.C. 1541 (1982).
21. The "right to die" is usually asserted in a suit brought by a hospital patient or by relatives on the patient's behalf seeking to compel the hospital and doctors to shut off devices necessary to support the patient's life or to cease intravenous feeding. The defendants would typically resist out of either fear of legal liability or a sense of moral obligation. Such cases do not raise any question under the U.S. Constitution unless the hospital is maintained by a governmental unit or the doctors and nurses are public officials or employees. Constitutional rights, with rare and irrelevant exceptions, run only against government.
22. McCulloch v. Maryland, 4 Wheat. 316, 407 (1819).
23. See Chapter 4.
24. *Federalist* No. 78 (New York: Modern Library), p. 510.
25. Dred Scott v. Sanford, 19 How. 393 (1857).
26. See Chapter 7.
27. See Chapter 6.
28. Pollock v. Farmers Loan & Trust Co., 158 U.S. 601 (1895).
29. L. Hand, *Mr. Justice Cardozo,* 52 Harv. L. Rev. 361 (1939).
30. The classic exposition is Justice Brandeis's concurring opinion in Ashwander v. Tennessee Valley Authority, 297 U.S. 288, 341 (1937).

31. 410 U.S. 113 (1973).
32. The cases are described in Cox, *The Effect of the Search for Equality upon Judicial Institutions,* Wash. Uni. L. Rev. 795 (1979).
33. 369 U.S. 186 (1962).
34. 1 Wheat. 304 (1816).
35. 6 Wheat. 264 (1821). The significance of the decision is discussed in Chapter 3.
36. *Ex parte* McCardle, 7 Wall. 506 (1869). Apparently other avenues of relief were left open. Cox, *Congress vs. The Supreme Court,* 33 Mercer L. Rev. 707, 713 (1982).
37. The bills are discussed in Cox, *op. cit.,* note 32.
38. Ratner, *Congressional Power over the Appellate Jurisdiction of the Supreme Court,* 109 U. Pa. L. Rev. 157, 201 (1960).
39. Bolling v. Sharpe, 347 U.S. 497 (1954).
40. See Chapter 11.
41. Gitlow v. New York, 268 U.S. 652 (1925).
42. See Chapter 13.
43. Local 28, Sheet Metal Workers v. EEOC, 106 S.Ct. 3019 (1986); Local 93, Int. Ass'n. of Firefighters v. City of Cleveland, 106 S.Ct. 3063 (1986).
44. Humphrey's Executor v. United States, 295 U.S. 602 (1935).
45. Interstate Commerce Act of 1887, 24 Stat. 383, 49 U.S.C. §10301 (1986).
46. The Warren Court rejected more settled precedents and accepted doctrines over a somewhat longer period. I put that experience to one side because we do not yet know whether the activism politicized constitutional adjudication to the point of impairing the legitimacy of Supreme Court rulings.
47. Humphrey's Executor v. United States, 295 U.S. 602 (1935).
48. Wygant v. Jackson Board of Education, 106 S.Ct. 1842 (1986). Justice O'Connor's separate opinion is less intrusive because it rests heavily upon procedural grounds.
49. Fullilove v. Klutznik, 448 U.S.; *Id.* at 448, 522 (1980).
50. Buckley v. Valeo, 424 U.S. 1 (1976).
51. Federal Election Comm. v. NCPAC, 105 S.Ct. 1459 (1985).
52. 424 U.S. at 290–294.
53. Katz v. United States, 389 U.S. 347 (1967).
54. Bickel, *The Original Understanding and the Segregation Decision,* 69 Harv. L. Rev. 1 (1955); *cf.* Raoul Berger, *Government by Judiciary* (Cambridge, MA: Harvard University Press, 1977), chapter 7.
55. The study by Peen & Schoen Associates was released during the 1966 Convention of the American Bar Association.
56. Sam Ervin, Jr., *Separation of Powers, Judicial Independence,* 35 Law and Contem. Probl. 108, 121 (1970).

57. 1 Annals of Congress 439 (1789).
58. *The Writings of Thomas Jefferson,* Paul L. Ford, ed. (New York: Putnam, 1892–1899), vol. 4, p. 257.
59. Walter Bagehot, *The English Constitution* (London: Henry S. King, 1872), p. 9.
60. Speech of Charles Evans Hughes at Elmira, NY, May 3, 1907, reprinted in *The Autobiographical Notes of Charles Evans Hughes,* David Danelski and Joseph Tulchin, eds. (Cambridge, MA: Harvard University Press, 1973), p. 144, and *Addresses and Papers of Charles Evans Hughes* (New York: Putnam, 1908), pp. 139–140.
61. See note 29.
62. Southern Pacific Co. v. Jensen, 244 U.S. 205, 222 (1917).

Index